COMPETITION LAW IN THE CARICOM SINGLE MARKET AND ECONOMY

Competition Law in the CARICOM Single Market and Economy provides a comprehensive introduction to and overview of the emerging competition law of the CARICOM Single Market and Economy (CSME). The book deals with both the current context and potential developments. It examines, *inter alia*, such topics as the possible objectives of CSME competition law, the concept of an 'enterprise', the prohibition of anti-competitive agreements, decisions and concerted practices, the prohibition of abuse by an enterprise of its dominant position, and the obligations imposed on Member States of the CSME deriving from CSME competition law. Additionally, the book pays special attention to the CARICOM Competition Commission – the main enforcer of CSME competition law. It also emphasises the importance of economics in the enforcement of competition law.

Offering the first major exploration of CSME competition law, this text will be an essential resource for lawyers, businesspersons and students alike.

Alina Kaczorowska-Ireland is Professor of International and EU Law at the University of the West Indies, Cave Hill Campus, Barbados.

COMPETITION LAW IN THE CARICOM SINGLE MARKET AND ECONOMY

Alina Kaczorowska-Ireland

Routledge
Taylor & Francis Group
LONDON AND NEW YORK

First published 2015
by Routledge
2 Park Square, Milton Park, Abingdon, Oxon, OX14 4RN

and by Routledge
711 Third Avenue, New York, NY 10017

Routledge is an imprint of the Taylor & Francis Group, an informa business

British Library Cataloguing in Publication Data
A catalogue record for this book is available from the British Library

Library of Congress Cataloging-in-Publication Data
Kaczorowska, Alina, author.
Competition law in the CARICOM single market and economy / Alina Kaczorowska-Ireland.
pages cm
ISBN 978-1-138-78732-2 (hbk) — ISBN 978-1-138-78731-5 (pbk) — ISBN 978-1-315-76467-2 (ebk) 1. Antitrust law—Caribbean Area. I. Title. II. Title: Competition law in the Caribbean Community single market economy.
KGJ759.K33 2014
343.272907′21—dc23

2014011119

ISBN: 978–1–138–78732–2 (hbk)
ISBN: 978–1–138–78731–5 (pbk)
ISBN: 978–1–315–76467–2 (ebk)

Typeset in Bembo
by RefineCatch Limited, Bungay, Suffolk

CONTENTS

PREFACE

'Fools rush in where angels fear to tread' is the expression in the forefront of my mind as I dispatch this book for printing and publication. I say this because the Revised Treaty of Chaguaramas (RTC), which created CARICOM Single Market and Economy (CSME) competition law, has not long been in force, and consequently there is a paucity of authorities. Indeed, the Caribbean Court of Justice (CCJ) has delivered only one judgment on CSME competition law, and this dealt with procedural, rather than substantive, aspects of that law. Further, the CARICOM Competition Commission (CCC), the main body created by the RTC to enforce CSME competition law, although currently investigating an alleged infringement of that law, has not yet made any determination as to whether or not any infringement has occurred. In this context, it may seem foolish of me to write a book on CSME competition law so early in its existence. Having said this, my knowledge and experience regarding EU competition law, on which the substantive provisions of CSME competition law are modelled, has persuaded me that what I am able to say should be 'outed' now rather than never said or, indeed, delayed.

I am very grateful to Dr Kevin Harriott, chief economist at the Jamaican Fair Trading Commission, for his numerous and extremely valuable contributions to the economic aspects of this book. I am hugely appreciative of the encouragement, professionalism, efficiency, kindness and assistance I have received from Fiona Briden, senior publisher at Routledge Law, her colleagues Emma Nugent and Rebekah Jenkins, and all other members of the Routledge Law team. I also wish to acknowledge the institutional support I have received from my faculty and my university.

I hope that this book will inspire further study in this new and fascinating area of law.

This book is up to date as at 15 March 2014.

Alina Kaczorowska-Ireland
15 March 2014
Cave Hill, Barbados

LIST OF ABBREVIATIONS

AAC	average avoidable cost
AC	average cost
AEC	as efficient competitor
AG	Advocate General
ATC	average total cost
AVC	average variable cost
CARICOM	Caribbean Community
CARIFORUM	Forum of the Caribbean Group of African, Caribbean and Pacific (ACP) States
CCC	CARICOM Competition Commission
CCJ	Caribbean Court of Justice
CFI	Court of First Instance (now the General Court)
CISAC	International Confederation of Societies of Authors and Composers (*Confédération Internationale des Sociétés d'Auteurs et Compositeurs*)
CJEU	Court of Justice of the European Union
CMLR	*Common Market Law Reports*
CML Rev	*Common Market Law Review*
Comp Law	*Competition Law Journal*
Comp L Rev	*Competition Law Review*
COTED	Council for Trade and Economic Development
CSME	CARICOM Single Market and Economy
CUP	Cambridge University Press
DG	Directorate-General (of the European Commission)
ECHR	European Convention on Human Rights

ECJ	European Court of Justice
ECLR	*European Competition Law Review*
ECR	*European Court Reports*
ECtHR	European Court of Human Rights
EEA	European Economic Area
EEC	European Economic Community
EFTA	European Free Trade Association
EHRR	*European Human Rights Reports*
EL Rev	*European Law Review*
EPA	economic partnership agreement
ESA	EFTA Surveillance Authority
EU	European Union
Euro CJ	*European Competition Journal*
FC	fixed costs
Fordham Int'l LJ	*Fordham International Law Journal*
FTA	free trade agreement
GATS	General Agreement on Trade in Services
GATT	General Agreement on Tariffs and Trade
GDP	gross domestic product
Harv L Rev	Harvard Law Review
HHI	Herfindahl-Hirschman Index
HMG	Horizontal Merger Guidelines
HMT	hypothetical monopolist test
ICLQ	*International and Comparative Law Quarterly*
ILR	*International Law Reports*
IPRs	intellectual property rights
J Comp L & Econ	*Journal of Competition Law and Economics*
JECLAP	*Journal of Competition Law and Practice*
J L & Econ	*Journal of Law and Economics*
Loyola L Rev	*Loyola Law Review*
LPP	legal professional privilege
LRAIC	long-run average incremental cost
MC	marginal cost
MCPs	merger control provisions
MEQRs	measures equivalent to quantitative restrictions
MES	minimum efficiency scale
MFN	most favoured nation
Mich L Rev	*Michigan Law Review*
MLR	*Modern Law Review*
MR	marginal revenue
MUPS	multiple unit pellet system
NAAT	non-appreciable affectation of trade
NCA	national competition authority

NYU L Rev	*New York University Law Review*
OECD	Organisation for Economic Co-operation and Development
OECS	Organisation of Eastern Caribbean States
OJ	*Official Journal*
OS	(desktop) operating system
OUP	Oxford University Press
PED	price elasticity of demand
PSO	public service obligation
QRs	quantitative restrictions
R&D	research and development
RGM	relevant geographic market
RJLSC	Regional Judicial and Legal Services Commission
RPM	relevant product market
RRA	reciprocal representation agreement
RTC	Revised Treaty of Chaguaramas Establishing the Caribbean Community including the CARICOM Single Market and Economy
RTM	relevant temporal market
SALISES	Sir Arthur Lewis Institute of Social and Economic Studies
SCP	structure–conduct–performance
SGEI	service of general economic interest
SGI	service of general interest
SMEs	small and medium-sized enterprises
SPC	supplementary protection certificate
SSNIP	small, but significant, non-transitory increase in price
TC	total costs
TEU	Treaty on European Union
TFEU	Treaty on the Functioning of the European Union
ToL	Treaty of Lisbon
TR	total revenue
TRIPS	Agreement on Trade-Related Aspects of Intellectual Property Rights 1994
U Colo L Rev	*University of Colorado Law Review*
UK	United Kingdom
UKCLR	*UK Competition Law Reports*
UKOFT	UK Office of Fair Trading (now superseded by the Competition and Markets Authority, or CMA)
UNCTAD	United Nations Conference on Trade and Development
U Penn L Rev	*University of Pennsylvania Law Review*

U Pitt L Rev	*University of Pittsburgh Law Review*
US	United States
VA L Rev	*Virginia Law Review*
VC	variable costs
WGOS	workgroup server operating system
WILJ	*West Indian Law Journal*
WMP	Windows Media Player
WTO	World Trade Organization
XED	cross-price elasticity of demand
Yale LJ	*Yale Law Journal*

TABLE OF CASES

Caribbean Court of Justice

EFTA court

EU courts

European Court of Justice

General Court

European Court of Human Rights

National courts

Decisions of the European Commission in competition cases

Decisions of the United Kingdom Office of Fair Trading (UKFTC)

TABLE OF TREATIES AND LEGISLATION

Caribbean treaties

European treaties

Universal treaties

EU secondary legislation

DECISIONS of the European Commission

DIRECTIVES

REGULATIONS

National legislation

BARBADOS

CANADA

JAMAICA

UNITED KINGDOM

UNITED STATES

1

INTRODUCTION

Chapter contents

1.1 Introduction

In 1973, four Caribbean States – Trinidad and Tobago, Barbados, Jamaica, and Guyana – entered into a Treaty Establishing the Caribbean Community and Common Market (CARICOM) at Chaguaramas. Eleven further Caribbean States subsequently became Contracting Parties to that Treaty.[1] The 1973 Treaty of Chaguaramas provided for the free movement of the factors of production and for the co-ordination of many policies. It has been described by Professor Duke Pollard as 'little more than an optical illusion in terms of positive enforceable rights and legally binding obligations'.[2] Revision was necessary in order to deepen regional economic integration and to respond to the challenges of globalisation. This need was acknowledged by the Heads of Government of the Member States of the CARICOM in 1989 at a Conference held in Grand Anse, which decided to establish the CARICOM Single Market and Economy

1 For an excellent introduction to the history of Caribbean integration, see D. Berry, *Caribbean Integration Law*, 2014, Oxford: OUP, pp 18–30.

2 D. Pollard, 'Governance Structure of the Caribbean Community', Paper presented at the inaugural seminar of the Caribbean Academy for Law and Court Administration, 6–10 December 2010, Trinidad and Tobago, p 4.

(CSME). As a result, the 1973 Treaty of Chaguaramas was, 16 years later, replaced by the Revised Treaty of Chaguaramas Establishing the Caribbean Community including the CARICOM Single Market and Economy (RTC). It entered into force on 1 January 2006.[3]

One of the vital elements of the RTC is its inclusion, under Chapter VIII, Part One, of competition policy and law as areas of CARICOM competence. Chapter VIII also provides for the establishment of a system for enforcement of competition law. This system comprises the CARICOM Competition Commission (CCC), which was inaugurated on 18 January 2008, the Caribbean Court of Justice (CCJ), which was established on 16 April 2005, and national competition authorities (NCAs) (see Chapter 8, section 8.2.1.3). A further organ of CARICOM, the Council for Trade and Economic Development (COTED), which consists of ministers designated by the Member States, is empowered to establish appropriate policies and rules of competition, including special rules for particular sectors,[4] as well as to exempt any sector of the economy or any enterprise or group of enterprises from the application of competition rules.[5] The enforcement system is in the process of construction. Nevertheless, the CCC conducted its first investigation, and the CCJ rendered its first judgment in competition matters, in the *Trinidad Cement Ltd v CCC* case.[6] This indicates that CSME competition law will grow in parallel with the development of the CSME.

CSME competition law is concerned with:

- agreements between enterprises, decisions of associations of enterprises and concerted practices by enterprises that have as their object or effect the restriction of competition within the Community. These being prohibited (subject to some exceptions);
- abusive business conduct by enterprises that are in a dominant position within the Community (although a dominant enterprise may justify such conduct on the grounds specified in the RTC);
- any other like conduct by enterprises, the object or effect of which is to frustrate the benefits expected from the establishment of the CSME, unless that conduct falls within justifications set out in the RTC; and
- public restrictions on competition, which occur when a Member State takes measures that restrict competition within the Community, which measures are prohibited.

It is important to note that, at the current stage of development of CSME competition law, mergers between enterprises are not within the scope of the

3 As at September 2013, 13 CARICOM States have ratified the RTC, the remaining two, the Bahamas and Montserrat, retain CARICOM membership under special bilateral agreements without being Contracting Parties to the RTC. See D. Berry, *Caribbean Integration Law*, 2014, Oxford: OUP, p 53.

4 Article 182 RTC.

5 Article 183 RTC.

6 [2012] CCJ 4 (OJ).

Community rules on competition. Although most mergers have pro-competitive effects, some may be harmful to competition, given that they reduce the number of competitors in the relevant market and thus increase merging enterprises' market power, and, at the extreme, can create a monopoly, thereby increasing the potential for abuse of that power. For that reason, Member States have already agreed that control of mergers should become part of CSME competition law[7] (see Chapter 3, section 3.2.2 and Chapter 9, section 5).

1.2 Should CSME competition law benefit from the experience of the United States, the European Union and other jurisdictions in the enforcement of competition law?

CSME competition law is a new area of law in the Caribbean Community. The novelty raises the matter of whether, in the enforcement of CSME competition law, the CCC, and ultimately the CCJ, should take account of the vast experience of other jurisdictions relating to the enforcement of competition law. It can be said that economic principles are the same everywhere and this may be a reason for paying attention to competition cases from other jurisdictions. However, this submission cannot be accepted. Although economic principles are the same, in each jurisdiction, competition law – and the way in which it is enforced – depends on the objectives that the competition law of that jurisdiction seeks to achieve. Therefore the underpinning philosophy of each regime of competition law is the vital factor in deciding whether and to what extent competition cases from elsewhere will be relevant to the enforcement of CSME competition law.

It is submitted that whilst it is always instructive and enriching to pay attention to competition cases from other jurisdictions, the similarity in the underpinning philosophy of CARICOM and the European Union, as well as the textual similarity between substantive provisions on competition set out in Articles 177–179 RTC and Articles 101 and 102 of the Treaty on the Functioning of the European Union (TFEU), entails that, in many instances, concepts and theories established under EU competition law may be transferred to CSME competition law. In any event, bearing in mind the similarities, substantive EU competition law may, at the very least, provide many valuable ideas for the interpretation of CSME competition law. Before underlining the similarities, it is necessary to stress that there are also important differences between CSME competition law and EU competition law – in particular, the enforcement regimes are very different procedurally.

7 See D. Bienen, *A Consultancy to Recommend a Policy for the Treatment of Mergers and Acquisitions within the CSME: Integrated Final Report*, 15 December 2010, available at http://csmeonline.org/website/images/documents/28/_1-1-2-1-1%20 Integrated%20Final%20Report%20-%20CSME%20Mergers%20(2).pdf [accessed 11 February 14].

With regard to similarities between the underpinning philosophies of CARICOM and the European Union, both are founded on the same values and both seek to achieve similar objectives, although integration in each region has reached differing stages of development. The values on which the Union is founded are similar to, if not the same as, the values on which CARICOM is based. Article 2 of the Treaty on European Union (TEU) lists those values:

> "The Union is founded on the values of respect for human dignity, freedom, democracy, equality, the rule of law and respect for human rights, including the rights of persons belonging to minorities. These values are common to the Member States in a society in which pluralism, non-discrimination, tolerance, justice, solidarity and equality between women and men prevail."

In CARICOM, the 1997 Charter of Civil Society for the Caribbean Community, although not a binding instrument, contains provisions that fully acknowledge the same values as those specified in Article 2 TEU as being fundamental to Caribbean society.

With regard to the objectives that each organisation strives to achieve, both are committed to the creation and maintenance of an internal market and single economy, the functioning of which must not be frustrated by anti-competitive conduct of enterprises, or restrictions imposed by Member States.

Textual similarity between the substantive provisions of Chapter VIII, Part One, RTC and Articles 101 and 102 TFEU strongly suggests that many RTC provisions are modelled on the TFEU provisions. Table 1.1 exemplifies this in relation to the prohibition of anti-competitive agreements, decisions and concerted practices.

TABLE 1.1 Textual similarity between Article 177 RTC and Article 101 TFEU

Prohibitions under the RTC	*Prohibitions under Article 101 TFEU*
Article 177(1) RTC states: A Member State shall, within its jurisdiction, prohibits as being anti-competitive business conduct, the following: (a) agreements between enterprises, decisions by associations of enterprises, and concerted practices by enterprises which have as their object or effect the prevention, restriction or distortion of competition within the Community.	**Article 101(1) TFEU states:** The following shall be prohibited as incompatible with the internal market: all agreements between undertakings, decisions by associations of undertakings, and concerted practices which may affect trade between Member States and which have as their object or effect the prevention, restriction or distortion of competition within the common market.
Article 177(2) RTC gives examples of prohibited agreements, decisions and concerted practices	**Article 101(1) TFEU gives examples of prohibited agreements, decisions and concerted practices**

Article 177(3) states:
Subject to Article 168, a Member State shall ensure that all agreements and decisions within the meaning of paragraph 1 of this Article shall be null and void within its jurisdiction.

Article 101(2) TFEU states:
Any agreements or decisions prohibited pursuant to this Article shall be automatically void.

Article 177(4) RTC states:
An enterprise shall not be treated as engaging in anti-competitive business conduct if it establishes that the activity complained of:

(a) contributes to:
  (i) the improvement of production or distribution of goods and services; or
  (ii) the promotion of technical or economic progress, while allowing consumers a fair share of the resulting benefit;
(b) imposes on the enterprises affected only such restrictions as are indispensable to the attainment of the objectives mentioned in sub-paragraph (a); or
(c) does not afford the enterprise engaged in the activity the possibility of eliminating competition in respect of a substantial part of the market for goods or services concerned.

Article 101(3) TFEU states:
The provisions of paragraph 1 may, however, be declared inapplicable in the case of:

- any agreement or category of agreements between undertakings;
- any decision or category of decisions by associations of undertakings;
- any concerted practice or category of concerted practices,

which contributes to improving the production or distribution of goods or to promoting technical or economic progress, while allowing consumers a fair share of the resulting benefit, and which does not:

(a) impose on the undertakings concerned restrictions which are not indispensable to the attainment of these objectives;
(b) afford such undertakings the possibility of eliminating competition in respect of a substantial part of the products in question.

It is submitted that the commonalities between CARICOM and the European Union, as well as the fact that the substantive centres of gravity of both EU and CSME competition law are the same as each other because they derive from the necessity to create and protect market integration, suggest that it is unlikely that the CCJ will ignore substantive EU competition law when interpreting substantive provisions of CSME competition law. Indeed, the CCJ has, when appropriate, been willing to follow precedents from the European Court of Justice (ECJ). For example, in *Myrie v Barbados*,[8] the CCJ defined the concept of 'public policy' by reference to the judgment of the ECJ in *R v Bouchereau*,[9] and

8 [2013] CCJ 3 (OJ).
9 Case 30/77 *Régina v Pierre Bouchereau* [1977] ECR 1999.

with regard to the concept of 'sufficiently serious threat to the fundamental interest of society', the CCJ stated:

> "[T]he Court finds persuasive the judgment of the European Court of Justice in Adoui[10] where that court stated that a Member State may not refuse a national of another Member State access to its territory by reason of or the threat of 'conduct which, when attributable to the former State's own nationals, does not give rise to repressive measures or other genuine and effective measures intended to combat such conduct."[11]

When appropriate, then, the CCJ is prepared to follow ECJ judgments. However, it is not appropriate, as the CCJ rightly noted, to follow European judgments in respect of procedural issues relating to the enforcement of competition law by the CCC and the European Commission. In *Trinidad Cement Ltd (TCL) v CCC*,[12] the CCJ stated that the reliance of TCL on judgments from the ECJ must be rejected:

> ". . . owing to the variances between the procedures of the European and CARICOM competition regimes. As between the two, there are considerable dis-similarities that flow from the significant differences in the wording, nature and effect of the underlying legal instruments and the overarching governing system of law."[13]

This book, when appropriate, refers to EU competition law. It also highlights differences between EU and CSME competition law with a view to suggesting novel approaches that may be considered useful in the enforcement of CSME competition law. In order to facilitate the understanding of important EU Law terms, concepts and institutions used or referred to in this book, some of the same are briefly explained below.

1. Only an enterprise within the meaning of the RTC is subject to CSME competition law. EU competition law uses the concept of an 'undertaking', which may not have the same meaning as the concept of an 'enterprise' (see Chapter 4).
2. The European Commission shares its enforcement powers in competition matters with NCAs and national courts. The Commission supervises the system for enforcement of EU competition law, and intervenes whenever necessary to ensure that that law is applied consistently and uniformly in the Member States. This arrangement allows the European Commission to

10 Joined Cases 115 and 116/81 *Rezguia Adoui v Belgian State and City of Liège; Dominique Cornuaille v Belgian State* [1982] ECR 1665.
11 *Myrie v Barbados* [2013] CCJ 3 (OJ), [71].
12 [2012] CCJ 4 (OJ).
13 Ibid., [27].

concentrate its limited resources on important matters and the most serious infringements of EU law, leaving less important tasks to NCAs and national courts. Only the Commission is empowered to initiate legislation at EU level in competition matters, as well as to draw up notices and guidelines to assist NCAs, national courts and undertakings in the application of EU competition rules and policies.

3. Within the European Commission, the Directorate-General for Competition (DG Competition) is in charge of EU competition policy and of enforcement of EU competition law. DG Competition comprises 10 directorates, covering management, antitrust and merger policy, cartel enforcement, sectoral expertise (four directorates) and state aid (three directorates). A Director General, who is a career manager, is responsible for DG Competition and reports directly to the European Commissioner for Competition.
4. The Treaty of Lisbon (ToL) contains the most recent amendments to the EU treaties. It has only seven Articles. The first two contain amendments to the TEU and to the EC Treaty. Article 1(3) TEU provides that the European Union is based on two treaties: the Treaty on European Union, as amended (TEU), and the Treaty on the Functioning of the European Union (TFEU), which amends and renames the EC Treaty. Both treaties are of equal legal value.
5. Under the ToL, the EU judiciary is collectively known as the Court of Justice of the European Union (CJEU). The CJEU comprises: the Court of Justice of the European Union, which was previously known as the Court of Justice of the European Communities and is colloquially known as the European Court of Justice (the ECJ); the General Court, which was previously known as the Court of First Instance (CFI); and various specialised courts, which were previously known as 'judicial panels'. There is only one specialised court at the time of writing – the Civil Service Tribunal, which has no jurisdiction in competition matters.

    (a) The General Court has jurisdiction to review decisions of the European Commission in competition matters. Judgments of the General Court may be appealed to the ECJ on points of law. However, the ECJ may also deal with competition cases *via* the preliminary ruling procedure, which is similar to that set out in Article XIV of the Agreement Establishing the Caribbean Court of Justice and in Article 214 RTC.
    (b) The ECJ is assisted by Advocates General (AGs). Article 252 TFEU defines the function of an AG as follows:

    > "It shall be the duty of the Advocate-General, acting with complete impartiality and independence, to make, in open court, reasoned submissions on cases which, in accordance with the Statute of the Court of Justice of the European Union, require his involvement."

Advocates General are required to be neutral as between the applicant and the defendant. They represent the interests of justice. They review the factual and legal aspects of a case, and must reach a conclusion that constitutes their recommendation of how the ECJ should decide the case. The conclusion is very detailed, and often suggests original and new legal approaches to the disputed matter, but is not binding on the ECJ. Even if rejected in a particular case, the opinion of an AG may be later referred to in a similar case, since it often indicates the direction in which EU law should evolve. Furthermore, the opinion is very useful in understanding the case, because the judgments of the ECJ are very short. Since 2003, AGs give an opinion only if the ECJ considers that a particular case raises a new point of law.

8. Article 101(1) TFEU prohibits agreements between undertakings, decisions of associations of undertakings, and concerted practices that may have appreciable effect on trade between Member States, and which have as their object or effect the prevention, restriction or distortion of competition. Article 101(1) TFEU provides a non-exhaustive list of prohibited arrangements. Under Article 101(2) TFEU, any such agreement or decision is void. Concerted practices are not mentioned because they are informal arrangements and therefore cannot be rendered void. However, arrangements that fall within the scope of Article 101(1) may escape the prohibition if they meet the criteria set out in Article 101(3) TFEU or in the relevant block exemption regulation (see Chapter 6, section 6.3.3.1A).
9. Article 102 TFEU prohibits the abuse of a dominant position by a single undertaking or by a number of undertakings, which abuse affects trade between Member States and cannot be objectively justified.

1.3 The structure of the book

This book contains nine chapters.

- **Chapter 1** briefly outlines the history of CARICOM. It examines the main concerns of CSME competition law and the system for its enforcement. It highlights commonalities among the underpinning objectives and values of CARICOM and the European Union, as well as textual similarities between substantive provisions on competition set out in Chapter VIII, Part One, RTC and Articles 101 and 102 TFEU. This being done mainly to justify references to EU competition law when examining substantive provisions of CSME competition law. However, it also emphasises that the enforcement regimes of EU competition law and CSME competition law are very different from each other in terms of procedure, and explains, as the CCJ stated in *Trinidad Cement Ltd (TCL) v CCC*, why the CCJ will be likely to find judgments of the ECJ persuasive only when appropriate.

- **Chapter 2** focuses on the economics of competition law. This is because economics has become an intrinsic part of competition law, as shown by the frequent references of competition law to economic concepts such as 'competition', 'monopoly' and 'barriers to entry', and the fact that competition law seeks to achieve economic objectives. As a result, economic evidence presented by forensic expert economists has a pivotal role to play in the litigation of competition cases. This means that lawyers, and other persons involved in the enforcement of competition law, must have sufficient knowledge of economics to be able to work with economists in the preparation and assessment of competition cases, and, if appropriate, to convey the relevant principles of economics to adjudicators who may not have been exposed to the discipline. This chapter covers the basic conceptual foundation of economics as applied to competition law. It also examines the main tools of economic analysis in competition law – that is, the concepts of 'market power' and 'market definition'. It is not intended to provide a comprehensive introduction to the economics of competition law, but to give the reader an insight into the interplay between competition law and economics.
- **Chapter 3** deals with the objectives of CSME competition law. At the time of writing, CSME competition policy and law are at a nascent stage, and therefore a discussion relating to the objectives of CSME competition law and policy is essential, bearing in mind that their determination is vital to the framing of a coherent body of substantive competition law. This chapter first identifies the various possible objectives of CSME competition policy and law by examining the provisions of the RTC; second, it suggests their ranking, with a view to achieving the wider political and economic goals set by the RTC. A submission is made in this chapter that two objectives should be given priority in the enforcement of CSME competition law: first, the objective of creating and maintaining the CSME; and second, the objective of protecting consumers.
- **Chapter 4** deals with the concept of an 'enterprise', which delimits the personal scope of application of CSME competition law. Article 1 RTC defines an enterprise as 'any person or type of organisation, other than a non-profit organisation, involved in the production of or the trade in goods, or the provision of services'. Each word of the definition is examined in this chapter and a special emphasis is placed on the concept of a 'non-profit organisation', the interpretation of which will be vital for the application of CSME competition law. Additionally, the meaning of an enterprise is examined in light of the activities and areas that are excluded from the scope of CSME competition law.
- **Chapter 5** deals with the concept of 'cross-border effects', which determines in what circumstances anti-competitive conduct will be within the scope of CSME competition law, and thus within the jurisdiction of the CCC. Because the RTC does not define the concept of 'cross-border effects', its interpretation raises many important issues, such as the applicability of CSME competition law to:

  - anti-competitive conduct that has potential and indirect effects on competition and trade in the CSME;
  - anti-competitive conduct of enterprises established outside CARICOM, but which has effects on competition and trade within the CSME; and
  - anti-competitive conduct of enterprises established within the CARICOM, but which has effects on competition and trade in a third country.

  The chapter also examines the concept of 'appreciability', which requires that alleged anti-competitive conduct must have appreciable effect on competition and trade in the Community (that is, be of some magnitude) in order to be of interest to CSME competition law.

- **Chapter 6** focuses on Article 177(1)(a) RTC, which prohibits, as being anti-competitive, any agreements between enterprises, decisions of associations of enterprises and concerted practices by enterprises that have as their object or effect restrictions on competition within the Community. It examines its potential applicability to vertical agreements and suggests some possible ways of interpreting the concepts of 'agreement', decision' and 'concerted practice'. It underlines the importance of distinguishing between agreements, decisions and concerted practices that restrict competition in the Community 'by object' and those that do so 'by effect'. It also explores the relationship between paragraphs (1)(a) and (4) of Article 177 RTC, the latter providing exemption for agreements, decisions and concerted practices that would otherwise be prohibited.
- **Chapter 7** deals with the treatment of an enterprise that has market power. Such an enterprise is prohibited from committing an abuse of its market power (that is, an abuse of its dominant position on the relevant market) where that abuse would have cross-border effects on trade and competition within the Community. The chapter examines the concept of 'dominance', and reflects on the most efficient ways of dealing with tacit collusion of enterprises operating in an oligopolistic market. It outlines the meaning of an 'abuse', and makes a distinction between exclusionary and exploitative abuses, whilst also paying attention to price discrimination. In the examination of exclusionary abuses, reference is made to the European Commission's Guidance on the Enforcement Priorities in Applying Article 102 TFEU to Abusive Exclusionary Conduct by Dominant Undertakings. This is because the approach outlined in the Guidance is based on sound economic principles and seems to be, at the very least, worth considering in the context of the efficient enforcement of the prohibition of abusive conduct by dominant enterprises in the CSME. This chapter concludes by examining possible justifications set out in the RTC for abusive conduct by dominant enterprises.
- **Chapter 8** focuses on the obligations relating to CSME competition law, general and specific, imposed on Member States by the RTC, aimed at

ensuring the enactment, proper enforcement, and efficiency of CSME competition law. It examines, in light of those obligations, the treatment of public undertakings and State monopolies. Additionally, it emphasises the importance of the economic partnership agreement (EPA) concluded between the CARIFORUM States, on the one hand, and the European Union and its Member States, on the other. All CARICOM Member States are signatories of the EPA. The chapter also explores the likely impact of the application of the EPA's provisions concerning competition on the development of CSME competition law.

- **Chapter 9** focuses on the enforcement of CSME competition law by the CCC, being the main body to which the RTC entrusts this task. It examines the composition of the CCC, and analyses its powers. The Rules of Procedure of the CCC are subjected to detailed consideration, and assessed in light of the judgment of the CCJ in *Trinidad Cement Ltd v CCC* and their compatibility with the requirements of human rights standards.

2

THE ECONOMICS OF COMPETITION LAW

Chapter contents

2.1 Introduction

Competition law enforcement involves the interdisciplinary application of law and economics. This is well illustrated by the fact that competition law prohibits conduct that distorts competition taking place within the confines of a market. Conduct prohibited by competition law includes collusive activities and abuses of a dominant position. Without an appreciation of economic concepts such as 'market definition', 'market structure' and 'barriers to entry', *inter alia*, it would be difficult to recognise conduct prohibited by competition law and even more so to litigate any competition case successfully. Additionally, the relevance of economic theory to the enforcement of competition law is highlighted by the fact that such law is used to achieve economic objectives. This forces policymakers to define these objectives clearly and to assess the normative consequences likely to flow from their choice (see Chapter 3).

Whichever economic theory is selected by policymakers to achieve the economic objectives, the involvement of economists is typically required. These are the experts qualified to carry out economic analysis, which has the following purposes.

- It explains how the relevant market works and the effects of any allegedly unlawful conduct on the part of an enterprise on that market.
- It strengthens a legal case by complementing it with economic analysis, as can be seen in relation to the difficulty experienced by competition enforcement agencies when establishing collusion. Indeed, collusive arrangements between enterprises are, by their nature, secret and difficult to prove because of the paucity of direct evidence. Economists have developed forensic methods for establishing indirect evidence of collusion. They use various models of collusive behaviour, based on market data, which are able to distinguish between parallel conduct that is collusive and that which is competitive, and thus lawful. In implementing these models, econometrics and other quantitative tools of analysis are employed.
- It shows whether and how the objectives of competition law have been undermined by the challenged conduct.

CARICOM Member States that have enacted competition law and established national competition authorities (NCAs) have acknowledged the fact that economic analysis is an intrinsic part of competition law. They have all created the post of 'chief economist'. The person holding this position works alongside the legal team of an NCA when it is investigating an alleged infringement of competition law.

As can be seen from this, lawyers and persons involved in the enforcement of competition law must have sufficient understanding of economics to be able to communicate effectively with economists. This was well noted by Brandeis J, who said, '[a] lawyer who has not studied economics . . . . is very apt to become a public enemy'.[1] However, in the context of CSME competition law, bearing in mind that, in the Caribbean Community, this is a new area of law, lawyers will be required not only to have knowledge of economics, but also, in some cases, to be able to explain clearly the relevant economic underpinnings of competition cases to the adjudicating body. This is because some Caribbean judges have not been sufficiently exposed to a competition culture to appreciate the relevance of economics to the enforcement of competition law. An example of this is provided in *The Jamaica Stock Exchange (JSE) v The Fair Trading Commission.*[2] In this case, the Jamaican Court of Appeal found, *inter alia*, that the JSE, which was the only entity monitoring firms listed on the local stock exchange, could not be

1 Quoted in R. Whish, *Competition Law*, 5th edn, 2003, London: LexisNexis Butterworths, p 1.

2 Supreme Court Civil Appeal No. 92/97, available at http://www.jftc.com/Libraries/Court_Judgements/Jamaica_Stock_Exchange_vs_The_Fair_Trading_Commission_-_January_2001.sflb.ashx [accessed 10 January 2014], 66. See also W. M. Duncan, 'Overview of Jamaican Stock Exchange Case' (2010) 35(1) WILJ 237.

considered as limiting competition 'where there is no evidence of the appellant being in competition with anyone else'.[3] Panton JA continued:

> The facts indicate that the field is wide open for the development of another stock exchange. However, there is no evidence of any such entity being even on the horizon. In the absence of such evidence, it is at least unfortunate that the respondent is alleging that the appellant is impeding that maintenance or development of effective competition to itself. The question of competition can only arise if there is another entity, real, or potential, that can offer competition.[4]

This statement clearly shows that the Court was unaware of the economic concept of a market or of a monopoly market structure. However, as Beckford noted, it is not only Caribbean judges who may show lack of understanding of economics when adjudicating cases.[5]

The purpose of this chapter is to outline, briefly, some of the economic concepts and theories relevant to competition law enforcement – in particular, those considered useful in understanding the competition matters dealt with in this book. The chapter does not seek to provide a comprehensive and detailed introduction to the economics of competition law, which are both outside the scope of this book.[6]

2.2 The economic benefits of competition

Economics has been described as 'the study of how individuals and societies choose between the alternative uses of scarce resources to satisfy their innumerable wants'.[7] Indeed, at any point in time, there is a fixed stock of resources available to satisfy innumerable wants and needs of individuals and societies. A competitive free-market mechanism allocates scarce resources in the most optimal way to satisfy the needs and wants of consumers.[8]

3 Supreme Court Civil Appeal No. 92/97, 66.
4 Ibid.
5 See D. S. Beckford, 'Enforcement of Competition Law in CARICOM: Perspectives on Domestic, Regional and Multilateral Obligations' (2010) 35(2) WILJ 109. He raises criticism with regard to the Judicial Committee of the Privy Council judgment in *National Commercial Bank Ltd v Olint Corp. Ltd* [2009] UKPC 16.
6 See an excellent introduction to economics of competition law by S. Bishop and M. Walker, *The Economics of EC Competition Law: Concepts, Application and Measurement*, 3rd edn, 2010, London: Sweet and Maxwell; also G. Niels, H. Jenkins and J. Kavanagh, *Economics for Competition Lawyers*, 2011, Oxford: OUP.
7 P. Maunder, D. Myers, N. Wall and R. Le Roy Miller, *Economics Explained*, 3rd edn, 2000, London: Collins, p 5.
8 In some circumstances, free-market mechanisms may fail to do this: ibid., pp 123–130.

Economists typically assess alternative market mechanisms based on how efficiently the mechanisms utilise the scarce productive resources of the society. A competitive market stands out from the other market mechanisms because it is the only one to be classified as efficient along the following distinct economic concepts of efficiency.

- Productive efficiency. This occurs when the economy is utilising all of its resources efficiently by producing goods and services at the minimum average cost.
- Allocative efficiency. This occurs when there is an optimal distribution of goods and services – that is, when goods are produced in the quantities desired by consumers.
- Total surplus (also known as 'total welfare' or 'social welfare', but see Chapter 3, section 3.2.3.3.A). This is the sum of consumer and producer surpluses. Consumer surplus measures the extent by which consumers' valuation of a product exceeds its price. Producer surplus measures the extent by which sales revenue exceeds the economic costs incurred to make the product available to consumers. Total surplus measures society's benefits by quantifying the extent by which consumers' valuation of a product exceeds the economic costs incurred in making the product available to consumers.

In a market that is perfectly competitive, competition law would be a redundant constraint on business conduct. In such a market, social welfare is maximised without the intervention of the State. Perfectly competitive markets do not exist in the real world. That is why competition law is necessary. Its enforcement constitutes a binding constraint on businesses and is deemed to be sufficient to promote the efficient use of scarce productive resources by the curbing of anti-competitive conduct of public and private entities.[9]

2.3 Basic economic concepts

This section deals with the basic economic concepts that are essential for understanding the economics of competition law and virtually all economics.

9 CSME competition law uses the term 'enterprise', whilst EU competition law uses the term 'undertaking' to describe an entity that is within the personal scope of competition law. Economists use the term 'firm', which can be defined as 'an organization that brings together different factors of production, such as labour, land and capital, to produce a product or service which it is hoped can be sold for a profit': ibid., p 343.

2.3.1 Demand and supply

The model of demand and supply is the foundation of all economic analysis. It explains why and how prices change. It combines two concepts: the 'demand curve'; and the 'supply curve'.

2.3.1.1 Demand

The theory of demand is rather simple. It can be described as follows: 'At higher prices, a lower quantity will be demanded than at lower prices, other things being equal.'[10] Examples of other non-price things that may influence demand include the tastes and preferences of buyers, the prices of related products and the income of buyers, which may affect their purchasing power. Provided that non-price factors (determinants) are held constant, prices have an inverse relationship with the quantity demanded. This is why a demand curve slopes downward, as illustrated in Figure 2.1.

If a non-price determinant of demand changes, then the entire demand curve shifts – either to the right or to the left. For example, if medical research is published showing that eating carrots increases life expectancy, then there will be an increase in demand for carrots, whereupon the demand curve will shift to the right. If medical research shows that eating carrots will decrease life expectancy, the demand curve will shift to the left. This is illustrated in Figure 2.2.

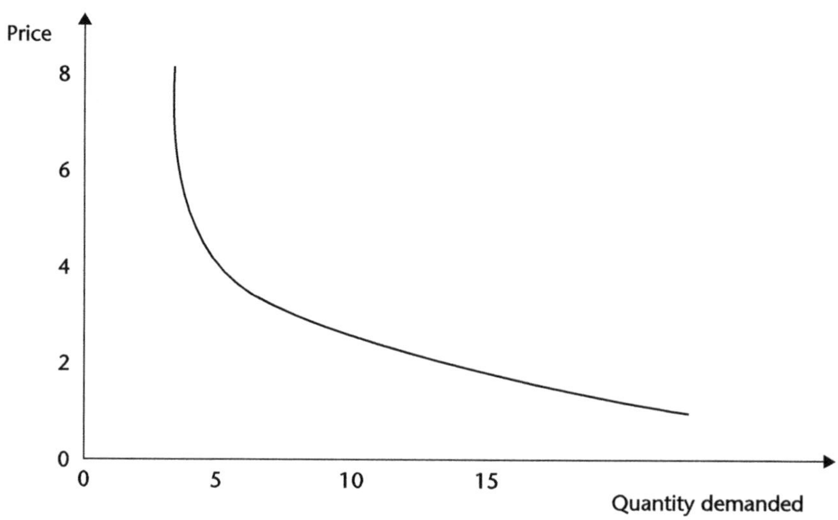

FIGURE 2.1 The demand curve

10 Supra note 7, p 42.

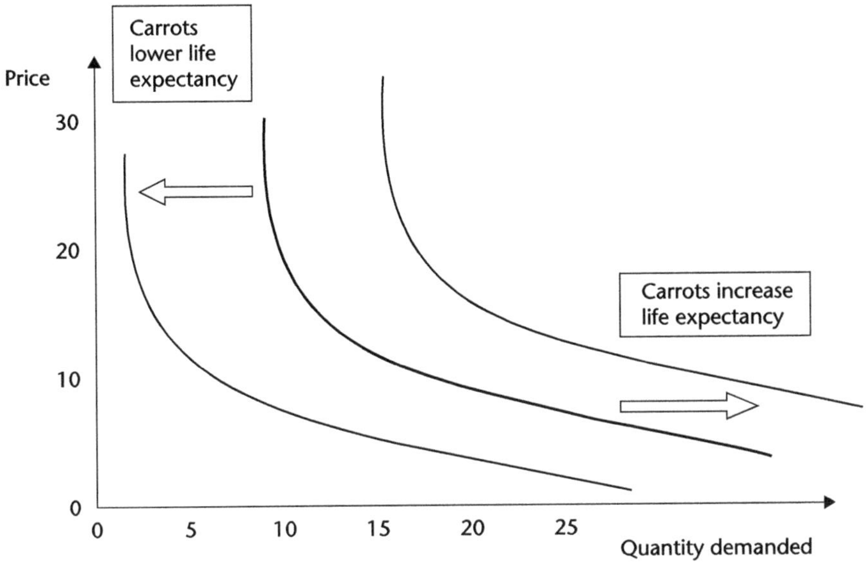

FIGURE 2.2 Shifts in the demand curve

It can be seen from Figure 2.2 that non-price determinants lead to change in demand, whilst changes in price lead to a change in quantity demanded.

2.3.1.2 Supply

The theory of supply says that, at higher prices, a larger quantity is supplied than at lower prices, all other things held constant. Examples of other non-price determinants include the prices of raw materials, changes in technology and the prices of related products. Provided that non-price factors are held constant, there is a direct relationship between quantity supplied and price. This is explained by the fact that suppliers have incentives for increasing production when prices increase. With the increase in quantity produced, there will be increase in the average costs of production, as illustrated in Figure 2.3.

A change in the non-price determinants of supply will shift the supply curve either to the left or to the right. For example, if an unknown disease kills half of the chicken population in Barbados, there will be a shift in the supply of chicken to the left. If a new drug is invented that makes chickens mature at a significantly faster pace, there will be a shift in the supply to the right. This is illustrated in Figure 2.4.

As can be seen from Figure 2.4, a change in a non-price determinant of supply leads to a change in supply, whilst a change in price leads to a change in the quantity supplied.

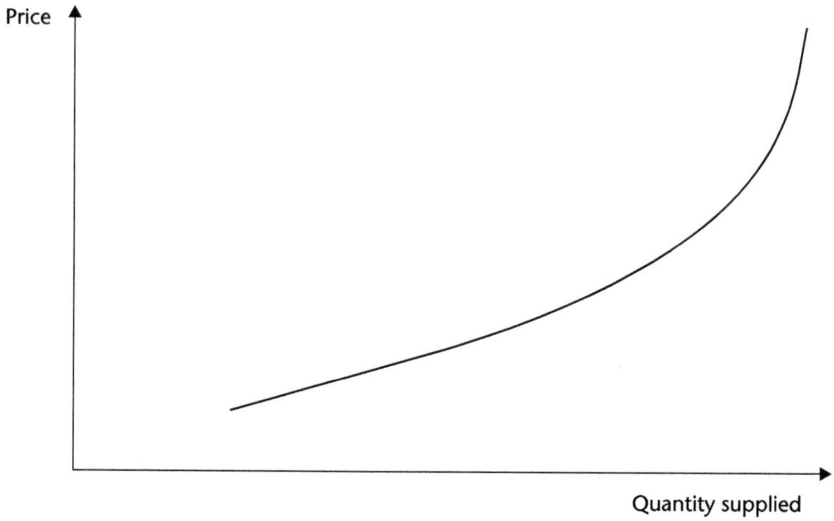

FIGURE 2.3 The supply curve

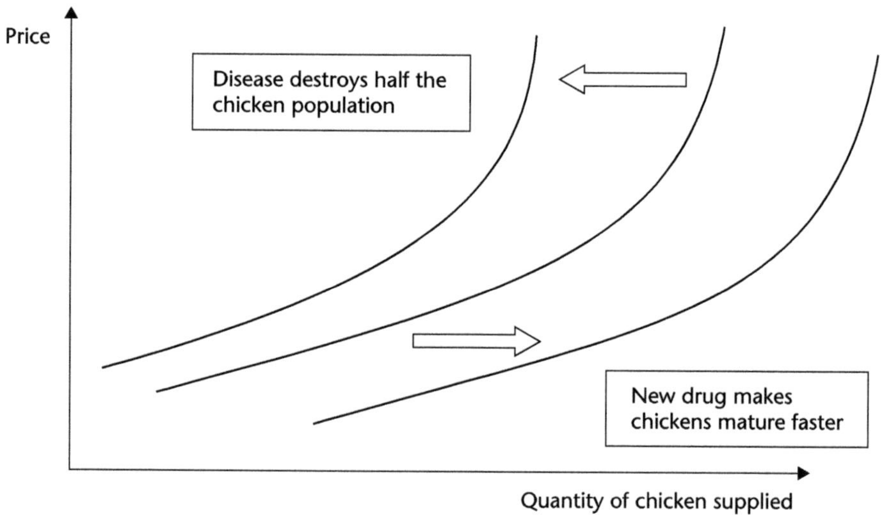

FIGURE 2.4 Shifts in the supply curve

2.3.1.3 The interaction between demand and supply

The interaction between demand and supply is essential to understanding how equilibrium prices and output are determined. This is illustrated in Figure 2.5.

As can be seen from Figure 2.5, the supply and demand curves intersect at point X. At that point, the market has determined the quantity of products that

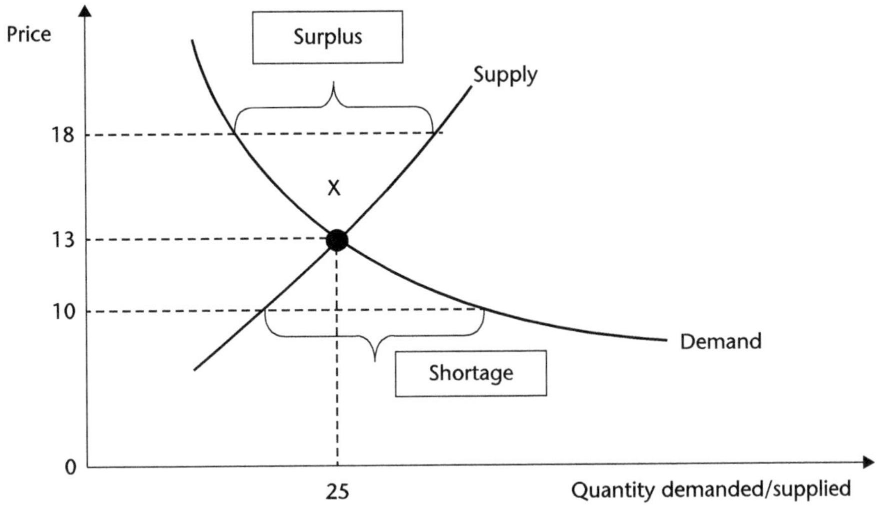

FIGURE 2.5 The interaction between demand and supply

would be supplied by the market and the prices at which they are sold. At the price of US$13 per unit, which is known as the 'market-clearing price', the quantity supplied equals the quantity demanded. There is neither an excess of quantity demanded (that is, a shortage) nor an excess of quantity supplied (that is, a surplus). The $13 price is called the 'market-clearing price' because it clears the market of all excess demand and excess supply. The market-clearing price is sometimes also referred to as the 'equilibrium price'.[11]

According to classical economists (see section 2.4.1), in a free-market economy, market forces have a tendency to adjust the price until the market clears. An example will illustrate why.

If the price is initially above the market-clearing price, producers will try to produce and sell more than consumers will be willing and able to buy. This will result in a surplus. To reduce the surplus, producers will lower prices. The fall in

11 The 'market clearing price' and the 'equilibrium price' are distinct concepts in economics and central to understanding the long-standing debate between the classical and Keynesian economic schools of thought. The equilibrium price is that price at which there is no longer a tendency for prices to increase or decrease in a market, whilst the market-clearing price is the price at which quantity demanded equals quantity supplied. The argument that the equilibrium price will always adjust to coincide with the market-clearing price is advanced by classical economists (see section 2.4.1). Keynesian economists, however, have demonstrated that some markets may come to rest in equilibrium at prices that do not clear the market. The Keynesian school of thought helps to explain the protracted high levels of unemployment (excess supply of labour) witnessed during the Great Depression of the 1930s. On this topic, see R. J. Gordon, 'What Is New-Keynesian Economics?' (1990) 28(3) *Journal of Economic Literature* 1115.

prices will stimulate an increase in the quantity demanded, which, in turn, will reduce the surplus, until prices fall to the market-clearing level.

The same mechanism will apply to a situation in which there is a shortage of demanded quantities – that is, a situation in which the quantity demanded by consumers exceeds the quantity supplied. When there is a shortage, some consumers will be unable to purchase product in the quantity desired, so they will try to outbid one another for existing quantities; suppliers will respond by increasing the price, and the output until the market-clearing price is reached.

2.3.1.4 Price elasticity of demand

The theory of demand, by itself, will not be helpful in deciding how much the quantity demanded will change when the price changes. Economists use the concept of 'price elasticity of demand' (PED) to define the responsiveness of consumers to changes in price. This is calculated as follows:

$$\text{PED} = \frac{\text{Percentage change in quantity demanded}}{\text{Percentage change in price}}$$

The elasticity measurement is about percentage change, not about absolute change. For example, if the price of a bicycle increases from US$2,000 to $2,200, the absolute increase is $200, but the percentage change is:

$$\frac{+200}{2{,}000} = +10\%$$

The key benchmark for measuring elasticity is whether a 1 per cent change in price elicits more or less than a 1 per cent change in the quantity demanded.

- If PED < 1, this means that demand for the product is price inelastic, i.e. that quantity demanded is not very sensitive to changes in price, and consequently changes by a smaller percentage than price changes.
- If PED $= 0$, this means that demand for the product is perfectly price inelastic. This entails that the quantity demanded will remain the same no matter the price. The best example of this is life-saving drugs: if a person needs a certain quantity of that drug to stay alive, he or she will pay any price asked.
- If PED $= 1$, this is called unit elasticity and occurs when a 1 per cent change in price causes a response of exactly 1 per cent change in the quantity demanded. This entails that if a firm raises its prices, its revenue will not change. If it decreases its prices, its revenue will not change either.
- If PED > 1, this means that demand for the product is price elastic. Accordingly, when a firm lowers its prices, its total revenue will rise, and if it raises its prices, its revenue will fall. The perfectly elastic demand situation is one in which the price elasticity of demand is approaching infinity – that

is, only one price can be charged because even a small increase in price will eliminate any quantity previously demanded for the product. This may occur, for example, if two products are perfect substitutes for each other. Suppose that a consumer normally buys 2 tons of one brand and 2 tons of another brand of margarine every month to make cakes for a big chain of supermarkets: both brands would sell for the same price because they are perfect substitutes. If the price for one brand were to be increased slightly, the consumer would simply switch to the other brand. He or she will buy only the cheapest brand of margarine and none of the higher priced brand.

As can be seen from the above, calculating PED is important because of its connection with a firm's total revenue (TR), which is in turn calculated by multiplying the price (P) by the quantity (Q) – that is:

$$\text{TR} = \text{P} \times \text{Q}$$

Accordingly, a firm will use PED to forecast its sales and to set prices for its products.

There are many factors that determine PED, such as the existence of close substitutes, the degree of necessity of the product, whether the product is habit-forming and the proportion of consumers' income which is spent on the product.

In the assessment of PED, it is important to consider the time factor – that is, how much time is allowed to pass before one measures the change in the quantity demanded. Depending upon the product, PED may be more elastic in the long run than in the short run, or *vice versa*. For example, in respect of petrol, an increase in price will have only a small effect on the quantity demanded in the short run. Consumers may decide to use their cars less often, but they will not rush to buy a new car. They will drive their existing cars until they decide to buy a new one. Their decision as to what car they want to buy will be motivated by the price of petrol. Accordingly, they will be likely to buy smaller and more fuel-efficient cars. As a result, PED will be more elastic in the long run than in the short run.

2.3.1.5 Cross-price elasticity of demand

'Cross-price elasticity of demand' (XED), or 'cross elasticity of demand', refers to the responsiveness of demand for one good to the price of another good. It is measured as follows:

$$\text{XED} = \frac{\text{Percentage change in quantity demanded for product A}}{\text{Percentage change in price of product B}}$$

For example, if the price for a loaf of bread increases by 10 per cent (say from US$1 to $1.10), the increase in price is likely to increase demand for bread rolls.

If the demand for bread rolls increases by 10 per cent (say, from 100 bread rolls to 110), then XED can be calculated as:

$$\frac{+10\%}{+10\%} = 1$$

When two products are substitutes, then XED > 0 (that is, XED is positive). When the products are complements, then XED < 0 (that is, it is negative). If XED = 0, the two products are considered to be unrelated in demand.

The determination of XED allows a firm to calculate the number of its rivals, as well as the importance of complementary products to its own products. It also demonstrates the risk to which a firm is exposed in terms of the change of prices of its rivals and producers of complementary products. In competition law enforcement, XED is an essential tool in the determination of the relevant product market (see section 2.5.1.1).

2.3.1.6 The maximisation of profit

Economists assume that, whatever the structure of the market (see section 2.4.2), a firm will seek to maximise its profit. This assumption has been challenged in respect of big firms in which managers are insufficiently controlled by the owners (the shareholders) and therefore, instead of focusing on profit maximisation, may be more concerned with revenue maximisation, or the payment of dividends to shareholders, or obtaining big bonuses. Notwithstanding this, the assumption serves as the basis for welfare economics.

Economists distinguish between two types of profit: accounting profit and economic profit.

Accounting profit equals total revenue (TR) less total explicit costs. 'Explicit costs' are actual payments made by a firm to acquire factors of production, such as labour, equipment, land and raw materials.

Economic profit equals total revenue (TR) less total costs explicit and implicit (TC). 'Implicit costs' can be defined as the value of the best forgone option to the factors of production employed by the firm. This includes, *inter alia*, the implicit cost of capital and the implicit cost of labour. The implicit cost of capital refers to the minimum amount of income that a firm's owner has forgone by deciding to invest in the firm rather than in any other venture.

The concept of implicit cost is best illustrated by the following example. Suppose that an owner of a firm left employment to run her own business selling brooms. In her previous employment, the owner received an annual salary of US$10,000. This salary represents an implicit cost of operating the business. Suppose that the new business makes a total accounting profit of $5,000. This means that the firm earns an economic loss of $5,000.

When a firm earns zero economic profit, economists say that the firm is making 'normal profits'. When a firm earns a normal profit, therefore, it earns revenues equal to its total costs (TC) – that is, explicit and implicit costs. Normal economic profit is an important threshold in economic analysis. It is the minimum level of profit required to ensure that the firm is prepared to remain in its present area of production in the long run.

As can been seen, the word 'profit' has a special meaning in economics: when referring to 'profits', economists mean economic profits.[12]

A firm maximises its profit when its marginal cost (MC) equals its marginal revenue (MR) and its marginal cost is rising. Profit is calculated as:

$$\text{Profit} = \text{Total revenue (TR)} - \text{Total costs (TC)}$$

To determine the production level associated with generating the maximum profit, it is necessary to explain various types of revenue and cost of a firm.

A Types of cost

The costs of a firm are calculated as:

$$\text{Total costs (TC)} = \text{Fixed costs (FC)} + \text{Variable costs (VC)}$$

The types of cost can be defined as follows.

- Fixed costs (FC) are costs to a firm that do not vary with the level of production, such as rent for its premises and repayment of a loan from a bank.
- Variable costs (VC) are costs to a firm that vary with the level of production. They include the costs of raw materials, the cost of electricity, and expenditure for wages and salaries.
- Marginal cost (MC), also known as 'incremental cost', refers to those costs that result from a one-unit change in the production level – that is, it is the increase in costs that results from producing one extra unit of output. It is calculated by using this formula:

$$\text{Marginal cost (MC)} = \frac{\text{Change in total cost}}{\text{Change in total quantity}}$$

B Types of revenue

The types of revenue are as follows.

12 See R. A. Arnold, *Economics*, 8th edn, 2008, Mason, OH: Thompson, p 411.

- Total revenue (TR). This is calculated by multiplying the quantity (Q) by price (P):

  $$TR = Q \times P$$

- *Marginal revenue* (MR) is the additional revenue that will be generated by increasing production by one unit. It is calculated as:

  $$\text{Marginal revenue (MR)} = \frac{\text{Change in total revenue}}{\text{Change in total quantity}}$$

C The relationship between costs and revenues

The example in Table 2.1 explains the relationship between various costs and revenues in the determination of circumstances in which a firm will maximise its profits.

TABLE 2.1 Profit maximisation

Quantity (units)	*Price (US$ per unit)*	*TR ($)*	*MR ($)*	*TC ($)*	*MC ($)*	*Profit ($) (TR − TC)*	*Profit maximisation condition (MR − MC)*
0	10	0	–	5	–	−5	–
1	9	9	9	10	5	−1	+4
2	8	16	7	12	2	4	+5
3	7	21	5	13	1	8	+4
4	6	24	3	16	3	8	0
5	5	25	1	20	4	5	−3
6	4	24	−1	22	2	2	−1

As Table 2.1 shows, profits will be at the highest when MR = MC – that is, when a firm produces four units at a price of US$6 per unit.[13] When MR > MC, an increase in output increases total profit; when MR < MC, then the total profit decreases.

2.3.1.7 Economies of scale and scope

'Economies of scale' is said to occur when inputs are increased by some percentage and output increases by a greater percentage, causing the cost of

13 The curious reader will observe that the firm earns maximum profit at US$8 at production levels of three units and four units. This occurs simply because, in this example, only discrete units of production are allowed (i.e. no production takes place between three and four units). We know that the equilibrium output level is four units and not three units because of a second condition for profit maximisation, i.e. MC must be increasing. At three units of output, MC decreased from $2 to $1, whereas at four units of production, MC increased from $1 to $3.

a unit of production to fall.[14] An example provided by Arnold illustrates this point.[15]

Suppose that product X is made of two inputs, Y and Z, each of which costs US$1. Suppose also that it takes 20Y and 10Z to produce five units of X. Thus the total cost of producing five units of X equals $30 ($20Y + $10Z = $30). The total average cost of X equals $6 per unit ($30 ÷ 5 units). If the cost of inputs Y and Z doubles, so that Y will cost $40 and Z will cost $20, and the output is more than doubled, say, to 15 units of X, the total cost of input will be $60, whilst the average total cost of each unit will be $4.

Many factors may result in a firm experiencing economies of scale.[16] Some may arise internally and others, externally.

- Internal factors are specific to an individual firm, for example arising from buying raw materials in bulk, or diversified production to ensure that a change in demand or supply will not put the firm out of business. Alternatively, a firm may use its profit to invest in research and development, which in turn will ensure high returns, or may benefit from the 'network effect' or 'learning effect' (see Chapter 7, section 7.4.1), or may acquire new technology that a smaller firm is not able to purchase.
- External factors may be factors that are external to the firm or factors external to the entire industry, for example improvements in a railway system that reduce the cost of transportation for all firms, or the relocation of a supplier of a firm closer to its plant, which will result in savings in transportation costs for that particular firm.

There is, however, a point at which the total average cost ceases to decrease and internal economies of scale are exhausted – that is, no further economies of scale can be achieved. This point is known as the 'minimum efficiency scale' (MES). In competition law, MES is important because of its implications for the structure of the industry and the assessment of barriers to entry. Industries in which MES is low will have a relatively large number of firms that are able to operate without making a loss. Conversely, in industries in which MES is high, a small number of firms – possibly only one – will be able to operate profitably. When MES can be achieved by only one firm, the market is said to be a 'natural monopoly'.

A natural monopoly is a type of a monopoly market structure where only one firm can profitably serve the market. It occurs in industries in which large scale

14 R. A. Arnold, *Economics*, 8th edn, 2008, Mason, OH: Thompson, p 427. In other words, economies of scale are said to occur when an expansion in output results in a lower average cost of production.
15 Ibid.
16 For examination of all factors see, ibid., pp 355–356.

infrastructure is required to ensure supply, such as cable and grits for electricity, and pipe lines for gas and water. Any new entrant will have to duplicate that infrastructure – that is, duplicate all fixed factors – and thus incur 'sunk costs' – that is, costs that it will not be able to recover when exiting the market. Wasteful duplication of resources creates losses for society, the result of which is that it is not profitable for a competitor to enter the market. Accordingly, there is a 'natural' reason for this industry being a monopoly – namely, that the economies of scale dictate that only one firm, rather than several, can profitably operate in the market.

Economies of scope occur when it is cheaper to produce two or more products together than it is to produce each separately. A good example of achieving economy of scope is that of a firm expanding its range of products to exploit the value of existing brands, for example McDonald's expanding its range of products to include healthy food.

2.4 Economic theories of competition

This section examines different schools of economic thought as they have changed over time, and can be expected to continue to change to address the challenges faced by the enforcement of competition law. It explains some economic concepts that are an integral part of 'competition economics', a discipline that deals specifically with the economics of competition law.

2.4.1 Classical theories of competition

Classical economists of the late eighteenth century, such as Adam Smith, David Ricardo, Jean-Baptiste Say and John Stuart Mill, were first to study competition matters. According to Smith, competition was a behavioural process. He posited that each individual pursues the satisfaction of his own self-interest, but nevertheless 'is led by an invisible hand to promote an end which was not part of his intention'.[17] This end was to achieve maximum social welfare for the nation. Competition was described as an endless rivalrous process through which natural prices – that is, prices close to the cost of production – were achieved.

2.4.2 The neoclassical theory of competition

Neoclassical economists of the late nineteenth and early twentieth centuries focused on the structural interpretation of competition. They developed two models of market structure: a perfectly competitive market and its opposite, a pure monopoly.

2.4.2.1 A perfectly competitive market

A 'perfectly competitive market' can be characterised as follows.

17 A. Smith, *The Wealth of Nations*, 1976, New York: The Modern Library, p 456.

- Buyers and sellers have no control over prices; they are 'price takers', rather than 'price makers'. In such a market, there are many firms that compete with each other. Each firm sells a sufficiently small proportion of the total market output that the decisions of its owners have no market impact on price. Similarly, there are many consumers in the market whose decisions will not affect the market price. The result is that the buyers and the sellers are price takers. The price is determined by the market and fixed at the market-clearing price – that is, at the price at which the quantity demanded is equal to the quantity supplied.
- There is product homogeneity – that is, the products of all of the firms in the market are perfectly substitutable with one another. Any rise of the price of a product above that being charged by other firms will result in a total loss of sales.
- Firms can freely enter and leave the market – that is, there are no special costs that make it difficult for a new firm to enter the market or to exit it if it cannot make a profit.
- Buyers and sellers have complete access to information, so allowing for free and rational decision-making.
- There are no externalities – that is, no uncompensated costs imposed by a firm on others. Each firm bears the full costs of its production process. For example, pollution produced by a firm is an externality, because the firm does not recompense the victims.

In a perfectly competitive market, firms have no control over prices. They are price takers. Prices are determined by the market forces of supply and demand. According to Marshall, one of the most prominent advocates of the neoclassical theory, in a perfectly competitive market, the equilibrium price of a product will be the market-clearing price – that is, a price that equates demand and supply (at which price the amount that buyers are willing to purchase will be just equal to the amount for which sellers are willing to take that price).[18] The equilibrium price will be equal to the average cost of the firm. The term 'average cost' (AC) is used interchangeably with the term 'average total cost' (ATC). The AC is equal to a firm's total costs divided by its level of output. The equilibrium price has to be accepted by all sellers as given. If they try to sell for more than the equilibrium price, they will find no customers, bearing in mind that customers will be able to acquire the same product elsewhere at a competitive price.

In a perfectly competitive market, the market demand curve slopes downwards. However, the demand curve for any particular firm is horizontal or perfectly elastic. This means that each firm can sell as much as it wants without lowering

18 See Marshall's theory on the equilibrium price in F. M. Machovec, *Perfect Competition and the Transformation of Economics*, 1995, London: Routledge, p 176.

the price. This difference between the two curves is explained by the fact that each firm is small in size, so that its output, whatever the amount, will not have any effect on the market price.

With regard to quantity, firms choose the level of output that maximises their profit, such maximisation of profit being achieved at the point at which marginal cost is equal to marginal revenue (MC = MR), and MC is rising (see section 2.3.1.6). Bearing in mind that firms know that they can sell any quantity that they want at competitive price, MR from selling an additional product will always equal the market price.

An implication of the equilibrium price being equal to average cost is that no firm makes a positive economic profit in the long run. If the price is high enough to make such a profit, firms that are not in the market will enter it, with a view to making positive profit. Because there are no barriers to entry, entry will continue until incumbent firms can no longer make positive profits. Once the price falls below the average cost, a firm will operate at a loss and thus will exit the market.

According to the neoclassical school of thought, in a perfectly competitive market there will be neither shortages nor surpluses. Accordingly, social welfare will be maximised (see section 2.2).

A perfectly competitive market is efficient in the economic sense. According to the paradigm of 'Pareto efficiency', which was developed by the Italian economist Vilfredo Pareto at the end of the nineteenth century, in a perfectly competitive market, resources are allocated in the most efficient way. No one wishes to produce more than demanded and all prices are fair. There is general equilibrium, entailing that no improvements can be made in the allocation of resources to one individual without it causing a loss to others. In other words, it is not possible to make one person better off without another being worse off. Pareto efficiency emphasises the welfare of the individual. Any change that increases the welfare of at least one person without decreasing the welfare of another is regarded as an improvement in social welfare. However, Pareto efficiency is indifferent to the equitable redistribution of wealth, in that those who have wealth and market power can increase their wealth and power so long as their conduct does not reduce the welfare of others.

In a perfectly competitive market, firms will be dynamically efficient as they will strive to produce new products and increase the quality of existing products. However, some economists posit that there is little scope for innovation in a perfectly competitive market, bearing in mind that products are homogeneous. Further, the fact that firms sell the products at a price that equals the production cost entails that they have no money to invest in research and development – a necessary and costly precondition to any innovation.

2.4.2.2 A monopoly

A pure monopoly exists where there is only one firm on the market supplying a particular product for which there is no close substitute. Its power to continue to exist in the long run is ensured by barriers that prevent other firms from entering the market for the supply of the particular product. These barriers may be legal or technical, or may result from the cost structure of the market. For example, a monopolist may control essential natural resources for which there is no close substitute, or be given by a government monopoly rights in a particular area, or be a holder of intellectual property rights, or operate in a market that needs large capital investment to enter it.

A monopoly, unlike a firm operating in a competitive market, is a price maker. A monopoly is the entire industry, thus it faces the entire market demand curve. The market demand curve, as in a perfectly competitive market, slopes downwards. Thus, to sell more units, a monopoly must lower the price. Unless it is able to discriminate between its consumers, it must lower the price on all units sold to sell more – that is, not only lower the price on the last unit sold. For example, if a monopolist sells one unit for US$5, but another unit for $4, the consumer who buys for $4 will buy a lot of units and sell each unit for a price of, say, $4.89 to a consumer who is willing to buy the unit for $5. For that reason, a monopolist must sell for a uniform price unless it can somehow prevent secondary transactions among the consumers in the relevant market.

Unlike a firm operating in a perfectly competitive market, a monopoly faces a downward-sloping marginal revenue curve, which entails that the more it sells, the lower the price it can charge its customers. A monopoly, as any firm, wants to maximise profits. Like a firm in a perfectly competitive market, a monopolist maximises profit when its revenue from selling an additional unit just equals the extra cost of producing the last unit of output – that is, profits are maximised where marginal revenue equals marginal cost (MR = MC) (see section 2.3.1.6). For a firm operating in a perfectly competitive market, its MR equals the market price, whilst for a monopoly MR is always less than price.

Why does a monopoly produce less and thus charge a higher price per unit than a firm operating in a perfectly competitive market? This is because the monopoly faces a downward-sloping marginal revenue curve, which means that it has to sell every additional unit for a lower price, and must lower that price on all units produced and sold. To maximise profits, a monopolist must restrict its production to ensure that MR = MC. Because a monopoly restricts its production, the monopoly price is always higher than the competitive price. By contrast, a firm operating in a perfectly competitive market faces a horizontal MR curve – that is, it does not have to reduce its revenue per unit if it increases its output. Whatever its output, it always sells each unit of production at a competitive price, which equals its MR. This is because its output is too small to affect the market price.

The fact that a monopoly charges consumers a higher price than a competitive price means that it makes a supranormal profit (the area between P1 and P2 in Figure 2.6). However, the worst harm caused by a monopoly is that it

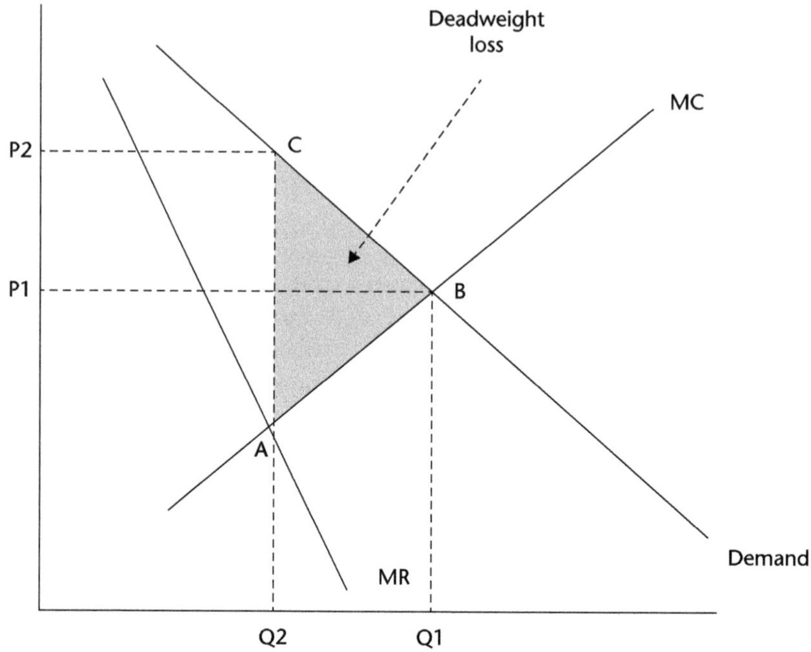

FIGURE 2.6 Deadweight loss from monopoly power

reduces output below the socially optimal level – that is, it creates the 'deadweight welfare loss' (see triangular area between A, B, and C in Figure 2.6). This is the reduction in consumer surplus that is not transferred to the monopoly or to anyone else.

As can be seen from Figure 2.6, a monopoly is inefficient with regard to the following.

- Allocative efficiency. This is because customers who are willing and able to pay for a product at a competitive price cannot purchase the product, given that the price is greater than marginal cost. For society, the loss of welfare is equal to the deadweight area.
- Productive efficiency. This is because monopolies do not produce enough to achieve economies of scale and thus do not produce at the lowest average cost possible.
- Dynamic efficiency. Many economists posit that monopolies are not dynamically efficient because they have no incentive to innovate. Others argue that such firms are dynamically efficient, because they are the only ones that can allocate the supranormal profits that they gain to research and

development, and thus, in the long-run bring innovation that benefits consumers.[19]

- X-efficency. This concept was introduced by Liebenstein, an American economist, who argued that, because of organisational slack resulting from lack of competitive constraints, monopolies are always likely to be technically or productively inefficient.[20] According to Liebenstein, X-inefficiency arises from losses of output attributable to the motivated deficiency of resource owners. The counter-argument is that monopolies, as any other firms, want to maximise profit, and therefore if improvement of the efficiency of operation increases profits, monopolies are likely to so improve.
- Distributive inefficiency. This refers to the distribution of resources between consumers and producers. Monopolists, because they make supranormal (above normal) profits and transfer them only internally, cause inequitable distribution of resources. For that reason, there is a suggestion that competition law should be concerned with controlling prices on concentrated markets. The concept of distributive efficiency is highly debated by economists, and political in nature.[21] The counter-argument is that the optimal distribution of profit can be ensured, bearing in mind that profits can be redistributed to shareholders (by means of dividends), to employees (by means of profit-sharing mechanisms) and to society (by imposing appropriate taxes on monopolies). Finally, a monopoly may keep its profits provided that it uses them to invest in research and development, so benefiting society.

2.4.2.3 Criticising neoclassical theory

The neoclassical theory has been criticised for a number of reasons, including:

- that it is based on unrealistic assumptions – that is, an idealistic concept of perfect competition that does not exist in the real world;
- that its highly abstract and theoretical content is of little usefulness for policymaking; and
- that it does not take account of the behavioural aspect of competition.

However, it can be said that the concept of perfect competition is useful because it serves as a benchmark against which the performance of actual markets can be measured. The closer the characteristics of an actual market to those of a perfectly

19 A. Schumpeter, *Capitalism, Socialism and Democracy*, 3rd edn, 1962, New York: Harper.
20 H. Leibenstein, 'Allocative Efficiency vs X-Efficiency' (1966) 56(3) American Economic Review 392.
21 See R. von den Berg and P. D. Camesasca, *European Competition Law and Economics: A Comparative Perspective*, 2001, Oxford: Hart Publishing, p 6.

competitive market, the more competitive the actual market will be. Marshal's contribution, in addition to the idea that the price and output are determined by both supply and demand law, is notable for introducing the concept of the 'price elasticity of demand', and the concepts of 'consumer surplus' and 'producer surplus', all of which continue to be used by modern economists (see section 2.3).

Dissatisfaction with the two extremes in the market structure led economists in the 1920s and 1930s to develop two new models of a market structure: monopolistic competitive market and oligopoly.

A A monopolistic competitive market

Monopolistic competition can be characterised as follows.

- There is a significant number of firms in a highly competitive market owing to low – or no – barriers to entry.
- Products are differentiated. Contrary to a perfectly competitive market, in which products are homogenous, in a monopolistic market, there is product differentiation. Each producer has a monopoly over its own product, which is slightly different from the products of its competitors. Each differentiated product has many substitutes and therefore price demand is elastic. This means that a firm's ability to increase price above the price of close substitutes is very small.
- Firms advertise and promote sales of their products. Unlike a perfectly competitive market, in a monopolistic market, firms promote their products. Advertisement is used to shift the demand curve to the right – or at least to maintain existing market share. The increase in sales resulting from advertisement can lead to economies of scale, but this strategy can be rational only if the reduction in costs arising from exploiting economies of scale outweighs the costs of advertising.

In the short run, in a monopolistic competitive market, it is possible for a firm to make economic profits, but in the long run economic profits may be competed away either because new firms enter the market to achieve a higher rate of returns, or because existing competing firms increase the quality of products or improve their advertisement strategies.

B An oligopolistic market

The main characteristics of an oligopolistic market are as follows.

- There is a limited number of firms in the market. As a result, the market is highly concentrated. The number of firms depends on the industry, but an oligopolistic market exists when firms dominating the market can effectively control the supply, and thus the price, thereby creating a seller's market.

- Firms are interdependent. This means that each firm will react to what other firms do in terms of changes in the price or non-price factors, such as output, quality and differentiation of products. Accordingly, each firm will try to predict reactions of its competitors.
- As would occur in the case of a monopoly, firms in an oligopolistic market maintain their dominance because of high barriers to entry, which may be divided into 'natural' or 'artificial'. Examples of natural barriers are economies of scale, high sunk costs, and high research and development costs, which are particularly apparent in respect of entry to the pharmaceutical industry. Examples of artificial barriers are the ownership of intellectual property rights and the conduct of firms in an oligopolistic market, which might charge predatory prices, ensuring that a new entrant will not be able to survive, or create loyalty schemes, which will ensure that their customers do not seek supplies from a new entrant.

An oligopoly poses a great challenge to the enforcement of competition law. Interdependency among firms means that it may be difficult to distinguish between a 'collusive oligopoly' and a 'competing oligopoly' because of the structure of the market: because each firm follows another in terms of price and non-price factors, it may appear that firms are colluding. Particularly difficult to establish is 'tacit collusion' – that is, a situation in which the enforcement authority cannot show that there was any direct or indirect contact between oligopolists, but they nonetheless display parallel behaviour by, for example, simultaneously changing prices (see Chapter 7, section 7.2.1).

2.4.3 The Harvard and the Chicago schools of competition theory

The theories of competition presented by the Harvard and the Chicago schools have greatly influenced the enforcement of competition law in the United States[22] and in other jurisdictions, including the European Union. Further, those theories have enriched debate on the objectives of competition law, emphasising the economic approach to the enforcement of competition law and the role of efficiency in assessing the business conduct of firms.

2.4.3.1 The Harvard school theory of competition

In the 1960s, economists and lawyers associated with the University of Harvard – Professor Joe Bain the most prominent amongst them – presented their theory of competition. They rejected the neoclassical theory as being too abstract and instead focused on empirical studies of US industries.

22 See E. Elhauge, 'Harvard, not Chicago: Which Antitrust School Drives Recent Supreme Court Decisions?' (2007) 3(2) Competition Policy International 59.

Their research led them to conclude that market structure, captured in the model or paradigm of 'structure–conduct–performance' (SCP), should be central to the enforcement of competition law.

- Structure refers to the structure of industry determined by such factors as the number of competitors, the product heterogeneity, and the barriers to entry and exit.
- Conduct concerns the behaviour of a firm in the relevant industry.
- Performance describes both the performance of an individual firm and the performance of the entire industry.

According to this theory, there is a stable causal SCP relationship in that the industry performance depends on the conduct of a firm, which in turn depends on the structure of the market. Thus structure determines conduct and conduct determines performance.

Harvard scholars, using the SCP paradigm, examined four market structures: a perfectly competitive market; a monopolistic competitive market; an oligopolistic market; and a monopolistic market. They noticed that each type of structure of the market has differing implications on the level of social welfare in that it is maximised in a perfectly competitive market and very low in a monopolistic market. They concluded that most US industries were more concentrated than necessary, that there were very high barriers to entry and that pricing above competitive level occurred at a low level of concentration in an oligopolistic market. Accordingly, they posited that competition policy should be used to decentralise the economic power of industries. In the 1960s, this was favourably viewed by the US government and US courts, which sought to protect small and medium-sized enterprises (SMEs). As a result, recommendations made by economists from the Harvard school resulted in very interventionist enforcement of US anti-trust law.[23]

The SCP paradigm came under fierce attack, *inter alia*, for its reliance on empirical evidence, its simplistic assessment of the relationship between conduct, structure and performance, and its assumption that there are no important differences between industries. In the United States, its influence petered out in the 1970s, as the influence of the Chicago school grew. Notwithstanding this, the Harvard school of competition theory has made an important contribution to the development of competition law. The structural analysis of the relevant market is the vital part of the assessment of anti-competitive behaviour of firms and of great importance in merger analysis.

23 See A. Jones and B. Sufrin, *EU Competition Law*, 4th edn, 2011, Oxford: OUP, p 22.

2.4.3.2 The Chicago school theory of competition

In the 1960s and 1970s, economists and lawyers associated with the University of Chicago – Aaron Director, Robert Bork and Richard Posner (a US Court of Appeal judge) the most prominent amongst them – developed a new anti-trust theory that greatly influenced the application of competition law in the United States under the Reagan and Bush administrations.[24]

The Chicago school rehabilitated neoclassical competition theory – in particular, elaborating on basic premises of neoclassical price theory and positing that the pursuit of allocative efficiency should be the sole objective of competition law, because it maximises consumer welfare. 'Consumer welfare' is understood as social welfare or total welfare. Under this theory, the distribution of wealth between consumers and producers is neutral. In other words, the matter of who gains and who loses from a particular business practice is irrelevant as long as there is maximisation of the aggregate welfare of producers and consumers.

The Chicago school economists posited that the pursuit of allocative efficiency requires unfettered free markets and no intervention from governments or competition law. Further, they believed that people behave rationally, and that the market corrects itself and achieves efficiency itself.

On monopolisation, Chicago scholars posited that its social cost is slight and that any exclusionary conduct should be allowed unless that conduct is shown to restrict output and is incapable of being justified as an attempt to better serve consumers. They also believed that the prohibition of exclusionary business strategies deters efficiency, coddles inefficient competitors and hurts consumers. The Chicago school of competition theory has, however, been challenged in light of the global financial and economic crisis of 2007–08, which demonstrated that 'markets are not perfect, imperfect markets do not always correct themselves, businessmen do not always behave rationally'.[25]

2.4.3.3 Post-Chicago and recent economic theories

It is outside the scope of this book to examine the economic theories put forward subsequent to those of the Chicago school. All of the more recent theories

24 For an overview of Chicago School economics, see W. H. Page, 'The Chicago School and the Evolution of Antitrust: Characterization, Antitrust Injury, and Evidentiary Sufficiency' (1989) 75 VA L Rev 1221.

25 See US Federal Trade Commission (FTC) Commissioner J. T. Rosch, 'Implications of the Financial Meltdown for the FTC', Speech made at the New York Bar Association Annual Dinner, 29 January 2009, New York available at http://www.ftc.gov/speeches/rosch/090129financialcrisisnybarspeech.pdf [accessed 16 October 2013]. The Chicago School theory, with its abiding faith in markets, has been subjected to a barrage of criticism: see e.g. R. Dibadj, 'Saving Antitrust' (2004) 75 U Colo L Rev 745; C. E. Mueller, 'Antitrust Economists and the "Flying Dutchman": How Economists Ruined Antitrust in Reagan's 1980s' (2008) 32 Antitrust Law and Economics Review 1.

recognise that markets are more complex than the model presented by Chicago school. These theories are part of new industrial economics and the most eminent among them are game theory, principal-and-agent theory, the theory of externalities, the contestable market hypothesis, the 'raising rival's costs' theory, the transaction costs theory and behavioural economics.[26]

2.5 The methodology of competition law

This section analyses the concept of 'market power', which is a key concept in the enforcement of competition law, bearing in mind that competition law is concerned with the power of enterprises to distort the competitive process. Competition legislation enacted around the world is founded on the unsubstantiated presumption that only firms with market power could stifle competition and abuse their power to the detriment of consumers. Professor Steven Salop, a prominent competition economist, demonstrated in a seminal paper that such a presumption is problematic, however, and warned against establishing lack of market power as a safe harbour for litigating alleged anti-competitive conduct.[27]

Notwithstanding the insightful comments of Professor Salop more than a decade ago, the determination of market power of an enterprise continues to be necessary in competition law to decide whether an agreement, decision or a concerted practice in which an enterprise participates has an appreciable cross-border effect on trade and competition within the Community (see Chapter 5, section 5.3) and to identify dominance under Article 178(a) RTC (see Chapter 7, section 7.2). Further, it is the key element in the assessment of mergers and acquisitions.

Market power can be exercised by a seller or by a buyer. However, economists generally refer to the position of a seller, rather than a buyer, to define market power.[28] In a perfectly competitive market, no enterprise has market power because no enterprise has the ability to affect individually either the total quantity of goods on the market or the prevailing prices in the market. Usually, economists refer to 'market power' to describe the ability of a seller to profitably impose prices above competitive prices for a sustainable period of time. The crucial issue is how to assess whether an enterprise has market power. Competition enforcement authorities, including the European Commission, usually determine whether market power exists by, first, defining the relevant market, second, measuring an individual firm's share and the industry concentration levels in that market, and, third, considering other relevant factors.[29]

26 See R. von den Berg and P. D. Camesasca, *European Competition Law and Economics: A Comparative Perspective*, 2001, Oxford: Hart Publishing, pp 11–74.

27 See S. C. Salop, 'The First Principles Approach to Antitrust: Kodak and Antitrust at the Millennium' (2001) 68 Antitrust Law Journal 187.

28 W. Landes and R. Posner, 'Market Power in Antitrust Cases' (1981) 94 Harv L Rev 939.

29 Steven Salop also warns against the practice, in litigation, to divorce the definition of the relevant market from the assessment of market power: Salop, op. cit.

2.5.1 Market definition

'Market definition' has been described by the Organisation for Economic Co-operation and Development (OECD) Competition Committee as 'one of the most important analytical tools to examine and evaluate the competitive constraints that a firm faces and the impact of its behaviour on competition'.[30]

The main purpose of market definition is to:

- identify all actual competitors of an enterprise under investigation – that is, all of its competitors operating in the same market;
- determine whether alleged anti-competitive business conduct has appreciable cross-border effect on trade and competition within the Community; and
- determine whether an enterprise has a dominant position on the relevant market, which position it can achieve only if it has market power.

To define the relevant market for competition law purposes, competition authorities use the 'hypothetical monopolist test' (HMT). It defines the relevant market as the smallest group of products in a geographical area for which a hypothetical monopolist, who controls that product group in that area, could profitably sustain a price at a level that was a small, but significant, amount above the 'competitive price'.

The HMT uses a range of between 5 and 10 per cent, which represents a 'small, but significant, non-transitory increase in price' (SSNIP).[31] This is known as the 'SSNIP test'. Accordingly, the objective of market definition is to find the smallest market in which a hypothetical monopolist could impose an SSNIP.

The relevant market has three components:

- the relevant product market (RPM), the determination of which is the most important and the most common issue in every case that raises competition concerns, but which poses a great challenge because of the interchangeability of many products (see section 2.5.1.1);[32]
- the relevant geographic market (RGM), the definition of which is necessary given that the prohibition applies only to enterprises that abuse their position 'within the Community'; and
- the relevant temporal market (RTM), if appropriate.

30 OECD Competition Committee, *Policy Roundtables Market Definition 2012*, October 2012, DAF.COM(2012) 19, p 11.

31 A price increase is regarded as non-transitory if it lasts at least for one year.

32 The release of the Horizontal Merger Guidelines (HMG) in 2010 signalled the intent of the US competition authorities to diminish the role that market definition plays in the economic assessment of a challenged conduct: US Department of Justice and the Federal Trade Commission, *Horizontal Merger Guidelines*, August 2010, available at http://www.ftc.gov/sites/default/files/attachments/merger-review/100819hmg.pdf [accessed 21 February 2014].

The Notice on the Definition of the Relevant Market for the Purposes of Community Competition Law[33] issued by the European Commission in 1997 is very helpful in understanding the concept of the relevant market. The Notice sets out the means (which are based on the practices ofboth the European Commission and the EU courts) of assessing the relevant product and geographical markets.

The European Commission identifies three main factors of competitive constraints to which undertakings are subject and which are used to identify the three relevant markets (RPM, RGM and RTM) – that is, demand substitutability, supply substitutability and potential competition. Regarding potential competition, it should be noted that this factor, although of relevance when supply substitutability is assessed, is essentially taken into consideration in the assessment of the market power of the enterprises concerned.

2.5.1.1 The relevant product market (RPM)

The 1997 European Commission Notice provides the following definition of the RPM: 'a relevant product market comprises all those products and/or services which are regarded as interchangeable or substitutable by the consumers, by reason of the products' characteristics, their prices and their intended uses'.[34]

The identification of the RPM depends on the determination of which products are substitutable, one for another. To determine whether products are or can be substituted, and thus to identify the RPM, two main factors of competitive constraints are taken into consideration: demand substitutability; and supply substitutability.

The enterprise under investigation will always seek a broad definition of the RPM, whilst the enforcement authority always seeks the opposite. The narrower the definition of a product market, the greater the market power of any one enterprise.

A Demand substitutability

The SSNIP assesses demand substitutability. If establishes if the hypothetical monopolist of the products under investigation would find it profitable to increase that product's price above the current level in a non-transitory way by 5 to 10 per cent. If yes, the product constitutes a separate market as there are no substitutes for it. If no (typically because a sufficently large number of consumers would switch some of their purchases to substitute products), it is assumed that the hypothetical monopolist controls both that product and its closest substitutes. The test is then repeated in relation to the larger set of products under the hypothetical monopolist's control until a separate market has been found.

33 [1997] OJ C 372/5.
34 Ibid., [7].

In assessing demand substitutability, economic evidence is used, such as market research surveys, interviews with competitors and customers, the price elasticity of demand for the product under investigation, and the cross-price elasticity of demand. Additionally, the time factor is important because customers may take time to respond to a sustained price increase. It is assumed that if substitution would take longer than one year, the product to which the customers would switch would be excluded from the relevant market.

The cellophane fallacy The SSNIP test yields erroneous conclusions about the relevant product if the competitive price is not used to benchmark the proposed price increase. If current prices are monopoly prices – that is, above competitive prices – it would be unprofitable for the hypothetical monopolist to increase prices further, since its products would probably be substituted with their closest substitutes. Therefore if current prices are above competitive prices, a further small increase of 5 per cent may encourage a critical level of consumers to switch to a product outside the relevant market. For example, if prices for railway tickets rise to that point, a significant number of consumers may decide to drive their own vehicle or take a coach. Thus the SSNIP test may include many substitutes (such as private cars and coaches) that should not have properly been included in the same product market as the hypothetical monopolist's product (trains). This problem is known as the 'cellophane fallacy' after a US case involving cellophane products.[35] In this case, the US Supreme Court erroneously accepted that cellophane was not a separate relevant market, but formed part of a market for flexible packaging materials, such as aluminium foil, polythene and wax paper. As a result, the Court failed to recognise that the price charged for cellophane was already a monopoly price.

The 1997 Notice recognises that the application of the SSNIP test may be inappropriate where the price of the relevant product has been determined in the absence of competition. Bearing in mind that the SSNIP test may be unreliable in a situation in which the current price is already a monopoly price, or the prevailing price is too low,[36] the European Commission has to take into account other factors to identify the relevant product market. These factors include excessive profit made by an undertaking and past fluctuations in prices, together with other evidence of market power and of the undertaking's conduct.[37] As the

35 *US v. El Du Pont de Nemours & Co.*, 351 US 377 (1956). This problem was acknowledged by the UK Office of Fair Trading (OFT) in Cases CA98/14/2002 *Aberdeen Journals Ltd v Office of Fair Trading* [2002] UKCLR 740 and CA98/20/2002 *BSkyB Investigation: Alleged Infringement of the Chapter II Prohibition* [2003] UKCLR 240.

36 See P. Crocioni, 'The Hypothetical Monopolist Test: What it Can and Cannot Tell You' [2002] ECLR 355.

37 For possible ways of solving the cellophane fallacy problem, see D. Geradin, A. Layne-Farrar and N. Petit, *EU Competition Law and Economics*, 2012, Oxford: OUP, pp 185–186.

Guidelines on Market Definition published by the UK Office of Fair Trading (OFT) emphasised, market definition is only a tool for assessing whether undertakings possess market power, not an end in itself.[38]

B Supply substitutability

'Supply substitutability' (the supply-side substitution) refers to the substitutability of products or otherwise, as assessed from the point of view of suppliers. The question to be asked is whether suppliers who do not currently supply the relevant products would be able to switch production to the relevant products and market them in the short term without incurring significant additional costs or risk, in response to small and non-transitory changes in prices. If this occurs, according to the 1997 Notice, 'the additional production that is put on the market will have a disciplinary effect on the competitive behaviour of the companies involved', and will be taken into consideration when defining the relevant product market, given that its effect in terms of effectiveness and immediacy is equivalent to the demand substitution effect.[39]

The important factor in assessing supply substitutability is time. If supply-side substitution would take place within a short time (usually one year, but it depends on the product), the supply-side substitution will be relevant to the definition of the RPM. Further, if a substantial investment would be needed, or if enterprises that might be involved in substitution were to have no excess capacity, or there would be substantial costs involving the advertisement or distribution of a substitute product, that product would not normally be included in the relevant product market.

C Power in aftermarkets

For many products, a customer must seek spare parts, or repair and maintenance services, or other supplementary or complementary products (for example cartridges for a laser printer and nails for use with nails guns, respectively) at a later date. The market for those products or services is referred to as an 'aftermarket'. The issue here is that an enterprise may not have market power with regard to its original product, but may nevertheless exercise it in respect of aftermarket products and services. Accordingly, if the RPM is defined as being confined to aftermarket products and services rather than the original products, the RPM may be very narrow and the undertaking concerned will be found to have market power.

38 UK OFT, '*Market Definition: Understanding Competition Law*, December 2004, available at http://www.oft.gov.uk/shared_oft/business_leaflets/ca98_guidelines/oft403.pdf [accessed 3 March 2014], p 4, [2.1].

39 European Commission, *Notice on the Definition of the Relevant Market for the Purposes of Community Competition Law* [1997] OJ C 372/5, [20].

It is important to note that the RPM in aftermarkets can be determined only after a factual inquiry into all of the circumstances of the case. A consumer may have already taken account of high prices of products and services in the aftermarkets when purchasing the original products. Accordingly, the high prices charged for spare parts or other supplementary or complementary products or services may constitute competitive restraints with regard to the original product market. In such a situation, there is only one RPM, not two separate product markets.

2.5.1.2 The relevant geographic market (RGM)

It is necessary to determine the RGM because the RTC requires that an enterprise must hold the alleged dominant position 'within the Community', or that a prohibited agreement, decision or concerted practice must have appreciable effect on trade and competition 'within the Community'.

Geographic markets are defined using the same criteria as those used to define the RPM. The demand side and the supply side are the main factors in determining the RGM. If customers will, or can, travel to obtain a different product in response to a 5 per cent increase in price, a hypothetical monopolist would not initiate a price increase, because this would lead to a large reduction in its sales and consequently its sales revenue would fall.

According to the 1997 European Commission Notice, a major factor in determining the geographic market is the consideration of whether, within that market, the cost and feasibility of transporting products are similar for all traders. Accordingly, when the cost of the product is low as compared with its transportation cost, as is the case for potatoes, the RGM is likely to be narrow; when the cost of the product is high as compared to its transportation cost, as is the case for cameras, the RGM is likely to be wide.

The 1997 European Commission Notice defines the RGM as:

> . . . the area in which the undertakings concerned are involved in the supply and demand of products or services, in which the conditions of competition are sufficiently homogeneous and which can be distinguished from neighbouring areas because the conditions of competition are appreciably different in those areas.[40]

To identify the RGM, criteria very similar to those used to define the RPM are to be applied, although not all of them will be relevant in any one case. The criteria are:

40 Ibid., [8].

- past evidence of diversion of orders to other areas;
- basic demand characteristics – that is whether there are local preferences based on brand, language, culture and the need for a local presence;
- the views of customers and retailers;
- the current geographic pattern of purchases;
- the trade flow or pattern of shipment when ascertaining the actual geographical pattern in the context of a large number of customers; and
- the barriers and costs associated with switching orders to companies situated in other areas.

2.5.1.3 The relevant temporal market (RTM)

The third dimension of the relevant market is that of the RTM. The existence of a temporal market affects the position of an enterprise in the market because, to be considered as being in a dominant position, an enterprise must be capable of sustaining such position for a considerable time.

The RTM takes account of how the timing of production and purchasing can affect markets. It may concern seasonal variations in a market, such as summer and winter months, or provision of peak and off-peak services. For example, the risk of customers changing their preferences according to the time of day in relation to peak and off-peak consumption of electricity, for which different prices are charged during the day from those charged at night, must be taken into consideration when identifying the RPM because the RPM may concern the peak supply of electricity only.[41]

The temporal market should be assessed both from the point of view of consumers, who may not consider, say, bananas and apples to be substitutes for each other, and from the point of view of suppliers' capacity, because they may be unable to supply, say, fresh strawberries in winter.

2.5.2 Measuring market power

There are different economic methods for measuring market power, each with its limitations.[42] For that reason, competition enforcement authorities rely on multifactor analysis, based on the shares of the relevant market and on other structural data. Article 178(a) RTC suggests that, in the determination of market power of an enterprise, effective constraints from its competitors or potential competitors will be relevant (see Chapter 7, section 7.2). A very similar approach is taken by the European Commission. The Guidance on the Commission's

41 On this topic, see S. Pype, 'Dominance in Peak-Term Electricity Markets' (2011) 32(2) ECLR 99.

42 See D. Geradin, A. Layne-Farrar and N. Petit, *EU Competition Law and Economics*, 2012, Oxford: OUP, pp 81–87.

Enforcement Priorities in Applying [Article 102 TFEU] to Abusive Exclusionary Conduct by Dominant Undertakings[43] identifies the constraints that will be taken into account when establishing market power as being:

- constraints imposed by existing rival suppliers and the position on the market of actual competitors (that is, the position of the undertaking concerned and its rivals);
- constraints imposed by credible threats of future expansion by actual competitors or entry by potential competitors (that is, expansion and entry); and,
- constraints imposed by the bargaining power of the undertaking's customers (that is, countervailing buyer power).

2.5.2.1 Effective constraints from actual competitors

To assess constraints from actual competitors of an undertaking under investigation, the European Commission focuses on the market share controlled by that undertaking and the structure of the market in which it operates. The issue of what weight should be given to the existence of a very large market share in the determination of market power has been highly debated.[44] Although holding a high percentage of the market is likely to indicate that an undertaking has market power, the opposite may also be true: some undertakings with high market shares may have relatively little market power if, for example, entry barriers are low.[45] Similarly, in an oligopolistic market, an undertaking may have market power while having a relatively low market share as a result of high brand differentiation. For these reasons, using the market share as a measure of market power is a highly contested issue, full treatment of which is outside the scope of this book.

Notwithstanding this debate, under EU competition law, the existing case law clearly indicates that high market shares have been regarded as conclusive in proving market power,[46] although market structure is also of relevance. For example, in *British Airways (BA)*,[47] BA, which held a steadily falling 39.7 per cent of the market, was nevertheless regarded as being in a dominant position – that

43 [2009] OJ C 45/7.
44 See A. Jones and B. Sufrin, *EU Competition Law*, 4th edn, 2011, Oxford: OUP, pp 325–326.
45 This is a direct conclusion of the contestable market hypothesis.
46 In Case T-30/89 *Hilti v Commission* [1990] ECR II-163, the General Court held that a very large share of the relevant market is in itself evidence of a dominant position. In this case, it was established that Hilti had a share of between 70 and 80 per cent of the relevant market. According to the General Court, this in itself constituted a clear indication of the existence of a dominant position.
47 Case C-95/04 *British Airways (BA) plc v Commission* [2007] ECR I-2331.

is, as having market power – given that its largest competitor had only 5.5 per cent of the relevant market. This shows that, under Article 102 TFEU, there is no safe harbour below which an undertaking may not be found to be in a dominant position. This is particularly important for undertakings that are far from being monopolies. Indeed, once an undertaking is aware of its dominant position, it will adjust its conduct to that position. If it is unaware, it may breach Article 102 TFEU by conduct that is normal so far as non-dominant undertakings are concerned, but prohibited with regard to dominant undertakings.

2.5.2.2 Market concentration

Competition enforcement authorities recognise that an enterprise's market share is better understood in the context of concentration of the entire market – that is, in light of the level of competition that exists within that market. To calculate the level of concentration, economists use the 'Herfindahl-Hirschman Index' (HHI), which is calculated by squaring the market share of each enterprise and then summing the resulting numbers. For example, if the market has four participants with shares of 30 per cent, 30 per cent, 20 per cent, and 20 per cent, the HHI is calculated as:

$$30^2 + 30^2 + 20^2 + 20^2 = 2{,}600$$

The HHI increases both as the number of firms decreases and as the disparity in size increases.

The theoretical value that the HHI can have ranges from close to zero to 10,000. The HHI is 10,000 when an enterprise has 100 per cent of the market share. The European Commission Guidelines on the Assessment of Horizontal Mergers[48] states that the concentration level is low when the HHI value is below 1,000, moderate when the HHI value is between 1,000 and 1,800, and high when it is above 1,800.

The HHI is useful in evaluating risks of parallel, oligopolistic behaviour in the relevant market and in assessing whether a merger between two firms should be allowed.

2.5.2.3 Effective constraints from potential competitors

Market shares indicate the current situation in the market. An undertaking may not have market power if existing competitors could easily expand or if potential competitors could easily enter the relevant market. The European Commission's Guidance on the Commission Enforcement Priorities in Applying [Article 102

48 [2004] OJ C 31/5.

TFEU] to Abusive Exclusionary Conduct by Dominant Undertakings[49] confirms this view. As a result, the Commission will take account of whether there are barriers to expansion or entry into the market.

The definition of 'barriers to entry' has been debated at length by both lawyers and economists.[50] There is no definition under EU competition law – but the European Commission's Guidance states that the entry or expansion barriers will be considered as impacting on a dominant undertaking if they are 'likely, timely and significant'.[51] Small-scale or niche entry will be insufficient in magnitude to deter attempts by an incumbent undertaking to increase prices.

The UK OFT's Guidelines on the Assessment of Market Power[52] and its Merger Assessment Guidance[53] describe some of the barriers as advantages to an 'existing' undertaking over new entrants.

- Absolute advantages include legal advantages (such as tariffs and non-tariff barriers, and governmental regulations limiting the number of participants on the relevant market) and technical advantages arising from access to important assets (such as raw materials or intellectual property rights).
- Intrinsic, or structural, advantages are those advantages arising from the technical or production method, or other factors, necessary to enter the market. In particular, this refers to a situation in which a new entrant will have to incur 'sunk costs' – that is, those that are necessary to enter the market, but which cannot be recovered on exit. If a new entrant expects to recover its entry costs, it will be tempted to enter a new market. However, if an undertaking already active in a market would compete fiercely with a new entrant, sunk costs may be irrecoverable and therefore prohibitive for a new entrant.
- First-mover advantage refers to the advantage that results from being on the market before competitors. Because of its presence on the market, a firm may have established reputation on the market, and it may also, by means of loyalty schemes and exclusive agreements, have tied its customers.
- Economies of scale (see section 2.3.1.7). In industries where economies of scale occur, a new entrant may have to incur substantive expenses to achieve low production costs which the existing firms have already achieved.

49 [2009] OJ C 45/7.
50 See R. Gilbert, 'Mobility Barriers and the Value of Incumbency', in R. Schmalensee and R. Willig (eds) *Handbook of Industrial Organisation*, 1989, Amsterdam: North Holland, ch. 8.
51 [2009] OJ C 45/7, [16].
52 UK OFT, *Assessment of Market Power: Understanding Competition Law*, December 2004, Pt 5, available at http://www.oft.gov.uk/shared_oft/business_leaflets/ca98_guidelines/ oft415.pdf [accessed 4 March 2014].
53 Competition Commission/OFT, *Merger Assessment Guidelines*, September 2010, CC2 (Revised)/OFT1254, available at http://www.oft.gov.uk/shared_oft/mergers/642749/OFT1254.pdf [accessed 1 October 2013], section 5.8.5, pp 59*ff.*

Additionally, a new entrant may be hampered by falling prices should it be able to enter on a high scale and flood the market with its products.

- Network effects occur when the value of a product or service increases as the number of users increases. The classical example is a telephone: the more people have them, the greater the number of telephone calls that an individual user might make, and the more valuable the telephone becomes to that user and to all other users. Other examples are online social media such as Twitter, Facebook and Google+. Network effects, just like economies of scale, may make new entry more difficult where the minimum viable scale (in terms of users of the network) is large in relation to the size of the market.
- Exclusionary behaviour refers to the behaviour of a firm already active in a market, such as predatory pricing and refusals to supply, and the extent to which that firm is 'tying up' its distributors or retailers.

An additional important consideration in connection with barriers to entering a market is the rate of innovation that exists in the particular market. If that rate is very high, it will be relatively easy for a firm to enter a new market.[54]

2.5.2.4 Countervailing buyer power

The European Commission's Guidance[55] provides that the Commission will take account of the bargaining power of customers of an undertaking, including a situation in which such an undertaking holds a high market share. This should be welcome given that, when a buyer can easily switch to competing suppliers, to promote a new entrant or to vertically integrate its power, important constraints are imposed on the market power of the undertaking under consideration. It is expected that the CARICOM Competition Commission will take account of the competitive constraints exerted by customers of a dominant enterprise when assessing its market power.

54 See C. Ahlborn, D. Evans and A. Padilla, 'Competition Policy in the New Economy: Is Competition Law up to the Challenge?' [2001] ECLR 156.

55 European Commission, *Guidance on the Commission Enforcement Priorities in Applying [Article 102 TFEU] to Abusive Exclusionary Conduct by Dominant Undertakings* [2009] OJ C 45/7.

3

THE OBJECTIVES OF CSME COMPETITION POLICY AND LAW

Chapter contents

3.1 Introduction

Identifying and, more importantly, ranking the objectives of CSME competition policy, with a view to establishing which of them are the most important to the achievement of the general objectives of the CARICOM Single Market and Economy, is essential to the framing of a coherent body of substantive competition rules. Indeed, Chapter VIII RTC and, in particular, its Part One, which concerns rules of competition, will be interpreted in the light of the objectives that CSME competition policy will strive to achieve, whilst not forgetting the wider political and economic goals set out by the Revised Treaty of Chaguaramas. Accordingly, on some occasions, the conduct of enterprises[1] operating within the CSME will be regarded as lawful or unlawful depending upon which of the objectives of the CSME competition policy is being given priority. This point is well illustrated when one compares US anti-trust law with EU competition law. For example, the priority given by the European Court of

1 The concept of 'enterprise' is defined in Article 1 RTC as meaning 'any person or type of organisation, other than a non-profit organisation, involved in the production of or the trade in goods, or the provision of services' (see Chapter 4).

Justice (ECJ) to the objective of integrating the markets of the Member States, and thus creating an internal market, has resulted in some business conduct of firms being condemned under EU law whilst the same conduct is perfectly lawful under US anti-trust law.

There is no doubt that Chapter VIII RTC will be interpreted in light of the objectives of the CSME. This is supported by the statement made by the Caribbean Court of Justice (CCJ) in *Trinidad Cement Limited (TCL), TCL Guyana Incorporated (TGI) v The State of the Co-operative Republic of Guyana*,[2] in which the CCJ recognised that the RTC is, in many instances, ambiguous, unclear and imprecise, and that this is to be expected bearing in mind that it constitutes a compromise of conflicting national interests and divergent perspectives. In that case, the CCJ explained that, in interpreting the RTC, it intends to have recourse to Article 31 of the Vienna Convention on the Law of Treaties, which states that '[a] treaty shall be interpreted in good faith in accordance with the ordinary meaning to be given to the terms of the Treaty in their context and in the light of its object and purpose'.

The CCJ has said that it does not intend to place undue reliance on a literal approach in the interpretation of the RTC and that it will give preference to the teleological method, which focuses on object and purpose, whilst paying attention to such factors as the intention of the Contracting Parties, the historical context, the subsequent conduct of the contracting parties, etc. Obviously, in the context of the RTC, the teleological approach is the most appropriate, because it will infuse common sense and flexibility into the interpretation of a very complex treaty. Indeed, literal interpretation of the provisions of the RTC relating to competition law seems inappropriate for many reasons.

1. The provisions of the RTC relating to competition law are written sparsely and contain general admonitions. Even when Article 177 RTC provides a non-exhaustive list of anti-competitive arrangements and abuses, it requires the enforcement authority to specify the elements of those offences. This can be done only in light of the objectives of CSME competition law.
2. Many words used in the RTC can have many meanings depending on the objectives that CSME competition law intends to attain. For example, 'promotion of competition' may be understood as referring to the maintenance of economic opportunities for small and medium-sized enterprises (SMEs), or as the promotion of consumer welfare in the economic sense, or as the imposition of a limitation on concentration of economic power, or as referring to the protection of competitors, or as promoting economic freedom and ensuring fairness.
3. In competition law, rarely can proscribed conduct be discerned from a literal interpretation of the words used in the RTC. This is because their meaning is often deeply embedded in economic concepts such as those of a 'market'

2 [2009] CCJ 1 (OJ).

> or 'consumer welfare'. Further, such concepts can have various meanings depending upon which economic theory is used to interpret them. Therefore not only does the meaning of the relevant economic concepts have to be defined, but also the methods of applying them must be specified. This can be done only in light of the objectives that the CSME seeks to attain.

This chapter first focuses on identifying the objectives of CSME competition policy; it then attempts to suggest the ranking of those objectives at a time when competition law is at a nascent stage within the CSME. The legal implications for enterprises carrying out their economic activities within CARICOM (or outside CARICOM in a situation in which such activities have detrimental effect on trade and competition in the Caribbean Community) of the suggested hierarchy of objectives of CSME competition policy on the interpretation and the application of substantive competition rules contained in Chapter VIII, Part One, of the RTC are also assessed.

3.2 The objectives of CSME competition policy

Competition policy can be defined as comprising measures and instruments used by governments (or regional integration organisations such as CARICOM or the European Union) to influence conditions of competition that exist in a market. This may include the well-motivated articulation of competition matters in industrial policy, trade policy, investment policy, service policy and consumer policy, as well as enactment of competition law. R. Whish rightly points out that competition policy does not exist in a vacuum, but 'is an expression of the current values and aims of society and is susceptible to change as political thinking generally'.[3]

Competition law is a vital part of competition policy. Competition law has been defined as being 'concerned with ensuring that firms . . . operating in the free market economy do not restrict or distort competition in a way that prevents the market from functioning optimally'.[4] More specifically, competition law prohibits arrangements between firms that restrict competition, abuses of market power by dominant firms and the creation of anti-competitive mergers. In light of the above definition of competition policy, it is clear that it has a broader scope than competition law, in that competition policy encompasses all aspects of government action (or of the actions of a supranational organisation such as CARICOM and the European Union) that affect the conditions under which firms compete in a particular market, while competition law is a servant of competition policy. The matter of what business conduct is allowed and what is prohibited will very much depend on the objectives pursued by the relevant competition policy.

Examination of the RTC reveals that CSME competition policy may pursue many objectives. It is submitted that they can be divided into three categories:

3 R. Whish, *Competition Law*, 5th edn, 2003, London: LexisNexis, p 17.
4 A. Jones and B. Sufrin, *EU Competition Law*, 4th edn, 2011, Oxford: OUP, p 1.

the overarching objectives set out in the Preamble to the RTC; the general objective expressly stated in Article 169(1) RTC; and the specific objectives laid down in Article 169(2) RTC.

3.2.1 The overarching objectives

Preambles to legislative acts or international treaties, although non-binding, are usually an important source of inspiration for courts in the interpretation of the substantive provisions of such instruments. The Preamble to the RTC is no exception: it is good guidance for determining the intention of the Contracting Parties to the RTC. Indeed, it contains statements made by them elucidating the objectives of the RTC. Those statements, in fact, encapsulate the overarching objectives that the Contracting Parties seek to attain.

In Recital 1 of the Preamble, the Contracting Parties, recalling the declaration of Grand Anse and other decisions of the Conference of Heads of Government, agree on their commitment to the deepening of regional economic integration through the establishment of the CSME in order to achieve sustained economic development based on international competitiveness, co-ordinated economic and foreign policies, functional co-operation, and enhanced trade and economic relations with third States.

The objective of creating a unified market and economy is vital, taking into account that the *reason d'être* of CARICOM is to establish the CSME, through which other general objectives stated in Article 6 RTC can be achieved. Therefore it can be assumed that any policy, including competition policy, should be formulated in such a way as to ensure the creation and maintenance of the CSME. The achievement of this objective is enhanced by Recital 6, which states that optimal production by economic enterprises requires the removal of barriers to the free movement of capital, labour and technology within the CSME. The importance of creating a fully integrated market is further emphasised in Recital 9, which states that such an integrated and liberalised internal market 'will create favourable conditions for sustained, market-led production of goods and services on an internationally competitive basis'. Accordingly, any business conduct that jeopardises the establishment and the proper functioning of the CSME should be regarded as anti-competitive.

Recital 5 of the Preamble may be relevant to the identification of the objectives of the CSME competition policy, because it states that the Contracting States are:

> ". . . conscious of the need to promote in the Community the highest level of efficiency in the production of goods and services especially with a view to maximising foreign exchange earnings on the basis of international competitiveness, attaining food security, achieving structural diversification and improving the standard of living of their peoples."

It is submitted that Recital 5 suggests that efficiency in the economic sense should be one of the main objectives of CSME competition policy.

Recital 12 of the Preamble recognises 'the potential of micro, small and medium enterprise development to contribute to the expansion and viability of national economies of the Community and the importance of large enterprises for achieving economies of scale in the production process'. The interpretation of Recital 12 is not easy: does it mean that CSME competition policy should protect SMEs from competitive pressures? Recognition of the importance of large enterprises makes any assumption that SMEs should be shielded from competition for their own sake rather doubtful. Perhaps, Recital 12 implies that SMEs should be protected only when they are as efficient as large enterprises – that is, in a situation in which large enterprises are not competing on merits (see Chapter 7, section 7.3), but are using anti-competitive business conduct to eliminate smaller rivals or to erect barriers to entry to the relevant market.

Recital 21 states that the contracting parties are conscious that 'disadvantaged countries, regions and sectors will require a transitional period to facilitate adjustment to competition in the CSME'. It is submitted that the impact of this Recital on CSME competition policy is that special exemption from the application of CSME competition law will be granted to disadvantaged countries, regions and sectors. This is confirmed in Article 183 RTC, which imposes an obligation on the Council for Trade and Economic Development (COTED) to develop and establish rules on competition within the CARICOM, including special rules for particular sectors, and gives COTED the power to exempt any sector, or any enterprise or group of enterprises, from the application of CSME competition law if the public interest so requires.

Recital 23 is restated in Article 169(1) RTC, which sets out the main objectives of CSME competition policy (see section 3.2.2).

Recital 24 states that the Contracting Parties are convinced that 'the application and convergence of national competition policies and the cooperation of competition authorities in the Community will promote the objectives of the CSME'. Recital 24 therefore implies that national competition policies are expected to follow CSME competition policy, or, at least, not to hinder any of the past, present and future achievements of the objectives of CSME competition policy.[5]

3.2.2 The general objective of CSME competition policy set out in Article 169(1) RTC

The goal of CSME competition policy is set out in Article 169 (1) RTC, which states that '[t]he goal of the Community Competition policy shall be to ensure that the benefits expected from the establishment of the CSME are not frustrated by anti-competitive business conduct'.

5 This is expanded upon in Article 170 RTC on 'Implementation of Community Competition Policy'.

If looked at superficially, it would seem that CSME competition policy has only one objective – that of ensuring that the benefits expected from the creation of the CSME are not endangered by anti-competitive business conduct. The issue that arises in this context is how to identify the expected benefits. In doing this, the relevant Recitals of the Preamble to the RTC – in particular, Recital 1, which refers to the objective of achieving an integrated market and economy within the CARICOM States, and Article 6 RTC, which sets out the general objectives of the Community – may be of assistance.

One can argue that the 'general objectives' are to be understood as the benefits mentioned in Article 169(1) RTC. If this reasoning is accepted, then it can be submitted that, for the purposes of competition policy, the following objectives set out in Article 6 RTC are of relevance:

(a) improved standards of living and work;
(b) full employment of labour and other factors of production;
(c) accelerated, co-ordinated and sustained economic development and convergence;
(d) expansion of trade and economic relations with third States;
(e) enhanced levels of international competitiveness;
(f) organisation for increased production and productivity;
(g) the achievement of a greater measure of economic leverage and effectiveness of Member States in dealing with third States, groups of States and entities of any description.

These objectives suggest that CSME competition policy will be used to serve social, employment, industrial and trade policies. If this occurs, however, it will be detrimental to the coherence of competition policy and difficult, if not impossible, to implement in practice, given that the various objectives of the CSME are likely to conflict with each other. For example, a merger[6] may lead to the loss of employment and thus be contrary to Article 6(b) RTC, but, at the same time, it may enhance the level of international competitiveness of the new enterprise and contribute to the expansion of trade and economic relations with third States, in accordance with Article 6(e) and (f) RTC.

It is submitted that the relationship between competition policy objectives and other objectives mentioned in Article 6 RTC should be that of mutual support: each should contribute to the achievement of the other and there should be no conflict between them. For example, no sound industrial or trade policy can be achieved without the support of a competition policy. However, in some

6 The RTC contains no provisions on merger control. However, following a meeting of representatives from the CARICOM Member States held on 24 October 2010 in Barbados, an agreement was reached that merger review provisions should be enacted at both the Community and national levels: see Jamaican Fair Trading Commission, 'Merger Review to be Implemented in the CSME' (2011) 15 Competition Matters 4.

areas in which a conflict is likely to arise, such as employment policy, the best approach may be to exclude the conflicting policy from the scope of application of competition law. This approach is evident in Article 168 RTC, which states that rules of competition do not apply to, *inter alia*, arrangements for collective bargaining on behalf of employers or employees for the purpose of fixing terms and conditions of employment. Further, the definition of an 'enterprise' contained in the RTC makes clear that non-profit-making entities are not enterprises and are therefore excluded from the scope of CSME competition law. Indeed, the objectives of the excluded areas are best advanced by using policies other than competition policy (see section 3.3.1).

3.2.3 The specific objectives of CSME competition policy, as laid down in Article 169(2) RTC

Whilst the RTC sets out multiple objectives within its competition policy, Article 169(2) RTC focuses on the specific objectives that are normally pursued by competition law in a free-market economy. Article 169(2) RTC states that, in order to achieve the general goal of the Community competition policy set out in Article 169(1) RTC, the Community:

> ". . . shall pursue the following objectives:
>
> (a) the promotion and maintenance of competition and enhancement of economic efficiency in production, trade and commerce;
> (b) subject to this Treaty, the prohibition of anti-competitive business conduct which prevents, restricts or distorts competition or which constitutes the abuse of a dominant position in the market; and
> (c) the promotion of consumer welfare and protection of consumer interest."

Each of these objectives is examined below.

3.2.3.1 The promotion and maintenance of competition and enhancement of economic efficiency in production, trade and commerce

Article 169(2)(a) RTC sets out two objectives: one is to promote and maintain competition; the other, the enhancement of economic efficiency in production, trade and commerce. Each is commented upon separately below.

A The objective of promotion and maintenance of competition

The words 'promote' and 'maintain' taken together mean that one of the objectives of competition law will be to ensure that competition is maintained and encouraged within the CSME – that is, that CSME competition law has as its objective the protection of competition. It is important to note that the objective of protecting competition is common to all systems of competition law, but that its meaning differs depending upon the objectives that the particular competition law aims to achieve. Therefore, in order to avoid confusion, the meaning under the RTC of the words 'the promotion and maintenance of competition' needs to be clearly established.

In the European Union, until the reform of EU competition law commenced in 1999,[7] the objective of protecting competition was understood as 'the protection of individual economic freedom of action as a value in itself, or vice versa, the restraint of undue economic power'.[8]

This approach was inspired by the 'ordoliberal' school of thought, which was born in Germany during the 1930s and further developed by scholars associated with the University of Freiburg during the Nazi regime in Germany.[9]

The ordoliberal influence on the interpretation of EU competition law, mainly on Article 101 TFEU and on Article 102 TFEU, was that these Articles were not interpreted in light of the objective of achieving economic efficiency, but as requiring that private power must be limited and controlled by the EU enforcement authorities in the interest of creating a free and fair political and social order.[10] The result of this, it has been emphasised, was that 'EU law has often been interpreted and applied to protect competitors themselves rather than the competitive process, to favour small and medium-sized enterprises, to keep markets open and to achieve "fairness"'.[11]

B The objective of enhancement of efficiency in production, trade and commerce

The reason why competition must be promoted and maintained is that competition is good for firms and is good for consumers. As far as competitors are

7 On this topic, see D. J. Gerber, 'Fifty Years of European Community: Two Forms of Modernization in European Competition Law' (2008) 31 Fordham Int'l LJ 1235.

8 W. Möschel, 'Competition Policy from an Ordo Point of View', in A. Peacock and H. Willgerodt (eds) *German Neo-Liberalism and the Social Market Economy*, 1989, London: Macmillan, p 149.

9 Ordoliberalism was a political and economic philosophy that served as the base for the post-war recovery of Germany and the era of a *Wirtschaftswunder* ('wonder economy') in Germany. Although ordoliberalism defended capitalism, it assigned a crucial role to the State, which was expected to create an appropriate legal environment for the economy and to maintain a healthy level of competition by taking active measures to foster competition. In particular, the State was to ensure that monopolies and oligopolies would not acquire power, which would not only negate the advantages offered by the market economy, but also undermine good government, given that strong economic power could be transformed into political power: see R. O'Donoghue and A. Padilla, *The Law and Economics of Article 82*, 2006, Oxford: OUP, p 9.

10 D. J. Gerber, *Law and Competition in the Twentieth Century Europe: Protecting Promotheus*, 1998, Oxford: Clarendon Press, pp 244–251.

11 A. Jones and B. Sufrin, *EU Competition Law*, 4th edn, 2011, Oxford: OUP, p 44.

concerned, when they compete with each other, instead of colluding, they are encouraged to innovate, given that the market rewards those who introduce new and better products, and that they are under pressure to achieve the lowest level of costs and prices in order to meet consumer needs more efficiently than their rivals. For consumers, competition is good because it preserves consumer choice and allows the purchase of products at the lowest price.

The process of competition creates three efficiencies in the market:

- productive efficiency. This occurs when the economy is utilising all of its resources efficiently by producing goods and services at the minimum average cost;
- allocative efficiency. This occurs when there is an optimal distribution of goods and services – that is, when goods are produced in the quantities desired by consumers; and
- dynamic efficiency. This is concerned with how well and how speedily a market delivers innovation and technological progress. A firm is dynamically efficient if it can respond quickly to changing economic circumstances. Dynamic efficiency leads to lower costs, or new products, or improved products.

According to economists, monopolies and oligopolies are regarded as neither productively efficient, because they can reduce the output to make greater profit, nor allocatively efficient, because they are less sensitive to consumer's demand than monopolistically competitive firms. However, many economists argue that monopolies and oligopolies are dynamically efficient, because they are the only firms that can allocate the supranormal profits that they gain to research and development, and thus in the long run drive innovation, which benefits consumers.[12] A counter-argument is that monopolies have no incentive to innovate. As to monopsonies,[13] they are productively inefficient, because they cause production to fall below the competitive level. In both a monopoly and a monopsony, there is a deadweight loss of consumer and producer surplus (see Chapter 2, section 2.4.2.2).

In the Caribbean context, economic conditions deriving from the small size of the economies of Caribbean islands and from historical circumstances, which are responsible for unequal distribution of wealth, result in markets in the CSME being dominated by monopolies and oligopolies. On the one hand, small economies are constrained by lack of economies of scale in production, export, distribution and infrastructure. For that reason, dominance may be inevitable and more efficient than fragmentation of the relevant market, which may result

12 J. A. Schumpeter, *Capitalism, Socialism and Democracy*, 3rd edn, 1962, New York: Harper.

13 A 'monopsony' is a market in which there is a single buyer and many sellers. In monopsony, a single buyer has the ability to affect the price of goods, i.e. holds monopsony power, which entails that the buyer is able to purchase goods for less than the price that would prevail in a competitive market.

in waste of resources and loss of international competitiveness. On the other hand, business profitability should be an important factor in the enforcement of competition law in the CSME because of the limited availability of investment capital. Indeed, in the Caribbean, profits are both a source of and an incentive for investment, given the high interest rates payable on loans, the poorly developed capital markets and the limited public resources to provide investment subsidies or even tax credits.

For many economists, such as Brodley, dynamic efficiency 'provides the single most important factor in the growth of real output in the industrial world'.[14] Brodley posits that dynamic efficiency is far more important than static efficiency – that is, allocative and productive efficiency. Singh argues that, in small economies, dynamic efficiency, rather than static efficiency, should be given priority,[15] whilst Dhanjee considers that:

> "[T]here is little empirical evidence that, in developed countries, large firm size or higher concentration are generally associated with innovation activity – but it is not clear whether this would necessarily be the case in developing countries which, in any event import a higher proportion of the technology they use than do the larger developed countries."[16]

He suggests that, in the Caribbean context, the giving of priority to dynamic efficiency over static efficiency should depend on the type of innovation and whether the matter is one of its creation, its introduction into a country or its diffusion.

In the light of the above, Article 169(2)(a) RTC poses a great challenge to the enforcement of CSME competition law. It requires determination of which of the three efficiencies should be given priority in seeking the attainment of the objectives of the CSME, given that the attainment of all three is almost impossible. Making the determination involves assessing both the trade-off between allocative and productive efficiency, and the trade-off between static efficiency and dynamic efficiency. For a decision to be made on the matter of which efficiency is most crucial to the achievement of the objectives of competition law, it is necessary to decide whose welfare competition law wants to maximise: that of society as a whole, or that of consumers.

14 J. Brodley, 'Proof of Efficiencies in Mergers and Joint Ventures' (1966) 64 Antitrust Law Journal 581, 581. Criticism by Professor J. Brodley of the enforcement of US anti-trust law in the 1980s has been acknowledged and incorporated into a new approach to different types of efficiency, and their respective contributions to wealth creation and resource distribution, by the US Federal Trade Commission.

15 A. Singh, *Multilateral Competition Policy and Economic Development: A Developing Country Perspective on the New European Community Proposals*, 2004, UNCTAD/DITC/CLP/2003/10.

16 R. Dhanjee, 'The Tailoring of Competition Policy to Caribbean Circumstances: Some Suggestions' [2004] Caribbean Dialogue 40, 40.

3.2.3.2 The prohibition of anti-competitive business conduct that prevents, restricts or distorts competition, or which constitutes the abuse of a dominant position on the market

The objective of prohibiting anti-competitive business conduct is impossible to achieve without first identifying what business conduct should be regarded as such. This can be done only in light of the objectives that CSME competition law seeks to attain.

3.2.3.3 The objectives of the promotion of consumer welfare and protection of consumer interests

Article 169(2)(c) RTC sets out two objectives: the promotion of consumer welfare and the protection of consumer interests. Each is examined below.

A The promotion of consumer welfare

It is important to clarify the meaning of 'consumer welfare', in particular in light of its usage by economists from the Chicago school (see Chapter 2, section 2.4.3.2). Professor Bork, one of Chicago's most eminent representatives, defined the meaning of 'consumer welfare' as follows:

> "[C]onsumer welfare is greatest when society's economic resources are allocated so that consumers are able to satisfy their wants as fully as technological constraints permit. Consumer welfare is, in this sense, merely another term for the wealth of the nation."[17]

Professor Bork's usage of the expression 'consumer welfare' differs from that used in traditional economics, in which consumer welfare means 'consumer surplus' – that is, the difference between the amount that a consumer is willing to pay for a product or service and its market price. A consumer surplus occurs when the consumer is willing to pay more for a given product than the current market price. The concept of consumer welfare is therefore a means of measuring the aggregate benefit that consumers obtain from buying a product or service in a market.

Bork's interpretation of 'consumer welfare' in traditional economics means 'total welfare' or 'social welfare', both of which refer to the aggregate of consumer surplus and producer surplus (see Chapter 2, section 2.2). Any increase, or decrease, in total surplus is reflected in an increase, or decrease, in social welfare, which latter is also referred to as the 'total welfare standard'.

17 R. H. Bork, *The Antitrust Paradox: A Policy at War with Itself*, 1978, New York: Basic Books, pp 107–108.

Economists are divided as to which standard – the total welfare standard or the consumer welfare standard – should be applied in the enforcement of competition law. Some, in particular those associated with the Chicago school, prefer the total welfare standard; others, such as Joseph Brodley, are in favour of the consumer welfare standard. According to Brodley:

> "[I]f consumer welfare is to serve as an operational principle of antitrust law, it must refer to the direct and explicit economic benefit received by the consumers of a particular product as measured by its price and quality. Using the more precise language of economics, consumer welfare can be defined as consumer surplus."[18]

This definition of consumer welfare entails that any conduct that reduces consumer welfare should be condemned as anti-competitive.

Some economists argue that it does not matter which standard is applied, because the distinction between the two standards is blurred, given that many businesses are owned by shareholders, many of which are pension funds. As a result, the maximisation of total welfare equates to the maximisation of consumer welfare.

Notwithstanding this debate, the distinction in economics between the total welfare standard and the consumer welfare standard is important, because the choice of welfare standard affects the entire assessment of efficiencies. The matter to be considered, when the choice is being made, is whose welfare the competition law wants to maximise – that of consumers or that of society as a whole.

If the consumer welfare standard is applied, competition law is concerned with the transfer of surplus from producers to consumers. Therefore any business conduct that prevents wealth transfer is anti-competitive. An example of this occurs where a monopoly charges consumers monopoly prices instead of competitive prices. The consumers suffer loss in the form of a wealth transfer to the monopolist. When the consumer welfare standard is applied, competition law prohibits business conduct that allows producers to capture consumer surplus.

The total welfare standard is concerned only with loss of efficiency and takes no account of the redistributory effects of efficiency gains – that is, it is not concerned with whether wealth is shifted to consumers or to producers, so long as society as a whole benefits. As a result, competition policy based on the total welfare standard will focus on efficiencies and does not require the transfer of efficiency benefits directly to consumers. For example, a merger between two competitors may increase efficiency, in that it may reduce the cost of production and thus increase the total welfare; at the same time, it may create

18 J. Brodley, 'The Economic Goals of Antitrust: Efficiency, Consumer Welfare and Technological Progress' (1989) 62 NYU L Rev 1020, 1033.

a monopoly and thus decrease consumer welfare, in that consumers will have to pay higher prices for the product in question. Such a merger will be allowed under the total welfare standard, but not under the consumer welfare standard. A further matter is that the consumer welfare standard has no concern for competitors unless the business conduct of an offending firm also harms consumers. This is not the case when the total welfare standard is applied, bearing in mind that the aggregate welfare is the surplus of all producers, including competitors, and all consumers.[19]

The RTC does not define the concept of consumer welfare. Therefore it is uncertain whether it refers to the total welfare standard or the consumer welfare standard, as defined in traditional economics. Further, it does not specify the method for applying those standards.

B The protection of consumer interests

Article 168 RTC states that one of the objectives of CSME competition law is the protection of consumer interests. Consumers and their interests are normally protected by consumer protection laws, the main objective of which is to ensure the ability of consumers to choose freely and effectively from among the options available to them in terms of suppliers or brands available on the market, by shielding them from unfair, deceptive and fraudulent practices by businesses, such as misleading advertising, double-ticketing, etc.

Competition law and consumer protection law have the common goal of providing consumers with access to a wide range of competitively priced goods and services in the marketplace. Convergence of the objectives of competition law and consumer protection laws has, in some jurisdictions, resulted in entrusting enforcement of both to one and the same body, for example in CARICOM to the CARICOM Competition Commission (CCC), in the United States to the Federal Trade Commission, and in Barbados to the Barbados Fair Trading Commission. However, although competition law and consumer protection law share the same goal, the approaches to achieving that goal differ: competition law focuses on promoting consumer welfare in the economic sense, while consumer protection law ensures that they have the necessary information to make informed choices. Obviously, consumers benefit when consumer welfare is maximised.

The protection of consumers' interests in a way that is compatible with, or even superior to, the existing approaches is examined in section 3.3.2.

3.3 The prioritisation of the objectives of CSME competition law

The rules on competition contained in the RTC are general and imprecise. The same can be said of US anti-trust provisions and the main provisions

19 Obviously, when the harm to competitors is offset by the gain to the offending firm, then producer surplus will not be diminished.

of the Treaty on the Functioning of the European Union (TFEU) on competition. The US Supreme Court described the language of the US anti-trust law as having 'a generality and adaptability comparable to that found . . . in constitutional provisions'.[20] The lack of precision is one of the reasons why the US anti-trust provisions have remained unchanged for many years. The same can be said about the provisions on competition law in the European Union. They have remained exactly the same for more than fifty years – that is, since the entry into force of the Treaty of Rome establishing the European Economic Community. This is despite the fact that the Treaty of Rome has been amended many times, most recently by the Treaty of Lisbon (ToL), which entered into force on 1 December 2009. The fact that no changes to treaties or statutes have been necessary can be explained by the fact that it is the interpretation of those provisions that is vital for the development of a coherent body of substantive competition rules. Indeed, in the European Union and in the United States, the interpretation of competition law provisions has, with time, evolved in such a way as to reflect the changing objectives that the US government or the European Commission have sought to attain. This shows that it is imperative for CSME competition law to assert clearly what objective(s) it wishes to pursue. This is vital for businesses, which need to know with certainty what business conduct will be regarded as anti-competitive so that they can adjust their business strategies accordingly. Further, as Professor Bork stated, 'only when the issue of goals has been settled it is possible to frame a coherent body of substantive rules'.[21]

As can be seen from section 3.2, many objectives, both economic and non-economic, are mentioned in the RTC and its Preamble. However, no competition law can pursue multiple objectives simultaneously, because various objectives of competition law conflict with each other and, further, because this would lead to inconsistent application of competition law. Therefore the prioritisation of objectives of competition law is necessary. In the context of Caribbean integration, it is submitted that CSME competition policy should pursue two objectives: first, the objective of creating and maintaining the CSME; and second, the objective of protecting consumers.

3.3.1 The creation and maintenance of the CSME

The main objective set out in the RTC is the creation and maintenance of the CSME. The issue of whether CSME competition policy should be only about economics or whether it should support the objective of maintaining the CSME is debatable. At a national level, many States have decided that their national competition laws should focus on economic objectives and that broader policy objectives, such as industrial policy, regional development, the protection of the

20 *Appalachian Coals, Inc. v US*, 288 US 344, 359–60 (1933).

21 R. H. Bork, *The Antitrust Paradox: A Policy at War with Itself*, 1978, New York: Basic Books, p 50.

environment and other public interests objectives, should be promoted through instruments other than competition law. In this respect, a survey conducted in 2003 by the Organisation for Economic Co-operation and Development (OECD) on the objectives of competition law and policy showed that, when a country reaches a certain level of development, it renounces the use of competition law to promote broader policy objectives, including public interest objectives.

The survey emphasised two reasons for the increasing exclusion of non-economic objectives from the objectives of competition law. First, it found that broadly specified policy objectives can be ambiguous and, as such, are sometimes used by strong private groups, such as producers or workers, to serve their own interests. Second, it recognised that non-competition policy mechanisms are more appropriate than competition law to achieve non-competition policy objectives.[22] In particular:

> "[R]estricting competition in an attempt to achieve broader policy objectives will have inevitable anti-competitive side effects, e.g. granting protected monopoly profit to a firm or firms. There is no reason to suppose that the State will have the capacity, even if it has the will, to control the extent and distribution of such side effects. In summary, restrictions on competition may be ineffective and socially wasteful."[23]

It is submitted that the objectives of CSME competition policy differ from the objectives of national competition policies in that CARICOM is not a State and therefore the objectives of its competition policy have direct relevance to the achievement of the goals for which it was established. The example of the European Union is instructive. EU competition law has been critical to the development and success of the internal market of the European Union. The effectiveness of the prohibition of obstacles to the free movement of goods, people, labour and capital addressed to the Member States would have been devoid of any practical effect had firms been allowed to create private barriers to trade between Member States. The ECJ, in *Consten and Grundig*,[24] held that:

> [A]n agreement . . . which might tend to restore the national division in trade between member states might be such as to frustrate the most fundamental objectives of the Community. The Treaty, whose preamble and content aim at abolishing the barriers between States, and which in

22 OECD Global Forum on Competition, *The Objectives of Competition Law and Policy: Note by the Secretariat*, 29 January 2003, CCNM/GF/COMP(2003)3, p 4.

23 OECD Global Forum on Competition, *The Objectives of Competition Law and Policy and the Optimal Design of a Competition Agency: Ireland*, 15 January 2003, CCNM/GF/COMP/WD(2003)17, [1.2].

24 Joined Cases 56 and 58/64 *Établissements Consten Sarl and Grundig-Verkaufs-GmbH v Commission* [1966] ECR 299.

several provisions gives evidence of a stern attitude with regard to their reappearance, could not allow undertakings to reconstruct such barriers.[25]

Since the judgment of the ECJ in that case, it has been accepted that the fundamental objective of EU competition law is to ensure that business conduct does not partition the European Union along national borders. On many occasions, the ECJ and the European Commission have emphasised that the creation and maintenance of the internal market is the most important objective of EU competition law.[26] Although, with the reform of EU competition law, new objectives have been set – that is, the promotion of economic efficiency and consumer welfare[27] – this does not mean that market integration is no longer relevant. The objective of market integration has not been abandoned. The 2000 European Commission Guidelines on Vertical Restraints provide that:

> "[T]he protection of competition is the primary objective of EC competition law, as this enhances consumer welfare and creates an efficient allocation of resources. In applying the EC competition rules, the Commission will adopt an economic approach which is based on the effects on the market. Market integration is an additional goal of EC competition law. Market integration enhances competition."[28]

Further, the 2009 Guidance on the Commission's Enforcement Priorities in Applying Article 82 of the EC Treaty [Article 102 TFEU] to Abusive Exclusionary Conduct by Dominant Undertakings provides that the Commission may intervene with regard to 'certain behaviour that undermines the efforts to achieve an integrated internal market'.[29]

It can be said that, nowadays in the European Union, the objective of market integration runs in parallel with the objective of the promotion of consumer welfare and efficient allocation of resources. When these two objectives clash, it seems that, despite the European Commission's policy statements, which appear to assign a secondary role to the objective of market integration, the ECJ will support the objective of market integration rather than the objective of the enhancement of efficiency and consumer welfare. This conclusion is drawn from

25 Ibid., [56] and [58]–[64].

26 See, e.g., European Commission, *Ninth Report on Competition Policy*, 1979, available at http://bookshop.europa.eu/en/ninth-report-on-competition-policy-pbCB2979603/?CatalogCategoryID=iuoKABstTO0AAAEjtZAY4e5L [accessed 10 December 2013], p 9, which stated that the first objective of competition law is to maintain an open and unified internal market.

27 See European Commission, *White Paper on Modernisation of Rules Implementing Articles [101 and 102 TFEU]* [1999] OJ C 132/1.

28 [2000] OJ C 291/1, [7].

29 [2009] OJ C 45/7, [7].

the Court's judgments in *GlaxoSmithKline*,[30] concerning the so-called 'dual pricing schemes' under which an undertaking operating on the pharmaceutical market had intended to charge differing prices for the same pharmaceutical products depending upon their destination, thereby reducing the scope for arbitrage (that is, preventing parallel trade) and leading to the partition of the internal market.

In dealing with the appeal against the judgment of the General Court,[31] the ECJ decided that the General Court had made an error in law when it ruled that the agreement at issue, which clearly intended to limit parallel trade in pharmaceutical products and thus partition the internal market, could be regarded as restricting competition by 'object' in so far as it may be presumed to deprive final consumers of the advantages of effective competition in terms of supply and price. This ruling meant that the General Court required the European Commission to establish that the restriction had to be to the detriment of final consumers in order for it to be regarded as restricting competition by 'object'. The ECJ held that there was no need to look at the effect of the agreement on consumers – that is, that there was no need for the European Commission to carry out an extensive effect analysis in respect of dual pricing arrangements in the situation in which it could be inferred from the context and the circumstances of the agreement that its object was to partition the internal market. In this respect, the ECJ held:

> The Court has . . . held in that regard, in relation to the application of Article 81 EC [Article 101 TFEU] and in a case involving the pharmaceuticals sector, that an agreement between producer and distributor which might tend to restore the national divisions in trade between Member States might be such as to frustrate the Treaty's objective of achieving the integration of national markets through the establishment of a single market. Thus on a number of occasions the Court has held agreements aimed at partitioning national markets according to national borders or making the interpenetration of national markets more difficult, in particular those aimed at preventing or restricting parallel exports, to be agreements whose object is to restrict competition within the meaning of that article of the Treaty.[32]

In light of the EU experience relating to the interpretation and application of the integrated market objective, it is submitted that the following practical

30 Joined Cases C-501/06 P, C-513/06 P, C-515/06 P and C-519/06 P *GlaxoSmithKline Services Unlimited v Commission* [2009] ECR I-9291.
31 Case T-168/01 *GlaxoSmithKline Services Unlimited v Commission* [2006] ECR II-2969.
32 Joined Cases C-501/06 P, C-513/06 P, C-515/06 P and C-519/06 P *GlaxoSmithKline Services Unlimited v Commission* [2009] ECR I-9291, [61].

consequences of the priority given to that objective would be likely to occur should it be adopted by the CARICOM Member States.

1. Under Article 177 RTC, which is similar in substance to Article 101 TFEU, not only anti-competitive horizontal agreements, but also vertical agreements will be within the scope of CSME competition law, because such agreements may result in the partitioning of the Community markets along national borders. It is important to note that Article 177 RTC does not expressly state that it applies to both horizontal and vertical agreements. In support of its application to vertical agreements, it can be said that the various prohibitions refer to 'agreements between enterprises' and not to 'agreements between *competing* enterprises'.
2. If the integrated market objective is adopted by the CARICOM States, any business conduct aimed at partitioning national markets according to national borders will constitute an infringement of CSME competition law unless such conduct is justified under Articles 177(4) or 179(3) RTC, or subject to exemption by COTED under Article 183(2) RTC, or by the CCC under Article 181 RTC. Further, if the EU approach to the distinction between an 'infringement by object' and an 'infringement by effect' (see Chapter 6, section 6.4) is adopted by the CSME competition authorities, then any conduct that is contrary to the integrated market objective will be regarded as anti-competitive by its object, and thus amount to a *per se* infringement of competition law. The similarity between Article 177(1) RTC and Article 101(1) TFEU, which both expressly state that any anti-competitive conduct that has as its 'object or effect' the restriction of competition is prohibited, suggests that CSME competition law is likely to recognise the distinction between the 'object' and 'effect' of anti-competitive conduct. Under EU law, the restriction of competition by object creates a rebuttable presumption that the conduct has anti-competitive market effect; not only actual, but also potential, anti-competitive effect is sufficient to trigger the application of the presumption. Obviously, any restriction that results in the partition of the internal market is anti-competitive by object – that is, a *per se* breach of competition law.
3. If any business conduct that results in the partitioning of the CSME will be regarded as an infringement of competition law by object, the task of the CCC to prove an infringement will be greatly alleviated in that it will not be required to demonstrate that the conduct in question has as its effect the restriction of competition in the CSME. Its anti-competitive object will be sufficient to establish an infringement (see Chapter 6, section 6.4).
4. The priority accorded to the integrated market objective may result in the condemnation of welfare-enhancing business practices (see Chapter 7, section 7.6).
5. Some sectors of the economy are particularly prone to the imposition of restrictions on parallel importers. Such restrictions result in the partition of

the internal market, for example the pharmaceutical sector or the car distribution sector. These sectors should be regarded by the CCC as priority enforcement targets. In order to ensure that competition is not distorted in those sectors, the CCC should be proactive and should carry out extensive investigations.

6. The European Commission considers that any anti-competitive conduct that results in partitioning of the internal market constitutes a 'very serious' infringement of EU competition law and therefore merits the maximum permissible fine. This fining policy applies not only to cartels and dominant undertakings abusing their market power, but also to parties to vertical agreements that result in the partition of the internal market.[33] It is submitted that a similar approach should be taken by the CCC.
7. The market integration objective entails that, despite an agreement or business conduct being confined to one Member State, it may nevertheless be of concern to EU competition law if it reinforces the compartmentalisation of the internal market[34] and thus affects trade between Member States. In this respect, the ECJ has condemned vertical agreements, even though they are not oriented towards import or export, as being capable of affecting trade between Member States.[35] In *The Lombard Club*,[36] the General Court held that, in a situation in which an agreement or a concerted practice covers the whole of the territory of a Member State, there is a strong presumption that, by its very nature, it has the effect of reinforcing the compartmentalisation of national markets and thus is capable of affecting trade between Member States. In this case, Austrian credit establishments, which were participating in a cartel, did not rebut this presumption, given that almost all Austrian banks were involved and that their agreement covered a wide range of banking products and services, in particular deposits and loans. Clearly, the existence of the cartel was capable of affecting trade between Member States.

   In the context of Article 102 TFEU, the General Court in *Michelin I*[37] found that a loyalty rebate system confined to one Member State affected trade between Member States, because it foreclosed competition from other Member States.
8. The market integration objective is of the utmost importance in relation to a merger policy. On the one hand, mergers facilitate market integration in

33 COMP/35.587 *PO Video Games*, COM/35.707 *PO Nintendo Distribution* and COMP/36.321 *Omega – Nintendo* [2003] OJ L 255/33.

34 Case 8/72 *Vereeniging van Cementhandelaren v Commission* [1972] ECR 977; Case 246/86 *Belasco and ors v Commission* [1989] ECR 2117.

35 *Brasserie Fire Insurance* (D) [1985] OJ L 35/20, confirmed by the ECJ in Case 45/85 *Verband der Sachversicherer v CommissionVerband* [1987] ECR 405.

36 Joined Cases T-259–264/02 and T-271/02 *Raiffeisen Zentralbank Österreich AG and ors v Commission (The Lombard Club)* [2006] ECR II-5169.

37 Case T-203/01 *Manufacture Française des Pneumatiques Michelin v Commission (Michelin I)* [2003] ECR II-4071.

that firms from different Member States, by means of mergers and acquisitions, acquire a Community dimension and thus increase not only their Community competitiveness, but also their ability to compete effectively on international markets. On the other hand, mergers may adversely affect the structure of the relevant market at the Community level by creating, or strengthening, a dominant position that would allow a newly merged firm to exploit consumers and may ultimately affect the fundamental values of a democratic society. For example, a merger resulting in all press being controlled by one firm would affect the fundamental principle of democracy, which requires the preservation of the plurality of the press. Indeed, as Jacquemin and de Jong stated, '[p]rivate power can cross economic boundaries and poses the threat of an "extra market" power which can change the rules of the game in favour of the dominant corporations'.[38] Further, the application of the market integration objective to merger reviews would not only be fundamental to the achievement of the CSME, but also protect the Caribbean region from the transformation by dominant firms of their economic power into political power, ensure that sensitive sectors (such as the oil industry) are not controlled by foreign powers, and support the industrial, social and other policies set out in the RTC. Finally, the 2007–08 global financial and economic crisis shows that tighter merger control is required to avoid situations in which a firm becomes so powerful that its collapse has repercussions for the entire economy of a country, a region, or indeed the global market.

The market integration objective may sometimes result in the prohibition of business conduct that is economically sound and welfare-enhancing for consumers. Notwithstanding this, it is submitted that the achievement of a single market and economy in the Caribbean region should be given priority over other economic objectives. Even economists who are critical of the market integration objective in the European Union do not suggest that its importance in the Union should be diminished or disregarded; instead, they suggest that 'assessing the impact of commercial practices against the objective of the EC Treaty [the ToL] can be made both more transparent and more coherent by considering each goal separately'.[39]

3.3.2 The protection of consumers

The interests of consumers should be at the forefront of any competition policy. However, the traditional approach to ensuring this, based on the efficiency model, has some deficiencies. A new approach, advocated by Averitt and Lande, appears

38 A. P. Jacquemin and H. W. de Jong, *European Industrial Organisation*, 1997, London: Macmillan, pp 198–199.

39 S. Bishop and M. Walker, *The Economics of EC Competition Law: Concepts, Application and Measurement*, 3rd edn, 2010, London: Sweet and Maxwell, p 8.

to avoid these. Their approach goes beyond the efficiency model to propose a 'consumer choice' approach as the unique goal of competition law[40] – that competition law should ensure optimal consumer choice. According to them, the efficiency standard, which is based on an analysis of price and demand (that is, it focuses on how prices co-ordinate the amounts produced and consumed in a perfectly competitive market) is inadequate to deal with non-price competition.

Averitt and Lande describe the consumer choice approach as follows:

> [The consumer choice approach] suggests that the role of antitrust should be broadly conceived to protect all the types of options that are significantly important to consumers. An antitrust violation can, therefore, be understood as an activity that unreasonably restricts the totality of price and non-price choices that would otherwise have been available.[41]

Averitt and Lande consider that the consumer choice approach is superior to the price and efficiency paradigms because it recognises that consumers do not only want competitive prices, but also want options.[42] According to them, the 'consumer choice' approach not only includes all of the benefits of the application of the efficiency paradigm, but also goes beyond it by truly promoting innovation, focusing on the benefits and consequences of business conduct on consumers, being easy to understand and apply, and ensuring better synergy between competition law and consumer protection law.

As to the methodology of the new approach, Averitt and Lande acknowledge that it is more complex to apply than the efficiency standard, in that it would require an additional layer of inquiry to be added to the inquiries traditionally made when using the efficiency standard, this layer being necessary to reflect a new focus on consumer choice. However, such inquiry would be required in only a limited number of cases (around 5 per cent). As a result, most cases would continue to be assessed in accordance with the efficiency standard. Nevertheless, an inquiry would not be unduly difficult in terms of gathering the relevant information and in terms of its incorporation into the Herfindahl-Hirschman Index (HHI) measure (see Chapter 2, section 2.5.2.2).[43]

The objective of maintaining consumer choice has been acknowledged as one of the objectives of US anti-trust law.[44] Commissioner Rosch of the US Federal

40 R. H. Lande, 'Consumer Choices as the Ultimate Goal of Antitrust' (2001) 62 U Pitt L Rev 503.

41 N. W. Averitt and R. H. Lande, 'Using the "Consumer Choice" Approach to Antitrust Law' (2007) 67 Antitrust Law Journal 175, 182.

42 Ibid., 178.

43 Ibid., 237–248.

44 In *FTC v Indiana Fed'n of Dentists*, 476 US 447, 459, 106 SCt2009, 90 L Ed 445 (1986), the court stated that a horizontal agreement that limits 'consumer choice by impeding the "ordinary give and take of the market place," cannot be sustained under the Rule of Reason'.

Trade Commission, in a speech addressed to the American Bar Association's Antitrust Section in April 2010,[45] endorsed this 'consumer choice approach' as the goal of anti-trust law. He pointed out the two main benefits flowing from the application of the approach as being, first, that it 'provides a means that is still tethered to a demonstrable standard to analyse anticompetitive conduct in dynamic industries where there is intense non-price competition', and second, that it brings the US approach closer to that of the European Union with regard to the assessment of anti-competitive business conduct.

It is submitted that the enforcement authorities should seriously consider adopting the consumer choice approach. It certainly demonstrates the inadequacy of the currently used price and efficiency models in the enforcement of competition law. Further, it deals properly with non-price restraints and emphasises the value of dynamic efficiency. It is also submitted that the protection of consumer interests, as an objective of CSME competition law, may be pursued by novel approaches appropriate to local conditions.

The local conditions in CARICOM are that all CSME countries are developing countries and thus suffer the usual constraints deriving from underdevelopment. Most of them are small, highly vulnerable economies, with limited availability of investment capital, excessive dependency on external sources for food and energy, a volatile rate of growth of gross domestic product (GDP), limited natural resources, high transportation costs and a limited range of exportable goods, such as bananas, sugar and tourism. Some of them have additional problems with the enforcement of their laws against smuggling, corruption, informal society, organised crime, etc.

The small size of most CSME countries, which prevents them from exploiting economies of scale, combined with historical circumstances results not only in CSME markets being highly concentrated, but also in a high concentration of company management and ownership into the hands of relatively few individuals, most of whom are descendents of the plantocracy, or foreign. Therefore even if a firm has no market power in the relevant product market, its owner is sufficiently powerful to be able to prevent new entrants into a market, or to eliminate existing competitors in that market, given his or her overall superior financial and economic resources in other markets, either vertically related or totally unrelated. Further, those who are wealthy are often in key positions in the government. Additionally, business culture is based on family relations and networks, and in some CSME countries there is no legislation protecting consumers.[46] These factors alone lead to exploitation of consumers and necessitate

45 See J. T. Rosch, 'Rewriting History: Antitrust not as we Know it Yet', Speech made at the ABA Antitrust Section 2010 Spring Meeting, 21 April 2010, Washington, DC, available at http://ftc.gov/speeches/rosch/100423rewritinghistory.pdf [accessed 17 December 2013].

46 See T. Stewart, 'The Role of Competition Policy in Regional Integration: The Case of the Caribbean Community', available at https://sta.uwi.edu/salises/workshop/papers/tstewart.pdf [accessed 20 January 2013].

the taking of a radical approach to the protection of consumers in the CSME. It can therefore be seen that consumer protection policy and competition policy should be in harmony with each other,[47] and thereby create a fair, efficient and accessible CSME consumer market.

3.4 Conclusion

The objectives of CSME competition policy are yet to be defined. Starting on a blank canvas has advantages. First, the CARICOM countries have the opportunity to create the ideal competition law enforcement system, or at least a system that will not repeat the mistakes made by more mature systems, such as those of the United States and the European Union.

Second, CSME competition law can easily incorporate the newest forms of economic thinking, such as the consumer choice approach or elements of behavioural economics,[48] or some new approach appropriate to local conditions, in the enforcement of competition law.

It is important to note that, when choosing the economic principles or an economic theory to be applied in the enforcement of competition law, it is necessary to take account of local conditions. Therefore the protection of consumers may require a strongly interventionist approach to the enforcement of CSME competition law on the part of the CCC. Indeed, in highly concentrated markets, the market forces cannot always be relied upon to regulate and wear down market power. In this respect, competition policies appropriate for a very large economy, as is the case in the United States, where economies of scale do not limit the number of competitive alternatives available to most buyers, may not be appropriate to small economies with non-tradable goods and services.[49]

Whichever objective or objectives the CARICOM Member States decide to embrace, as appropriate to the requirements of the CSME, it is vital that the economic principles and theories to be applied to attain them are transparent, appropriately theorised and explained to all concerned, including businesses, consumers, national law enforcement authorities and courts.

47 On the interface between consumer protection and competition law, see UNCTAD, *Model Law on Competition (2010): Chapter VIII*, August 2010, TD/RBP/CONF.7/L.8.

48 See D. H. Ginsburg and D. W. Moore, 'The Jevons Colloquium: Behavioral Economics in Consumer Protection and Competition Law—The Future of Behavioral Economics in Antitrust Jurisprudence' (2010) 6 Competition Policy International 89.

49 On this topic, see M. Gal, *Competition Policy for Small Market Economies*, 2003, Cambridge, MA: Harvard University Press.

4

THE CONCEPT OF 'ENTERPRISE'

Chapter contents

4.1 Introduction

This chapter deals with the concept of an 'enterprise', which delimits the personal scope of application of CSME competition law.

Only entities that are enterprises within the meaning of the Revised Treaty of Chaguaramas (RTC) are within the personal scope of CSME competition law. Article 1 RTC defines an enterprise as 'any person or type of organisation, other than a non-profit organisation, involved in the production of or the trade in goods, or the provision of services'. Additionally, the meaning of an enterprise should be examined in light of Article 168 RTC, which lists areas excluded from the application of competition rules.

4.2 The meaning of 'any person or type of organisation'

The words 'any person' indicate that competition rules apply to both natural and legal persons. Natural persons will qualify as enterprises if they are involved in the production of, or the trade in, goods or the provision of services – that is, commercial activity. Accordingly, this definition excludes from the scope of competition law a consumer who purchases goods or services as an end user – that is, for individual consumption.

It is clear from the Article 1 RTC definition of an enterprise that, for the purposes of CSME competition law, an entity's legal status is irrelevant. If it is engaged in commercial activity, it will be regarded as an undertaking. A similar approach is taken under EU competition law. The case law of the European Union shows that not only companies and partnerships are undertakings, but also entities such as a Committee organising the World Cup,[1] a professional sports club,[2] and an agricultural co-operative.[3] In *Commission v Italy*,[4] the ECJ confirmed the European Commission's decision that customs agents in Italy, who were carrying out customs formalities in respect of export, import and goods in transit in exchange for fees, were undertakings.

The matter of whether the way in which an entity is financed – that is, whether from public or private funds – will be relevant to its being classified as an enterprise is examined in section 4.5.

4.3 The meaning of a 'non-profit organisation'

Article 1 RTC clearly excludes non-profit organisations from falling within its definition of an enterprise and therefore excludes them from the ambit of CSME competition law.

The scope of this exclusion will depend on the interpretation by the Caribbean Court of Justice (CCJ) of the concept of 'non-profit organisation'. On the one hand, the CCJ may interpret the words 'non-profit organisation' literally – that is, the Court may accept that entities registered as non-profit organisations, or bodies that are entrusted by a Member State with the provision of goods or services, such as education, health, etc., are exempt from the application of competition law. On the other hand, the CCJ may choose to provide its own definition of 'a non-profit organisation'. The latter would be the better approach,

1 Commission Decision Cases 33384 and 33378, *Distribution of Package Tours during the 1990 World Cup* [1992] OJ L 326/31.
2 For example, Commission Decision 2001/478/EC *UEFA's Broadcasting Regulations* [2001] OJ L 171/12.
3 For example, Case C-250/92 *Gøttrup-Klim Grovvareforening and ors v Dansk Landbrugs Grovvareselskab AmbA* [1994] ECR I-5641.
4 Case C-35/96 *Commission v Italy* [1998] ECR I-3851; see also Commission Decision 93/438/EEC *CNSD* [1993] OJ L 203/27, confirmed by the General Court in Case T-513/93 *CNSD v Commission* [2000] ECR II-1807.

bearing in mind that a private or public non-profit organisation may nevertheless be involved in production of, or trade in, goods or the provision of services within the meaning of Article 1 RTC, and thus may compete with enterprises on the relevant market. The exclusion of such organisations from competition rules would therefore distort competition on the relevant market.

This section first outlines the reasons why a literal interpretation of the words 'non-profit organisation' is inappropriate for the purposes of CSME competition law; second, it examines a suggested definition that the CCJ may be willing to consider. That definition is as follows:

> A 'non-profit organisation' means an entity that is subject to the non-distribution constraint, and either provides public goods and services or carries out social activities based on the principle of solidarity as defined by the CCJ.

4.3.1 Reasons why the literal interpretation of the concept of 'non-profit organisation' contained in Article 1 RTC is inappropriate from the perspective of the applicability of CSME competition law

At first glance, the exclusion of a non-profit organisation from the scope of CSME competition law may seem justified. The popular perception (perhaps even illusion) of non-profit entities is that they have loftier objectives than simply making money, do not seek to maximise profit, will normally pass efficiencies to consumers and would not exercise their market power even if they had it. However, the reality is more complex.

First, in law and economics, the distinction between a for-profit and non-profit entity is that the 'non-distribution constraint' is imposed on the latter[5] – that is, profit must be devoted to the purpose for which a non-profit entity has been established and must not be paid out to its owners or equivalents (shareholders). However, there is no restriction imposed in terms of the type of activity that may generate profit, whether economic, charitable or philanthropic, and none on how much profit a 'non-profit' entity can generate. Accordingly, non-profit entities operate on the same basis as profit-making entities: both aim at maximising profit in order to stay in business. Indeed, this entails that non-profit entities can be, and often are, highly profitable.

5 On the law and economics of non-profit legal entities, see H. B. Hansmann, 'The Role of Non-Profit Enterprise' (1980) 89 Yale LJ 835; H. B. Hansmann, 'Reforming Non-Profit Corporation Law' (1981) 129 U Penn L Rev 497; H. B. Hansmann, *The Ownership of Enterprise*, 1996, Cambridge, MA: Harvard University Press. For a useful introduction to the legal theory of non-profit legal entities in the United States, see H. L. Oleck, *Non-Profit Corporations and Associations: Organization, Management and Dissolution*, 1956, Englewood Cliffs, NJ: Prentice-Hall.

Second, even though, in the past, most non-profit organisations were mainly financed by charitable donations from individuals, grants from governments and returns on investment, nowadays a major proportion of revenue of non-profit organisations comes from the provision of goods and services. This trend has been accentuated by the current economic downturn, resulting in a sharp decrease in private charitable donations and in subsidies from governments, and a decline in interests and dividends. As a result, non-profit organisations have been forced to seek alternative sources of revenue, mainly by engaging in commercial activities. Examples are numerous. For example, the famous Smithsonian Institute, a museum, derives substantial revenue from the operation of its retail shops, restaurants, educational tours, IMAX theatres, licensing, and sales of its catalogue and magazines. The American Association of Museums reported that, in 2006, approximately one-third of total revenue of US museums was earned from commercial activities.[6] In many countries, universities are, as a response to reductions in government funding, engaged in commercial activities such as letting their student accommodation during summer vacations, organising income-generating conferences, running stores, bookshops and restaurants, performing contracted research and testing, and operating publishing houses. The same can be said about many hospitals registered as non-profit entities. For example, in 2005 in the United States, non-profit organisations providing education and health care derived 56 per cent of their revenue from the provision of services.[7] From the perspective of competition law, what is of importance is that, when non-profit organisations carry out commercial activities, they compete with for-profit entities and thus should play by the same rules.

Third, non-profit organisations are highly heterogeneous. They include a wide range of organisations, including the mega-wealthy Bill and Melinda Gates Foundation (which has assets of more than US$39 billion), neighbourhood associations, churches, soup kitchens, chambers of commerce, labour unions, fraternal organisations, credit unions, medical research charities, social and recreational clubs, employee benefit funds, hospitals, nursing homes and sports tournament organisations.

Fourth, the importance of non-profit organisations to national economies has been steadily growing. This is well exemplified in the United States where, between 2001 and 2011, the number of non-profit organisations increased by 25 per cent: from 1,259,764 million to 1,574,674 million. The growth rate of the non-profit sector has surpassed the rate of both the business and government sectors. In 2010, non-profit organisations contributed products and services that

6 N. G. Kotler, P. Kotler and W. I. Kotler, *Museum Marketing and Strategy: Designing Missions, Building Audiences, Generating Revenue and Resources*, 2nd edn, 2008, San Francisco, CA: Jossey-Bass, p 196.

7 M. F. Sherlock and J. G. Gravelle, *An Overview of Nonprofit and Charitable Sector*, November 2009, CRS R40919, available at http://www.fas.org/sgp/crs/misc/R40919.pdf [accessed 10 March 2014], p 19.

added $779 billion to the United States' gross domestic product – that is, 5.4 per cent of GDP. Non-profit organisations are also a major employer, accounting for 9 per cent of the economy's wages and over 10 per cent of jobs in 2009. With regard to their source of revenue, in 2010 sales receipts, including tuition fees and medical payments, amounted to $836.6 billion, which constituted 72.4 per cent of revenue of non-profit organisations operating in the United States. In 2010, income from assets of non-profit organisations amounted to only 4.3 per cent of their revenue.[8]

It is submitted, then, that the literal interpretation of Article 1 RTC, which entails that all non-profit organisations should be exempted from the application of CSME competition law, is inappropriate for at least four reasons.

1. As outlined above, the nature of non-profit organisations has changed, with the result that they are now often engaged in commercial activities. Further, the size of the non-profit sector and its importance for national economies is growing, as evidenced by its contribution to GDP. Although, in developing countries, the size and importance of the non-profit sector is not the same as that in developed countries, it can be expected that, in developing countries, the non-profit sector will expand once the conditions for its evolution are satisfied.
2. The assumption that non-profit organisations do not compete with for-profit organisations is false, bearing in mind that the majority of revenue of non-profit organisations now comes from the provision of goods and services – that is, from commercial activities.
3. Any assumption that non-profit organisations, when engaged in commercial activities, do not use anti-competitive practices is false. The US anti-trust case law[9] and EU competition law[10] provide many examples of anti-competitive conduct by non-profit organisations. This is why US anti-trust law and EU competition law make no distinction between non-profit and for-profit organisations. Further, prominent economists have demonstrated that:

> "[T]he same incentives to restrain trade exist in the nonprofit sector as in the for-profit sector. Altruistic firms benefit from exploiting market power, just as non-altruistic ones do, even when the altruistic firms would price below marginal cost without the spur of competition.

8 K. L. Roeger, A. S. Blackwood and S. L. Pettijohn, The *Nonprofit Almanac 2012*, 2012, Baltimore, MD: Urban Institute Press.

9 See T. J. Philipson and R. A. Posner, 'Antitrust in the Not-for-Profit Sector' (2009) 52(1) J L & Econ 1.

10 See, e.g., Case C-41/90 *Klaus Höfner and Fritz Elser v Macrotron GmbH* [1991] ECR I-1979; Commission Decision Cases 33384 and 33378, *Distribution of Package Tours during the 1990 World Cup* [1992] OJ L 326/31.

Therefore promoting competition is socially valuable regardless of the particular objectives of producers, and the fact that antitrust law does not distinguish between two sectors is efficient."[11]

4. The literal interpretation is incompatible with the main objectives of the RTC – that is, the creation and maintenance of the CARICOM Single Market and Economy, and the protection of consumers (see Chapter 3, section 3.3). The exemption of all non-profit organisations from the application of CSME competition law would undermine both objectives.

Notwithstanding these reasons militating against a literal interpretation of the RTC's concept of non-profit organisation, it is important to note that Article 1 RTC cannot be interpreted *contra legem*. The CCJ's task is to interpret and apply the RTC, not to revise it. Accordingly, the best way of reconciling the express wording of Article 1 RTC with the objectives of CSME competition law would be to provide an autonomous Community definition of 'non-profit organisation' for the purposes of CSME competition law. This approach is consistent with the teleological interpretation of the RTC and has been often used by the ECJ. The most appropriate example is that of the establishment by the ECJ of an autonomous uniform definition of the concept of an 'undertaking'. Under EU competition law, any natural or legal person (i) engaged in any economic activity[12] and (ii) enjoying some autonomy in determining their conduct on the relevant market is regarded as an undertaking (see Chapter 4, section 4.6).

4.3.2 The suggested definition of 'non-profit organisation' under CSME competition law

The following definition of 'non-profit organisation' is suggested:

> A 'non-profit organisation' means an entity that is subject to the non-distribution constraint, and either provides public goods and services or carries out social activities based on the principle of solidarity as defined by the CCJ.

11 Philipson and Posner, op. cit., pp 27–28.

12 For example, in Case C-41/90 *Klaus Höfner and Fritz Elser v Macrotron GmbH* [1991] ECR I-1979, [21], the ECJ held that 'the concept of an undertaking encompasses every entity engaged in an economic activity, regardless of the legal status of the entity and the way in which it is financed'; in Case C-309/99 *J. C. J. Wouters and ors v Algemene Raad van de Nederlandse Orde van Advocaten* [2002] ECR I-1577, [57], it stated that EU competition law does not apply 'to activity which, by its nature, its aim and the rules to which it is subject does not belong to the sphere of economic activity'.

This definition would ensure that when a non-profit organisation is not engaged in economic activity – that is, is not involved in the production of, or trade in, goods or the provision of services – it will be outside the scope of CSME competition law. It also ensures that when such an organisation is engaged in commercial activity, it will be subject to CSME competition law rules unless the activity in question consists of providing public goods or services, or is based on the principle of solidarity. This definition is examined in more depth below.

4.3.2.1 The non-distribution constraint

It is submitted that, for the purposes of CSME competition law, some latitude may be given to Member States in their determination of what should be regarded as a non-profit organisation. However, Community law should require that, whatever the definition of a non-profit organisation under national law, only an entity subject to the non-distribution constraint will satisfy the Community definition. The 'non-distribution constraint' refers to the prohibition imposed on a non-profit organisation of the distribution of profits (that is, net income) to its owners or equivalents. Accordingly, a non-profit organisation must devote any profit (any surplus left after reasonable organisational expenses) to the advancement of the organisation's mission. Economists and lawyers agree that the non-distribution constraint constitutes a defining characteristic of a non-profit organisation.[13]

4.3.2.2 The provision of public goods and services

According to economists, it is impossible to make profit from the provision of public goods or services. For that reason, enterprises are not likely to produce or provide them. Examples of public goods or services are fresh air, knowledge, national defence, law enforcement, public parks, public street lighting, and other things for the use and benefit of all.

Public goods or services have two characteristics:

- they are non-excludable in that they cannot be withheld from those who do not pay for them, which means that it is difficult or impossible to charge for their use (when a non-profit organisation operates a lighthouse, for example,

13 See H. Hansmann, *The Ownership of Enterprise*, 2000, Cambridge, MA: Harvard University Press, p 17: 'The defining characteristic of a nonprofit organization is that the persons who control the organization – including its members, directors and officers – are forbidden from receiving the organization's net earnings.' The non-distribution constraint is also considered by the ECJ as being the essential defining factor of a non-profit organisation: see Case C-174/00 *Kennemer Golf & Country Club v Staatssecretarisvan Financiën* [2002] ECR I-329, [28] and [33].

the world at large benefits from it and it is impossible to charge people for using it);[14] and

- they are non-rivalrous, which means that, once produced, an infinite number of consumers can enjoy the goods without increased production cost or diminished enjoyment by other consumers (once the lighthouse is in operation, its use by any additional ship adds nothing to its running costs).

As a result of the non-excludability of public goods or services, private producers cannot earn sufficient revenue from their provision, and thus have no incentive to produce and provide the socially optimal level of such goods or services. Such providers would face the free-rider problem: on the one hand, consumers have an incentive to free-ride – that is, not to pay for the goods or services that they receive; and on the other, the costs incurred in keeping non-payers from enjoying the benefit of goods or services is prohibitive.

In order to ensure the socially optimal level of provision of public goods or services, the government must step in to produce unanimously desired public goods that would otherwise not be produced, or would be under-produced, if they were to be left to the private sector. A government will source the funds necessary to pay for those goods by various means, most commonly by imposing general taxation. A government may itself create non-profit governmental organisations, or subsidise private non-profit organisations, or provide such organisations with various incentives, to ensure that public goods or services are provided in sufficient amounts and that they are provided at a proper price.

In light of this, it is submitted that, when defining the concept of 'non-profit organisations', one element in determining whether they should be subject to CSME competition law that should be taken into account is whether they provide public goods and services. If they do so, they should be excluded from the scope of CSME competition law. This exclusion is justified by the fact that the provision of public goods or services contributes to a nation's standard of living and creates positive externalities.[15]

14 See R. Coase, 'The Lighthouse in Economics' (1974) 17 J L & Econ 357.

15 A positive externality can be defined as 'a benefit that is enjoyed by a third-party as a result of an economic transaction. Third-parties include any individual, organisation, property owner, or resource that is indirectly affected. While individuals who benefit from positive externalities without paying are considered to be free-riders, it may be in the interests of society to encourage free-riders to consume goods which generate substantial external benefits': see Economics Online, 'Positive Consumption Externalities', available at http://www.economicsonline.co.uk/Market_failures/Positive_externalities.html [accessed 13 January 2014]. For example, a positive externality exists when a person is inoculated against a disease. Such a person benefits from inoculation by not becoming ill. Those around him or her benefit as well, because the risk that the inoculated individual will spread the disease is diminished or even eliminated. Although the transaction is between the doctor and the patient, the entire community derives benefit from it.

4.3.2.3 Social activities based on the principle of solidarity

It is submitted that, when a non-profit organisation is engaged in a social activity based on the principle of solidarity, it should be exempted from the application of CSME competition law. A similar exemption is well rooted in EU competition law, which not only excludes social activities from the ambit of competition law, but also excludes procurement pursuant to such activities on the ground that both are of a non-economic nature and, as a result, entities performing them cannot be regarded as undertakings.

In a number of cases concerning social protection schemes, many concerning pension funds, the ECJ has made a distinction between situations in which such protection is provided on the basis of the principle of solidarity[16] and those in which it is provided in a market context. In *Poucet and Pistre*,[17] the ECJ held that entities that fulfil an 'exclusively social' function based on 'national solidarity' are not undertakings because they do not perform economic activities. Advocate General Fennelly in *Sodemare*[18] described the principle of solidarity as 'the inherently uncommercial act of involuntary subsidisation of one social group by another'.

From the EU case law, it is not easy to establish what criteria should be used to distinguish commercial activities from social activities based on the principle of solidarity – that is, to establish how to carry out what has been known as the 'solidarity test'. In this respect, the Opinion of Advocate General Jacobs in *Albany*,[19] which lists the most significant criteria for making the distinction, is very useful. He submitted that the ECJ must apply a functional approach to the determination of whether an entity is an undertaking and therefore subject to EU competition law. Accordingly, the ECJ must focus on the nature of the activity, rather than the status of the entity under national law. Jacobs listed three criteria indicative of an economic activity, as follows.

- Membership of the insurance scheme or system must be optional.
- The contributions made by a beneficiary must be based on the principle of capitalisation rather than the principle of allocation. This means that contributions made by a specific beneficiary must finance his or her own future social security benefits rather than be used immediately to finance the current social benefits of other beneficiaries.

16 On this topic, see N. Boeger, 'Solidarity and EC Competition Law' (2007) 32(3) EL Rev 319.

17 Joined Cases C-159/91 and C-160/91 *Christian Poucet v Assurances Générales de France and Caisse Mutuelle Régionale du Languedoc-Roussillon; Daniel Pistre v Caisse Autonome Nationale de Compensation de l'Assurance Vieillesse des Artisans (Cancava)* [1993] ECR I-637, [18].

18 Case C-70/95 *Sodemare SA, Anni Azzurri Holding SpA and Anni Azzurri RezzatoSrl v Regione Lombardia* [1997] ECR I-3395, [29].

19 Case C-67/96 *Albany International BV v Stichting Bedrijfspensioenfonds Textielindustrie* [1999] ECR I-5751.

- A beneficiary must receive correlated benefits rather than uncorrelated benefits. This means that contributions paid by a beneficiary must correlate to the benefits that he or she receives.

It might be said that the ECJ uses these three criteria, but also pays attention to other factors, such as the involvement of a Member State in the supervision of the relevant social protection scheme and the absence of a profit motive.[20] The following ECJ cases exemplify this.

- *Fédération Française des Sociétés d'Assurance.*[21] In this case, the ECJ found that a body managing a supplementary old-age insurance scheme was engaged in economic activity because it was in competition with life assurance companies. Given that its members could opt for other schemes that guaranteed better returns, the body applied the principle of capitalisation, and the benefits depended solely on the amount of the contributions paid by the beneficiaries and on the financial results of the investments made by the managing organisation.
- *Albany.*[22] In this case, the ECJ found that a body in charge of managing a supplementary pension fund was an undertaking because it could itself determine the amount of contributions of its members, and their benefits, and because it operated in accordance with the principle of capitalisation. Thus it was engaged in competition with insurance companies.
- *AOK.*[23] Here, the ECJ had to determine whether the latitude given to the German sickness insurance funds to determine the fixed maximum amounts payable in respect of medicinal products constituted an activity of an economic nature unrelated to the sickness funds' functions. The ECJ found that the following factors indicated that the sickness insurance funds were not engaged in economic activities and therefore were not undertakings:
    - determination of the fixed maximum amounts constituted a task imposed upon them by statute;
    - the procedure for determination was established by statute; and
    - the sickness funds' discretion was limited – that is, they could determine the maximum amounts, but if they could not determine these amounts, the competent minister had to decide them.

20 See D. Geradin, A. Layne-Farra and N. Petit, *EU Competition Law and Economics*, 2012, Oxford: OUP, p 44.

21 Case C-244/94 *Fédération Française des Sociétés d'Assurance and ors v Ministère de l'Agriculture et de la Pêche* [1995] ECR I-4013.

22 Case C-67/96 *Albany International BV v Stichting Bedrijfspensioenfonds Textielindustrie* [1999] ECR I-5751.

23 Joined Cases C-264/01, C-306/01, C-354/01 and C-355/01 *AOK Bundesverband and ors v Ichthyol-Gesellschaft Cordes, Hermani & Co.* [2004] ECR I-2493.

- *Kattner*[24] The ECJ found that MMB, a body that provided insurance in Germany against accidents at work and occupational diseases, was not an undertaking. This was for the following reasons.
    - It pursued social objectives consisting of preventing, by all appropriate means, accidents at work and occupational diseases, and on the occurrence of accidents or occupational diseases, restoring, by all appropriate means, the health and the capacity to work of insured persons, and by providing financial compensation to insured persons or their dependants. Further, it was a non-profit-making body to which affiliation of undertakings established within a specific geographical area was mandatory and was governed by public law.
    - It was based on the principle of solidarity as a result of the fact that, *inter alia*, amounts of benefits paid under the insurance scheme were not necessarily proportionate to the insured person's contributions.
    - It was subject to State supervision. In this respect, the ECJ held that although MMB had some latitude – that is, it could decide on factors to be taken into consideration when calculating amounts of contributions and benefits payable under the scheme – this latitude was established and strictly delimited by law.

Examination of the case law of the ECJ shows that the solidarity test is not easy to carry out. This is because it is uncertain whether, in order to establish the level of solidarity warranting the exclusion of a particular activity from the scope of competition law, the abovementioned criteria are to be applied cumulatively, or whether some are more important than others, or whether their importance varies depending on the circumstances of each particular case.

It is interesting to note that the ECJ in *FENIN*[25] held that if public bodies that perform social functions purchase goods and services for the purpose of using them for activities of a purely social nature, they are not to be regarded as undertakings. This is particularly unfair to suppliers when a public body is in a dominant position on the relevant market, because this may have important implications on the suppliers' market, for example it may lead to the disappearance of innovative and competitive suppliers.[26]

24 Case C-350/07 *Kattner Stahlbau GmbH v Maschinenbau- und Metall-Berufsgenossenschaft (MMB)* [2009] ECR I-1513.

25 Case C-205/03P *Federación Española de Empresas de Tecnología Sanitaria (FENIN) v Commission* [2006] ECR I-6295.

26 On this topic, see L. Montana and J. Jellis, 'The Concept of Undertakings in EC Competition Law and its Application to Public Bodies: Can You Buy Your Way into Article 82 [102 TFEU]?' [2003] Comp Law 110.

4.3.3 Conclusion

High moral rhetoric should not shield non-profit organisations from the application of CSME competition law when they are engaged in commercial activities. Accordingly, the exemption set out in Article 1 RTC, as any exemption from the application of competition law, should be interpreted 'narrowly, with beady eyes and green eyeshades',[27] bearing in mind that it is rarely justified on economic or other grounds.

The proposed definition of a non-profit organisation is very narrow. However, the restrictions that it imposes are necessary in the light of the fact that non-profit organisations, in order to achieve financial sustainability, have increasingly been engaged in commercial activities. When they act as enterprises, they should be treated as such and subjected to competition law. This would not only be good for competition in the CSME, but also for non-profit organisations themselves, in that they would be required to get closer to their markets and stakeholders, and thus to become more innovative, flexible and accountable.

4.4 The meaning of 'involvement in the production of or the trade in goods, or the provision of services'

Article 1 RTC provides definitions of 'goods', 'trade', 'services' and 'provision of services'. The definitions are examined below.

4.4.1 The definition of 'goods'

Article 1 RTC defines the concept of goods 'as encompassing all kinds of property other than real property, money, securities or choses in action'. It is a definition that merits further examination.

'Goods' are defined by exclusion in that, apart from real property, money, securities or choses in action, all other things are goods within the meaning of Article 1 RTC.

With regard to real property, it is obvious that, by its nature, it cannot freely move and, accordingly, cannot be subject to provisions relating to the free movement of goods. However, it is submitted that real property investment and purchase are within the scope of the free movement of capital, as well as subject to the RTC rules relating to the right of establishment and the provision of services.

27 *Chi Prof'l Sports Ltd. P'ship v Nat'l Basketball Ass'n*, 961 F2d 667, 671-672 (7th Cir. 1992).

The exclusion of money needs some clarification. Distinction must be made between money that is legal tender in a Member State, and coins and banknotes that used to be legal tender in a Member State. With regard to money that is legal tender, it is subject to the free movement of capital and thus cannot be treated as falling with the definition of 'goods'. However, it is submitted that any coins or banknotes that used to be legal tender should be considered as goods. Similar views were expressed by the ECJ in *R v Thompson and ors*[28] and in *Criminal Proceedings against Bordessa and ors.*[29]

Securities are not goods. They are covered by the rules on the free movement of capital.

Choses in action refer to 'all personal rights of property which can only be claimed or enforced by action, and not taking physical possession'.[30] Accordingly, their nature entails that they cannot be considered to be 'goods'.

4.4.2 The definition of 'trade'

'Trade' is defined in Article 1 RTC as 'includ[ing] any business, industry, profession or occupation relating to the supply or acquisition of goods or services'. It is submitted in Chapter 5, section 5.3.3, that the definition of trade should cover all cross-border economic activities, including establishment. In this section, the definition of trade set out in Article 1 RTC is examined.

4.4.2.1 The meaning of 'any business'

The words 'any business' can have many meanings. The common understanding of the word 'business' is that it refers to an economic activity relating to the supply or acquisition of goods and services for money or money's worth. The activity needs to be carried out on a regular basis. Therefore, when a person is involved in only one transaction, that person is not involved in business. Further, business is carried on with the intention of earning a profit, and is subject to risks and uncertainties.

4.4.2.2 The meaning of 'industry'

The word 'industry' usually means the production of economic goods and services.

28 Case 7/78 *Regina v Ernest George Thompson, Brian Albert Johnson and Colin Alex Norman Woodiwiss* [1978] ECR 2247.

29 Joined Cases C-358/93 and C-416/93 *Criminal Proceedings against Aldo Bordessa, Vicente Marí Mellado and Concepción Barbero Maestre* [1995] ECR I-361.

30 *Torkington v Magee* [1902] 2 KB 427, 430 *per* Channel J.

4.4.2.3 The meaning of 'profession'

'Profession' refers to any occupation, practice or vocation requiring mastery of complex knowledge and skills through formal education and/or practical experience. Members of professions, being involved in the provision of services to consumers, are enterprises and thus subject to CSME competition rules. However, because most professions are subject to either State regulation or self-regulation by a professional body, their freedom with regard to the terms of carrying out the provision of professional services is usually greatly curtailed. The RTC takes a wise approach to regulation of the competition aspects of activities relating to the provision of professional services.[31]

First, the RTC states that any anti-competitive restrictions on the provision of professional services imposed by a Member State must be removed in accordance with Article 9 RTC, which requires Member States to take all appropriate measures to comply with their obligations arising out of the Treaty, or a decision taken by organs and bodies of the Community, and to abstain from taking measures that could jeopardise the attainment of objectives pursued by the RTC. Article 169(1) RTC states that the goal of CSME competition policy is 'to ensure that the benefits expected from the establishment of the CSME are not frustrated by anti-competitive business conduct'. Accordingly, a Member State will be in breach of the RTC if it maintains or introduces unjustified restrictions.

Second, Article 168(e) RTC provides that competition rules shall not apply to 'activities of professional associations designed to develop or enforce professional standards of competence reasonably necessary for the protection of the public and approved by the Commission'.

In light of this, the CARICOM Competition Commission (CCC) will be in charge of ensuring that the rules of professional associations do not restrict competition. It should accordingly be noted that the RTC does not, in fact, remove rules and regulations adopted by professional bodies from the scope of CSME competition law; instead, the RTC has subjected them to the scrutiny of the CCC, which will ensure that only those rules and regulations that are justified as benefiting consumers will be retained. In light of Article 168(e) RTC, it seems that, with the entry into force of the RTC, professional associations – under the guidance of the CCC and preferably with input from consumer protection bodies – should commence the process of reviewing professional rules and regulations in order to make them compatible with CSME competition law if they are not currently so.

31 See, in particular, the difficulties encountered by the ECJ and the European Commission in regulating professional services: I. E. Wendt, *EU Competition Law and Liberal Professions: An Uneasy Relationship*, 2012, Leiden: Martinus Nijhoff Publishers.

In the European Union, the importance of removing anti-competitive restrictions imposed either by a State or professional associations on the provision of professional services was examined by the European Commission in its Report on Competition in Professional Services.[32] The Report shows that the quality and competitiveness of professional services have spillover effects across the entire EU economy in that the removal of anti-competitive restrictions will improve the competitiveness of undertakings, foster growth in GDP, and offer consumers more innovative, more competitive and better quality professional services on more advantageous terms.

Anti-competitive restrictions imposed by professional bodies and governments on providers of professional services most commonly take the following forms.

- Fixed prices. Fixing price prevents a customer and a service provider from freely negotiating the price for a particular professional service. Fixing a price, or fixing a minimum price, is clearly anti-competitive; imposing a maximum price may arguably have some beneficial effects, in that it may protect consumers from paying excessive prices, but it impinges on the freedom of the provider to charge more if appropriate.
- Recommended prices. On the one hand, recommended prices may facilitate collusion between providers of services; on the other, they may mislead consumers as to what is the reasonable price for a service.
- Advertising restrictions. These may take various forms, from a total prohibition of advertising, to the prohibition of advertising comparisons of fees among members of the same profession, or the prohibition of seeking business by telephoning potential clients directly (so-called 'cold calling'). Advertising is of great importance for consumers because it contributes to their ability to make informed choices.
- Entry restrictions and reserved rights. Professional rules and regulations may impose excessive entry restrictions, which might be qualitative (for example minimum periods of education, minimum periods of professional experience, formal entry requirements, usually in the form of approved examinations) and/or quantitative (for example limiting the number of professionals permitted to be admitted to a given profession during a particular year or in a particular geographical area). Further, members of professional organisations may be holders of reserved rights, in that only members of that professional body will be allowed to provide certain services. Such entry restrictions and reserved rights may result in a reduction of the number of possible professional providers, protecting existing providers from competitive pressures and negatively impacting on the quality, price and availability of services for consumers.

32 European Commission, *Report on Competition in Professional Services*, February 2004, COM(2004) 83 final.

- Restrictions on the formation of partnerships between members of different professions. Such restrictions negate the possibility of consumers being offered a more cost-effective service, for example by means of an integrated legal and accountancy advice on taxation matters.
- Restrictions on business structure. These are likely to consist of, *inter alia*, restrictions relating to the ownership structure of professional service providers and on the opening of branches.

It is necessary to emphasise that a certain level of regulation is needed. The European Commission's Report on Professional Services lists three reasons why, the first of which is based on the concept of 'asymmetry of information' between customers and service providers. Professionals have high levels of knowledge and experience in areas of their expertise. Consumers usually do not have the same level of knowledge and thus find it difficult to assess the quality of a service.

The second reason is based on the concept of 'externalities' – that is, the impact of the provision of a service on third parties. A badly constructed building may jeopardise public safety, for example. The provider and the recipient of a service may fail to take appropriate account of those external effects.

Further, the Commission points out that certain professional services produce public goods or services (see section 4.3.2.2). Accordingly, regulation is necessary to ensure that such services are adequate and supplied at the appropriate level.

In light of this, it is clear that some restrictions are necessary to protect consumers from malpractice, misleading advertising, poor quality of services, etc. It will be the task of the CCC to decide which restrictions are justified as pursuing legitimate public policy objectives and which should be removed, to ensure that professional rules and regulations do not distort competition in the CSME.

4.4.2.4 The meaning of 'occupation'

The word 'occupation' normally means any job relating to the supply or acquisition of goods or services.

4.4.3 The definition of 'services'

Article 1 RTC defines 'services' as meaning services provided against remuneration other than wages in an approved sector. It also defines 'provision of services' as concerning the supply of services:

> "(a) from the territory of one Member State into the territory of another Member State;
> (b) in the territory of one Member State to a service consumer of another Member State;
> (c) by a service supplier of one Member State through commercial presence in the territory of another Member State; and

(d) by a service supplier of one Member State through the presence of natural persons of a Member State in the territory of another Member State."

This definition emphasises two characteristics of services: for the RTC to apply, they must be offered for remuneration; and there must be a cross-border element.

Implied in the Article 1 definition is that, in order to be regarded as a service, the activity must be of an economic nature. Further, Article 36(2) RTC refers to services as being of a temporary duration, thus distinguishing between the freedom of establishment and the freedom to provide services. For the purposes of CSME competition rules, this distinction may be of importance when a Member State imposes certain restrictions on the right to provide services that may distort competition, for example requiring that a provider of services has its principal establishment in that Member State, or prohibiting certain activities as unlawful (such as gambling services). However, such restrictions will be dealt with under Chapter 3 RTC concerning 'Establishment, Services, Capital and Movement of Community Nationals', rather than Chapter VIII, Part One, which deals with 'Competition Policy' (but see Chapter 5, section 5.3.3).

For the purposes of determining the personal scope of application of CSME competition rules, the term 'remuneration' needs further clarification given that the definition of 'services' contained in Article 1 RTC states that they must be provided for remuneration. This entails that a gratuitous service – that is, one that is 'provided for nothing' – is excluded from the scope of the RTC.

The case law of the ECJ indicates that the term 'remuneration' has been interpreted broadly. Remuneration is not restricted to direct payment by the beneficiary of the service to the provider, but also encompasses payments that bear indirect relation to the service provided and payments by a third party. This is exemplified in relation to payments for medical services covered by a social security scheme of a home Member State, provided to a person insured under that scheme in a host Member State. In *Geraets-Smits and Peerbooms*,[33] the ECJ held that:

> Payments made by the sickness insurance funds . . . albeit set at a flat rate are indeed the consideration for the hospital services and unquestionably represent remuneration for the hospital which receives them and which is engaged in an activity of an economic character.[34]

33 Case C-157/99 *B. S. M. Geraets-Smits v Stichting Ziekenfonds VGZ and H. T. M. Peerbooms v Stichting CZ Groep Zorgverzekeringen* [2001] ECR I-5473.

34 Ibid., [58].

It is expected that the CCJ will, like the ECJ, interpret the term 'remuneration' broadly.

The RTC's definition of 'services' explicitly excludes wages from being regarded as 'remuneration'. This exclusion solves any disagreement on the issue of whether employees may be regarded as enterprises, bearing in mind that one could argue that employees offer labour against remuneration and thus are within the personal scope of competition law. In the EU context, this matter was examined by AG Jacobs in *Albany*.[35] He submitted powerful arguments against the classification of employees as undertakings. He stated that although, from an economic perspective, one could argue that the offering of labour in exchange for remuneration is an economic activity, important legal considerations justify the exclusion of employees from the application of EU competition law. The main justification was that:

> "Dependent labour is by its very nature the opposite of the independent exercise of an economic or commercial activity. Employees normally do not bear the direct commercial risk of a given transaction. They are subject to the orders of their employer. They do not offer services to different clients, but work for a single employer. For those reasons there is a significant functional difference between an employee and an undertaking providing services. That difference is reflected in their distinct legal status in various areas of [EU] or national law."[36]

Jacobs further submitted that the EU competition rules are not drafted to be applicable to employees and that, in any event, employees neither provide goods nor services to the employer, but are engaged in work, which is a concept distinct from those of 'goods' and 'services' under EU law.

The ECJ subsequently stated its position in *Becu*,[37] in which it held that employees, whether taken individually or collectively, cannot be regarded as undertakings, given that they are incorporated into the undertaking that employs them and thus form an economic unit with it (see section 4.6.1). However, an ex-employee who carries on an independent business would be considered to be an undertaking.[38]

Bearing in mind that employees cannot be regarded as enterprises, their trade unions or associations cannot be regarded as 'associations of enterprises' within the meaning of Article 177(1)(a) RTC. However, can trade unions or other associations of employees be regarded as 'enterprises'? The answer is subject to the following considerations.

35 Case C-67/96 *Albany International BV v StichtingBedrijfspensioenfondsTextielindustrie* [1999] ECR I-5751.
36 Ibid., [215].
37 Case C-22/98 *Criminal Proceedings against Jean Claude Becu and ors* [1999] ECR I-5665.
38 Commission Decision 76/743/EEC *Reuter/BASF* [1976] OJ L 254/40.

1. Article 168(a) RTC states that CSME competition law does not apply to 'combinations or activities of employees for their own reasonable protection as employees'. Accordingly, when a trade union or other association representing employees acts as an agent for employees – that is, carries out decisions adopted only by its members and not in its own right, with a view to achieving social objectives consisting of protecting interest of employees as employees – it will not be regarded as an enterprise for the purposes of CSME competition law. This conclusion is reinforced by Article 168(b) RTC, which states that competition rules do not apply to 'arrangements for collective bargaining on behalf of employers or employees for the purpose of fixing terms and conditions of employment'. In such a situation, a trade union or an association of employees will be engaged in collective bargaining with employers and thus will act as an agent for employees in order to achieve an important social objective – that is, improving terms and conditions of employment. Obviously, it is inherent in such arrangements that they restrict competition in the relevant sector, but as the ECJ held in *Albany*,[39] the application of competition law here would seriously undermine the social policy objectives pursued by such agreements. The same can be said in the context of Article 6(a) RTC, which states that the improvement of standards of living and work in the Community constitutes the priority objective to be pursued by the Community. Accordingly, social policy objectives will prevail over the objectives of CSME competition law, with the result that collective bargaining agreements, because of their nature and purpose, will be outside the scope of CSME competition law.
2. Trade unions (and some associations of employees) are non-profit-making organisations and therefore whether they are within the definition of an enterprise when engaged in economic activities such as running a travel agency, or a bank, or a supermarket, will depend on the interpretation by the CCJ of the concept of 'non-profit-making organisations' (see section 4.3).
3. Subject to point 2 above, there is no valid reason why associations of employees, when acting outside the scope of Article 168(a) and (b) RTC, should not be subject to competition law.

4.5 The exclusion of public entities involved in the exercise of governmental authority from the definition of an enterprise

Article 30(2) RTC excludes from the scope of Chapter 3 RTC, which is entitled 'Establishment, Services, Capital and Movement of Community Nationals', 'activities in a Member State involving the exercise of governmental authority . . . in so far as that Member State is concerned'.

39 Case C-67/96 *Albany International BV v Stichting Bedrijfspensioenfonds Textielindustrie* [1999] ECR I-5751.

Article 30(3) RTC further defines those activities as meaning 'activities conducted neither on a commercial basis nor in competition with one or more economic enterprises'. It goes on to provide the following list of such activities:

> "(a) activities conducted by a central bank or monetary authority or any other public entity, in pursuit of monetary or exchange rate policies;
> (b) activities forming part of a statutory system of social security or public retirement plans;
> (c) activities forming part of a system of national security or for the establishment or maintenance of public order; and
> (d) other activities conducted by a public entity for the account of or with the guarantee or using financial resources of the government."

In light of this, it can be said that, when an entity exercises governmental authority, it will not be regarded as an enterprise and thus competition rules will not apply to its activities. However, Article 30(3) RTC does not exclude all activities of public authorities from the scope of Chapter 3 RTC and consequently from CSME competition law, but only those that 'are neither conducted on a commercial basis nor in competition with one or more economic enterprises'. Accordingly, it is submitted that the RTC has espoused the functional approach to the determination of whether an activity exercised by a public authority is within the scope of competition law. It focuses on the type of activity, rather than on the characteristics of the entity that carries it out. This entails that the concept of an enterprise is not only an objective concept, but also a relative one, in that an entity will be an enterprise with regard to some of its activities, but not in respect of others.

The application of the functional approach requires that the nature of a particular activity should be assessed on a case-by-case basis in order to decide whether that activity falls within the scope of competition rules. In this context, the importance of the establishment of appropriate criteria for determining whether certain activities of public bodies fall within the exercise of public powers or prerogatives and thus are excluded from the scrutiny of competition law is vital. This is because of the impact that such exclusion has on the relevant market in that, in respect of the relevant activity, there will be no competitive market and therefore no competition therein.

The choice of the appropriate criteria must be examined in light of Article 30(3) RTC, which states that activities of public entities that are 'conducted neither on a commercial basis nor in competition with one or more economic enterprises' are subject to CSME competition rules. The words used in Article 30(3) RTC may be interpreted in various ways. However, it is submitted that the following considerations may be of relevance.

1. The RTC clearly distinguishes between commercial and non-commercial activities of public entities. One may suggest that, in determining the

commercial nature or otherwise of a particular activity, the distinction known in public international law between *acte jure imperii* and *acte jure gestionis* may be of relevance. This distinction has been accepted by most States and entails that a foreign State may claim immunity from the jurisdiction of national courts of another State only in respect of *acte jure imperii* – that is, only in respect of 'sovereign' acts, or acts performed in the exercise of a public service. Accordingly, a State will be denied immunity for acts of a commercial or private law nature. The possible transposition of the distinction between *acte jure imperii* and *acte jure gestionis* to competition law is not without difficulty. Indeed, such a transposition would require the establishment of the determinative factors on the basis of which the identification of commercial activities would be made.

In public international law, States have used various criteria to identify *acte jure gestionis*. Some have focused on the nature of a transaction; some, on its purpose. For example, under section 1603(d) of the US Foreign Sovereign Immunities Act of 1976 and section 2 of the Canadian State Immunity Act 1985, the classification of an act is based on the nature of the State transaction or the resulting legal relationship, rather than on its purpose.[40] The UK State Immunity Act 1978 does not address this issue. However, the position embraced by the United Kingdom seems to be that taken by Lord Wilberforce in the House of Lords' decision *I Congreso del Partido*.[41] He stated that the 'whole context' of a transaction should be taken into consideration. This entails that both the nature and the purpose of the relevant transaction are relevant in making the distinction between *acte jure imperii* and *acte jure gestionis*. The lack of an agreement as to whether the nature or the purpose of a transaction should be the determinative factor is reflected in Article 2.2 of the 2004 United Nations Convention on Jurisdictional Immunities of States and their Property, which states:

> "In determining whether a contract or transactions is a commercial transaction under paragraph 1(c), reference should be made primarily to the nature of the contract or transaction, but its purpose should also be taken into account if the parties to the contract or transaction have so agreed, or if, in the practice of the State of the Forum, that purpose is relevant to determining the non-commercial character of the contract or transaction."

40 See German Federal Constitutional Court (30 April 1963) *Claim against the Empire of Iran* (1963) 45 ILR 57, in which the German Federal Constitutional Court held that '[a]s a means for determining the distinction between acts *jure imperii* and *jure gestionis* one should rather refer to the nature of the State transaction or the resulting legal relationships; and not the motive or purpose of the State activity'.

41 *I Congreso del Partido* [1983] 1 AC 244, 64 ILR 307 (HL). A similar approach is taken in France: see P. Mayer and V. Heuzé, *Droit International Privé*, 9th edn, 2007, Paris: Montchrestien, p 325.

It is submitted that, for the purposes of competition law, the establishment of whether a particular activity is of a commercial nature should be based on a case-by-case examination of the activity in question, in particular its nature and purpose, and if relevant other factors should be assessed. In other words, the whole context in which the activity is performed by a public entity should be taken into account in order to determine its nature.

It is interesting to note that the ECJ, when determining the nature of an activity – that is, whether it is of an economic or non-economic nature – has, in numerous cases, focused on the nature, aim and content of the rules governing the activity in question. For example, in *Calì & Figli*,[42] the ECJ held that activity consisting of surveillance intended to prevent pollution in the oil port of Genoa was, by its nature, its aim, and the rules to which it was subject, connected 'with the exercise of powers relating to the protection of the environment which are typically those of a public authority', and thus of a non-economic nature. More recently, this approach was applied in *Compass-Datenbank*.[43]

Case C-138/11 *Compass-Datenbank GMBH v Austria* [2012] ECR I-449

Facts

Under Austrian law businesses are required to place certain information (such as the name, address and details of any liquidation proceedings) on the publicly accessible national register of undertakings. By 1991, the register had been computerised, with the result that, from 1994, the general public could gain access to the register online. However, in 1999, Austria created billing agencies, which were put in charge of providing access to the register via the internet. These billing agencies impose a levy on users for accessing the register, the amount of which is fixed by the State and which, after being collected by the billing agencies, is passed on to the State. They also charge for their service an amount that must be approved by the Ministry of Justice.

The register is a protected database. Under Austrian law, the billing agencies and the final customers are prohibited from making their own data collections

42 Case C-343/95 *Diego Calì &Figli Srl, paras v Servizi Ecologici Porto di Genova SpA (SEPG)* [1997] ECR I-1547, [23].

43 Case C-138/11 *Compass-Datenbank GmbH v Austria* [2012] ECR I-449.

reproducing the data in the register, supplying that data themselves, or adding advertising to the content or presentation of that data. As a result, only the Austrian State has the right to engage in acts of distribution of the database. Accordingly, any redistribution of information placed on the register is prohibited.

Compass-Datenbank, an Austrian company, running a trade and industry datebase *via* the internet, provided information additional to that appearing in the register, but, in order to run its services efficiently, it needed to have daily updates of the data that had been recorded in the register. Until 2001, Compass-Datenbank had no problem with reutilising information received from the register. However, in 2001, the Austrian State started proceedings against Compass-Datenbank, seeking, *inter alia*, an injunction prohibiting Compass-Datenbank from using data from the register, in particular from storing it, reproducing it or transmitting it to third parties.

The dispute between the Austrian State and Compass-Datenbank was long and complex, and finally reached the *Oberster Gerichtshof* (the Austrian Supreme Court for civil and commercial matters), which made a request for a preliminary ruling to the ECJ. In order to decide the case, the ECJ had to determine whether the Austrian State was 'an undertaking' within the meaning of EU competition law, bearing in mind that if this were the case, the prohibition of abuse of a dominant position set out in Article 102 TFEU might have become relevant to the proceedings between the Austrian State and Compass-Datenbank.

Held

The ECJ held, first, that when a public authority stores data reported by undertakings on the basis of statutory reporting obligations and allows the public to search that data in return for remuneration laid down by law, it is not acting as an undertaking within the menaing of EU competition law. This is because those activities do not constitute economic activities.

Second, a public entity does not engage in an economic activity when, in reliance on intellectual property rights (IPRs), it prohibits the reuse of its data.

Comment

In accordance with EU case law, the ECJ looked separately at each activity of the Austrian State relating to the management of the register and the protection of the database. In fact, there were three separate activities.

1. The first consisted of storing in a database information provided by businesses on the basis of statutory reporting duties and the exercising of

powers to enforce those. The ECJ held that this activity was not of an economic nature, because it fell within the exercise of public powers of the Austrian State. This classification causes no controversy.

2. The second consisted of the maintenance and making available to the public of the data collected by the Austrian State, in return for payment. In this respect, the ECJ held that the activity was of a non-economic nature, because:

> "the maintenance of a database containing such data and making that data available to the public are activities which cannot be separated from the activity of collection of the data. The collection of the data would be rendered largely useless in the absence of the maintenance of a database which stores the data for the purpose of consultation by the public."[44]

The fact that the provision of facilities for searching the register and/or obtaining printouts were provided for remuneration was not in itself sufficient to classify the activity as being of an economic nature.

In earlier judgments, the ECJ had decided that if an economic activity cannot be separated from the exercise of public powers by the relevant entity, that activity as a whole remains connected with the exercise of public powers and thus falls outside the scope of EU competition law.[45] The ECJ applied this reasoning to the activity consisting of the maintenance and exploitation of the database, and thus considered it unable to be separated from the activity consisting of the creation of the database. This reasoning is not convincing, in that the maintenance and exploitation of the database is clearly an economic activity. There are no economic or technical obstacles preventing that activity from being severed from the activity consisting of the creation of the database. Indeed, in several Member States (such as Spain), those activities are in fact separated, thus allowing private undertakings to exploit databases created by public authorities.

The consequence of the judgment of the ECJ is that it has not only excessively protected the activity of public authorities connected with the maintenance and exploitation of the database from the scrutiny of EU competition law, but also prevented the existence of a competitive market in this area. It is regrettable that the ECJ did not explain its reason for treating the activity consisting of the maintenance and exploitation of the database as being non-severable from the activity relating to the creation of the database.

44 Ibid., [41].
45 Case C-113/07P *SELEX Sistemi Integrati v Commission* [2009] ECR I-2207, [72]*ff.*

3. The third activity consisted of the issuing of prohibitions against reutilisation of the information contained in the register. The ECJ held that the Austrian State, being the creator of the register and thus having *sui generis* IPRs over it, was 'not obliged to authorise free use of the data which it collects and make available to the public'.[46] The reason for the exclusion of the exploitation of activities related to IPRs by the Austrian State from the scope of EU competition law was that it was legitimate for a public authority to consider:

> ". . . that it is necessary, or even mandatory in the light of provisions of its national law, to prohibit the re-utilisation of data appearing in a database such as that at issue in the main proceedings, so as to respect the interest which companies and other legal entities which make the disclosures required by law have in ensuring that no re-use of the information concerning them is possible beyond that database."[47]

The justification of the ECJ for refusing to categorise the exploitation of IPRs as an economic activity is surprising in that the widest possible reuse of any non-confidential public-sector documents is certainly in the public interest and, in any event, if any information additional to that contained in the register is provided by private operators, they may be held responsible if such information is misleading. It is difficult to understand how the reuse of information already provided by undertakings may affect their interests, bearing in mind that the relevant information is in the public domain. Further, the extensive reuse of public-sector documents is in line with Recital 9 of Directive 2003/98/EC on the reuse of public sector information, which states that 'public-sector bodies should be encouraged to make available for re-use any [non-confidential] documents held by them'. The exclusion of the exploitation of IPRs by the Austrian State entailed that the prohibition of reutilisation of the data contained in the register was not examined by the ECJ in light of the 'essential facilities' doctrine' (see Chapter 7, section 7.4.2.3B).

The position of the ECJ in this case was therefore criticised as undermining the functional approach to the identification of an undertaking under EU competition law and as being economically unsound.[48]

46 Case C-138/11 *Compass-Datenbank GmbH v Austria* [2012] ECR I-449, [47].
47 Ibid.
48 A. Sánchez Graells, 'How to Crack a Nut', 16 July 2012, available at http://howtocrackanut.blogspot.com/2012/07/another-step-back-in-definition-of.html [accessed 5 July 2013].

2. Article 30(3) RTC states that activities involving the exercise of governmental authority are not those that are conducted in competition with one or more economic enterprises. It is not easy to interpret the words 'activities conducted . . . in competition with one or more economic enterprises'. The words have two possible interpretations.

   (a) Under one interpretation, the relevant factor in determining the nature of a particular activity will be whether that activity could be carried out only by a public body or whether it could also be carried on by a private operator with a view to making profit.[49] The use of this factor ensures that the determination of the nature of an activity is independent of individual circumstances, and thus independent from political, historical and other considerations. Accordingly, the existence of a potentially competitive market in the relevant area will be decisive in determining whether a specific activity can be classified as being of an economic nature and thus within the scope of competition law. The drawback of the use of this criterion is that almost all activities with economic importance will potentially be within the scope of competition law. Indeed, there is nothing preventing a State from contracting out its defence activities or law enforcement.
   (b) Under the other interpretation, the relevant factor in the determination of the nature of a particular activity will be the fact that the particular activity is, or has been in the past, carried out under market conditions.[50] Accordingly, the fact that governmental authorities have allowed partial competition to arise with regard to a particular activity will entail that there is a competitive market with regard to that activity.

   It is submitted that the first interpretation should be preferred, bearing in mind that Article 30(3) RTC suggests that, in the determination of the nature of a particular activity, the factors mentioned in point 1 above should also apply.
3. Under Article 30(3) RTC, activities of public authorities are outside the scope of CSME competition law when they 'are neither conducted on a commercial basis nor in competition with one or more economic enterprises'. The wording

49 This is similar to the comparative criterion used by the ECJ in the determination of the nature of a particular activity carried on by a public body. See E. Wendt, *EU Competition Law and Liberal Professions: An Uneasy Relationship*, 2012, Leiden: Martinus Nijhoff Publishers. See also Case C-222/04 *Ministero dell'Economia e delle Finanze v Cassa di Risparmio di Firenze SpA, Fondazione Cassa di Risparmio di San Miniato and Cassa di Risparmio di San Miniato SpA* [2006] ECR I-289, Opinion of AG Jacobs, [76]–[83], esp. [78].

50 This criterion is similar to the 'participation in the market' criterion used by the ECJ to limit the scope of the comparative criterion by placing the relevant activity in the context of the circumstances of existing markets: see Case C-205/03 P *Federación Española de Empresas de Tecnología Sanitaria (FENIN) v Commission* [2006] ECR I-6295, AG Opinion, [13].

of Article 30(3) RTC seems to suggest that, in order to classify a particular activity as falling within the scope of competition law, one must decide, first, that the activity under consideration is not conducted by a public body on a commercial basis, and second, that the activity in question is not carried out in competition with one or more economic enterprise. Accordingly, an activity will be within the scope of Article 30(3) RTC if it satisfies a double test – that is, it must be carried out on a commercial basis *and* in competition with one or more economic enterprises. This is a very restrictive test. The literal interpretation of Article 30(3) RTC therefore suggests that activities of public bodies will rarely be within the scope of CSME competition law. Even if they are carried out on a commercial basis, but there are no actual competitors, they will be outside CSME competition law. It is submitted that a better view is to interpret the term 'in competition' as suggested in point 2 above.

4. Article 30(3)(d) RTC states that, apart from activities expressly stated in Articles 30(3)(a)–(c), 'other activities conducted by a public entity for the account of or with the guarantee or using financial resources of the government' are excluded from the scope of Chapter III. This provision clearly follows the EU approach in that, under EU law, the method of financing – that is, private or public – has been used to determine the scope of provisions on the free movement of workers, establishment and services.[51] However, the ECJ did not transpose this approach to competition matters. In *Höfner and Elser*,[52] the ECJ held that the way in which an entity is financed is irrelevant for the purposes of competition law; what is important is whether the entity carries out an activity of an economic nature. This reasoning was applied in *Enirisorse*,[53] in which the ECJ held that an entity formed by public institutions and entirely financed by a Member State was an undertaking because it carried out economic activities within the meaning of EU competition law. It is submitted that CSME competition law should follow the EU approach in that whether a body is funded publicly or privately should be irrelevant for the purpose of ascertaining whether that body is an enterprise.

51 See O. Odudu, 'Economic Activity as a Limit to Community Law', in C. Barnard and O. Odudu (eds) *The Outer Limits of European Union Law*, 2009, Oxford: Hart Publishing, pp 226–230; European Commission, *Communication on a Single Market for 21st Century Europe: Services of General Interest, including Social Services of General Interest—A New European Commitment*, November 2007, COM(2007) 725 final, [2.1].

52 Case C-41/90 *Klaus Höfner and Fritz Elser v Macrotron GmbH* [1991] ECR I-1979, [21]; Case C-67/96 *Albany International BV v Stichting Bedrijfspensioenfonds Textielindustrie* [1999] ECR I-5751, [77]; Joined Cases C-180/98–C-184/98 *Pavel Pavlov and ors v Stichting Pensioenfonds Medische Specialisten* [2000] ECR I-6451, [74]; Case C-222/04 *Ministero dell'Economia e delle Finanze v Cassa di Risparmio di Firenze SpA, Fondazione Cassa di Risparmio di San Miniato and Cassa di Risparmio di San Miniato SpA* [2006] ECR I-289, [107].

53 Case C-237/04 *Enirisorse SpA v Sotacarbo SpA* [2006] ECR I-2843.

4.6 Autonomy in determining conduct on the market as an essential characteristic of an enterprise

The definition of an 'enterprise' in Article 1 RTC does not mention that an entity, in order to be regarded as an enterprise, must enjoy autonomy in determining its course of action on the relevant market irrespective of whether it has a separate legal personality. Examples of entities that do not enjoy such autonomy include a subsidiary owned and controlled by a parent company, a genuine agent and a subcontractor.[54] Further, the autonomy of an enterprise may be undermined when it is required to follow national legislation that is in breach of competition law. Finally, public bodies, when they act 'as public authority', have no autonomy in determining their course of action on the relevant market and therefore cannot be regarded as enterprises.

4.6.1 The doctrine of a single economic unit

It can be inferred from Article 179(b) RTC that autonomy in determining conduct on the market is an essential characteristic of an enterprise. This Article states that 'any two enterprises shall be treated as interconnected enterprises if one of them is a subsidiary of the other or both of them are subsidiaries of the same parent enterprise'.

It is submitted that Article 179(b) RTC endorses the doctrine of the 'single economic unit' well known in EU and US competition law.[55] Under EU law, a number of entities, although legally distinct, may nevertheless form one legal entity when they are controlled by a common mind and in a cohesive manner. In *Shell*,[56] the ECJ, in the context of an alleged infringement of Article 101(1) TFEU, stated that an economic unit 'consists of a unitary organization of personal, tangible and intangible elements which pursues a specific economic aim on a long-term basis and can contribute to the commission of an infringement of the kind referred to in that provision'.

Bearing in mind the legal implications flowing from the 'single economic unit' doctrine, it is necessary to be more specific about the criteria relevant to the determination of circumstances in which an entity, owing to its lack of independence from another entity, will be regarded as the same entity for the purposes of competition law. The consequences of the application of the single economic unit doctrine are, *inter alia*, the following.

54 See European Commission, *Notice on Subcontracting Agreements* [1979] OJ C 130/1.
55 See A. Jones, 'The Boundaries of an Undertaking in EU Competition Law' (2012) 8(2) ECJ 301.
56 Case T-11/89 *Shell International Chemical Company Ltd v Commission* [1992] ECR II-757, [311].

1. Unilateral conduct of an enterprise cannot breach Article 177(1)(a) RTC. Accordingly, any commercial arrangements between connected entities are outside the scope of competition law. If a parent and its subsidiary, which is not capable of independent policymaking, enter into an agreement that would, in other circumstances, be prohibited under Article 177(1) RTC, there will not be a breach of that provision, since that agreement (or concerted practice) will reflect the allocation of functions within the corporate body.
2. A controlling entity can be liable for the conduct of a subordinate entity.[57]
3. In the assessment of whether an enterprise is in a dominant position in the relevant market, the enforcement authority will consider as one enterprise all companies forming part of a corporate group located within the Community.
4. In the application of the *de minimis* rule contained in Article 181 RTC (see Chapter 5, section 5.3.2), the CCC will assess the business conduct of all entities belonging to the same corporate group in order to decide whether such conduct may be exempt from the application of competition rules.
5. An aggrieved party will be entitled to bring an action for damages against either a parent company or a subsidiary, or both. This entails that such a party will have a wider choice of jurisdictions when commencing civil proceedings against an alleged infringement of competition law.[58]
6. The CCC will not be prevented from carrying out inspections in the premises of an entity forming part of an economic unit merely because another entity belonging to that conglomerate group is allegedly in breach of competition law.[59]
7. With regard the imposition of fines for breaches of competition law, the CCC has not set out its policy. In the context of EU law, the maximum fine permitted under Article 23(2) of Council Regulation (EC) 1/2003 is 10 per cent of an undertaking's worldwide turnover. This includes the turnover of all entities belonging to the same corporate group, as opposed to the turnover of the entity that has actually infringed EU competition law. As a result, an

57 Case 15/74 *Centrafarm v Sterling Drug Inc.* [1974] ECR 1147. The matter of the attribution of responsibility for an infringement of EU competition law by a subsidiary to its parent company is highly debated: see M. Bronckers and A. Vallery, 'No Longer Presumed Guilty? The Impact of Fundamental Rights on Certain Dogmas of EU Competition Law' (2011) 34 World Competition 535; S. Thomas, 'Guilty of a Fault that One Has not Committed: The Limits of the Group-Based Sanction Policy Carried out by the Commission and the European Courts in EU-Antitrust Law' (2012) 3(1) JECLAP 11; L. La Rocca, 'The Controversial Issue of the Parent-Company Liability for the Violation of EC Competition Rules by the Subsidiary' (2011) 32(2) ECLR 68.

58 See *Provimi Ltd v Aventis Nutrition SA* [2003] All ER (S) 59 (May).

59 See Case T-66/99 *Minoan Lines v Commission* [2003] ECR II-5515.

infringement of EU competition law by a small subsidiary of a large corporate body may trigger the imposition of a huge fine.

Article 179(b) RTC states that two enterprises are interconnected – that is, form part of a single economic entity – if they belong to the same group of companies. It does not, however, specify the factors to be applied in order to establish that a parent company and its subsidiary form a single economic unit. In this context, examination of the application of the doctrine of a single economic unit under EU competition law may be useful.

Under EU competition law, a subsidiary will not be regarded as a separate undertaking if both the parent undertaking and the subsidiary form a single economic unit within which the subsidiary has no real freedom to determine its course of action on the market.[60]

In order to decide whether a subsidiary enjoys autonomy, the test of 'decisive control', which was established in *Viho*,[61] applies. In this case, Parker Pen had established an integrated distribution system *via* which its subsidiaries in Belgium, France, Germany, the Netherlands and Spain distributed its products. Parker Pen held 100 per cent of the shares in its subsidiaries, and directed their sales and marketing activities. Viho, a third party that marketed office equipment on a wholesale basis, complained, *inter alia*, that it was unable to obtain Parker products on conditions equivalent to those granted to Parker's subsidiaries. Viho alleged that agreements between Parker Pen and its subsidiaries divided the internal market along national borders, and thus were contrary to Article 101 TFEU. The ECJ held that there was no agreement between Parker Pen and its subsidiaries, because the subsidiaries did not enjoy any real autonomy in determining their conduct on the relevant market: they simply had to 'carry out the instructions issued by the parent company controlling them'.[62] Thus Parker Pen and its subsidiaries formed a single economic unit – that is, were part of the same undertaking.

In *Akzo Nobel NV*,[63] the ECJ confirmed that where a parent company has a 100 per cent shareholding in its subsidiary, there is a rebuttable presumption that the parent exercises a decisive influence over the conduct of its subsidiary and thus it will be held responsible for the conduct of its subsidiary. When a parent company's shareholding in its subsidiary is less than 100 per cent, the matter of 'decisive influence' or otherwise is assessed according to the facts, such as whether

60 See Case 48/69 *ICI v Commission* [1972] ECR 619, [134]; Case T-102/92 *Viho Europe BV v Commission* [1995] ECR II-17, [47].
61 Case T-102/92 *Viho Europe BV v Commission* [1995] ECR II-17, upheld by the ECJ in Case C-73/95P [1996] ECR I-5457.
62 Ibid., [16].
63 Case C-97/08P *Akzo Nobel NV v Commission* [2009] ECR I-8237.

the parent company appoints the directors and whether it imposes its commercial policy on the subsidiary.[64]

The doctrine of a single economic unit applies not only to the parent–subsidiary relationship, but also, when appropriate, to relationships between principal and agent, employer and employee (see section 4.4.3), and contractor and subcontractor. In *Hydrotherm*,[65] the ECJ held that three undertakings – a natural person, a limited partnership and another undertaking – constituted a single economic unit because they pursued the identical interest as, and were completely controlled by the same natural person.

With regard to the relationship between principal and agent, the position of EU competition law is stated in the Commission's 1962 Notice, as confirmed in its Guidelines on Vertical Restraints.[66] A genuine commercial agent who acts on behalf of a principal is not considered to be an undertaking within the meaning of EU competition rules. In order to decide whether an agent acts as a genuine agent, the European Commission will assess whether the activities that the agent carries out are associated with a commercial risk. If an agent bears no risk, or bears only a minimal risk, on the contracts that it negotiates, it will be considered to be a 'genuine' agent[67] and therefore not regarded as an undertaking within the meaning of EU competition law.

4.6.2 The doctrine of 'State compulsion'

EU competition law endorses the doctrine of 'State compulsion'. Under this doctrine, when an undertaking is required by national legislation to act in breach of EU competition law, or when the national legal framework is such as to eliminate any possibility of competitive activity on the part of an undertaking, EU competition law will not apply.[68] The justification is that, in these circumstances, it cannot be said that the undertaking concerned has freely participated in anti-competitive conduct. However, for the doctrine to apply, the legislation in question must have a 'decisive influence' on the undertaking's conduct. This is not the case when a State simply encourages an undertaking to adopt anti-competitive conduct without compelling it so to do. It is submitted that it would be appropriate for the doctrine of 'State compulsion' to be endorsed by CSME competition law.

64 Case T-102/92 *Viho Europe BV v Commission* [1995] ECR II-117.

65 Case 170/83 *Hydrotherm Gerätebau GmbH v Compact del Dott. Ing. Mario Andreoli & C. Sas* [1984] ECR 2999, [10].

66 SEC(2010) 411 final, [12]–[21].

67 Case 311/85 *ASBL Vereniging van Vlaamse Reisbureaus v ASBL Sociale Dienst van de Plaatselijke en Gewestelijke Overheidsdiensten* [1987] ECR 3801; Case C-266/93 *Bundeskartellamt v Volkswagen AG and VAG Leasing* [1995] ECR I-3477; Case C-217/05 *Confederación Española de Empresarios de Estaciones de Servicio v Compañía Española de Petróleos SA* [2006] ECR I-11987.

68 Case T-4/96 *Commission v Bayer* [2000] ECR II-3383.

5

THE CONCEPT OF 'CROSS-BORDER EFFECT'

Chapter contents

5.1 Introduction

This chapter deals with the concept of 'cross-border effect', which determines the circumstances in which anti-competitive conduct will be within the scope of CSME competition law and thus within the jurisdiction of the CARICOM Competition Commission (CCC).

Article 173(1)(a) RTC states that the CCC will 'apply the rules of competition in respect of anti-competitive cross-border business conduct', whilst Article 174(1) RTC provides that the CCC will have jurisdiction in respect of 'cross-border transactions or transactions with cross-border effects'. These provisions clearly establish that CSME competition law applies to anti-competitive conduct that has cross-border effect or to cross-border transactions. However, the Revised Treaty of Chaguaramas (RTC) neither defines 'cross-border effects' nor 'cross-border transactions'. The lack of definitions raises important questions:

- Whether for CSME competition law to apply, the cross-border effect of anti-competitive conduct must be actual and direct, or whether CSME competition law should also apply to anti-competitive conduct that has potential and indirect effects on competition and trade in the CSME?
- Whether for the application of CSME competition law, the cross-border effect of anti-competitive conduct must be appreciable – that is, of a certain magnitude?
- Whether CSME competition law will apply to anti-competitive conduct that is confined to a single Member State or a part of it?
- Whether CSME competition law will apply to anti-competitive conduct of enterprises established outside the Community territory, but which has effect on competition and trade within the CSME?
- Whether CSME competition law will apply to anti-competitive conduct of enterprises established within the Community, but which has effect on competition and trade in a third country?

Answers to these questions are vital for the application of CSME competition law, bearing in mind that the CCC will have jurisdiction to apply CSME competition law only in situations in which anti-competitive conduct has cross-border effect.

It is suggested that, in examining these questions, it will be helpful to refer to EU competition law, bearing in mind that similar issues have been dealt with on the other side of the Atlantic. Having said this, it must be remembered that the European Union's way of dealing with competition matters may not always be appropriate in the Caribbean context.

5.2 Whether, for CSME competition law to apply, the cross-border effect of anti-competitive conduct must be actual and direct, or whether CSME competition law should also apply to anti-competitive conduct that has potential and indirect effect on competition and trade in the CSME?

EU competition law applies when a prohibited agreement, decision or concerted practice (Article 101 TFEU), or an abuse of a dominant position (Article 102 TFEU), 'may affect trade between Member States'. The requirement that conduct prohibited under both Articles 101 and 102 TFEU must affect trade between Member States defines the boundaries between the application of EU competition law and national competition law of the Member States.[1] It is often referred to as the 'inter-Member State clause',[2] because it establishes the jurisdictional limitation on the scope of application of Articles 101 and 102 TFEU – that is, if the activity does not affect trade between Member States, it is outside the scope of EU competition law.

In *Société Technique Minière (STM)*,[3] the European Court of Justice (ECJ) held that, for the requirement that anti-competitive conduct may have effect on trade between Member States:

> ". . . to be fulfilled, it must be possible to foresee with a sufficient degree of probability on the basis of a set of objective factors of law or fact that the agreement in question may have an influence, direct or indirect, actual or potential, on the pattern of trade between Member States."[4]

This broad interpretation of the concept of effect on trade brings within the scope of EU competition law even arrangements that indirectly or potentially may affect trade between Member States, although the effect must not be purely hypothetical (see below).

1 It is to be noted that, first, under Council Regulation 1/2003 of 16 December 2002 on the implementation of the rules on competition laid down in Articles [101 and 102 TFEU] [2003] OJ L 1/1, which decentralised the application of EU competition law, the determination of whether prohibited conduct has effect on trade between Member States is very important for a number of reasons, *inter alia*: (i) under Article 3, NCAs and national courts are obliged to apply EU competition law when prohibited conduct has effect on trade between Member States; (ii) under Article 11(4), NCAs must give the European Commission at least 30 days' notice of their intention to apply Article 101 or 102 TFEU before adopting a decision requiring that an infringement be brought to an end, accepting commitments or withdrawing the benefit of a block exemption regulation (see Chapter 6, section 6.3.3.1A); and (iii) under Article 11(6), the Commission, upon receipt of notice specified in Article 11(4), may decide to initiate its own proceedings, thereby terminating the proceedings of the NCA.

2 R. Whish and D. Bailey, *Competition Law*, 7th edn, 2012, Oxford: OUP, pp 144*ff*.

3 Case 56/65 *Société Technique Minière (STM) v Maschinenbau Ulm* [1966] ECR 235.

4 Ibid., 249.

In 2004, the European Commission published its Guidelines on the Effect on Trade Concept Contained in Articles 101 and 102 TFEU.[5] The Guidelines restate the relevant case law. They provide that the above mentioned requirement constitutes 'an autonomous Community [EU] law criterion, which must be assessed separately in each case'.[6]

The assessment of effect on trade is based on objective factors; subjective intent on the part of the undertakings concerned is not required. However, if there is evidence that undertakings intended to affect trade between Member States, for example because they sought to hinder exports to or imports from other Member States, this is a relevant factor to be taken into account.

The broad interpretation of the requirement entails that it is irrelevant whether the prohibited conduct will affect trade favourably or unfavourably. In *Consten and Grundig*,[7] the ECJ held that even if an agreement results in a large increase in the volume of trade between Member States, this does not 'exclude the possibility that the agreement may "affect" such trade within the meaning of Article [101]'. This is because anti-competitive conduct may increase trade whilst having harmful effects on competition. The existence of a cartel, for example, may increase trade between Member States because its customers may desert it in favour of purchasing the relevant goods or services from undertakings located in Member States in which the cartel does not operate.

In *Consten and Grundig*, a large German manufacturer of electrical equipment entered into an exclusive distribution agreement with a French distributor, Consten, according to which Consten was appointed as Grundig's exclusive distributor in France, Corsica and the Saar region. Under the contract, Consten agreed not to sell outside its territory, and Grundig undertook not to compete with Consten, nor to deliver to third parties, even indirectly, products intended for the territory assigned to Consten, and to obtain assurances from its distributors in other Member States that they would not sell to buyers from outside their exclusive territories. This 'airtight' exclusive distribution agreement was reinforced by a clause allowing Consten to use the Grundig emblem and trade mark 'GINT' in its promotions. On the basis of this authority, Consten registered the Grundig trade mark in France. The argument submitted by Consten and Grundig to the European Commission was that the agreement resulted in Grundig's products being sold in France and that, without this agreement, those products would not be available for sale in France; thus, because of the agreement, there was a significant increase in trade between the two Member States. This argument was rejected by the ECJ, which focused on the nature of the agreement. The Court found that its nature was to isolate the national markets for Grundig products and consequently to partition the internal market along national lines,

5 [2004] OJ C 101/81 (hereafter 'the Guidelines').

6 Ibid., [19].

7 Joined Cases 56 and 58/64 *Établissements Consten SaRL and Grundig-Verkaufs-GmbH v Commission* [1966] ECR 299, 341.

which in itself distorted competition in the internal market. Although the agreement did not explicitly exclude parallel imports, it discouraged it. In short, it restricted competition by object (see Chapter 6, section 6.4.1).

The ECJ interpreted the requirement that an agreement may affect trade between Member States in light of the objective of the Treaty, which is not to increase trade between Member States, but to ensure that competition in the internal market is not distorted. The agreement in question led to distortion of competition and thus, as the ECJ held, 'indisputably' affected trade between Member States. As such, it was within the jurisdiction of the European Commission.

The Guidelines confirm the case law of the ECJ. They state that EU competition law applies when an agreement or a concerted practice has influenced the 'pattern of trade between Member States'. The term 'pattern of trade' is neutral, in that it does not require that trade be restricted, or reduced, or increased; rather, it encompasses all diversions of trade. Accordingly, EU jurisdiction is established 'if trade between Member States is likely to develop differently with the agreement or practice compared to the way in which it would probably have developed in the absence of the agreement or practice'.[8]

An example of indirect effect provided in the Guidelines is that of an agreement by which a manufacturer limits warranties to products sold by distributors established in other Member States.[9] This would create disincentives for consumers from other Member States to buy the products because they would not be able to invoke the warranty.[10] Export by official distributors and parallel traders would be made more difficult because, in the eyes of consumers, without the manufacturer's warranty the products would be less attractive.[11]

The taking into account of potential effect means that, in order to be within the jurisdiction of the European Union, an agreement, decision of association of undertakings, concerted practice, or abuse of a dominant position does not have to actually affect trade between Member States. Instead, it is sufficient to show that it has potential to have such an effect – that is, that it is capable of constituting a threat to freedom of trade between Member States.

The Guidelines list factors to be considered when assessing whether an anti-competitive agreement is capable of affecting trade between Member States.

8 The Guidelines, [34]. See also Case 71/74 *Nederlandse Vereniging voor de fruit- en groentenimporthandel, Nederlandse Bond van grossiers in zuidvruchten en ander geimporteerd fruit 'Frubo' v Commission of the European Communities and Vereniging de Fruitunie* [1975] ECR 563, [38]; Joined Cases 209/78–215/78 *Heintz van Landewyck SARL and ors v Commission* [1980] ECR 3125, [172]; Case T-61/89 *Dansk Pelsdyravlerforening v Commission* [1992] ECR II-1931, [143]; Case T-65/89 *BPB Industries plc and British Gypsum Ltd v Commission* [1993] ECR II-389, [135].

9 The Guidelines, [39].

10 See Commission Decision 78/59/EEC *Zanussi* [1978] OJ L 322/36, [11].

11 See Case 31/85 *ETA Fabriques d'Ébauches v SA DK Investment and ors* [1985] ECR 3933, [12] and [13].

They are the nature of the agreement, the nature of the products covered by the agreement or practice, the legal and factual environment in which the agreement or practice operates,[12] and the position and importance of the undertaking concerned.[13] The last mentioned factor, however, is more relevant to the assessment of the appreciability than it is to the ability of anti-competitive conduct to affect trade between Member States (see section 5.3.1).

It is submitted that it is imperative that CSME competition law encompasses the indirect and the potential effect of anti-competitive conduct in the examination of its impact on competition and trade within the CSME. This is well justified, *inter alia*, on the following grounds:

1. The purpose of the CCC's enforcement duties is not only to correct existing distortions of competition, but also to prevent such distortions. For that reason, potential effect of anti-competitive conduct need to be assessed by the CCC. In the EU context, this was well explained by Neelie Kroes, then European Commissioner for Competition, when speaking about Article 102 TFEU, which prohibits a dominant undertaking from engaging in conduct that is likely to lead to anti-competitive foreclosure. She said:

   > "We will not wait until actual [foreclosure] effects have manifested themselves. If we wait until rivals are forced to leave the market then we have two serious problems. First, you cannot resuscitate a corpse. No matter how effective the regulatory intervention, if it only happens after exit has occurred, then the damage to the market may be permanent. Second, such intervention will completely miss many examples of consumer harm that weaken competitors, but do not kill them. Competitors may be wounded, confined to a small corner of the market, but not killed. Leaving these cases to one side is a recipe for serious under-enforcement."[14]

2. The inclusion of the 'potential' effect of anti-competitive conduct would allow the CCC to take account of foreseeable development of the relevant market. In this respect, the European Commission's Guidelines provide that:

   > ". . . Even if trade is not capable of being affected at the time the agreement is concluded or the practice is implemented, Articles [101] and [102] remain applicable if the factors which led to that conclusion

12 The Guidelines, [32].
13 Ibid., [19].
14 N. Kroes, 'Exclusionary Abuses of Dominance: The European Commission's Enforcement Priorities', Speech at Fordham University Symposium, 25 September 2008, New York, available at http://europa.eu/rapid/press-release_SPEECH-08-457_en.htm?locale=en [accessed 14 January 2014].

- the aggregate market share of the parties on any relevant market within the European Union affected by the agreement does not exceed 5 per cent; and
- for horizontal agreements, the aggregate EU turnover of the parties does not exceed €40 million or, for vertical agreements, the turnover of the supplier of the product does not exceed €40 million.

However, the NAAT does not apply to Article 102 TFEU, which deals with abuses of a dominant position. With regard to markets that do not yet exist, the market share or turnover of which it is therefore impossible to determine, the European Commission will assess appreciability on the basis of the position of the parties in a related product market or their strength in technologies relating to the agreement.[20]

Paragraph 52 of the Guidelines provides short-term exemption for parties who have exceeded the above figures for turnover by up to 10 per cent and for market share, by up to 2 per cent, in no more than two successive calendar years.

The NAAT does not apply to cross-border cartels, because they are deemed by their nature to have appreciable effect on trade. Further, it results from the judgment of the ECJ in *Expedia*[21] that it does not apply to agreements that have as their object the restriction of competition (see Chapter 6, section 6.4.1).

In order to apply the NAAT, it is necessary to determine the relevant product market (RPM) and the relevant geographic market (RGM), given that the presumption is based on market-share thresholds. As explained in Chapter 2, section 2.5, this is not an easy task.

The Guidelines set out a rebuttable presumption regarding agreements between small and medium-sized enterprises (SMEs). In principle, such agreements are not capable of affecting trade between Member States given that SMEs are normally local or regional undertakings. However, when SMEs are engaged in cross-border activities, their agreements or practices may be found to be capable of affecting trade between Member States.

The Guidelines establish a positive rebuttable presumption of appreciability. This presumption operates in respect of agreements that are, by their very nature, capable of affecting trade between Member States – that is, agreements that cover several Member States or concern export and/or imports. The presumption applies when:

- the aggregate market share of the relevant parties exceeds 5 per cent; or
- the turnover of the parties in the product covered by the agreement exceeds €40 million.

20 The Guidelines, [52].

21 Case C-226/11 *Expedia Inc. v Autorité de la Concurrence and ors* [2012] ECR I-795.

This presumption operates if, at least, either the market share criterion is met or the turnover thresholds are met.[22] However, it does not apply when the agreement covers only part of a Member State.

It is submitted that the concept of appreciability developed under EU competition law is of relevance to CSME competition law. In particular, the assessment of appreciability by reference to the NAAT is useful, although not easy to carry out in practice, because it requires determination of the RPM and the RGM in each case. Further, it is certainly helpful to rely on factors specified in the European Commission's Guidelines to establish whether an agreement, decision or concerted practice is capable of appreciably affecting competition and trade in the Community.

The proof required to establish indirect or potential effect of business conduct must not be based on its remote or hypothetical effect, but, as the Guidelines state, 'must be explained by the authority or party claiming that trade between Member States is capable of being appreciably affected'.[23]

5.3.2 The de minimis *rule*

Article 181 RTC enshrines the *de minimis rule* in the following terms: 'The Commission may exempt from the provisions of this part any business conduct referred to it if it considers that the impact of such conduct on competition and trade in the CSME is minimal.'

Article 181 RTC establishes that the CCC will assume jurisdiction in respect of anti-competitive agreements, decisions and concerted practices, as well as abuses of a dominant position, only if their effect on competition and trade in the CSME warrant the Commission's intervention. In determining whether business conduct of enterprises is within the scope of the *de minimis* rule, it would seem appropriate for the CCC to follow the example of the European Commission: it would be very helpful if the CCC were to publish a notice on this matter. It is submitted that, in the preparation of such a notice, it may be instructive to examine how the European Commission and the ECJ have applied the *de minimis* rule, in particular in the light of the judgment of the ECJ in *Expedia*.[24]

The *de minimis* rule was established by the ECJ in *Völk*.[25] In this case, Völk, a small undertaking manufacturing washing machines, concluded an exclusive distribution agreement with Vervaecke, a Dutch distributor. Völk's share of the market in washing machines was less than 1 per cent. When a dispute arose between the parties, a Dutch court referred to the ECJ, asking whether the agreement was in breach of Article 101(1) TFEU, taking into account the small share of the market held by Völk. The ECJ held that the exclusive distributorship

22 Ibid., [53].

23 The Guidelines, [43].

24 Case C-226/11 *Expedia Inc. v Autorité de la Concurrence and ors* [2012] ECR I-795.

25 Case 5/69 *Franz Völk v SPRL ets J. Vervaecke* [1969] ECR 295.

agreement ensuring absolute territorial protection was outside the scope of Article 101(1) TFEU, because the effects produced on trade between Member States were not appreciable (the agreement concerned only 600 units).

Following establishment of the *de minimis* rule, the European Commission issued non-binding Notices on Agreements of Minor Importance (most recently in 2001).[26] The 2001 Notice is not binding on anyone, not even on the European Commission, but is very useful for undertakings in that if their agreement falls below the fixed thresholds, they can reasonably assume that it is outside the scope of EU competition rules. The Commission states in its Notice that no infringement proceedings will be commenced in respect of any such agreement.

The 2001 Notice quantifies in the following manner, by using market-share thresholds, what constitutes an 'appreciable effect on trade' between Member States within the meaning of Article 101(1) TFEU.

- Agreements between competitors (actual or potential). In the case of undertakings operating at the same level of production or marketing, the threshold is fixed at 10 per cent – that is, the aggregate market share held by an undertaking participating in any part of the relevant market must not exceed 10 per cent.
- Agreements between non-competitors. Agreements between undertakings operating at different economic levels in the distribution process are within the scope of the Notice if the aggregate market share of participating undertakings does not exceed 15 per cent in any of the relevant markets.
- Mixed agreements. For a mixed horizontal/vertical agreement (or in the event that the classification of an agreement is difficult), a threshold of 10 per cent is applicable.
- Networks of agreements. Paragraph 8 relates to networks of agreements. It provides that where competition in the relevant product market is restricted by the cumulative effect of agreements entered into by different suppliers and distributors, a reduced threshold of 5 per cent applies. The matter addressed here is that the cumulative effect of agreements may lead to foreclosure of the market. Paragraph 9 states that foreclosure is unlikely to occur if the cumulative effect of parallel networks of agreements affects less than 30 per cent of the relevant market.

The Notice states that the Commission will treat agreements as being within the scope of the Notice if they exceed the fixed market-share threshold by no more than 2 per cent in relation to the market share over two successive financial years.

The Notice does not apply to agreements containing so-called 'hard-core restrictions', for example horizontal agreements that are within the scope of the *de minimis* rule, but which have as their object price fixing, the restriction of

26 [2001] OJ C 368/13 (hereafter 'the Notice').

production or sales, or market sharing, any of which are *per se* contrary to Article 101(1) TFEU. However, the Commission will usually not commence proceedings in respect of such agreements unless the interests of the European Union require it. This will be the case if an undertaking participates in a cartel.[27] Similar treatment is applied to vertical agreements that fix resale prices, or confer absolute territorial protection upon the participating undertakings or third undertakings.

The Notice acknowledges that agreements between SMEs – that is, undertakings that have fewer than 250 employees and have either an annual turnover not exceeding €40 million or an annual balance sheet total net worth not exceeding €27 million[28] – are unlikely to have appreciable effect on trade between Member States.

The 2001 Notice is in the process of being redrafted[29] in the light of the ECJ judgment in *Expedia*.[30]

Case C-226/11 *Expedia Inc. v Autorité de la Concurrence and ors* [2012] ECR I-795

Facts

Expedia, an online travel agency, formed a joint venture, Agence VCS, with the French State railways company Société Nationale des Chemins de Fer (SNCF) for sale of rail tickets and other travel services. As a result of this joint venture, Expedia obtained privileged access to the 'voyagessncf.com' website created by SNCF and thus enjoyed preferential treatment for its services, while similar

27 In Case T-56/99 *Marlines SA v Commission (Greek Ferries Cartel)* [2003] ECR II-5225, the General Court confirmed the Commission's decision that even if an undertaking is small and its market share is below the threshold of 10 per cent (in this case, the ferry company operated between the Ports of Patras and Ancons, carrying very few passengers and vehicles, and had no ship of its own), but is a member of a cartel, it is not excluded from the application of Article 101 TFEU. Marlines argued, *inter alia*, that, because of its limited size and very limited commercial influence, it was not in a position to conclude price agreements with its competitors and thus did not participate in a cartel. The General Court replied that the fact that, despite its size, the other undertakings participating in the cartel perceived it to be an undertaking the opinion of which should be ascertained in order to establish a common position constituted a factor indicating its participation in the cartel.

28 The Notice, [3].

29 On this topic, see European Commission, *Revision of the* De Minimis *Notice (Antitrust)*, 2013, available at http://ec.europa.eu/competition/consultations/2013_de_minimis_notice/index_en.html [accessed 7 February 2014].

30 Case C-226/11 *Expedia Inc. v Autorité de la Concurrence and ors* [2012] ECR I-795.

treatment was withheld from other travel agents. Because of this, the French competition authority decided that the joint venture was in breach of Article 101 TFEU, and imposed fines on both Expedia and SNCF. Expedia appealed, arguing that, because the market share of Agence VCS was below the threshold specified in the 2001 Notice (under French law, the threshold was the same as under the Commission's Notice), the agreement was outside the scope of Article 101 TFEU. The referring court asked the ECJ whether the threshold specified by the Commission in the *de minimis* notice was binding on the authorities of the Member States.

Held

The ECJ held that the notice was non-binding, but added that an agreement that has as its object the restriction of competition constitutes, by its nature and independently of any concrete effect that it may have, an appreciable restriction on competition.

Comment

It was not surprising that the ECJ found that the Commission's Notice was not binding: the Notice itself makes it clear that it is of a non-binding nature. The ECJ held that the thresholds in the Notice are among many factors to be considered in the determination of whether a restriction set out in an agreement is appreciable. Other relevant factors include the factual circumstances of the case, in particular the content of the allegedly anti-competitive provision, its objective, the economic and legal context of which it forms part, the nature of the goods or services affected, and the real conditions of the functioning and structure of the relevant markets.

With regard to agreements that have restriction of competition as their object, the ECJ held that 'an agreement that may affect trade between Member States and that has an anti-competitive object constitutes, by its nature and independently of any concrete effect that it may have, an appreciable restriction on competition'.[31] This means that when an agreement restricts competition by object – that is, contains 'hard-core' restrictions – it always has appreciable effect on competition irrespective of the parties' weak position on the relevant market. This also means that the enforcement of EU competition law will be simplified given that, with regard to such agreements, it is not necessary to assess their effect on trade between Member States because it is presumed that they may have only negative effect.

31 Ibid., [37].

In this case, the ECJ closed the loophole for exemption of minor agreements that restrict competition by object from the application of EU completion law. The judgment is therefore one of the rare judgments in which the ECJ overturned its previous case law. Accordingly, *Völk* is no longer good law.[32]

The relevance of the judgment of the ECJ in *Expedia* for the enforcement of CSME competition law is that the CCC, if it ever decides to publish a notice on Article 181 RTC, should clearly state that agreements that restrict competition by object, irrespective of the size of the market shares and turnover of the parties, cannot escape the application of CSME competition law. Further, the CCC should establish a list of the types of agreement that are deemed to have the object of restricting competition and thus avoid any doubts as to their classification.[33] This will be beneficial, first, to the parties, because they will have a strong incentive to amend agreements that restrict competition by object, no matter how small their market share or turnover, and second, to NCAs, which will have clear guidance on this point.

5.3.3 The concept of 'trade'

Article 1 RTC provides a definition of 'trade'. It states that 'trade includes any business, profession or occupation relating to supply or acquisition of goods and services'. This concept is examined in Chapter 4, section 4.4.2. In light of the very clear wording of Article 1, the issue arises as to whether the term 'trade' also covers establishment in another Member State. In other words, the issue is whether a measure that impedes an enterprise from establishing itself in another Member State with a view to providing services there may affect cross-border trade within the meaning of competition law.

With regard to EU competition law, the Commission's Guidelines state that 'the concept of trade is not limited to traditional exchanges of goods and services across borders. It is also a wider concept, covering all cross-border economic activity, including establishment.'[34]

32 Case 5/69 *Franz Völk v SPRL ets J. Vervaecke* [1969] ECR 295. See also Case C-260/07 *Pedro IV Servicios SL v Total España SA* [2009] ECR I-2437, [68], in which the ECJ held that an exclusive purchasing agreement breaches Article 101(1) if it 'perceptibly' restricts competition.

33 See D. Bailey, 'Restrictions of Competition by Object under Article 101 TFEU' (2012) 49 CML Rev 559; M. R. Mahtani, 'Thinking Outside the Object Box: An EU and UK Perspective' (2012) 8(1) ECJ 1.

34 The Guidelines, [19].

In a number of cases, the ECJ held that restrictions on establishment may affect trade between Member States.[35] In *Pronuptia*,[36] the Court held that franchising agreements containing provisions for sharing markets between the franchisor and the franchisees, or among the franchisees themselves, are liable to affect trade between Member States even if entered into by undertakings established in the same Member State, in so far as they prevent franchisees from establishing themselves in another Member State. Such agreements constitute a restriction on competition contrary to Article 101(1) TFEU.

Ambulanz Glöckner[37] concerned provision of an emergency and non-emergency patient transport service in Germany. This service was subject to a procedure for an authorisation by administrative authorities in each German *Lande* (province) and in the towns, which are administrative districts in their own right. Under German law, the administrative authorities assigned the operation of the public ambulance services to medical aid organisations such as the German Red Cross and St John Ambulance (that is, to non-profit-making organisations), whilst exercising supervision over them by giving directions and bearing the costs of the services. Only if those organisations were unwilling or unable to guarantee a permanent public service did the administrative authorities assign the public ambulance services to private operators. Ambulanz Glöckner, a provider of private ambulance services, applied for a renewal of its authorisation to provide emergency and non-emergency transport services in a district of the *Lande* of Rheinland-Pfalz. Under German law, any such authorisation was to be refused if it would be likely to have an adverse effect on the general interest in the operation of an effective ambulance service. In assessing this interest, the relevant authorities had to take account of such factors as the reserve capacity of the public ambulance service throughout the territory, the actual use made of the public ambulance service within the operational area concerned, and changes in the expenditure and revenue situation. The administrative authorities of the district in which Ambulanz Glöckner wished to operate, after consultation with two medical aid organisations that were providing emergency and non-emergency patient public transport services in that district, refused the renewal. This was on the grounds that, in that district, the medical aid organisations then operated at only 26 per cent of their capacity and made no profit, and that, in those

35 See Case C-41/90 *Klaus Höfner and Fritz Elser v Macrotron GmbH* [1991] ECR I-1979, [33]; Joined Cases C 215/96 and C 216/96 *Carlo Bagnasco and ors v Banca Popolare di Novara soc. coop. arl. (BNP) (C-215/96) and Cassa di Risparmio di Genova e Imperia SpA (Carige) (C-216/96)* [1999] ECR I-135, [51]; Case C-309/99 *J. C. J. Wouters, J. W. Savelbergh and Price Waterhouse Belastingadviseurs BV v Algemene Raad van de Nederlandse Orde van Advocaten* [2002] ECR I-1577, [95].

36 Case 161/84 *Pronuptia de Paris GmbH v Pronuptia de Paris Irmgard Schillgallis* [1986] ECR 353, [26].

37 Case C-475/99 *Firma Ambulanz Glöckner v Landkreis Südwestpfalz* [2001] ECR I-8089.

circumstances, to have an additional provider would result in either increasing charges for the public service or reducing its availability. Ambulanz Glöckner challenged the decision.

One of the aspects of this case was whether trade between Member States may be affected by German law. The ECJ made a general statement that 'trade between Member States may be affected by a measure which prevents an undertaking from establishing itself in another Member State with a view to providing services there on the market in question'.[38] However, the ECJ left it to the referring court to determine whether this would occur in this particular case, in light of the local nature of the service at issue.

It is submitted that the main reason for including 'establishment' in the concept of trade is that such inclusion would bring establishment within the scope of CSME competition law. This would result in claimants having an additional, or alternative, or, in some cases, the one and only route for challenging particular conduct, or transactions, or measures on the basis of the RTC. It is important to note that competition rules are concerned with the business conduct of enterprises, whilst rules on free movement and State aid are mainly addressed to States. This distinction is not absolute, however, because – as exemplified by the case law of the ECJ – measures enacted by Member States may be subject to competition rules (see in particular Chapter 8) and rules on freedoms may apply to some non-State measures.

It is submitted that the concept of trade should be interpreted widely to cover not only supply and acquisition of goods and services, but also establishment of enterprises in another Member State with a view to providing services there. This is consistent with the main objective of the RTC to create the CARICOM Single Market and Economy in which goods, services and capital circulate freely, and in which enterprises are free to establish themselves in any Member State. For as long as establishment is not included in the RTC's definition of trade, a large gap will remain in that definition. It is to be hoped that the CCJ will close the gap by means of the teleological interpretation of the RTC.

5.3.4 The concept of 'competition'

Article 181 RTC, which establishes a *de minimis* rule, states that the CCC has discretion to exempt from the application of competition rules any business conduct that has minimal impact on competition and trade within the Community. It is submitted that the reference to 'impact on competition' means that the CCC will have jurisdiction not only in a situation in which the cross-border effect of anti-competitive business conduct has appreciable effect on trade within the Community, but also when it impacts on

38 Ibid., [51].

competition – that is, when such conduct alters the competitive structure within the Community.

Normally, when cross-border business conduct or transactions alter the competitive structure of the relevant market, trade within the Community is also affected. However, the reference in Article 181 RTC to 'impact on competition' is very important in that it unequivocally condemns business conduct that may have no real or potential impact on trade within the Community, but which may alter the competitive structure of the relevant market in the Community. The judgment of the ECJ in *Commercial Solvents*[39] illustrates this point. In this case, anti-competitive conduct of a dominant undertaking consisted of eliminating a competitor established within the European Union, whose production was almost entirely exported outside the Union. The dominant undertaking argued that its conduct was outside the scope of Article 102 TFEU because it did not affect trade between Member States. It is important to note that the TFEU neither defines the concept of 'effects on trade between Member States', nor the concept of 'trade'. Accordingly, it was the task of the European Commission, and ultimately the ECJ, to define those concepts. In *Commercial Solvents*, the ECJ interpreted Articles 101 and 102 TFEU teleologically. This interpretation allowed the ECJ to extend the application of Articles 101 and 102 TFEU beyond economic or industrial activities consisting of supplying the Member States. Accordingly, under EU competition law, in order to decide whether business conduct alters the competitive structure within the European Union, it is irrelevant whether production is intended for sale within the Union or for export. In this respect, the ECJ held that:

> "When an undertaking in a dominant position within the common market abuses its position in such a way that a competitor in the common market is likely to be eliminated, it does not matter whether the conduct relates to the latter's export or its trade within the common market, once it has been established that this elimination will have repercussions on the competitive structure within the common market."[40]

The *Commercial Solvents* case shows that, under EU competition law, trade between Member States may be affected when business conduct alters the competitive structure of the relevant EU market. The teleological interpretation by the ECJ of the concept of 'effect on trade' is certainly correct, but a better approach would be to include the cross-border effect of anti-competitive business

39 Joined Cases 6 and 7/73 *Istituto Chemioterapico Italiano SpA and Commercial Solvents Corporation v Commission* [1974] ECR 223.

40 Ibid., [33].

conduct on competition expressly within the scope of CSME competition law and thus within the jurisdiction of the CCC. Article 181 RTC clearly confirms that any cross-border conduct or transaction that has impact on competition within the Community is within the scope of CSME competition law. Additionally, Article 174(1) RTC refers to 'cross-border transactions or transactions with cross-border effects' as being within the competence of the CCC when they prevent, restrict or distort competition within the CSME – that is, when they constitute a restriction on competition.

5.4 Whether CSME competition law will apply to anti-competitive conduct that is confined to a single Member State or a part of it?

The concept of appreciability entails that, for the purposes of CSME competition law, it is irrelevant whether anti-competitive conduct is confined to a single Member State, or a part of a Member State, or covers several Member States. What is important is to establish whether it has appreciable effect on trade and competition between Member States. This has been acknowledged by EU competition law under which anti-competitive agreements, decisions or concerted practices, as well as abuses of a dominant position, covering one Member State, or even a part of a Member State, may have an appreciable effect on trade between Member States and thus fall within the scope of EU competition law.

With regard to an agreement, decision or a concerted practice between undertakings in a single Member State, such arrangements may appreciably affect trade between Member States if they create or reinforce partitioning of the internal market in accord with national borders,[41] or limit the capacity of production in a Member State by, for example, fixing prices to be charged in that Member State,[42] or by creating a common subsidiary there responsible for production and commercialisation of their products.[43]

In *The Lombard Club*,[44] the General Court held that, in a situation in which an agreement or concerted practice covers the whole of the territory of a Member State, there is a strong presumption that such an agreement or concerted practice, by its very nature, has the effect of reinforcing the compartmentalisation of national markets and thus is capable of appreciably affecting trade between

41 Case 8/72 *Vereeniging van Cementhandelaren v Commission* [1972] ECR 977; Case 246/86 *SC Belasco v Commission* [1989] ECR 2117.

42 Commission Decision 89/93/EEC *Flat Glass* [1989] OJ L 33/44.

43 Commission Decision 93/48/EEC *Fiat-Hitachi* [1993] OJ L 20/10.

44 Joined Cases T-259–264/02 and T-271/02 *Raiffeisen Zentralbank Österreich AG and ors v Commission (The Lombard Club)* [2006] ECR II-5169, confirmed by the ECJ in Joined Cases C-125/07P, C-133/07P and 135/07P *Erste Group Bank and ors v Commission* [2009] ECR I-8681.

Member States. In this case, Austrian credit establishments involved in a cartel did not rebut this presumption, given that almost all Austrian banks were involved, and their agreement covered a wide range of banking products and services, in particular deposits and loans. Thus it was capable of affecting trade between Member States.

In the context of the requirement that, to be in breach of Article 101(1) TFEU, the conduct of undertakings must appreciably affect trade between Member States, it is important to emphasise that the agreement as a whole must be taken into consideration, not only each clause restricting competition.[45] If there is a network of agreements, the actual circumstances, both economic and legal, in which each agreement was made must be taken into consideration.[46] In the case of abuse of a dominant position, it is necessary to take into account the entirety of the commercial activities of an undertaking, including those outside the internal market.[47]

With regard to abuses of a dominant position by an enterprise that operates in a single State, or a part of a single State, they are often capable of having effect on competitive structures within the Community. In this context, it can be said that the very presence of an enterprise in a dominant position covering a single Member State entails that competition is weak in that Member State in respect of the relevant market. When an enterprise abuses its dominant position by, for example, eliminating competitors in that single Member State, the abuse will have no effect on trade between Member States if the enterprises that are being eliminated operate in that single Member State alone – that is, if they do not export to or import from other Member States and have no subsidiaries in any other Member State. However, the abusive conduct will affect the competitive structures of the relevant Community market in that fewer enterprises will operate in that market and its penetration may be more difficult for enterprises from other Member States than those from the Member State in which a dominant enterprise operates. Furthermore, competitors from other Member States may be reluctant to compete if the dominant undertaking has acquired a reputation for adopting aggressive exclusionary practices towards competitors that attempt to enter the relevant market in that Member State.

In determining whether an abuse by a dominant enterprise, which covers only part of a Member State, is capable of appreciably affecting competition and trade within the Community, the size of the relevant market held by that enterprise, in terms of volume, will be of relevance. For example, when an enterprise that owns or controls a facility or an infrastructure such as a port, or

45 Case 193/83 *Windsurfing International* [1986] ECR 611.

46 Case 23/67 *Brasserie de Haecht v Wilkin-Janssens (No. 1)* [1967] ECR 407.

47 Joined Cases 6 and 7/73 *Istituto Chemioterapico Italiano SpA and Commercial Solvents Corporation v Commission* [1974] ECR 223; Case 22/79 *Greenwich Film Production v SACEM and Société des Editions Labrador* [1979] ECR 3275.

airport, which is used to provide important cross-border services, refuses access to that facility or infrastructure to enterprises from other Member States, or provides access only on discriminatory or unfavourable terms, trade between Member States is capable of being affected.

5.5 Whether CSME competition law will apply to anti-competitive conduct of enterprises established outside the Community territory, but which has effect on competition and trade within the CSME?

In considering whether CSME competition law will apply only to undertakings established within the CSME or whether it will also apply to those established outside the CSME in a situation in which their unlawful conduct has cross-border effect within the Community, the experience of the European Union and of the United States is instructive.

EU competition law applies not only to undertakings established in the European Union, but also to those established outside it. The extraterritorial application of EU law is based, first, on the 'single economic unit' doctrine (see Chapter 4, section 4.6.1), second, on the 'implementation doctrine' established by the ECJ in the *Wood Pulp Cartel* cases[48] (which has many similarities with the US 'effects doctrine'), and third, on the EU Merger Regulation,[49] which applies to undertakings satisfying the turnover threshold in the European Union.

The application of competition law to foreign firms was initially developed in the United States under the 'effects doctrine', which was first applied in *Aluminium Co. of America*.[50] The question in that case was whether a Canadian company could be liable under US anti-trust legislation. The US court held that it had jurisdiction because the acts of the Canadian company were intended to, and did indeed, have effects within the United States.

The US effects doctrine was reformulated in 1982 in the Foreign Trade Antitrust Improvement Act, which amended the Sherman Act and provided for application of US anti-trust law in situations in which the conduct of a foreign company has direct, substantial and reasonably foreseeable effect on US commerce or US export. In *Hartford*,[51] the US Supreme Court held that conduct by foreign parties violates the Sherman Act if it satisfies both the 'intent' and 'effects' tests. As to the intent, the party must have intended to hurt, and in fact have hurt, competition in the US market. With regard to the effect, its conduct must have

48 Joined Cases 89, 104, 114, 116, 117 and 125–129/85 *A. Ahlström Osakeyhtiö and ors v Commission (Re Wood Pulp Cartel)* [1988] ECR 5193.

49 Council Regulation (EC) 139/2004 on the control of concentrations between undertakings [2004] OJ L 24/1.

50 *US v. Aluminium Co. of America*, 148 F.2d. 416 (1945).

51 *Hartford Fire Insurance Co. v. California*, 509 US 764,113 S.Ct 2891, 125 L.Ed.2d 612 (1993).

had a direct, substantial and reasonably foreseeable effect on US commerce or US exports. The only defence available to the defendant is based on foreign legal compulsion. This means that comity will limit the assertion of jurisdiction of US courts only when a foreign State compels particular conduct that US anti-trust law prohibits. The intent and effect tests have also been applied in criminal proceedings against foreign companies and their officials.[52] However, following from the *Empagran* case,[53] the Sherman Act does not apply in a situation in which foreign claimants seek damages in respect of conduct prohibited under the Act, which conduct has produced harmful effects only outside the United States.

The ECJ endorsed the extraterritorial application of EU competition law in *Wood Pulp Cartel*,[54] in which the Commission found 40 undertakings supplying wood pulp in violation of EU competition law, despite the fact that they were not resident within the European Union. The ECJ held that:

> "It should be observed that an infringement of [Article 101 TFEU], such as the conclusion of an agreement which has had the effect of restricting competition within the Common Market, consists of conduct made up of two elements: the formation of the agreement, decision or concerted practice and the implementation thereof. If the applicability of prohibitions laid down under competition law were made to depend on the place where the agreement, decision or concerted practice was formed, the result would obviously be to give undertakings an easy means of evading these prohibitions. The decisive factor is therefore the place where it is implemented."[55]

This statement established the doctrine of 'implementation'. The doctrine is particularly relevant where a foreign undertaking has no subsidiaries, no agents and no branches in the European Union, and thus the Union has no jurisdiction under the doctrine of the single economic unit (see Chapter 4, section 4.6.1). In *Wood Pulp Cartel*, the ECJ held that it had jurisdiction in a situation in which a foreign undertaking sells directly to EU purchasers.

Under the implementation doctrine, it is irrelevant for the application of EU law where an agreement, decision or a concerted practice was formed; what counts is where it was implemented. Implementation in the European Union is the first condition for the application of the doctrine. The second is that the agreement, decision or concerted practice in question must have appreciable effect on intra-Union trade.[56]

52 *United States v. Nippon Paper Indus. Co.*, 109 F.3d 1 (1st Cir. 1997).
53 *Hoffmann-La Roche Ltd v. Empagran SA*, 124 S.Ct 2359 (2004).
54 Joined Cases 89, 104, 114, 116, 117 and 125–129/85 *A. Ahlström Osakeyhtiö and ors v Commission (Re Wood Pulp Cartel)* [1988] ECR 5193.
55 Ibid., [16].
56 Case T-329/01 *Archer Daniels Midland Co. v Commission (Re: Sodium Gluconate Cartel)* [2006] ECR II-3255.

The implementation doctrine developed by the ECJ does not exactly match the US effects doctrine: intent to harm intra-Union trade is irrelevant; what counts is the place of implementation of the relevant agreement, decision, concerted practice or abusive practice, and its appreciable impact on intra-Union trade. Further, in the European Union, the implementation doctrine will not apply to a situation in which undertakings conclude an agreement outside the Union under which they agree not to sell within the Union, or not to purchase from EU producers, whilst the US effect doctrine will apply if such an agreement is directed at the US market.[57]

There is no doubt that the CCC should have jurisdiction in respect of anti-competitive conduct originating outside the Community, but having appreciable cross-border effect within the Community. It is submitted that the EU approach to the extraterritorial application of competition law should be preferred to that of the United States, the reason being that reliance on the single economic unit doctrine, under which the European Union asserts jurisdiction based on the principle of nationality, and the implementation doctrine, under which the Union asserts jurisdiction based on the principle of territoriality, is more than sufficient to ensure the application of EU competition law to foreign enterprises located outside the European Union. Furthermore, these doctrines are less politically sensitive than the US effects doctrine.[58]

The ECJ has never formally recognised the US effects doctrine as part of EU competition law.[59] This is for many reasons, the most important being that the US effects doctrine ignores the role of comity in dealing with issues of extraterritorial jurisdiction. This is well illustrated in the *Hartford* case, in which the UK government's *amicus* to the US Supreme Court submitted that US courts had no jurisdiction over conduct occurring in London, because the United Kingdom had a regulatory scheme in place for the reinsurance industry and the challenged reinsurance agreements were exempt, under that scheme, from UK competition law.[60] Nevertheless, UK law, although it permitted the agreements, did not compel them. Accordingly, under UK law, a defendant was not required to act in the impugned manner and thus the defence based on foreign legal compulsion was not available to it. Bearing in mind that most competition laws are normally prescriptive in nature and thus do not require undertakings to act

57 J. Griffin, 'Reactions to US Assertions of Extraterritorial Jurisdiction' [1998] ECLR 64.

58 See D. Geradin, M. Reysen and D. Henry, 'Extraterritoriality, Comity, and Cooperation in EU Competition Law', in A. T. Guzman (ed.) *Cooperation, Comity, and Competition Policy*, 2011, New York: OUP, pp 27–28.

59 It is to be noted that the General Court in Case T-102/96 *Gencor Ltd v Commission* [1999] ECR II-753, [87], seemed to recognise the effects doctrine. Some AGs and the European Commission endorse it: Geradin, Reysen and Henry, supra op. cit., pp 27–28.

60 *Hartford Fire Insurance Co. v. California*, 509 US 764,113 S.Ct 2891, 125 L.Ed.2d 612 (1993).

in any particular manner, under the effects doctrine, US courts have no discretion to take account of foreign interests, because the only instance in which a defence pursuant to comity is accepted is when a foreign sovereign compels a foreign firm to act in a manner prohibited by US anti-trust law.[61] The wide extraterritorial scope of the US effects doctrine, combined with the manner in which US anti-trust law is enforced (for example the possibility of imposition of treble damages, the possibility of foreign individuals being sentenced to imprisonment, because antitrust violations are criminal offences, and the possibility of class action), has led to the enactment of blocking legislation in many States,[62] such as the UK, and to accusations that US anti-trust law is 'imperialistic' in nature.

The extraterritorial application of competition law creates many problems, including, *inter alia*, that it is contrary to international comity and fairness, encourages confrontation between countries rather than co-operation and leads to overregulation. The best example of the last is the enactment of merger control laws, which often subject firms to investigations in numerous countries and force them to comply with divergent laws. Further, enforcement of competition law against foreign-based offenders requires assistance from foreign authorities, and this is unlikely to be achieved unless powerful countries, like the United States, or powerful blocks, like the European Union, press for enforcement against foreign offenders.

It is submitted that CARICOM is unlikely to enforce its competition law against powerful US, or EU, or other firms. Unfortunately, the absence of harmonised substantive competition rules and their enforcement at international level[63] leaves CARICOM with limited options. The option that may well be the best is for CARICOM to enter into bilateral co-operation agreements on competition with its most important trading partners.[64] It is to be noted that Chapter 1 of the Economic Partnership Agreement (EPA) between the CARIFORUM States and the European Community and its Member States,[65] contains principles relating to exchange of information and enforcement co-operation between the European Commission and the CCC (see Chapter 8, section 8.2.2).

61 C. Ryngaert, *Jurisdiction in International Law*, 2008, Oxford: OUP, pp 134*ff.*

62 Under blocking statutes, States prohibit national firms from providing documents to foreign competition authorities or courts. See D. A. Sabalot, 'Shortening the Long Arm of American Antitrust Jurisdiction: Extraterritoriality and the Foreign Blocking Statutes' (1982) 28 Loyola L Rev 213. An example of a blocking statute is the UK Protection of Trade Interests Act 1980.

63 See D. J. Gerber, *Global Competition: Law, Markets and Globalisation*, 2010, Oxford: OUP.

64 On external co-operation of the European Union with third countries and, in particular bilateral co-operation agreements, see V. Demedts, 'International Competition Law Enforcement: Different Means, One Goal?' (2012) 8(3) Comp L Rev 223.

65 [2008] OJ L 289/3.

5.6 Whether CSME competition law will apply to the anti-competitive conduct of enterprises established within the Community, but which has effects on competition and trade in a third country?

It is submitted that CSME competition law is not interested in prohibiting and penalising anti-competitive conduct that originates within the Community, but produces anti-competitive effect only in a third country. Article 177(1)(a) RTC supports this submission. It prohibits agreements, decisions by associations of enterprises and concerted practices that have as their object or effect the restriction of competition 'within the Community'. Similarly, Article 179 RTC prohibits abusive practices by dominant enterprises that 'frustrate the benefits expected from the establishment of the CSME'. Additionally, Article 174(1) RTC, which concerns powers of the CCC, states that the CCC may, with regard to conduct or transactions that have cross-border effects, 'monitor, investigate, detect, make determinations or take action to inhibit and penalise enterprises whose business conduct prejudices trade or prevents, restricts or distorts competition within the CSME'. A similar approach is taken by the European Commission.[66]

It may be the case that anti-competitive conduct or transactions originate within the Community, have as their main target a third country, but, as a side effect, have appreciable prejudicial effects on trade and competition within the Community. In such a situation, anti-competitive conduct or transactions will be within the scope of CSME competition law. In the context of the European Union, the Commission's Guidelines provide an example of export cartels, which may agree to export certain surplus quantities to third countries and, by so doing unintentionally create shortage of supply within the European Union, resulting in reducing price competition within the Union.[67] Such conduct will have impact within the European Union, bearing in mind that, without any export agreements, these quantities might have been sold within the Union. An export cartel may also decide to export certain surplus quantities in order to intentionally create a shortage in the European Union, with a view to increasing prices for the relevant products there. In such a situation, the agreement will have effect on trade within the Member States.

In a situation in which enterprises established in CARICOM form a cartel with enterprises established outside CARICOM and it is clear from the facts that activities of foreign enterprises have not had any actual or direct cross-border effect on trade and competition within the Community, the question arises whether the activities of the foreign enterprises are within the scope of

66 Case 30/78 *Distillers Company Ltd v Commission* [1980] ECR 2229; Commission Decision 69/202/EEC *VVVF* [1969] OJ L 168/22. With regard to export cartels, see D. D. Sokol, 'What Do We Really Know about Export Cartels and What is the Appropriate Solution?' (2008) 4(4) J Comp L & Econ 967.

67 The Guidelines, [105].

Community law. A matter of this sort was examined by the European Commission and, on appeal, by the General Court in *JFE Engineering*.[68]

Joined Cases T-67/00, T-68/00, T-71/00 and T-78/00 *JFE Engineering Corp., Formerly NKK Corp. (T-67/00), Nippon Steel Corp. (T-68/00), JFE Steel Corp. (T-71/00) and Sumitomo Metal Industries Ltd (T-78/00) v Commission* [2004] ECR II-2501, Confirmed By The ECJ In Joined Cases C-403/04P and C-405/04P *Sumitomo Metal Industries Ltd (C-403/04 P) and Nippon Steel Corp. (C-405/04 P) v Commission* [2007] ECR I-729

Facts

Four European undertakings, including some from the United Kingdom, and four Japanese undertakings, all of which were producers of seamless steel tubes, formed a market-sharing cartel, according to which each cartel member agreed not to sell on the domestic market of any other party to the cartel. The European Commission discovered the cartel and imposed heavy fines on all of its participants for anti-competitive activities.[69] The Japanese undertakings argued that their conduct had no impact on trade between EU Member States because they were not selling the product concerned either directly or indirectly in the European Union.

Held

On appeal, the General Court held as follows.

1. It reiterated a well-established principle in EU competition law that an undertaking may be held responsible for an overall cartel, even though it is shown that it has participated directly in only some of its aspects, if it knew, or must have known, that the collusion in which it participated was part of an overall plan intended to distort competition and that the overall

68 Joined Cases T-67/00, T-68/00, T-71/00 and T-78/00 *JFE Engineering Corp., formerly NKK Corp. (T-67/00), Nippon Steel Corp. (T-68/00), JFE Steel Corp. (T-71/00) and Sumitomo Metal Industries Ltd (T-78/00) v Commission* [2004] ECR II-2501, confirmed by the ECJ in Joined Cases C-403/04P and C-405/04P *Sumitomo Metal Industries Ltd (C-403/04 P) and Nippon Steel Corp. (C-405/04 P) v Commission* [2007] ECR I-729.

69 The European Commission imposed a €99 million fine on the members of the cartel.

plan included all constituent elements of the cartel (see Chapter 6, section 6.3).

2. Because the agreement between European and Japanese undertakings restricted competition by object, it was not necessary for the European Commission to prove actual adverse effect of the cartel on competition, potential effect being sufficient. There were no doubts that the cartel had intra-Union aspects – that is, its participants, *inter alia*, divided the EU markets between themselves and thus, at least potentially, restricted trade between Member States. Accordingly, the requirement relating to the agreement having effect on trade between Member States was satisfied.
3. In any event, the fact that the European members of the cartel were convinced that the cessation of production of seamless tubes by its UK participants may create a risk that the Japanese producers would decide to enter the UK market was sufficient to establish the existence of potential impact on trade between Member States.[70]

It is rare that vertical export agreements that contain a clause prohibiting re-import will be within the scope of CSME competition law. An EU case on the point is *Javico*.[71]

Case C-306/96 *Javico International and Javico AG v Yves Saint Laurent Parfums SA (YSLP)* [1998] ECR I-1983

Facts

A French undertaking, Yves St Laurent Parfums SA (YSL), had appointed Javico as its authorised distributor of luxury cosmetics in Russia, Ukraine and Slovenia (the last not an EU Member State at the relevant time). Under the contract, Javico was expressly prohibited from selling the contract products outside the authorised territories either by direct marketing or through re-export. When YSL found that Javico was selling the contract products in many EU States, it

70 Joined Cases T-67/00, T-68/00, T-71/00 and T-78/00 *JFE Engineering Corp., formerly NKK Corp. (T-67/00), Nippon Steel Corp. (T-68/00), JFE Steel Corp. (T-71/00) and Sumitomo Metal Industries Ltd (T-78/00) v Commission* [2004] ECR II-2501, [394].

71 Case C-306/96 *Javico International and Javico AG v Yves Saint Laurent Parfums SA (YSLP)* [1998] ECR I-1983.

terminated the contract and started proceedings against Javico in a French court. When the French court upheld the termination and awarded compensation to YSL, Javico appealed on the grounds that the clause prohibiting re-import was in breach of Article 101(1) TFEU and thus, by virtue of Article 101(2) TFEU, void. The case was referred to the ECJ.

Held:

The ECJ held that, by their very nature, agreements that prohibit re-import to the European Union, are not contrary to Article 101(1) TFEU – that is, they do not restrict competition by object (see Chapter 6, section 6.4.1), because they do not restrict parallel imports of contract products within the Union. However, they may have effect on trade between Member States. Appraisal of the effect requires the examination of the agreement within its economic and legal context. The ECJ left to the referring court to decide whether the agreement at issue had such effect, but set out the following criteria to be considered:

- the structure of the relevant market, in particular whether it was oligopolistic and thus allowed only limited competition within the EU distribution network of those products;
- whether there was a substantial difference in the price charged for the contract product outside the European Union and that charged for it inside (in which respect, the profitability of re-import may be undermined by customs duties imposed on contract products and thus the agreement may have had no effect on competition or trade); and
- the re-import must be of appreciable magnitude in order to be capable of affecting trade within the European Union.

Comment

These criteria have been expanded in subsequent cases. In *Silhouette*,[72] the ECJ established that the principle of the exhaustion of intellectual property rights (IPRs)[73] does not apply to imports from outside the European Economic Area

72 Case C-355/96 *Silhouette International Schmied GmbH & Co. Kg v Hartlauer Handelsgesellschaft MbH* [1998] ECR I-4799.

73 The principle of exhaustion of IPRs means that once a holder of IPRs has marketed, or consented to the marketing of, the protected product in more than one EU Member State, the IPRs are exhausted – that is, the owner cannot rely on them subsequently to prevent parallel imports of the protected products from other Member States.

(EEA).[74] This means that a holder of IPRs is entitled to stop parallel imports of protected goods from outside the EEA. Accordingly, there is nothing to prevent the holder from setting up whatever differing commercial arrangements he or she likes outside the EEA. Some other criteria include, *inter alia*, the cost of transportation of goods and the accumulated profit margin in the chain of distribution, in that this may make sale of re-imported goods unprofitable.

In the light of the above, it can be said that each case must be carefully assessed and all relevant criteria must be taken into consideration to decide whether an agreement has appreciable cross-border effect on trade and competition within the Community.

74 In 1992, three out of four the EFTA countries – Iceland, Liechtenstein and Norway – concluded an agreement with the European Union creating the EEA. Under the agreement, the EFTA States accept the EU internal market rules. Switzerland is not part of the EEA, but has signed a series of bilateral agreements with the European Union, which define the relationship between them (see Chapter 9, section 9.6.1).

6

AGREEMENTS, DECISIONS AND CONCERTED PRACTICES PROHIBITED UNDER CSME COMPETITION LAW

Chapter contents

6.1 Introduction

Article 177(1)(a) RTC prohibits, as being anti-competitive, any agreement between enterprises, any decision of associations of enterprises and any concerted practice by enterprises that has as its object or effect restriction of competition within the Community. In order to be within the prohibition, any arrangement within the scope of Article 177(1)(a) RTC must have appreciable cross-border effect (see Chapter 5). Article 177(2) RTC provides some examples of the types of prohibited arrangements set out in Article 177(1)(a) RTC. Under Article 177(3) RTC, any prohibited agreement or decision is null and void (see Chapter 9, section 9.7.1.4D); concerted practices are not mentioned, because they are informal arrangements and therefore cannot be rendered void. However, arrangements that fall within the scope of Article 177(1)(a) RTC may escape the prohibition if they meet the criteria set out in Article 177(4) RTC. This occurs when some form of collaboration between enterprises may have overall beneficial effects that prevail over the restrictions that they impose on competition. Further, what would otherwise be prohibited arrangements may escape the prohibition set out in Article 177(1)(a) RTC if they are within the scope of the *de minimis* rule (see Chapter 5, section 5.3.2) or are exempted by the CARICOM Competition Commission (CCC) under Article 180 RTC (see Chapter 9, section 9.7.2.1) or by the Council for Trade and Economic Development (COTED) under Article 183 RTC (see Chapter 3, section 3.2.1).

Parts of Article 177 RTC relevant to the prohibition of anti-competitive agreements, decisions and concerted practices contain many concepts that need to be defined. However, the Revised Treaty of Chaguaramas (RTC) provides no such definitions. As a result, it will be the task of the CCC, and of the Caribbean Court of Justice (CCJ) when exercising its supervisory function over the CCC, to elucidate the meaning and effect of the prohibition set out in Article 177(1)(a) RTC. Bearing in mind that this Article is modelled on Article 101 TFEU, and that the European Court of Justice (ECJ) has interpreted Article 101 TFEU extensively, this chapter often refers to EU competition law in this area. Notwithstanding this, it is important to note that interpretation of Article 177(1)(a) RTC will depend on the objectives that CSME competition law seeks to achieve. This is particularly relevant with regard to the application of CSME competition law to the so-called 'vertical agreements'.

6.2 Horizontal and vertical agreements

- Horizontal agreements are those that are entered into between enterprises that compete with each other at the same level of the production and distribution chain, for example agreements between producers, or manufacturers, or retailers.
- Vertical agreements are those that are entered into by enterprises that operate at different levels of the production and distribution chain, for example agreements between producers and retailers. The enterprises involved do not, in any event, compete with each other, because they operate at different levels of the market. The most common vertical agreements are distribution agreements and franchising agreements.

A short assessment of horizontal and vertical agreements is provided below.

6.2.1 Horizontal agreements

Horizontal agreements may be perfectly lawful, for example co-operation and specialisation agreements, even though they may contain anti-competitive clauses that may bring them within the scope of Article 177(1)(a) RTC. However, these types of agreement are not the main concern of Article 177(1)(a) RTC, which will be used primarily to combat collusive arrangements between competitors and potential competitors. Those arrangements are the most harmful to competition because, instead of competing with each other, rival enterprises collude and therefore can act as one undertaking in the relevant market. An arrangement between rival enterprises is called a 'cartel'. It is the nature of a cartel that participating enterprises considerably increase their market power and, in some cases, can monopolise the relevant market. As a result, they can reduce output to increase prices and are not subjected to pressure to improve the products that they sell, to create new products or to find new ways of commercialising those products. Thus cartels stifle creativity and innovation, impose higher prices for lower quality goods and narrow the choice of products. Additionally, they harm consumers, who have to pay cartel prices. Further, they dampen opportunities for new enterprises to enter the relevant market. In short, the existence of cartels runs counter to the objectives of competition law and adversely affects the competitiveness of the economy as a whole.

Stewart submits that, in the Caribbean context, cartelisation is not a major problem, noting that:

> "[I]n the very small economies, businesses have a robust sense of independence and do not like to collude to fix prices. Even so, at the same time, these very small economies abhor fierce competition. This may be due to the social culture and the small communities these people live in, where businessmen are friends and interact with each other socially as well."[1]

It is submitted that even if this assessment of cartelisation is correct, bearing in mind that cartels are normally secret and that the interpersonal culture in countries with small economies makes the detection of cartels very difficult, with the creation of the CARICOM Single Market and Economy (CSME), business opportunities will increase, so encouraging enterprises to cartelise. Interestingly, Stewart submits that regional and international cartels involving new emigrants from China, Taiwan, India and Syria are in operation in CARICOM,[2] and that some sectors of the economy, such as the banking sector, need to be scrutinised in terms of cartel detection. She also provides examples of cartelisation with regard to trading associations of enterprises.[3] This highlights the relevance of Article 177(1)(a) RTC in ensuring that competition in the CSME is not distorted by cartels.

1 T. Stewart, 'CARICOM Countries', in P. S. Mehta (ed.) *Competition Regimes in the World: A Civil Society Report*, 2006, Jaipur: CUTS Centre for Competition, Investment & Economic Regulation, p 537.

2 T. Stewart, 'The Role of Competition Policy in Regional Integration: The Case of the Caribbean Countries', available at http://sta.uwi.edu/salises/workshop/papers/tstewart.pdf [accessed 15 January 2014], pp 9–14.

3 Ibid.

It is also submitted that Article 177(1)(a) RTC will be relevant to deal with the issue of interlocking directorates – that is, a situation in which a director on the corporate board of one company sits on the board of directors of another company, or companies. The argument that, in small economies, there is an insufficient number of qualified persons to serve across several boards of directors has been challenged by the fact that, in Trinidad and Jamaica, interlocking directorates are widespread. The practice of interlocking directorates seems to be highlighted in the Caribbean region by the fact that businesses are dominated by family firms.[4] Article 177(1)(a) RTC is an appropriate tool for dealing with a situation in which the same person serves as a director on the boards of directors of companies that are supposedly competitors. It is to be noted that, under Article 23 of the Barbados Fair Competition Act, of 2002, the Barbados Fair Trading Commission (FTC) is empowered to order a person who sits as a director on the board of more than one company to serve on no more than one board of directors if:

- the relevant companies are significant competitors; and
- the director's conduct has the effect of welding together the policies of those companies in such a way as to reduce significantly, or to eliminate, competition in the relevant market.

The 2012 Annual Report of the Barbados FTC noted one prohibited interlocking directorship, which matter is under investigation.[5]

6.2.2 Vertical agreements

The matter of whether so-called 'vertical agreements' are encompassed within the meaning of an agreement set out in Article 177(1)(a) RTC has not been settled by the RTC. There are powerful arguments in favour of including vertical agreements within the concept of agreements (see Chapter 3, section 3.3.1), in particular that such agreements may perpetuate national boundaries as obstacles to the free movement of goods and services, and thus undermine the creation of the CSME. Teleological interpretation of the RTC entails that any agreement that divides the Community market is within the scope of CSME competition law.

Under EU competition law, vertical agreements are treated less severely than horizontal agreements. They are, in general, less obviously anti-competitive than

4 See T. Stewart (ed.) *An Empirical Examination of Competition Issues in Selected CARICOM Countries: Towards Policy of Formulation*, February 2004, Trinidad & Tobago: SALISES, pp 148–149.

5 Fair Trading Commission Barbados, *2012 Annual Report*, July 2012, available at http://www.ftc.gov.bb/library/2013-01-29_ftc_annual_report_2012.pdf [accessed 16 January 2014], p 13.

horizontal agreements. This is because each party to such an agreement exercises its power independently of any rivals. If any party is in a dominant position and abuses that position, the matter is dealt with under Article 102 TFEU. Usually, the only anti-competitive effect of such agreements is when there is insufficient inter-brand-competition.[6] Many economists (in particular those allied to the Chicago school) emphasise that vertical agreements offer many pro-competitive benefits.[7] This is also the view of the European Commission, which, under Regulation 330/2010 on the Application of Article 101(3) TFEU to Categories of Vertical Agreements and Concerted Practices,[8] introduced a rebuttable presumption of compatibility with Article 101(1) TFEU of vertical agreements where each of the parties to a vertical agreement has a share in the relevant product market of less than 30 per cent. This is subject to some exceptions, and to a limited number of 'hard core' restrictions, which are set out in Regulation 330/2010. Such restrictions are considered by the European Commission as restricting competition by object (see section 6.4).

6.3 The meaning of 'agreements, decisions and concerted practices'

EU competition law, as well as CSME competition law, distinguishes between various forms of prohibited co-operation between undertakings. None is defined by either the RTC or the EU Treaties. The ECJ, when confronted by the need to define them, has embraced an expansive and flexible approach, rather than a narrow, legalistic one. This can be explained, on the one hand, by the need to ensure that conditions of competition in the internal market are not distorted by collusive conduct of undertakings, irrespective of the form that it takes, and on the other by the need to respond to the probatory difficulties of the European Commission in meeting the requisite legal standard to prove the existence of cartels.

The expansive interpretation of 'agreements, decisions and concerted practices' makes it difficult to identify and separate one from the other. This was acknowledged by the ECJ in *Anic*,[9] in which it held that although Article 101 TFEU distinguishes between 'concerted practices', 'agreements between undertakings' and 'decisions by associations of undertakings', its objective is to catch different forms of co-ordination and collusion between undertakings, and

6 'Inter-brand competition' refers to competition between suppliers of competing brands. 'Intra-brand competition' concerns competition between distributors of the same brand.
7 W. S. Comanor, 'Vertical Price-Fixing, Vertical Market Restrictions, and the New Antitrust Policy' (1985) 98 Harv L Rev 986.
8 [2010] OJ L 142/1.
9 Case C-49/92P *Commission v Anic Partecipazioni SpA* [1999] ECR I-4125, [3]. See also Case T-62/98 *Volkswagen AG v Commission* [2000] ECR II-2707.

therefore the General Court had been correct in considering that 'patterns of conduct by several undertakings were a manifestation of a single infringement, corresponding partly to an agreement and partly to a concerted practice'. Therefore the two concepts are not incompatible and certain conduct may be qualified as being, in the first place, a concerted practice, and in the second place, an agreement, or as being at the same time an agreement and a decision of associations. Accordingly, under EU law, a joint classification is in conformity with the objectives that Article 101(1) TFEU seeks to achieve – that is, to distinguish between conduct of an undertaking on the relevant market that is collusive and thus prohibited, and that which is independent and thus lawful. As the European Commission stated in its *Polypropylene* decision:[10]

> "The importance of the concept of a concerted practice does not thus result so much from the distinction between it and 'an agreement' as from the distinction between forms of collusion falling under Article [101(1) TFEU] and mere parallel behaviour with no element of concertation."[11]

The approach based on distinguishing between collusive and non-collusive conduct rather than on a formal distinction between various forms of collusion not only allows a joint classification, but also gave rise to the concept of a 'single, overall agreement', which is especially useful for the European Commission because it eases the burden of proof imposed on it in respect of complex cartels of considerable duration involving many undertakings (see section 6.3.1.1).

Notwithstanding this, under EU competition law, each of 'agreement', 'decision' and 'concerted practice' has been defined, albeit that, as the ECJ held in *T-Mobile*,[12] those definitions 'are intended, from a subjective point of view, to catch forms of collusion having the same nature which are distinguishable from each other only by their intensity and the forms in which they manifest themselves'. These definitions are examined below.

6.3.1 The concept of 'agreement'

The term 'agreement' indicates that the prohibition set out in Article 177(1)(a) RTC applies to joint conduct of enterprises or to an association of enterprises. As a result, unilateral conduct of an enterprise is outside the scope of the prohibition.

A distinction must be made between vertical agreements and horizontal agreements.

- With regard to vertical agreements, provided that they are within the scope of the RTC (see section 6.2.2), they are normally concluded in a form of

10 Commission Decision 86/398/EEC *Polypropylene* [1986] OJ L 230/1.
11 Ibid., [97].
12 Case C-8/08 *T-Mobile Netherlands BV and ors v Commission* [2009] ECR I-4529, [23].

contract, such as a distributorship agreement or a franchising agreement. If a contract contains anti-competitive clauses and produces cross-border effects, it will be regarded as an 'agreement' falling within the prohibition of Article 177(1)(a) RTC.

- With regard to horizontal agreements, some of them will be in the form of a contact drawn up between enterprises, such as co-operation and specialisation agreements, but it is unlikely that two or more enterprises from different Member States will sign a formal contract in which each party promises, for example, to fix prices for the relevant product and not to effect sales to each other's territory. In this situation, the parties will enter into less formal, clandestine arrangements. For this reason, EU law has adopted a pragmatic approach to the identification of an agreement within the meaning of Article 101(1) TFEU. In *Bayer*,[13] the General Court offered the following definition:

> "[T]he concept of an agreement within the meaning of [Article 101(1) TFEU], as interpreted by the case-law, centres round the existence of a concurrence of wills between at least two parties, the form in which it is manifested being unimportant so long as it constitutes the faithful expression of the parties' intention."[14]

Accordingly, the form in which the parties to an agreement have expressed their joint intention is unimportant; what is important is that there is a concurrence of wills, constituting the faithful expression of the parties' intention. Resulting from this, under EU law, the following have been identified as agreements within the meaning of Article 101(1) TFEU: standard sale conditions;[15] out-of-court settlements; correspondence between undertakings; conversations between representatives of those undertakings;[16] and rules adopted by a trade association that were binding on its members (such rules are considered as agreements with regard to the members and as a decision with regard to the association).[17] An informal agreement such as a 'gentlemen's agreement' also falls within the scope of Article 101(1) TFEU.[18] Even if a contract is contrary to the economic interests of one of the parties,[19] or was legally terminated,

13 Case T-41/96 *Bayer AG v Commission* [2000] ECR II-3383.
14 Ibid., [69].
15 Case C-277/87 *Sandoz Prodotti Farmaceutici SpA v Commission* [1990] ECR I-45; Case T-168/01 *GlaxoSmithKline Services Unlimited v Commission* [2006] ECR II-2969.
16 Case T-7/89 *Hercules Chemicals NV v Commission* [1991] ECR II-1711.
17 Commission Decision 84/191/EEC *Nuovo Cegam* [1984] OJ L 99/29.
18 Case 41/69 *Chemiefarma NV v Commission (Quinine Cartel)* [1970] ECR 661.
19 *Johnson and Johnson* [1980] OJ L 377/16, [1981] 2 CMLR 287; Case T-48/98 *Acerinox v Commission* [2001] ECR II-3859.

but still produces unlawful effects,[20] or was concluded subject to a condition,[21] it is regarded as an agreement within the meaning of Article 101(1) TFEU. Further, an undertaking will be regarded as being a party to an agreement even if it was bullied into it,[22] or had no intention to follow it and had adopted an 'aggressive commercial policy' with regard to other parties to the agreement.[23] The legal nature of an agreement is determined by the EU institutions or national competition authorities (NCAs) in light of factual considerations and not by the parties to it.[24]

There is no concurrence of wills between the parties at the stage of negotiations, preparatory discussions, and so on,[25] because at that stage no agreement has been reached. However, such conduct may, depending upon the circumstances, amount to a concerted practice.

The broad interpretation of an agreement was further expanded by the General Court in *AC-Treuhand*.[26] In this case, the Court classified conduct of a consultancy company, which was not active on the relevant market, but which contributed to the implementation and maintenance of a cartel by, *inter alia*, organising meetings for the three producers of organic peroxides that set it up and, later, by covering up evidence of its existence, as an agreement between undertakings within the meaning of Article 101 TFEU. The General Court held that although the consultancy company was only an accessory, and not a party, to the cartel, the element of 'joint intention' that is essential to the existence of an 'agreement' does not require the relevant market, on which the undertaking that is the 'perpetrator' of the restriction of competition is active, to be exactly the same as the one on which that restriction is deemed to have materialised.

With regard to proof, in order to establish the existence of an agreement, the European Commission is required to show that there is indirect or direct concurrence of will between undertakings.

20 Case 51/75 *EMI Records Ltd v CBS United Kingdom Ltd* [1976] ECR 811.

21 Commission Decision 2001/716/EC *SAS/Maersk Air* [2001] OJ L 265/15.

22 Case T-141/89 *Tréfileurope Sales SARL v Commission* [1995] ECR II-791, [58]; Joined Cases T-25/95, T-26/95, T-30/95–T-32/95, T-34/95–T-39/95, T-42/95–T-46/95, T-48/95, T-50/95–T-65/95, T-68/95–T-71/95, T-87/95, T-88/95, T-103/95 and T-104/95 *Cimenteries CBR and ors v Commission* [2000] ECR II-49, [2557]. It is to be noted that the defect in consent will be taken into account by the European Commission when it determines the amount of the fine to be imposed on the undertaking concerned.

23 COMP/E-3736.700 *Industrial and Medical Gases* [2003] OJ L 84/1.

24 Commission Decision 93/668/EC *Auditel and AGB Italia SpA* [1993] OJ L 306/50.

25 Case T-60/02 *Deutsche Verkehrsbank AG v Commission* (General Court, 14 October 2004 unpublished).

26 Case T-99/04 *AC-Treuhand AG v Commission* [2008] ECR II-1501.

6.3.1.1 The concept of a 'single, overall agreement'

The concept of a 'single, overall agreement', having been initially developed by the European Commission, was endorsed by the ECJ in *Anic*.[27] In this case, the European Commission found that undertakings participating in a cartel were engaged in a single and continuous infringement. Anic submitted that, when various actions amount to a single infringement, the European Commission must show that the undertaking concerned participated in all aspects of the infringement – that is, in all actions forming the infringement – in order to make it responsible for all aspects of the conduct of all of the undertakings charged. Because Anic participated in only some concerted actions, but not all of them, it argued that it was wrongly held responsible for actions of other undertakings that participated in the infringement.

The ECJ emphasised that, taking into account the nature and degree of the ensuing penalties, responsibility for infringements of Article 101 TFEU is personal in nature. It added, however, that it flows from Article 101 TFEU that anti-competitive conduct results from collaboration by several undertakings, and therefore each undertaking is a co-perpetrator of the infringement, even if it participates in different ways depending on a number of factors, such as its position in the market, the characteristics of the market itself, the objectives pursued and the means of implementation of anti-competitive practices chosen or envisaged by it. The ECJ held that an undertaking may be held responsible for the conduct of other undertakings that participated in the same infringement:

> ". . . where it is proved that the undertaking in question was aware of the unlawful conduct of the other participants, or could reasonably foresee such conduct, and was prepared to accept the risk. Such a conclusion is not at odds with the principle that responsibility for such infringements is personal in nature, nor does it neglect individual analysis of the evidence adduced, in disregard of the applicable rules of evidence, or infringe the rights of defence of the undertakings involved."[28]

The concept of a 'single, overall agreement' eases the evidentiary burden imposed on the European Commission in that it establishes a presumption that an undertaking will be liable for all aspects of a cartel, even though it had not participated in all arrangements made by the cartel, if it can be shown that it was aware of the unlawful conduct of other participants, or could reasonably foresee such conduct, and was prepared to accept the risk. Accordingly, the European Commission is not required to show that every participating undertaking took

27 Case C-49/92 P *Commission v Anic Partecipazioni SpA* [1999] ECR I-4125. See also Case T-334/94 *Sarrió SA v Commission* [1998] ECR II-1439.

28 Case C-49/92P *Commission v Anic Partecipazioni SpA* [1999] ECR I-4125, [203].

part in every aspect of a cartel over a long period of time.[29] Further, aggregation into a single infringement of various complex arrangements made by a cartel that take place over a lengthy period of time and often involve many countries entails that the European Commission is not required to make a distinction between various form of collusion. As the European Commission stated in the *Consumer Detergents* case:[30]

> It would be artificial to split up such continuous conduct, characterised by a single purpose, by treating it as consisting of several separate infringements, when what was involved was a single infringement which progressively would manifest itself in both agreements and concerted practices.[31]

Nevertheless, an alleged participant in a cartel may rebut the presumption. Further, its degree of participation in the infringement will be taken into consideration in the determination of the fine to be imposed on it.[32]

6.3.1.2 Participation in meetings

Under EU law, there is a presumption that, when an undertaking participates in a meeting during which its competitor discloses its future policy regarding the relevant market, that undertaking takes account of such information for the purpose of determining its own conduct on the market. This is a rebuttable presumption in that, unless an undertaking distances itself publicly from what was discussed during an anti-competitive meeting, it will be presumed to have participated in an anti-competitive agreement or a concerted practice.

The General Court held that the concept of an undertaking publically distancing itself must be interpreted narrowly.[33] Accordingly, it seems that, apart from a situation in which an undertaking reports to the relevant administrative authorities, it must not only make a statement to other participants of a cartel expressing its intention to terminate its participation in an agreement or concerted practice, but also ensure that other participants are convinced that it has terminated its participation in the cartel. For example, in *ADM*,[34] ADM argued that it had publicly dissociated itself from a cartel when it had publicly stated its wish to end its participation by leaving before the end of a meeting. The ECJ

29 Commission Decision 94/599/EEC *PVC II* [1994] OJ L 239/14.
30 COMP/39579 *Consumer Detergents*, 13 April 2011, C(2011) 2528 final.
31 Ibid., [36].
32 The controversies surrounding the concept of a 'single, overall agreement' are well explained by D. Bailey, 'Single, Overall Agreement in EU Competition Law' (2010) 47 CML Rev 473.
33 Case T-61/99 *Adriatica di Navigazione SpA v Commission* [2003] ECR II-5349, [135].
34 Case C-510/06 P *Archer Daniels Midland Co. (ADM) v Commission* [2009] ECR I-1843.

stated that 'it is indeed the understanding which the other participants in a cartel have of the intention of the undertaking concerned which is of critical importance when assessing whether that undertaking sought to distance itself from the unlawful agreement'.[35] In this case, it was clear that ADM had left the meeting because it could not resolve a disagreement between the participants of the cartel in the manner that it wished. Accordingly, by leaving the meeting, ADM indicated a negotiating strategy rather than the end of its involvement in the cartel. This was confirmed by the fact that, subsequent to the meeting, other participating undertakings sent documents to ADM – that is, they obviously did not understand that, by leaving the meeting before its end, ADM had expressed its wish to end its participation in the cartel.

Non-implementation by an undertaking of any unlawful policy discussed at a meeting will not be sufficient to exclude it from liability under Article 101(1) TFEU. In *Sarrió*,[36] the General Court rejected the argument of Sarrió that, despite its participation in an agreement that co-ordinated prices, it applied its own prices to each individual transaction. The Court held that the agreement had an impact on transaction prices, because it provided the basis for price negotiation in each transaction, and that, solely by participating in the agreement, Sarrió had infringed Article 101(1) TFEU. The General Court rejected Sarrió's argument concerning no implementation of the agreement. It stated that a serious anti-competitive intent is contrary to Article 101(1) TFEU whether or not the agreement is in fact implemented.

Subsequent conduct on the relevant market contrary to what was discussed at an anti-competitive meeting will not be enough to exclude the liability of an undertaking. In *Industrial and Medical Gases*,[37] two undertakings that participated in anti-competitive meetings, Air Liquide and Westfalen, tried to convince the Commission that their conduct in the market subsequent to those meetings (which consisted of pursuing an 'aggressive commercial policy' towards their competitors) provided sufficient evidence that they neither participated in the agreements nor implemented them. The Commission rejected this argument.

Silence at an anti-competitive meeting will amount to tacit approval and thus render the participating undertaking liable under Article 101 TFEU.[38]

6.3.2 Decisions by associations of undertakings

Normally, trade and other associations provide a comprehensive range of services to their members, are guardians of professional standards for the benefit of their

35 Ibid., [120].
36 Case T-334/94 *Sarrió SA v Commission* [1998] ECR II-1439.
37 COMP/E-3736.700 *Industrial and Medical Gases* [2003] OJ L 84/1.
38 Case T-208/06 *Quinn Barlo Ltd, Quinn Plastics NV and Quinn Plastics GmbH v Commission* [2011] ECR II-7953, [50]; Case T-303/02 *Westfalen Gassen Nederland* v *Commission* [2006] II-4567, [103] and [124].

members and their customers, provide professional training and support, and lobby on behalf of their members. However, because they provide a forum for discussion and exchange of their members' views, they may also facilitate collusion between their members. They may act in such a way as to control entry to a given market and block potential competitors.

Trade associations may either actively participate in collusive actions of members,[39] or may be used as a means by which members exchange information on prices, outputs and other matters, which will enable undertakings to be aware of the market position and strategy of their rivals, and thus increase the probability of collusion, or even facilitate it. In such circumstances, conduct of members of an association of undertakings may be identified as an agreement or a concerted practice. However, both Article 177(1)(a) RTC and Article 101(1) TFEU also catch conduct that is described as a 'decision' – that is, conduct that cannot, in the strict sense, be identified as an agreement or a concerted practice.

Under EU law, both the concept of an 'association' and the concept of a 'decision' have been interpreted broadly. With regard to the concept of an association, it is unimportant for the application of EU law whether a group of undertakings is registered as an association or not; what matters is whether it constitutes an entity formed to pursue economic objectives of its members. Accordingly, under EU law, the concept of association encompasses: agricultural cooperatives;[40] professional associations,[41] including a body set up by statute that has public functions, the members of which are appointed by the government;[42] international organisations such as the International Railways Union;[43] groupings such as the European Broadcasting Union,[44] which co-ordinates the Eurovision system; and even a maritime conference.[45] In *BNIC*,[46] the ECJ held that an agreement concluded between two groups of traders must be regarded as 'an agreement between undertakings or associations of undertakings'. A decision

39 Case 246/86 *Belasco v Commission (Re Belgian Roofing Felt Cartel)* [1989] ECR 2117.

40 Case C-250/92 *Gøttrup-Klim e.a. Grovvareforeninger v Dansk Landbrugs Grovvareselskab AmbA* [1994] ECR I-5641.

41 Commission Decision 95/188/EC *COAPI* [1995] OJ L 122/37; Case C-309/99 *Wouters v Algemene Raad van de Nederlandse Orde van Advocaten* [2002] ECR I-577.

42 For example, the Examination Committee of the Italian Bar: Case C-250/03 *Mauri (Ord)* [2005] OJ C 115/8.

43 Case T-14/93 *UIC v Commission* [1995] ECR II-1503. Additionally, the International Olympic Committee, the supreme authority of the Olympic movement, which brings together the various international sporting federations, is regarded as an association of undertakings: see Case C-519/04 P *Meca-Medina and Majcen v Commission* [2006] ECR I-6991.

44 Joined Cases T-528, 542, 543/93 and 546/93 *Metropole Télévision SA and Reti Televisive Italiane SpA and Gestevisión Telecinco SA and Antena 3 de Televisión v Commission* [1996] ECR II-649.

45 Joined Cases C-395 and 396/96P *Compagnie Maritime Belge Transport SA and ors v Commission* [1996] ECR I-1365.

46 Case 123/83 *Bureau National Interprofessionnel du Cognac (BNIC) v Guy Clair* [1985] ECR 391.

adopted by a federation-type association – that is, an association the members of which are themselves associations – is also within the Article 101(1) TFEU prohibition.[47]

The concept of a decision is intended to catch all forms of prohibited co-ordination organised by an association with regard to its members. These may include, *inter alia*, binding resolutions of associations,[48] binding rules relating to operation of a certification scheme[49] and a written constitution of an association.[50] The matter of whether a non-binding recommendation may amount to a decision within the meaning of Article 101(1) TFEU was considered by the ECJ in *Cementhandelaren*.[51]

Case 8/72 *Vereeniging van Cementhandelaren v Commission* [1972] ECR 977

Facts

A Dutch trade association, of which most Dutch cement dealers were members, recommended the prices at which cement should be sold in the Netherlands. The trade association actually controlled the Dutch cement industry, because it imposed detailed trading rules on its members (for example the obligation to notify any change in management), supervised its members' accounts, required that they sell to each other (and thus eliminated the possibility of the building up of stocks of cement by third parties) and was empowered to expel its members for non-compliance with these rules.

Held

The ECJ held that a non-binding recommendation amounts to a decision in so far as its acceptance by undertakings actually influenced their conduct on the market.

Comment

Cementhandelaren's decision recommending target prices had great impact on the level of prices: first, its members were actually complying with the

47 Commission Decision 85/76/EC *Milchförderungsfonds* [1985] OJ L 35/35.
48 Case 246/86 *Belasco v Commission (Re Belgian Roofing Felt Cartel)* [1989] ECR 2117.
49 Joined Cases T-213/95 and T-18/96 *Stichting Certificatie Kraanverhuurbedrijf (SCK) and Federatie van Nederlandse Kraanbedrijven (FNK) v Commission* [1997] ECR II-1739.
50 Commission Decision 80/917/EEC *National Sulphuric Acid Association* [1980] OJ L 260/24, [1980] 3 CMLR 429.
51 Case 8/72 *Vereeniging van Cementhandelaren v Commission* [1972] ECR 977.

recommendation; and second, it removed to a great extent the uncertainty as to prices, because almost all dealers were charging the same as each other. Consequently, the recommendation was regarded as a decision within the meaning of Article 101(1) TFEU.

It flows from this case that the term 'decision' covers non binding recommendations, informal decisions, circulars, etc. if it can be shown that such non-binding measures taken by an association have influenced, or might influence (in which respect, past conduct of its members will be taken into account), conduct of its members on the relevant market resulting in restricting competition.

In the context of trade associations, the matter of the kind of information exchange system that can be put in place by a trade association without falling foul of being in breach of Article 101(1) TFEU was examined in *John Deere*.[52] The ECJ held that the compatibility of an exchange of information system with competition law must be assessed in the context of the economic conditions of the market and the particular characteristics of the system in question. However, it seems that the following three factors will decide whether such a system is compatible with EU law:

- the degree of concentration of the market, so in an oligopolistic market,[53] for example, competition is already greatly reduced and thus any exchange of information substantially risks impairing the competition that exists between traders;
- whether such a system reveals to all of the competitors the market positions and strategies of the various individual competitors – thus an exchange of information system must not reduce or remove uncertainty regarding the conduct of competitors in the relevant market; and
- whether non-discriminatory access to the system is available, in law and in fact, to all operators in the relevant area.

It results from the case law that any scheme for the exchange of information will be permitted if the market in question is not highly concentrated, if it excludes any information from which the behaviour of individual members can be identified and if it ensures that all operators have access to the scheme. Such a scheme will be helpful and neutral, while assisting undertakings, and often consumers, in making informed choices.

52 Case C-7/95P *John Deere Ltd v Commission* [1998] ECR I-3111. This was confirmed in Case C-238/05 *ASNEF-EQUIFAX v Ausbanc* [2006] ECR I-11125, [54].

53 On oligopoly, see Chapter 2, section 2.4.2.3.B.

6.3.3 Concerted practices

It derives from the very nature of a concerted practice that it does not have all of the elements of a contract, but it constitutes a form of informal co-ordination between undertakings.

Concerted practices are difficult to discover and evidence, taking into account that:

- they are secret arrangements that participating undertakings will try to hide from the public view at all costs; and
- when there is no documentary evidence (such as meeting minutes, plans, exchange of emails, etc.), parallel conduct may nevertheless indicate that an undertaking is engaged in a concerted practice.

However, when a finding of an infringement is based on parallel conduct alone, EU law imposes on the European Commission a very heavy burden of proof (see section 6.3.3.3).

6.3.3.1 The meaning of a 'concerted practice' under EU competition law

Three cases decided by the European courts have, for the purposes of EU law, defined the meaning of a concerted practice.

- *ICI (Dyestuffs).*[54] The ECJ held that a concerted practice refers to a form of co-operation between undertakings that, without having been taken to the stage at which an agreement properly so-called has been concluded, knowingly substitutes for the risk of competition practical co-operation between them. This case shows that co-ordination and co-operation between undertakings constitute an essential feature in determining whether or not they had been engaged in a concerted practice.
- *Suiker Unie.*[55] The ECJ held that:

  > [T]he criteria of co-ordination and co-operation must be understood in the light of the concept inherent in the provision of the Treaty relating to competition that each economic operator must determine independently the policy which he intends to adopt on the [internal market].[56]

54 Case 48/69 *Imperial Chemical Industries (ICI) Ltd v Commission (Dyestuffs)* [1972] ECR 619.

55 Joined Cases 40–48, 50, 54–56, 111, 113 and 114–73 *Coöperatieve Vereniging 'Suiker Unie' UA and ors v Commission* [1975] ECR 1663.

56 Ibid., [4].

- The ECJ emphasised that the autonomy of an undertaking must not be altered. This autonomy is called into question when competing undertakings intentionally exchange information, directly or indirectly, in order to influence the conduct of actual or potential competitors or to disclose to such a competitor an adopted or envisaged course of conduct.
- It also held that, for a concerted practice to exist, no actual plan is required, but it is necessary that undertakings have direct or indirect contact, the object or effect of which is to either influence the conduct of an actual or potential competitor, or to disclose to such a competitor the course of action that the colluding undertakings have agreed to adopt, or envisage adopting, in the relevant market.

- *Cimenteries.*[57] The General Court held as follows.
  - First, it made a distinction between passive reception of information and active reception of information. It stated that, to amount to a concerted practice, there must be an intention to communicate information to the other party and the latter must be aware that it is receiving such communication not accidentally, but on purpose. The exchange of information must go beyond mutual awareness of what the other party is doing based on normal sources of information, such as the terms and conditions quoted to customers, which are easy to obtain and which will influence prices and policies adopted by competitors.
  - Second, the General Court stated that 'a concerted practice implies, besides undertakings concerting together, conduct on the market pursuant to those collusive practices, and a relationship of cause and effect between the two'.[58]

The above case law can be summarised as follows. For there to be a concerted practice, there must be direct or indirect contact between competing undertakings that influences the conduct on the market of an actual or potential competitor, the object or effect of such contact must be 'to create conditions of competition which would not correspond to the normal conditions of the market in question',[59] and there must be a relationship of cause and effect between the concertation and the market conduct.

A Direct or indirect contact between undertakings

Any direct or indirect contact between competitors that undermines the requirement of independence – that is, the requirement according to which each

57 Joined Cases T-25–104/95 *Cimenteries CBR and ors v Commission* [2000] ECR II-491.
58 Ibid., [1852].
59 Case T-208/06 *Quinn Barlo Ltd, Quinn Plastics NV, and Quinn Plastics GmbH v* Commission [2011] ECR II-7953, [37].

economic operator must determine independently the policy that it intends to adopt on the market – is prohibited.[60] This requirement raises two questions:

1. What kind of information can be exchanged between competing undertakings without breaching Article 101(1) TFEU? Information can be exchanged directly by competitors (for example, during a meeting, by phone, etc.), or indirectly, through a common agency such as a trade association, or a third party such as market research organisations, or suppliers, or retailers.

   The European Commission's position on exchange of information between undertakings is stated in its Guidelines on the Applicability of Article 101 [TFEU] to Horizontal Co-operation Agreements.[61] The Guidelines reiterate the case law on this matter.[62] They state, on the one hand, that exchange of information may generate various types of efficiency gain (for example it may improve internal efficiency of undertakings through benchmarking against each other's best practices), and, on the other, that exchange of information may be harmful to competition, because it may facilitate collusive behaviour and lead to anti-competitive foreclosure.

   The Guidelines recognise that information may be exchanged in various contexts, for example in the context of research and development (R&D) or specialisation agreements. Such exchange of information may be vital and necessary to the implementation of agreements, and thus benefit from the relevant block exemption regulation.[63] However, it may also support an unlawful cartel, in which case it will be unlawful.[64]

60 See Joined Cases 40–48, 50, 54–56, 111, 113 and 114–73 *Coöperatieve Vereniging 'Suiker Unie' UA and ors v Commission* [1975] ECR 1663, [173]; Case 172/80 *Züchner* [1981] ECR 2021, [13]; Joined Cases C-89/85, C-104/85, C-114/85, C-116/85, C-117/85 and C-125/85–C-129/85 *Ahlström Osakeyhtiö and ors v Commission (Re Wood Pulp Cartel)* [1993] ECR I-1307, [63]; Case C-7/95 P *John Deere v Commission* [1998] ECR I-3111, [86].

61 [2011] OJ C 11/1.

62 Case C-7/95 P *John Deere v Commission* [1998] ECR I-3111; Case C-238/05 *Asnef-Equifax v Ausbanc* [2006] ECR I-11125; Case C-8/08 *T-Mobile Netherlands* [2009] ECR I-4529.

63 Until the entry into force of Regulation 1/2003, which decentralised the enforcement of EU competition law, the European Commission had exclusive competence to grant individual exemptions under Article 101(3) TFEU. In order to ease the Commission's workload, the Council, under Regulation 19/65, empowered it to adopt block exemption regulations exempting classes or blocks of agreements (hence 'block' exemption regulations), such as exclusive distribution agreements, purchasing agreements and agreements licensing IPRs, so long as they conform to any exemption regulation. Each block exemption is contained in a separate regulation and is legally binding. If an agreement strictly complies with every condition and term of a block exemption regulation, it is outside the scope of Article 101(1) TFEU, i.e. there is no need to examine the agreement under Article 101(3) TFEU.

64 See Joined Cases T-117/07 and T-121/07 *Areva v Commission* [2011] ECR II-633.

The Guidelines set out two factors that will be decisive in determining whether an exchange of information can produce anti-competitive outcomes:

(a) the characteristics of the relevant market – that is, whether the market is highly concentrated, stable, transparent, complex, symmetric, etc.; and
(b) the types of information that is exchanged – that is, strategic data such as actual or proposed prices, discounts, customer lists, production costs, quantities, turnovers, sales, capacities, qualities, marketing plans, risks, investments, technologies and R&D programmes, and their results.

In this second respect, the European Commission considers that information related to prices and quantities is the most strategic, followed by information about costs and demand. However, if companies compete with regard to R&D programmes, it is the technology data that may be the most strategic for competition. The strategic usefulness of data depends on its aggregation (if it is individualised, it is more likely to have an anti-competitive outcome than aggregated data, which normally makes recognition of the data of an individual undertaking difficult), the age of the information (exchange of historic data is unlikely to have a collusive outcome), the market context, the frequency of the exchange and whether information is public or non-public.

Exchange of information may restrict competition by object or effect (see section 6.4). It restricts competition by object when strategic information is exchanged between competitors. The Guidelines state that exchanges of information relating to intended future prices or quantities should be considered a restriction of competition by object unlikely to be exempted under Article 101(3) TFEU.[65] With regard to restriction of competition by effect, the Guidelines provide that the economic conditions of the relevant market and the nature of information exchanged will determine whether 'pure exchange' of information between competitors in itself infringes Article 101(1) TFEU.[66]

2. Will participation in meetings attended by competitors be sufficient to prove the existence of a concerted practice? In some cases, in which the European Commission was unable to establish the existence of any agreement based on the participation of an undertaking in an anti-competitive meeting, it nevertheless had enough evidence to prove the existence of a concerted practice. In *PVC Cartel*,[67] the General Court held that the European

65 European Commission, Guidelines on the Applicability of Article 101 [TFEU] to Horizontal Co-operation Agreements [2011] OJ C 11/1, [74].

66 Ibid., [74].

67 Commission Decision 94/599/EEC *PVC Cartel* [1994] OJ L 239/14, appealed as Joined Cases T-305/94, T-306/94, T-307/94, T-313/94–T-316/94, T-318/94, T-325/94, T-328/94, T-329/94, and T-335/94 *Limburgse Vinyl Maatschappij NV and ors v Commission (PVC II)* [1999] ECR II-931, [696].

Commission had been correct in classifying a meeting as either an agreement or a concerted practice.

The ECJ in *T-Mobile*[68] held that the finding of a concerted practice does not require that competitors meet regularly over a period of time; a single meeting between competitors may constitute a sufficient basis for them to concert their market conduct. Accordingly, the number, frequency and form of meetings are irrelevant; what counts is whether a meeting allows, or meetings allow, the participating undertakings to take account of information exchanged with their competitors so as to influence future conduct on the relevant market. Obviously, the presumption is stronger when undertakings are involved in a concerted practice on a regular basis over a long period of time.[69]

B Conduct pursuant to direct or indirect contact, and the relationship of cause and effect between the concertation and the market conduct

In *Hüls*,[70] the ECJ established a rebuttable presumption that concertation is followed by anti-competitive conduct if an undertaking taking part in the concertation remains active on the relevant market. This presumption is almost impossible to rebut bearing in mind that, in *AC-Treuhand*,[71] the General Court had stated that Article 101(1) TFEU does not require the relevant market on which the undertaking that is the 'perpetrator' of the restriction of competition is active to be exactly the same as the one on which that restriction is deemed to materialise. Accordingly, as long as the relevant undertaking exists, it is unlikely to escape liability for participation in a cartel. In *T-Mobile*,[72] the ECJ held that this presumption is substantive, rather than procedural, and thus must be applied by national courts when they apply Article 101 TFEU.

The second rebuttable presumption that the ECJ established in *Hüls* is that a concerted practice (as well as an agreement or a decision) is within the scope of Article 101(1) TFEU, even in the absence of anti-competitive effects on the market. When a concerted practice imposes restrictions on competition by object, it is not necessary for the European Commission to prove anti-competitive effects (see section 6.4); a potential negative impact on competition will suffice.[73]

68 Case C-8/08 *T-Mobile Netherlands BV and ors v Raad van bestuur van de Nederlandse Mededingingsautoriteit* [2009] ECR I-4529.
69 COMP/39.188 *Bananas*, 15 October 2008, C(2008) 5955 final.
70 Case C-199/92 *Hüls AG v Commission* [1999] ECR I-4287.
71 Case T-99/04 *AC-Treuhand AG v Commission* [2008] ECR II-1501.
72 Case C-8/08 *T-Mobile Netherlands BV and ors v Raad van bestuur van de Nederlandse Mededingingsautoriteit* [2009] ECR I-4529.
73 Case C-209/07 *Competition Authority v Beef Industry Development Society and Barry Brothers (Carrigmore) Meats* [2008] ECR I-8637.

6.3.3.2 Parallel behaviour in an oligopolistic market

The line between independent conduct and collusive conduct is particularly difficult to draw in the case of an oligopolistic market, in which undertakings act in parallel. The matter of whether parallel conduct over a period of time will constitute sufficient evidence of a concerted practice where there is no evidence of any contact, direct or indirect, between undertakings was examined by the ECJ in *Re Wood Pulp Cartel*.[74]

Joined Cases C-89/85, C-104/85, C-114/85, C-116/85, C-117/85 and C-125/85–C-129/85 *Ahlström Osakeyhtiö and ORS v Commission (Re Wood Pulp Cartel)* [1993] ECR I-1307

Facts

The Commission found more than forty suppliers of wood pulp in violation of EU competition law. Fines were imposed on 36 of these companies for violation of Article 101(1) TFEU. A number of these companies appealed against the decision to the ECJ. They challenged the Commission's finding that they breached Article 101(1) TFEU through concertation of prices for their products by means of a system of quarterly price announcements. The factors that the Commission took into account, *inter alia*, were the system of early announcements of prices, which made prices transparent, the uniform fluctuation of prices and the uniform approach to prices, which could be explained in a narrow oligopolistic situation in which undertakings had to follow a market leader. However, at that time, there were more than fifty producers of wood pulp. On this basis, the Commission had concluded that the market was not oligopolistic and that the uniform market behaviour could be explained only by a concerted practice.

Held

The ECJ annulled the decision of the European Commission on the ground that the Commission had not provided a firm, precise and consistent body of evidence of infringement.

The ECJ held that parallel conduct could not be regarded as furnishing proof of concertation unless concertation constituted the only plausible explanation.

74 Joined Cases C-89/85, C-104/85, C-114/85, C-116/85, C-117/85 and C-125/85–C-129/85 *Ahlström Osakeyhtiö and ors v Commission (Re Wood Pulp Cartel)* [1993] ECR I-1307.

Comment

The ECJ appointed its own experts to analyse the market. Their findings convinced the ECJ that there may be explanations of parallel behaviour other than concertation, such as the natural structure of the market. In the present case, the market was cyclical. In respect of transparency of prices, the early announcements were requested by customers; taking into account the cyclical nature of the market, they wanted to know the price for wood pulp as soon as possible. The ECJ held that:

> "[I]t must be stated that, in this case, concertation is not the only plausible explanation for the parallel conduct. To begin with, the system of price announcements may be regarded as constituting a rational response to the fact that the pulp market constituted a long-term market and to the need felt by both buyers and sellers to limit commercial risks. Further, the similarity in the dates of price announcements may be regarded as a direct result of the high degree of market transparency, which does not have to be described as artificial. Finally, the parallelism of prices and the price trends may be satisfactorily explained by the oligopolistic tendencies of the market and by the specific circumstances prevailing in certain periods. Accordingly, the parallel conduct established by the Commission does not constitute evidence of concertation."[75]

It flows from this judgment that the standard of proof is very high in cases concerning parallel behaviour in an oligopolistic market. In such cases, the European Commission is required to establish that parallel behaviour is the only plausible explanation of the concerted action. This seems to entail that the European Commission must eliminate all other justifications for parallel behaviour in order to prove infringement of Article 101(1) TFEU, which is almost an impossible task. In the Opinion of Advocate General Darmon in *Re Wood Pulp Cartel*, the European Commission could not shift the burden of proof onto the undertakings by a finding of parallel conduct.[76] As Jones and Sufrin said: 'It would seem inadvisable to rely solely on economic evidence to establish the existence of a cartel. Rather, other evidence is required to corroborate a case.'[77] Further, they referred to the European Commission decision in *Cartonboard*,[78] in which this view was acknowledged by the Commission when it stated that 'unless direct proof of collusion were forthcoming – which the undertakings concerned would go to some length to ensure it was not',[79] undertakings in an oligopolistic

75 Ibid., [126].
76 Ibid., [195].
77 A. Jones and B. Sufrin, *EU Competition Law*, 2011, Oxford: OUP, p 834.
78 Commission Decision 94/601/EEC *Cartonboard* [1994] OJ L 243/1.
79 Ibid., [73].

market may rely on the defence of oligopolistic interdependence to justify parallel price increases. Finally, the General Court in *CISAC*[80] (see section 6.3.3.3) seems to say that the standard of proof in cases in which the European Commission's finding of infringement is based on parallel conduct alone is very close to that required in criminal cases. In this respect, the Court stated that any doubt that the Commission entertains 'must benefit the undertaking to which the decision finding an infringement was addressed'.[81]

6.3.3.3 The burden of proof

The burden of proof is particularly difficult to discharge in cases relating to cartels bearing in mind that participants are aware of their anti-competitive conduct, and thus organise their meeting in remote places, falsify documents and use modern technology with the intention of ensuring that their activities are undetected. In the EU context, one of the main means of uncovering cartels is the leniency programme. This offers immunity to undertakings participating in a cartel, or smaller fines than would have been imposed had the Commission discovered the cartel, in exchange for self-reporting and co-operation in the Commission's ensuing investigation. Currently, most cartels are discovered by the European Commission *via* its leniency programme. As a result, the burden of proving the existence of cartels resting on the European Commission has been greatly alleviated, or even removed, in most cases.

Stewart posits that, in CARICOM, any leniency programme is unlikely to be successful, for two reasons.

- First, participants in a cartel will be likely to expose it only if they fear the possibility of incurring serious consequences, such as large fines and perhaps imprisonment. Such fear is unlikely to be inspired by any NCA. However, the existence of the CCC may change this perception. It is to be noted that the CCC is in the process of establishing its fining policy.
- Second, the social culture of small economies means that businessmen are friends and interact with each other socially, and that any whistleblower may not only become a social pariah, but also be in real danger of being physically attacked or intimidated.[82]

In the context of EU competition law, the European Commission is always required to prove an alleged infringement. The requisite legal standard comprises

80 Case T-442/08 *International Confederation of Societies of Authors and Composers (CISAC) v European Commission* [2013] ECR II-188.

81 Ibid., [92].

82 T. Stewart, 'CARICOM Countries', in P. S. Mehta (ed.) *Competition Regimes in the World: A Civil Society Report*, 2006, Jaipur: CUTS Centre for Competition, Investment & Economic Regulation, p 537.

three requirements[83] – that is, the European Commission must prove (i) the existence of a prohibited form of co-operation between undertakings, (ii) which has as its object or effect the prevention, restriction or distortion of competition (a requirement examined in section 6.4) and (iii) which has effect on trade within the European Union (which requirement was examined in Chapter 5).

The first requirement, as discussed in section 6.3, is intended to catch all forms of prohibited co-operation. The reliance on the leniency programme, as well as the existence of presumptions, attenuates the need for the Commission to infer cartels from complicated factual evidence. In *Hüls*,[84] (one of the *Cartonboard Cartel* cases), the ECJ held that it was the task of the European Commission to establish that Hüls participated in the meetings at which price initiatives were decided, organised and monitored. However, it was incumbent on Hüls to prove that it had not subscribed to those initiatives if that was the case. Consequently, there was no reversal of the burden of proof. The ECJ emphasised that the right to be presumed innocent constitutes one of the fundamental principles of the EU legal order and, as such, applies to competition procedures. Notwithstanding this, it is submitted that the existence of presumptions under EU competition law, which are almost impossible to rebut, entails that the ECJ is more concerned with ensuring the efficiency of EU competition law than it is with the strict application of the presumption of innocence. On the one hand, it can be said that this approach may be in breach of Article 6 ECHR,[85] but on the other it is clear that reliance on the leniency programme lessens the importance of the presumption of innocence in cartel cases.

Notwithstanding this, in cases in which the European Commission's allegations of infringement of Article 101(1) TFEU are based solely on parallel conduct of undertakings, the standard of proof imposed on the Commission is very high. This is illustrated in the recent judgment of the General Court in *CISAC*.[86]

83 Case C-185 /95P *Baustahlgewebe v Commission* [1998] ECR I-8417, [58].

84 Case C-199/92P *Hüls AG v Commission* [1999] ECR I-4287.

85 However, the ECtHR in *Salabiaku v France* [1991] 13 EHRR 379, [28], held that, in criminal matters, the right to be presumed innocent and the requirement that the prosecution bears the onus of proving all relevant allegations is not absolute. It accepted the existence of presumptions of fact and law 'as long as States remain within the reasonable limits, taking into account the importance of what is at stake and maintaining the rights of the defence'.

86 Case T-442/08 *International Confederation of Societies of Authors and Composers (CISAC) v European Commission* [2013] ECR II-188.

Case T-442/08 *International Confederation of Societies of Authors and Composers (CISAC) v European Commission* [2013] ECR II-188

Facts

The International Confederation of Societies of Authors and Composers (CISAC, from the French *Confédération Internationale des Sociétés d'Auteurs et Compositeurs*), a non-profit non-governmental organisation, which has as its main task the promotion of reciprocal representation between collecting societies around the world, brought proceedings before the General Court for annulment of the European Commission's Decision of 16 July 2008[87] in which the European Commission found 24 European collecting society members of CISAC to be in breach of Article 101(1) TFEU.

Collecting societies manage their members' copyright in musical works within their respective countries. Each collecting society acquires the relevant rights either by direct transfer from the original holders or by transmission from another collecting society managing the same categories of rights in another country. The management of copyright by the collecting societies means that they enjoy the exclusive right to grant exploitation licences to commercial users, such as broadcasting undertakings and organisers of live shows. The price of those licences constitutes the source of the royalties for the holders after the expenses of the relevant collecting society are deducted. Each collecting society pays the royalties for the exploitation of works to the holder of the works whose copyright it manages, irrespective of the territory in which those rights are exploited.

In order to carry out the efficient management of copyright, CISAC prepared a non-binding model contract in 1936, which has been amended many times ('the model contract'). Collecting societies have adapted this model into reciprocal representation agreements (RRAs) whereby they mutually confer on each other the right over their repertoires for the purpose of their exploitation in the territory of each collecting society. Accordingly, each collecting society can propose a worldwide portfolio of musical works to commercial users, but only for use in its territory, thus restricting the ability to engage in multi-territorial licensing (this is the national territorial limitation set out in the RRAs). The RRAs cover both the traditional exploitation of copyrights (that is, concerts and radio) and exploitation *via* internet, satellite or cable broadcast.

Following complaints from radio and television broadcasting groups concerning the refusal of members of CISAC to grant to them a licence

87 COMP/C2/38.698 *CISAC*, 16 July 2008, C(2008) 3435 final.

covering the entire territory of the European Union for their music broadcasting activities, the European Commission found, *inter alia*, that the national territorial limitation contained in the RRAs was a result of a concerted practice that restricted competition in the European Union and could not be justified under Article 101(3) TFEU. The European Commission's view was that the existence of a concerted practice was evidenced, *inter alia*, by:

- discussions between collecting societies concerning standardisation of their model contracts within the framework of CISAC's activities; and
- the existence of the Santiago Agreement, which was a result of discussion between the collecting societies, in particular in relation to the national territorial limitations and the use of licences for internet, and under which the collecting societies undertook to grant global licences to users established in their national territory with regard to internet use. The Santiago Agreement was exempted by the European Commission under Article 101(3) TFEU. However, it had not been renewed upon its expiry in 2004 on the basis of the Commission's objections, with the result that the collecting societies had since returned to their national territorial limitations. In the contested decision, the Commission had considered that the abandoning of the Santiago Agreement showed that the collecting societies had coordinated their behaviour with regard to licences for internet use.
- Parallel behaviour of the collecting societies in relation to territorial national limitations, to which the collecting societies had returned after the expiry of the Santiago Agreement. For the Commission the only plausible explanation of the parallel behaviour was collusion.

Held

The General Court held that the European Commission had not proved the existence of a concerted practice.

Comments

The General Court confirmed that the European Commission must provide precise and consistent evidence in order to establish the existence of an infringement. However, the Court took account of evidential difficulties experienced by the Commission when seeking to prove the existence of collusive conduct. It held that:

> [I]t is not necessary for every item of evidence produced by the Commission to satisfy those criteria in relation to every aspect of the

> infringement. It is sufficient if the set of indicia relied on by the Commission, viewed as a whole, meets that requirement.[88]

The General Court emphasised the importance of the principle of the presumption of innocence, which requires that any doubt regarding the proof of an infringement must be interpreted by the Court in favour of the alleged perpetrator.

The General Court stated that a distinction must be made between a situation in which the European Commission seeks to prove the existence of concertation based on documents in its possession and that based on a mere finding of parallel conduct. In a situation in which allegations of an infringement are based on documents produced by the Commission, the burden is on the applicants 'not merely to submit another explanation for the facts found by the Commission but to challenge the existence of those facts established on the basis of the documents produced by the Commission'.[89] However, when an infringement is based on a mere finding of parallel conduct, the applicant is required only 'to prove circumstances which cast the facts established by the Commission in a different light and thus allow another explanation of the facts to be substituted for the one adopted by the Commission'.[90] Accordingly, an undertaking needs only to submit a credible alternative explanation to allow the Court to accept this explanation and reject that put forward by the European Commission. The General Court held that any doubt on its part as to the existence of an infringement 'must benefit the undertaking to which the decision finding an infringement was addressed'.[91] It is submitted that this statement does not mean that the European Commission must establish beyond a reasonable doubt the existence of an infringement when its evidence is solely based on parallel conduct, but implies that the burden proof that the Commission must bear is very high: somewhere beyond the civil law standard based on the balance of probabilities, but still not as high as that in criminal cases – that is, the proof beyond reasonable doubt.

In light of this, it is not surprising that the General Court did not find that CISAC was engaged in a concerted practice. The Court accepted the explanations of CISAC that the national territorial limitations were necessary to ensure, first, the effectiveness of the fight against the unauthorised use of musical works, and second, that the amount of royalties received by the authors does not diminish. The Court found that the evidence submitted by the Commission did not render these explanations implausible.

88 Case T-442/08 *International Confederation of Societies of Authors and Composers (CISAC) v European Commission* [2013] ECR II-188, [97].
89 Ibid., [99].
90 Ibid., [99].
91 Ibid., [92].

With regard to documents produced by the European Commission, the General Court found that neither the discussions of the collecting societies within the framework of CISAC activities, nor the existence of the Santiago Agreement, provided evidence of concertation relating to the national territorial limitations. With regard to the discussions of the collecting societies within the framework of CISAC's activities, the General Court established that they were necessary to deal collectively with important issues and did not have an anti-competitive objective. With regard to the Santiago Agreement, the General Court found, *inter alia,* that, after the expiry of the agreement, the national territorial limitations again became applicable to the collecting societies. The Court emphasised that, contrary to the allegations of the Commission, the collecting societies did not then return to national territorial limitations, but returned to the *status quo ante* – that is, the situation prior to the existence of the Santiago Agreement. The General Court stated that the application of the national territorial limitations after 2004 by the collecting societies could not constitute evidence of concertation in the absence of proof that the collecting societies acted in concert for that purpose.

6.4 The distinction between 'infringement by object' and 'infringement by effect'

In *STM,*[92] the ECJ stated that the terms 'object' and 'effect' are to be read disjunctively. The consequence of this is that the European Commission will, first, seek to establish whether an agreement, decision or concerted practice has as its object the restriction of competition, and second, if there is no restriction by object, then it is required to assess whether an agreement, decision or a concerted practice has a restrictive effect on competition.

6.4.1 Infringement by 'object'

The restriction of competition by object entails a rebuttable presumption that collusive conduct has anti-competitive market effects. Not only actual, but also potential, effects are sufficient to trigger the application of the presumption. Accordingly, it is almost impossible to rebut this presumption, bearing in mind that neither non-implementation of an agreement, decision or a concerted practice,[93] nor the practical impossibility of implementing an agreement, decision or a concerted practice,[94] removes its potential to restrict competition.

92 Case 56/65 *Société Technique Minière v Maschinenbau Ulm GmbH* [1966] ECR 235.
93 Case T-13/89 *ICI v Commission* [1992] ECR II-102, [273]–[294].
94 Joined Cases C-189/02 P, C-202/02 P, C-205/02 P–C-208/02 P and C-213/02 P *Dansk Rørindustri A/S and ors v Commission* [2005] ECR I-5425, [146].

In its Guidelines on the Application of [Article 101(3) TFEU],[95] the European Commission summarised the case law of the ECJ in relation to determining whether an agreement restricts competition by object. This determination requires the examination of the terms of the agreement, its legal and economic context, and the actual conduct and behaviour of the parties on the relevant market.[96]

In *T-Mobile*,[97] the ECJ stated that the intent of the parties is relevant, although not an essential factor in determining whether a concerted practice is restrictive of competition. It explained that:

> "[T]he distinction between 'infringement by object' and 'infringement by effect' arises from the fact that certain forms of collusion between undertakings can be regarded, by their very nature, as being injurious to the proper functioning of normal competition."[98]

As a result, when restriction of competition is an inevitable consequence of an agreement, decision or concerted practice, it will be regarded as having an anti-competitive object irrespective of whether it has actually restricted competition or whether it has only the potential to have restrictive effect on competition. Examples of restriction by object in respect of horizontal agreements include price fixing, exchange of information that reduces uncertainty about future conduct of competitors in the relevant market, market-sharing agreements and collective exclusive dealing.[99] With regard to vertical agreements, examples of restrictions by object include the imposition of export bans,[100] the 'hard core' restrictions specified in Article 4 of Regulation 330/2010 (see section 6.2.2), such as fixing prices, and prohibiting cross-supply by authorised distributors.

The concept of the restriction of competition by object alleviates the task of the European Commission in terms of the burden of proof. Once it has been established that an agreement, decision or concerted practice restricts competition by object, then the European Commission is not required to prove its actual effect, or even its potential effect, on competition.

95 [2004] OJ C 101/97.

96 Ibid., [22]. See also Joined Cases C-501/06 P, C-513/06 P, C-515/06 P and C-519/06 P *GlaxoSmithKline Services Unlimited, formerly Glaxo Wellcome plc v Commission* [2009] ECR I-9291, [58].

97 Case C-8/08 *T-Mobile Netherlands BV and ors v Raad van bestuur van de Nederlandse Mededingingsautoriteit* [2009] ECR I-4529.

98 Ibid., [29].

99 See Case T-5/00 and T-6/00 *Nederlandse Federative Vereniging voor de Groothandel op Elektrotechnisch Gebied and Technische Unie BV v Commission* [2003] ECR II-5761.

100 See, e.g., Joined Cases C-501/06 P, C-513/06 P, C-515/06 P and C-519/06 P *GlaxoSmithKline Services Unlimited, formerly Glaxo Wellcome plc v Commission* [2009] ECR I-9291.

6.4.2 Infringement by 'effect'

If an agreement, decision or a concerted practice does not restrict competition by object, the European Commission is required to assess whether it restricts competition by effect. The case law shows that the European Commission is required to determine, at least, what would be the state of competition, actual and potential, in the relevant market if the agreement, with its alleged restrictions, did not exist. This is known as a 'counterfactual standard', or 'but for' analysis.[101] It entails a three-step approach, as follows.

1. The Commission must establish the hypothetical degree of competition in the relevant market if the agreement did not exist.
2. It must determine the degree of competition in light of the existing agreement.
3. It must compare the first two factors or conditions.

If the comparison reveals that the degree of competition has been reduced, there will have been an infringement of Article 101(1) TFEU. Introduction of the 'counterfactual standard' was an important development in EU law given that the comparison between the potential and the actual degree of competition in the relevant market entails that 'the specific factors or conditions that differ between the two must be identified and how those factors or conditions lead (or potentially will lead) to consumer harm must be explained. This alone provides some rigour to the analysis.'[102]

The Commission's Guidelines on the Interpretation of [Article 101(3) TFEU] explain how to apply the counterfactual standard.[103]

The matter of whether an agreement, decision or a concerted practice is restrictive of competition by its effect is one of the most controversial in competition law. This is because, eventually, everything boils down to economic matters – that is, how, why and in light of what general objectives an economic assessment is carried out. Thus expert economic evidence plays a very important role in the fact-finding part of proceedings.

It is submitted that CSME competition law should embrace the distinction between a restriction of competition by object and a restriction of it by effect. Cartel agreements fixing prices or sharing markets, or vertical agreements fixing minimum prices, are *per se* anti-competitive and thus it would be a waste of the resources of the CCC to require it to establish that they also have anti-competitive effect. In any event, under CSME competition law, any agreement, decision or

101 See Case 56/65 *Société Technique Minière v Maschinenbau Ulm GmbH* [1966] ECR 235, [39].
102 D. Geradin, A. Layne-Farrar and N. Petit, *EU Competition Law and Economics*, 2012, Oxford: OUP, p 128.
103 [2004] OJ C 101/97, [16]–[23].

concerted practice may escape the prohibition of Article 177(1)(a) RTC if an enterprise can show that the criteria set out in Article 177(4) RTC are met (see section 6.6).

6.5 The advantages of the expansive interpretation of 'agreements, decisions and concerted practices'

The matter of whether the CCC, and ultimately the CCJ, should adopt a legalistic, formalistic approach to the definition of agreements, decisions and concerted practices, or whether they should follow the expansionist approach adopted by the European Commission and the ECJ, merits consideration. It is submitted that preference should be given to the expansionist EU approach. This can be justified by the following:

1. CSME competition law should be concerned with catching different forms of collusion between enterprises rather than making formal distinction between those different forms of collusion. The bottom line is that an economic operator must independently determine the policy that it intends to adopt on the relevant market. Accordingly, the purpose of Article 177(1)(a) RTC is to make a distinction between collusive behaviour, which is prohibited, and independent behaviour, which is lawful.
2. Distinguishing between various forms of collusion is of interest only from a theoretical perspective. It is submitted that Article 177(1)(c) RTC confirms this view. This provision states that any conduct by enterprises that is not within the scope of Article 177(1)(a) and (b) RTC (which prohibits abuses of a dominant position), the object or effect of which is to frustrate the benefits expected from the establishment of the CSME, is in breach of competition law. Article 177(1)(c) RTC therefore ensures that CSME competition law applies to all types of anti-competitive arrangement irrespective of the form that they take. It ensures, first, that there is no *lacuna* in the scope of application of CSME competition law, and second, that CSME competition law is well equipped to deal with any new form of collusion that the ingenuity of cartelists may produce.
3. The RTC makes no distinction between the legal consequences deriving from participation by an enterprise in a concerted practice, or an unlawful agreement, or any other form of collusive behaviour. In all cases, they are the same. Accordingly, the adoption of an expansionist approach would be well justified from the perspective of sanctions that may be imposed on an offending enterprise.
4. Under EU law, the difference between anti-competitive agreements and concerted practices lies in the intensity of prohibited co-operation between or amongst undertakings, in that it is stronger when an undertaking enters into an anti-competitive agreement than when it is engaged in a concerted practice. Notwithstanding this, the anti-competitive effect of collusive

> conduct on the relevant market is the same. CSME competition law is about elimination of restriction on competition and thus should not be concerned with the manner in which enterprises collude. Whether managing directors of enterprises that are competitors sign a legally binding contract or whether there is only 'a nod and a wink', but no formal consensus *ad idem*, or whether one of them makes a statement relating to the pricing policy of its undertaking and others remain silent, ensuing anti-competitive conduct produces the same restrictive effect on the relevant market.

It is submitted that Article 177(1)(a) RTC, instead of using the three terms 'agreements', 'decisions' and 'concerted practices', could have used one term – that is, 'arrangements' – to capture all forms of prohibited co-operation. This approach would not create any change in the objective of Article 171(1)(a) RTC, which is to capture and punish illicit collective action of enterprises; what is of real importance is the matter of proof. Under EU law, the European Commission must prove the infringement to the requisite standard – that is, it must provide reliable evidence of concertation, or if there is no convincing evidence, it must show that the explanation provided by the parties to an alleged infringement is implausible and that the only reasonable explanation of parallel conduct is concertation.

6.6 Exemption under Article 177(4) RTC

Article 177(4) RTC states:

> "An enterprise shall not be treated as engaging in anti-competitive business conduct if it establishes that the activity complained of:
>
> (a) contributes to:
>
> (i) the improvement of production or distribution of goods and services; or
> (ii) the promotion of technical or economic progress,
>
> while allowing consumers a fair share of the resulting benefit;
>
> (b) imposes on the enterprises affected only such restrictions as are indispensable to the attainment of the objectives mentioned in sub-paragraph (a); or
>
> (c) does not afford the enterprise engaged in the activity the possibility of eliminating competition in respect of a substantial part of the market for goods or services concerned."

Article 177(4) RTC sets out two positive and two negative criteria relating to the eligibility of anti-competitive conduct for exemption. The positive criteria are that:

- the conduct must contribute to improving the production or distribution of goods, or the promotion of technical or economic progress; and
- consumers must be allowed a fair share of the resulting benefit.

The negative criteria are that:

- the conduct must not impose on the affected enterprises restrictions that are not indispensable to the attainment of the objectives set out in Article 177(4)(a) RTC; and
- it must not afford an enterprise engaged in the activity complaint of the possibility of eliminating competition in respect of a substantial part of the market for the goods or services concerned.

It is for an enterprise seeking exemption to establish that the necessary criteria for exemption set out in Article 177(4) RTC are satisfied, by means of convincing arguments and evidence. Once this has been established, the CCC will examine whether the enterprise has discharged the burden of proof. It will weigh the benefit flowing from prohibited conduct against the disadvantage resulting from the restriction that it imposes on competition. If the benefit outweighs the disadvantage, the conduct will merit exemption.

It is clear from the terms of Article 177(4) RTC that any conduct, irrespective of whether it restricts competition by object or by effect, may qualify for exemption.

While Article 177(4) RTC is modelled on Article 101(3) TFEU, there are important differences between them.

1. Article 177(4) RTC applies to any anti-competitive conduct. It covers not only anti-competitive agreements, decisions or concerted practices, but also abuses of a dominant position and any other conduct, the object or effect of which is to frustrate benefits expected from the establishment of the CSME. Article 101(3) TFEU applies only to anti-competitive agreements, decisions and concerted practices. However, the ECJ has developed the concept of 'objective justification', under which abusive conduct of a dominant undertaking may escape the application of Article 102 TFEU. Under this concept, one of the justifications available to a dominant undertaking is based on efficiencies. It involves a weighing of efficiency gains against the anti-competitive effects of conduct, and thus is similar to the economic assessment carried out under Article 101(3) TFEU. It is important to note that further justifications for abuses of a dominant position are provided in Article 179(3) RTC (see Chapter 7, section 7.7.2).
2. The literal interpretation of Article 177(4)(b) and (c) RTC suggests that the two negative criteria for exemption are alternative, rather than cumulative. Accordingly, it seems that if both positive criteria set out in Article 177(a) RTC are satisfied, anti-competitive business conduct will be eligible for

exemption if it satisfies either of the criteria set out in Article 177(4)(b) or (c) RTC.

It is submitted that the literal interpretation of Article 177(4) RTC must be rejected as incompatible with the objectives of CSME competition law. Whilst the criteria set out in Article 177(4)(a) RTC focus on the short-term efficiency gains and Article 177(4)(b) RTC ensures that the restrictions imposed by anti-competitive conduct are indispensible to the achievement of efficiencies mentioned in Article 177(4)(a), Article 177(4)(c) RTC takes account of long-term losses flowing from anti-competitive conduct. Accordingly, Article 177(4)(c) ensures that anti-competitive conduct will not eliminate rivalry on the relevant market. Its application is essential to protect the competitive process. It is difficult, if not impossible, to accept that only one negative criterion will need to be satisfied for anti-competitive conduct to be within the scope of exemption. This would mean that, for example, an agreement that meets the indispensability criterion, but which allows the parties to it the opportunity of eliminating competition on the relevant market, would qualify for exemption. Further, because the burden of proof lies on the party that seeks exemption, such a party would have discretion to choose which of the two negative criteria its conduct satisfies, and consequently avoid the criterion that its conduct obviously fails to meet. Such a result defeats the basic objectives of CSME competition law, because it provides an easy escape for enterprises the conduct of which may have detrimental effect on the relevant market. An additional argument against the literal interpretation of Article 177(4)(b) and (c) RTC is that, under EU law, all four criteria laid down in Article 101(3) TFEU must be satisfied: if one of them is not fulfilled, the agreement will not be exempted.[104]

In the examination of the criteria set out in Article 177(4) RTC, reference to EU law is helpful – in particular, to the European Commission's Guidelines on the Application of [Article 101(3) TFEU][105] and to its Guidance on Enforcement Priorities in Applying [Article 102 TFEU] to Abusive Exclusionary Conduct of Dominant Undertakings.[106]

The criteria set out in Article 177(4) RTC are examined below.

6.6.1 Criterion 1: Improvement in the production or distribution of goods, or the promotion of technical or economic progress

The first positive criterion expressed in Article 177(4)(a) RTC is very broad. It refers to '(i) the improvement of production or distribution of goods and services;

104 Joined Cases T-528, 542, 543 and 546/93 *Métropole Télévision and ors v Commission* [1996] ECR II-649; Case T-395/94 *Atlantic Container Line AB v Commission* [2002] ECR II-875.

105 [2004] OJ C 101/97.

106 [2009] OJ C 45/7, [30].

or (ii) the promotion of technical or economic progress'. The criterion clearly states that it does not require that all four possibilities are present; it is sufficient if only one of the four possibilities set out in Article 174(4)(a) RTC occurs.

In applying the first criterion, any advantages flowing from the activity complained of must be compared with any disadvantages resulting from the restriction that it imposes on competition. In order to qualify for exemption, the advantages must prevail over the disadvantages. According to the European Commission Guidelines on the Application of [Article 101(3) TFEU], only objective benefits can be taken into account.[107] This entails that efficiencies are not assessed from the subjective point of view of the parties.[108] Accordingly, as the Guidelines state, cost savings arising from the mere exercise of market power by the parties, for example from fixing prices or sharing markets, which reduce output and thereby production costs, cannot be taken into account.[109]

According to the European Commission's Guidelines on the Application of [Article 101(3) TFEU], all types of objective economic efficiency can be claimed by undertakings.[110] The Guidelines examine two types of efficiency, as examples: cost efficiencies and qualitative efficiencies. They state that each efficiency must be substantiated by the undertaking claiming the benefit of the exemption in order that the following can be verified:

> "(a) The nature of the claimed efficiencies;
> (b) The link between the agreement and the efficiencies;
> (c) The likelihood and magnitude of each claimed efficiency; and
> (d) How and when each claimed efficiency would be achieved."[111]

Under EU law, there is a debate as to whether only economic improvements should be taken into account or whether non-economic improvements, such as full employment and the protection of the environment, should also be considered when applying Article 101(3) TFEU.[112] The Guidelines are clear on this matter: the only improvements relevant to the application of Article 101(3) TFEU are 'objective economic benefits' or 'pro-competitive effects', which are achieved 'by way of efficiency gains'.[113] The rejection by the European Commission of

107 [2004] OJ C 101/97, [49].
108 Cases 56 and 58/64 *Établissements Consten SaRL and Grundig-Verkaufs-GmbH v Commission* [1966] ECR 299.
109 [2004] OJ C 101/97, [49].
110 Ibid., [59].
111 Ibid., [51].
112 See J. Bougeois and J. Bocken, 'Guidelines on the Application of Article [101(3) TFEU] or How to Restrict a Restriction' (2005) 32(2) Legal Issues of Economic Integration 111.
113 European Commission, Guidelines on the Application of [Article 101(3) TFEU] [2004] OJ C 101/97, [33].

non-economic improvements is explained by its fear that, since the entry into force of Regulation 1/2003, which abolished the Commission's monopoly on granting exemption under Article 101(3) TFEU, NCAs and national courts, which assess the exemption, may exempt anti-competitive agreements, decisions and concerted practices on grounds of national public policy considerations to the detriment of the competitive process. This would undermine uniformity in the application of EU competition law.

This debate is irrelevant for the application of the criterion set out in Article 177(4)(a) RTC, however, because, in the CSME, the assessment of improvements will be carried out by the CCC and ultimately reviewed by the CCJ.

It is submitted that, in the application of the criterion set out in Article 177(4)(a) RTC, the CCC should take account of non-economic improvements when deciding whether anti-competitive conduct qualifies for exemption. In particular, in a situation in which non-economic improvements are compatible with the objectives set out in Article 6 RTC, such as the protection of employment, the improvement of standards of living and work of nationals of CARICOM, and the advancement of their social and cultural development, the CCC should be allowed to take such improvements into consideration in order to decide whether anti-competitive conduct merits exemption under Article 177(4) RTC. This may be thought to be supported by the fact that both the European Commission, prior to the entry into force of Regulation 1/2003, and the EU's courts accepted non-economic improvements as factors relevant to the application of the first criterion set out in Article 101(3) TFEU.[114]

6.6.2 Criterion 2: Benefit to consumers

The second positive criterion requires that the activity complained of must not only contribute to improving the production or distribution of goods, or to promoting technical or economic progress, but also must allow consumers a fair share of the resulting benefit.

In the interpretation of the second criterion, reference to EU case law and to the European Commission's Guidelines on the Application of [Article 101(3) TFEU] is of interest.

Under EU law, the term 'consumers' applies not only to final consumers, but also to wholesalers and retailers who purchase products in the course of their

114 See A. Komninos, 'Non-Competition Concerns: Resolution of Conflicts in the Integrated Article [101 TFEU]', University of Oxford Centre for Competition Law and Policy Working Paper (L) 08/05, available at http://intranet.law.ox.ac.uk/ckfinder/userfiles/files/CCLP%20L%2008-05.pdf [accessed 20 March 2014], pp 4*ff.* Komninos examines many decisions of the European Commission in which non-economic improvements were accepted. Examples of their acceptance by the ECJ are provided in Case 26/76 *Metro SB-Großmärkte GmbH & Co. KG v Commission* [1977] ECR 1875 and Case 42/84 *Remia BV and ors v Commission* [1985] ECR 2545.

trade and business.[115] The European Commission takes into consideration the interests of the majority of consumers. In *VBVB/VBBB*,[116] the European Commission refused to grant exemption to an agreement between associations of booksellers and publishers operating in the Netherlands and Belgium. The agreement imposed collective prices on books in the Dutch language to be sold in Belgium and in the Netherlands. It provided that less popular books on specific subjects published in a limited number of copies were to be subsidised by more popular books. The European Commission condemned the agreement on the ground that it would be unfair to the majority of consumers, taking into account that they prefer popular books rather than specialised books, which have a limited number of readers.

The 'fair share' concept entails that 'the pass-on of benefits must at least compensate consumers for any actual or likely negative impact caused to them by the restriction of competition found under Article 101(3) TFEU'.[117] As a result, the net effect of an agreement on the affected consumers must at least be neutral. If they are worse off, the second criterion will not be fulfilled.

As to the term 'benefit', it covers not only reduction of purchase prices, but also improvements in the quality of products, improvement of after-sales service, the possibility of a greater range of products, an increase in the number or quality of outlets from which the products may be purchased and quicker delivery.[118]

6.6.3 Criterion 3: Indispensable restrictions

This first negative criterion requires that the anti-competitive activity complained of must not impose on the enterprises affected restrictions that are not indispensable to the attainment of the objectives specified in Article 177(4)(a) RTC. This requires that the anti-competitive effects of the activity in question must not go beyond what is absolutely necessary to achieve the objectives regarded as beneficial. This will be assessed in light of the principle of proportionality. Accordingly, it will be for the enterprise concerned to show that there are no less restrictive alternatives to achieve the benefits that its conduct seeks.

6.6.4 Criterion 4: No possibility of eliminating competition

The second negative criterion is that the anti-competitive activity complained of must not result in eliminating competition in respect of a substantial part of the

115 Commission Decision 75/494/EEC *Kabel und Metallwerke Neumeyer/Luchaire* [1975] OJ L 222/34.

116 Commission Decision 82/123/EC *Vereniging ter Bevordering van het Vlaamse Boekwezen (VBVB) and Vereeniging ter Bevordering van de Belangen des Boekhandels (VBBB)* [1982] OJ L 54/36.

117 European Commission, Guidelines on the Application of [Article 101(3) TFEU] [2004] OJ C 101/97, [85].

118 Ibid., [88]*ff.*

market for the goods or services concerned. The application of this criterion ensures the protection of reasonable rivalry on the relevant market.

The European Commission, in its Guidelines on the Application of [Article 101(3) TFEU], stated that this criterion recognises the importance of rivalry as an essential driver of economic efficiency, including dynamic efficiencies in the shape of innovation. The Guidelines emphasise that:

> "When competition is eliminated the competitive process is brought to an end and short-term efficiency gains are outweighed by longer-term losses stemming inter alia from expenditures incurred by the incumbent to maintain its position (rent seeking), misallocation of resources, reduced innovation and higher prices."[119]

For these reasons, the protection of rivalry must prevail over potentially pro-competitive efficiency gains, which could result from the activity complained of.

In order to apply the second negative criterion, the CCC will have to carry out an economic assessment of the competitive restriction on the relevant geographic and product markets. It will have to assess the degree of competition prior to the existence of the restriction and analyse its impact not only on actual, but also on potential, competitors.

119 Ibid., [105].

7

THE PROHIBITION OF ABUSES OF A DOMINANT POSITION

Chapter contents

7.1 Introduction

Article 177(1)(b) RTC prohibits actions by which an enterprise abuses its dominant position within the Community. Article 177(2) RTC provides some examples of abuse, whilst Article 177(4) sets out exemptions from the prohibition.

Article 178 RTC is entitled 'Determination of Dominant Position'. Article 178(a) sets out factors that will allow the determination of a dominant position, whilst Article 178(b) clarifies the concept of 'interconnected enterprises'. Article 178(b) embodies the doctrine that is known under EU competition law as the doctrine of the 'single economic unit' (see Chapter 4, section 4.6.1). For the purpose of CSME competition law, enterprises are interconnected 'if one of them is a subsidiary of the other or both of them are subsidiaries of the same parent enterprises'. For the purpose of the determination of a dominant position, they will be regarded as one enterprise.

Article 179(1) RTC is entitled 'Abuse of a Dominant Position'. It provides examples, additional to those set out in Article 177(2)(e)–(j) RTC, of possible abuses of a dominant position that result in the frustration of the benefits expected from the establishment of the CSME. Article 179(2) RTC lists factors that should be taken into account when determining whether an enterprise has abused its dominant position, although the factors listed are relevant specifically to the determination of the existence of exclusionary abuses (see section 7.4) rather than to the determination of all possible abuses. Article 179(3) RTC specifies the circumstances in which a dominant enterprise shall not be treated as abusing its dominant position. It is important to note that abusive conduct on the part of a dominant enterprise may also be exempted by the Council for Trade and Economic Development (COTED) under Article 183(2) RTC or by the CARICOM Competition Commission (CCC) if it is within the *de minimis* rule (see Chapter 5, section 5.3.2). Further, when the CCC, under Article 180 RTC, gives a negative clearance ruling in respect of business conduct, its ruling is conclusive, although the Caribbean Court of Justice (CCJ) may, on the application of the CCC, review the Commission's decision in circumstances under which that decision was induced by deceit or improper means (see Chapter 9, section 9.7.2.1).

The structure of Chapter VIII, Part One, of the Revised Treaty of Chaguaramas (RTC) regarding the prohibition of abuses of a dominant position by an enterprise seems rather chaotic. Examples of abuses are scattered between Articles 177(2) and 179(1) RTC. Some examples given in Article 177(2) RTC are repeated in Article 179(1) RTC, such as Article 177(2)(e) RTC and Article 179(1)(f) RTC. Other so-called 'abuses' are the results of abuses rather than abuses *per se*, for example Article 179(1)(a)–(c) RTC (see section 7.7.2.3). Finally, the provisions of the RTC relating to the justifications available to an enterprise in a dominant position for its abusive conduct are unclear.

As can be seen from the above, it is not easy to interpret some of the provisions of the RTC in relation to the prohibition of abusive conduct by a dominant enterprise. It is clear from Chapter VIII, Part One, however, that the RTC prohibits neither a dominant position nor its creation. Once an enterprise is in a dominant position on the relevant market, CSME competition law imposes on it a standard of conduct different from that required of an undertaking that is not in a dominant position. The European Court of Justice (ECJ), when interpreting Article 102 TFEU, which prohibits abuses of a dominant position, emphasised that an undertaking in a dominant position 'has a special responsibility not to allow its conduct to impair genuine undistorted competition on the [internal] market'.[1] When applied to CSME competition law, this means that an enterprise in a dominant position may breach the prohibition if it engages in conduct that, if it were to be carried out by its competitors rather than by it, would be lawful. The imposition of a different standard of conduct on an enterprise in a dominant

1 Case 322/81 *Nederlandische Banden-Industie Michelin NV v Commission (Michelin I)* [1983] ECR 3461, [57].

position from that required of a non-dominant enterprise is explained by the fact that the former has greater capacity to distort competition on the relevant market than the latter.[2] For example, if an enterprise that is not in a dominant position grants loyalty discounts or concessions to its customers on the condition that, over a long period of time, they buy all of their requirements exclusively from it, such practices are normal business practices, which raise no competition law concerns. However, when an enterprise in a dominant position grants similar loyalty discounts or concessions to its customers, its conduct is severely detrimental to the competitive structure of the relevant market. Customers so tied to a dominant enterprise will not purchase from its existing competitors and it will be impossible for potential competitors to enter the relevant market. Accordingly, such practices lead to foreclosure of the relevant market and are unlikely to be justified under either of Articles 177(4) or 179(3) RTC.

In order to show a breach of the prohibition of abuses of a dominant position, it is necessary to establish that (i) an enterprise (for a definition of which, see Chapter 4), (ii) in a dominant position within the Community, (iii) has abused that position, and that (iv) the abuse has appreciable cross-border effects on trade and competition within the Community (see Chapter 5), and that (v) there are no justifications for the abuse.

In examining these elements, reference to EU competition law is useful, particularly in light of the fact that the European Commission has revised its approach to the enforcement of Article 102 TFEU. As a result of the modernisation of EU competition law, which started in the late 1990s and aimed at developing a more economic-based approach to the enforcement of EU competition law (often referred to as the 'effects-based approach'), the main purpose of the enforcement of EU law on the abuse of a dominant position is now the protection of competition by means of ensuring economic efficiency and enhancing consumer welfare. The European Commission's Guidance on the Commission Enforcement Priorities in Applying [Article 102 TFEU] to Abusive Exclusionary Conduct by Dominant Undertakings[3] confirms the applicability of the effects-based approach to the establishment of exclusionary abuses under Article 102 TFEU. It makes clear that, under Article 102 TFEU, there are no *per se* abuses. Additionally, the Guidance establishes a generalised system of justifications for abusive practices.

7.2 The concept of 'dominance'

Article 178(a) RTC defines 'dominance' in the following terms:

2 It is to be noted that the ECJ seems to attach a particular importance to the origin of the dominant position. In Case C-209/10 *Post Danmark A/S v Konkurrencerådet* [2012] ECR I-172, [23] the Court stated that '[w]hen the existence of a dominant position has its origins in a former legal monopoly, that fact has to be taken into account'.

3 [2009] OJ C 45/7 (hereafter 'the Guidance').

> "[A]n enterprise holds a dominant position in a market if by itself or together with an interconnected enterprise, it occupies such a position of economic strength as will enable it to operate in the market without effective constraints from its competitors or potential competitors."

According to this definition, for dominance to exist, the enterprise concerned must not be subject to effective competitive constraints.

The Article mentions two such constraints: first, from existing competitors; and second, from potential competitors – that is, from potential entry by new competitors on the relevant market and from expansion by existing ones. It is submitted that, in addition to these constraints, in the assessment of dominance, the CCC will be likely to take account of constraints imposed by the bargaining power of the undertaking's customers (that is, of countervailing buyer power).

For detailed treatment of how an enforcement authority identifies whether an enterprise has market power and thus is in a dominant position on the relevant market, see Chapter 2, section 2.5.1.

7.2.1 Collective dominance

Under EU law, the main reason for introducing the concept of 'collective dominance' was to combat tacit collusion, which, although it may take place in any kind of market, typically occurs in an oligopoly.

Firms in an oligopolistic market are, at the same time, both independent from each other and interdependent. In such a market, a firm is always unsure as to what will be the impact of another firm's change in market conduct, bearing in mind that decisions of one firm have consequences for all. Accordingly, in such a market, there is a strong incentive to minimise, by explicitly or tacitly colluding with competitors, the uncertainty that all firms face.[4] As a result of the fact that the number of firms in such a market is limited, each firm, after a period of repeated action, will become conscious of other firms' pricing strategies and other competitive parameters, such as output, capacity, investment and advertisement, and may consciously align its own strategy with those of its competitors. Accordingly, without any need to communicate with each other, firms in an oligopolistic market may act as one entity on the relevant market by consciously aligning their strategies to gain monopolistic profits. There is a debate as to whether this tacit collusion, also known as 'conscious parallelism', should be within the scope of competition law. On the one hand, it can be said that to require firms operating in an oligopolistic market to ignore conduct of their competitors would amount to requiring them to act irrationally, bearing in

4 The patterns of behaviour of oligopolists have been analysed in terms of game theory (and prisoner's dilemma). On this topic, see M. Franzosi, 'Oligopoly and the Prisoner's Dilemma: Concerted Practices and "as if" Behaviour' (1988) 9 ECLR 385.

mind their interdependence (see below). On the other hand, tacit collusion, like any form of collusion, generates large welfare losses and, for that reason, needs to be addressed by competition authorities. The European Commission tried to tackle this situation by establishing the concept of 'collective dominance'.

In EU law, tacit collusion in an oligopolistic market is dealt with under Article 102 TFEU. It was possible to establish the concept of collective dominance by giving a wide interpretation to Article 102 TFEU, which prohibits the abuse of a dominant position 'by one or more undertakings'. Under a wide interpretation, it can be said that Article 102 TFEU applies not only to interconnected undertakings, but also to legally and economically independent undertakings when they collectively control the relevant market, and thus hold a collective dominant position. The General Court in *Italian Flat Glass*[5] relied on the wording of Articles 102 and 101(1) TFEU, which refer to more than one undertaking, when it stated that:

> "[T]here is no legal or economic reason to suppose that the term 'undertaking' in Article [102 TFEU] has a different meaning from the one given to it in the context of Article [101 TFEU]. There is nothing, in principle, to prevent two or more independent economic entities from being, on a specific market, united by such economic links that, by virtue of that fact, together they hold a dominant position vis-à-vis the other operators on the same market."[6]

Indeed, Article 102 TFEU seems to be suitable to deal with tacit collusion of oligopolies.

Additionally, under EU law, in the *Wood Pulp* cases,[7] the ECJ closed the door on the possibility of applying Article 101 TFEU to tacit collusion by allowing reliance on the so-called 'oligopoly defence'(see Chapter 6, section 6.3.3.2). The Court clearly established that parallel conduct cannot be regarded as furnishing proof of concertation unless concertation constitutes the only plausible explanation of such conduct. In this case, it stated that 'the parallelism of prices and the price trends may be satisfactorily explained by the oligopolistic tendencies of the market'.[8] The failure of Article 101 TFEU to apply to tacit collusion in oligopolistic markets, combined with the fact that Article 102 expressly refers to 'one or more undertakings', resulted in the establishment of the concept of collective dominance.

5 Joined Cases T-68/89, T-77/89 and T-78/89 *Società Italiana Vetro SpA, Fabbrica Pisana SpA and PPG Vernante Pennitalia SpA v Commission* [1992] ECR II-1403.

6 Ibid., [358].

7 Joined Cases C-89/85, C-104/85, C-114/85, C-116/85, C-117/85 and C-125/85 to C-129/85 *A. Ahlström Osakeyhtiö and ors v Commission* [1993] ECR I-1307.

8 Ibid., [126].

In the context of CSME competition law, the following questions arise: whether tacit collusion in an oligopolistic market should be addressed by the CCC; if so, whether the RTC allows the establishment of the concept of collective dominance; and how to prove the existence of tacit collusion. These questions are examined below.

1. Whether tacit collusion in an oligopolistic market should be addressed by the CCC? With regard to the first matter, it is submitted that, bearing in mind that many markets in the Community are oligopolistic, the CCC must address tacit collusion and deal with situations in which competitors in an oligopolistic market achieve cartel-like effects by tacitly co-ordinating their conduct on the relevant market. This view is supported by Petit,[9] who first accepts that, even though tacit collusion in an oligopolistic market is rare, it needs to be dealt with, bearing in mind its effects on society. He compares the tacit collusion of oligopolistic firms with such events as 'terrorist attacks, nuclear meltdowns and systematic financial crisis', which, although rare, result in immense welfare losses for society, and the prevention or correction of which cannot be challenged by any reasonable person.

   Second, Petit challenges the view that competition law should not apply to tacit collusion among oligopolists because tacit collusion involves rational conduct. He attacks this view on two bases: flawed moral justifications and remedial concerns.

   (a) With regard to moral justifications, Petit rightly points out that the justification for tacit collusion based on the fact that the structure of the market is such that oligopolists have no rational choice but to collude, should be rejected. This is because competition law prohibits market conduct that, despite being entirely rational, has the effect of distorting competition, for example the rational conduct of a dominant firm that has the effect of forcing equally efficient rivals from the market. Thus rationality cannot constitute a defence under competition law. Further, Petit cites Posner, who observes that tacit collusion is a strategy that an oligopolist deliberately chooses. Finally, Petit points out that oligopolists often take additional measures to facilitate, adjust and protect situations of tacit collusion. Accordingly, he states that 'depicting oligopolists as passive spectators of tacitly collusive dynamics is a fraud'.[10]
   (b) With regard to remedial concerns – that is, the submission that there are no workable remedies applicable to tacit collusion[11] – Petit points out that

9 N. Petit, 'The Oligopoly Problem in EU Competition Law', in I. Lianos and D. Geradin (eds) *Handbook on European Competition Law: Substantive Aspects*, 2013, Cheltenham: Edward Elgar, ch. 7.

10 Ibid., p 281.

11 OECD, *Note by the US Department of Justice and the US Federal Trade Commission: Mini-Roundtable on Oligopoly*, 30 April 1999, DAFFE/CLP/WD(99)13.

this matter is relevant to the enforcement of US anti-trust law under section 1 of the Sherman Act, which condemns any contract, combination or conspiracy in restraint of trade, and which may be applied to tacit collusion.[12] US courts, which are the primary enforcers of the Sherman Act, can issue injunctions and impose sanctions, but cannot pronounce remedies.[13] This is not the case in the European Union, where the European Commission has at its disposal a wide range of behavioural and structural remedies, in addition to orders to cease and desist. With regard to remedies, Petit emphasises that, because tacit collusion has a variety of causes, a large variety of remedies should be used by enforcement authorities to fight and prevent tacit collusion. Accordingly, they should disregard the simplistic, 'one size fits all' approach of the Harvard school, which advocates the application of only structural remedies, such as deconcentration measures and structural divestitures, and should instead attack the causes of tacit collusion on a case-by-case basis.[14]

2. If the answer to the first question is in the affirmative, whether the RTC allows the establishment of the concept of collective dominance? With regard to the second matter, it is to be noted that Articles 177(1)(b) and 178(a) RTC state that only one enterprise can be in a dominant position on the relevant market, and thus the concept of 'collective dominance' cannot be implied from these provisions. It may, however, be introduced by:

   (a) interpreting Articles 177(1)(b) and 178(a) RTC in light of the objectives of CSME competition law, which entails that it will be contrary to the objectives of the RTC to ignore a situation in which a number of enterprises present themselves on the market as a single entity rather than separate entities, and thus hold a collective dominant position on that market, with a view to collectively abusing it to the detriment of consumers;
   (b) interpreting the concept of a concerted practice in such a way as to include tacit collusion; and/or
   (c) relying on Article 177(1)(c) RTC, which states that CSME competition law applies not only to anti-competitive agreements, decisions, concerted practices and abuses of a dominant position, but also to 'any other like conduct by enterprises whose object or effect is to frustrate the benefits expected from the establishment of the CSME'.

12 On existing and proposed approaches to the suitable evidentiary standards for finding that conscious parallelism constitutes a violation of §1 of the Sherman Act, see W. E. Kovacic, R. C. Marshall, L. M. Marx and H. L. White, 'Plus Factors and Agreement in Antitrust Law' (2011) 110 Mich L Rev 393.

13 OECD, op. cit.

14 See also R. H. Bork, *The Antitrust Paradox: A Policy at War with Itself*, 2nd edn, 1993, New York: The Free Press, pp 178–196. Bork notes that the negative impact of structural remedies on efficiency of firms may consist of hampering economies of scale or scope or of depriving firms of the minimum efficient size.

It is submitted that the third of these approaches would be the least controversial, and the most appropriate, to deal with tacit collusion of oligopolists. Indeed, the purpose of Article 177(1)(c) RTC is to catch all anti-competitive conduct that does not fit into the categories of either prohibited agreements, decisions and concerted practices or abuses by a dominant enterprise.

3. How to prove the existence of tacit collusion? The third and final matter is the most challenging, bearing in mind that a situation of tacit collusion can be established only by economic circumstantial evidence.

   Under EU law, the General Court in *Airtours*[15] set out three cumulative conditions necessary for a finding of collective dominance:

   "(a) mutual awareness on the part of the colluding parties concerning the adoption and execution of the common policy;
   (b) sustainability, which means that there must be a retaliatory mechanism put in place that secures unity within an oligopoly and thus dissuades its members from deviating from their common policy adopted in the relevant market; and
   (c) an absence of competitive constraints, so allowing undertakings within a dominant oligopoly to act independently of their customers and consumers, actual or potential."

   With regards to the second of these points, on the retaliatory mechanism, the General Court understands retaliation not as a punishment mechanism, but as referring to:

   > ". . . adequate deterrents to ensure that there is a long-term incentive in not departing from the common policy, which means that each member of the dominant oligopoly must be aware that highly competitive action on its part designed to increase its market share would provoke identical action by the others, so that it would derive no benefit from its initiative."[16]

   If there is any agreed punishment mechanism, then it evidences the existence of a cartel and thus entails the application of Article 101 TFEU

It is important to note that, under EU competition law, the concept of collective dominance has been developed and applied mainly in the context of the control of mergers. Therefore some scholars have challenged the suitability of its application to Article 102 TFEU proceedings.[17] However, the EU courts have

15 Case T-342/99 *Airtours plc v Commission* [2002] ECR II-2585.

16 Ibid., [62]. This was clearly stated in Case T-193/02 *Laurent Piau v Commission* [2005] ECR II-209, [111].

17 See J. Temple Lang, 'Oligopolies and Joint Dominance in Community Anti-Trust Law' (2002) 26 Fordham Corporate Law Institute 269, 314.

confirmed that the concept of collective dominance has the same meaning under the EU Merger Regulation[18] as it does under Article 102 TFEU.[19]

To conclude on the topic of the EU experience of tackling situations of tacit collusion under the concept of collective dominance, the following points can be made. First, as Petit points out, there has been no case under Article 102 TFEU in which tacit collusion alone has been held to constitute the sufficient element required for the establishment of a collective dominant position.[20] This is mainly because the European Commission has shown an 'enduring' disinterest in using the concept to fight tacit collusion; instead, it focuses on the prevention of tacit collusion situations by having recourse either to the EU Merger Regulation or to sector-specific regulatory frameworks.

Second, under Article 102 TFEU, the concept of collective dominance has been used in respect of market settings remote from oligopolistic tacit collusion. For example, in *Piau*,[21] which has no connection with any situation of tacit collusion, the General Court found that the Commission was wrong in deciding that the Fédération Internationale de Football Association (FIFA), a Swiss-based association, the members of which are national associations of professional and amateur football clubs, did not hold a collective dominant position in the market for players' agents' services. FIFA could be regarded as acting on behalf of football clubs, which, by virtue of their membership of FIFA and the fact that they were required to follow FIFA's regulations under threat of being excluded from the market, held a collective dominant position on that market. Therefore the collective dominant position was based on the links between FIFA and its members, which had to implement its regulations. Although the Court decided that the three conditions set out in *Airtours* were satisfied,[22] it did not find that FIFA had abused its position of collective dominance.

It is submitted that, in the context of CSME competition law, Article 177(1)(c) RTC may be used to establish the concept of collective dominance. The main purpose of using that Article would be to attack the conduct of independent enterprises in circumstances under which they are connected by some economic or contractual links, such as interlocking directorships or cross-shareholdings, and thus present themselves on the relevant market as a collective entity. The EU experience shows that the concept of collective dominance is not the preferred

18 Council Regulation 139/2004 on the Control of Concentrations between Undertakings [2004] OJ L 24/1.

19 Case T-193/02 *Laurent Piau v Commission* [2005] ECR II-209; Case C-413/06P *Bertelsmann AG and Sony Corporation of America v Independent Music Publishers and Labels Association (Impala)* [2008] ECR I-4951.

20 N. Petit, 'The Oligopoly Problem in EU Competition Law', in I. Lianos and D. Geradin (eds) *Handbook on European Competition Law: Substantive Aspects*, 2013, Cheltenham: Edward Elgar, p 306.

21 Case T-193/02 *Laurent Piau v Commission* [2005] ECR II-209.

22 Case T-342/99 *Airtours v Commission* [2002] ECR II-2585, [111]–[116].

means by which the European Commission deals with a situation of tacit collusion of oligopolists. The European Commission clearly prefers to take preventive measures to deal with situations of tacit collusion – namely, to act under the Merger Regulation to ensure that a proposed merger will not create or exacerbate a situation of tacit collusion. With regard to the CCC, it is expected that merger control provisions will be introduced into CSME competition law (see Chapter 9, section 9.5). In addition, it should not be forgotten that, under Article 173(2)(b) RTC, the CCC is required to keep Community competition policy under review and to make recommendations to COTED to enhance its effectiveness. Accordingly, the CCC should investigate sectors of the economy that are dominated by oligopolies and then, if appropriate, make recommendations to COTED for necessary adjustments. Obviously, there is no easy answer as to how to deal with the existing situations of tacit collusion. The EU's experience, although discouraging, may nevertheless serve as a basis for discussion, in particular helping to establish the factors that will show that it is more likely than not that the collective dominance position of enterprises operating in an oligopolistic market has resulted from tacit collusion.

7.3 The concept of 'abuse'

The RTC does not provide a definition of abuse. However, Article 179(2) RTC lists factors that will be taken into account in determining whether an abuse exists. These are economic factors and it is therefore submitted that economists will be the persons best qualified to establish an abuse. Reliance on economic factors means that bad faith, or subjective, intent of a dominant undertaking to distort competition will be irrelevant for the establishment of an abuse. Further, the economic approach to enforcing the prohibition of abuses of a dominant position will highlight the importance of the purpose of the prohibition. In this respect, it is submitted that the CCC is likely to follow the European Commission with regard to the determination of the purpose of prohibition. Under EU law, the purpose of Article 102 TFEU is to protect the competitive process for the benefit of consumers rather than competitors. This entails that competitors that are not as efficient as a dominant undertaking are not protected by Article 102 TFEU.

It is important to note that Article 179(2) RTC will be of relevance to the determination of the existence of some abuses of a dominant position. Abuses such as refusal of access to networks or essential infrastructure, or the making by a dominant enterprise of misleading representations to patent authorities and national courts to block or delay its competitors from market entry for generic versions of pharmaceutical products,[23] are not amenable to examination under

23 Case T-321/05 *AstraZeneca AB and AstraZeneca plc (AZ) v Commission* [2010] ECR II-2805.

Article 179(2) RTC. Accordingly, it is expected that the CCJ, in due course, will provide a comprehensive definition of an abuse.

It is to be noted that the ECJ defined the concept of an abuse in *Hoffmann-La Roche*[24] as:

> ". . . an objective concept relating to the behaviour of an undertaking in a dominant position which is such as to influence the structure of a market where, as the result of the very presence of the undertaking in question, the degree of competition is weakened and which, through recourse to methods different from those which condition normal competition in products or services on the basis of the transactions of commercial operators, has the effect of hindering the maintenance of the degree of competition still existing in the market or the growth of that competition."[25]

The case law of the ECJ on the concept of abuse can be summarised as follows.

1. In *Hoffmann-La Roche*, the ECJ held that the concept of abuse is an objective concept. This means that, in general, bad faith, or a subjective, intent of a dominant undertaking to distort competition is irrelevant for the application of Article 102 TFEU,[26] although in some circumstances intent can be used as evidence of an abuse (see section 7.4.1.1). Further, conduct of an undertaking in a dominant position may be found abusive even when such conduct did not bring any financial or competitive advantage to the undertaking concerned. For example, in *1998 Football World Cup*,[27] the European Commission found a French body that had been in charge of organising the 1998 World Cup to be in breach of Article 102 TFEU for distributing tickets in a manner that discriminated against fans who were not French. This practice did not bring any commercial or other advantage to that body.
2. Under Article 102 TFEU, a dominant undertaking is allowed to compete on the merits, but is not allowed to use methods that are different from those governing normal competition in products and services based on traders' performance.[28] This means that only 'abnormal' conduct of a dominant undertaking is prohibited. The difficulty here is how to define what constitutes 'normal' conduct – that is, how to establish an appropriate benchmark to decide whether a dominant undertaking competes on the

24 Case 85/76 *Hoffmann-La Roche & Co. AG v Commission* [1979] ECR 461.
25 Ibid., [91].
26 Case T-321/05 *AstraZeneca AB and AstraZeneca plc (AZ) v Commission* [2010] ECR II-2805, [2010] CMLR 1585.
27 Commission Decision 2000/12/EC *1998 Football World Cup* [2000] OJ L 5/55.
28 See Case 322/81 *NV Nederlandsche Banden Industrie Michelin v Commission (Michelin I)* [1983] ECR 3461.

merits. In this respect, economists have proposed a number of tests, such as the 'as efficient competitor' test, the 'profit sacrifice' test, the 'consumer welfare balancing' test and the 'no economic sense' test.[29] The European Commission's Guidance endorses these tests.

3. The ECJ in *Michelin I*[30] held that an undertaking in a dominant position has a 'special responsibility' towards the competitive process. It stated that:

    > "A finding that an undertaking has a dominant position is not in itself a recrimination but simply means that, irrespective of the reason for which it has such a dominant position, the undertaking concerned has a special responsibility not to allow its conduct to impair genuine undistorted competition on the common market."[31]

4. In reforming the enforcement of Article 102 TFEU, the European Commission and the ECJ have emphasised that the purpose of Article 102 TFEU is to protect the competitive process for the benefit of consumers rather than competitors.[32] This entails that competitors that are not as efficient as a dominant undertaking are not protected by Article 102 TFEU.
5. In order to establish the existence of an abuse, it is sufficient to show that the practice has a potential anti-competitive effect. It is not necessary to show that the practice has actual anti-competitive effect.[33]
6. Article 102 TFEU applies only when an abuse committed by a dominant undertaking has an appreciable effect on trade between Member States (see Chapter 5, section 5.3).
7. Article 102 TFEU applies to a situation in which an undertaking is in a dominant position in one market, but commits an abuse in a different market in which it is not dominant (see sections 7.7.2.2, 7.4.2.1, 7.4.1.3 and 7.4.2.3B).

7.3.1 Categories of abuse

Article 177(2)(f)–(j) RTC provides examples of abuses. Further, Article 179(1) RTC states that, subject to Article 179(2) RTC – that is, subject to the determination that an abuse exists – an enterprise abuses its dominant position when, for example, it restricts the entry of any enterprise into a market, or eliminates or removes any enterprise from a market. These so called 'abuses' listed in Article 179(1)(a)–(c) RTC seem to be consequences of a particular practice of

29 See A. Jones and B. Sufrin, *EU Competition Law*, 4th edn, 2011, Oxford: OUP, p 371.

30 Case 322/81 *NV Nederlandsche Banden Industrie Michelin v Commission (Michelin I)* [1983] ECR 3461.

31 Ibid., [57].

32 See Case C-209/10 *Post Danmark A/S v Konkurrencerådet* (ECJ, 27 March 2012), [21]–[22].

33 Case C-280/08 P *Deutsche Telekom v Commission* [2010] ECR I-9555.

a dominant enterprise rather than abuses in the strict sense. If an efficient enterprise, as a result of its superior performance, eliminates competitors from the relevant market, there is no abuse of a dominant position. Perhaps this is what prompted the drafters of the RTC to insert Article 179(3)(c) RTC, which states that a dominant undertaking does not abuse its position on the market when 'the effect or likely effect of its behavior on the market is the result of superior competitive performance of the enterprises concerned' (see section 7.7.2.3).

Most commentators categorise abuses as follows:

- exclusionary abuses are aimed at foreclosing the relevant market;
- exploitative abuses occur when an undertaking is, at the expense of customers or consumers, using its economic power to obtain benefits, or to impose burdens, which are not obtainable, or imposable, within normal competition on the merits; and
- discriminatory prices. These occur when a dominant undertaking treats its customers in a dissimilar manner without costs-based or legally acceptable justification.

An abuse may be, at the same time, exploitative, exclusionary, and discriminatory at the same time.

7.4 Exclusionary abuses

With regard to exclusionary abuses, the European Commission's Guidance is very instructive. It is likely, at the least, to serve as a useful document to stimulate debate within the CCC on how to enforce the prohibition of abuses of a dominant position by enterprises. Alternatively, the CCC may simply follow some of the Guidance's suggested solutions, given that it incorporates sound economic-based principles and that the economic approach to the enforcement of the prohibition of abuses by dominant enterprises has been recognised by Article 179(2) RTC. For that reason, exclusionary abuses are examined here in light of the European Commission's Guidance.

It is important to note that the Guidance is not a binding document. The ECJ has exclusive jurisdiction to interpret Article 102 TFEU. Further, when drafting the Guidance, the European Commission was, to some extent, a 'prisoner' of the formalistic case law of the ECJ, and thus drafted it in a cautious manner to ensure that its decisions subsequent to the adoption of the Guidance would not become subject to successful appeals. No such restrictions are imposed on the CCC, which has the advantage not only of taking account of the experience of the European Union in the enforcement of Article 102 TFEU, but also of the opportunity to choose the most suitable approach to the enforcement of CSME competition law without any historic constraints.

The Guidance defines anti-competitive foreclosure as a situation in which:

> "... effective access of actual or potential competitors to supplies or markets is hampered or eliminated as a result of the conduct of the dominant undertaking whereby the dominant undertaking is likely to be in a position to profitably increase prices to the detriment of consumers."[34]

This definition encompasses two elements, as follows.

- Foreclosure. The concept of foreclosure is understood as a situation in which 'access of actual or potential competitors to supplies or markets is hampered or eliminated'. To prove anti-competitive foreclosure, the Commission must establish that foreclosure has actually occurred or is likely to occur. The Guidance states that, in deciding whether the allegedly abusive conduct is likely to lead to anti-competitive foreclosure, the Commission must submit cogent and convincing evidence.[35] It goes on to list factors which will be taken into account in the determination of a credible risk of foreclosure.[36] Those factors are:

    - the position, on the relevant market, of the dominant undertaking;
    - the conditions on the relevant market;
    - the position of the dominant undertaking's competitors;
    - the position of the customers or input suppliers – that is, those with which the dominant undertaking has concluded exclusive supplies arrangements;
    - the extent of the alleged abusive conduct;
    - possible evidence of actual foreclosure; and
    - direct evidence of any exclusionary strategy.

  However, in some situations – that is, those in which anti-competitive conduct may be inferred – the Commission will not carry out a detailed assessment of the likely consumer harm caused by anti-competitive conduct based on the listed factors. This occurs in particular, 'if it appears that the conduct can only raise obstacles to competition and that it creates no efficiencies'.[37] The Guidance provides two examples of conduct that it considers to be within this category: when a dominant undertaking prevents its customers from testing the products of competitors (either by making this a condition of sale or by offering payment not to test competitors' products); and when a dominant undertaking pays a distributor or a customer to delay the introduction of a competitor's product.
- Consumer harm. This occurs when a dominant undertaking 'is likely to be in position to profitably increase prices, to the detriment of consumers' once its competitors are eliminated. The concept of 'consumer harm' is the main

34 The Guidance, [19].
35 Ibid., [20].
36 Ibid.
37 Ibid., [22].

> factor distinguishing anti-competitive foreclosure from foreclosure arising from competition 'on the merits'. The exclusion of competitors, being a preliminary step to the exploitation of consumers, is therefore a key element in the assessment of adverse impact on consumer welfare.

The Guidance distinguishes between 'price-based' and 'non-price-based' exclusionary conduct of a dominant undertaking.

7.4.1 Price-based exclusionary conduct and the 'as efficient competitor' test

The Guidance states that the European Commission will intervene 'where the conduct concerned has already been or is capable of hampering competition from competitors which are considered to be as efficient as the dominant undertaking'.[38] This indicates that the Commission will use the test of hypothetical rivals that are 'as efficient' as the dominant undertaking – the so-called 'as efficient competitor' (AEC) test – in order to determine whether the price-based conduct of a dominant undertaking leads to foreclosure. If a rival is less efficient, the Commission will normally assume that foreclosure results from mere competition on merits and thus is not anti-competitive. However, this is subject to an exception. In some circumstances, the Commission will depart from the AEC test, such as when the relevant market is one in which network and/or learning effects are important.[39] In such a situation, the European Commission will use the hypothetical 'prospective entrant' standard.

Departures from the AEC test have been criticised as introducing uncertainty in that a dominant undertaking will not be able to assess whether its conduct is potentially exclusionary and this may lead to it adopting an overly cautious response to competition, which might result in higher prices for consumers. Further, some authors have criticised the use of the AEC test on the basis that failure to protect a less efficient rival may have negative effects on consumers. The presence of a less efficient rival on the market may constitute a competitive constraint on the market power of a dominant undertaking, and thus prevent it from raising prices and reducing consumer surplus.[40]

38 Ibid., [23].

39 Network effects occur when the value of a product or service increases as the number of users increases. The classical example is a telephone: the more people who have them, the greater the number of possible calls that an individual user can make, and the more valuable the telephone becomes to that user and to all other users. Other examples are online social media such as Twitter, Facebook and Google+. Learning effects entail that the value that customers attach to a durable, reusable product rises over time as they become acquainted with it. In order to switch to another product, they have to undertake a costly training investment.

40 I. Lianos, 'The Price/Non-Price Exclusionary Abuses Dichotomy: A Critical Appraisal' (2009) 2 Concurrences Review, available at http://papers.ssrn.com/sol3/papers.cfm?abstract_id=1398943 [accessed 27 February 2014].

In order to determine whether a hypothetical rival is as efficient as a dominant undertaking, the European Commission will examine economic data relating to cost and sale prices. This will require detailed analyses of sufficiently reliable data. The Guidance states that, 'where available, the Commission will use information on the costs of the dominant undertaking itself'.[41]

The Guidance identifies two cost benchmarks for determining whether a dominant undertaking's pricing should be regarded as exclusionary:

- the average avoidable cost (AAC);[42] and
- the long-run average incremental cost (LRAIC).[43]

The Guidance explains that failure to cover the AAC indicates that the dominant undertaking is sacrificing profits in the short term (that is, that the undertaking is not recovering its fixed and variable costs) and that an equally efficient rival could not serve the targeted customers without incurring a loss.[44] The LRAIC is usually above the AAC. This is because, in contrast to the AAC (which includes only fixed costs incurred during the period under examination), the LRAIC includes product-specific fixed costs incurred before the period during which allegedly abusive conduct took place. Failure to cover the LRAIC indicates that the dominant undertaking is not recovering all of the (attributable) fixed costs of producing the goods or services in question and that an equally efficient competitor could be eliminated from the market.

7.4.1.1 Predatory pricing

Article 177(2)(g) RTC states that predatory pricing constitutes an abuse under CSME competition law. 'Predatory pricing' refers to a situation in which a dominant undertaking sets prices below costs over a long enough period of time that it can drive competitors out of the market or obstruct potential competitors from entering the market, with the objective of solidifying its market position and obtaining long-term profit. The practice is profitable because a dominant undertaking, after predation, can recoup its short-term lost profits (referred to as

41 The Guidance, [25].
42 AAC is the average of the costs that could have been avoided if the undertaking had not produced a discrete amount of (extra) output that is allegedly the subject of abusive conduct. In most cases, AAC and the average variable cost (AVC) are the same. AVC is calculated as a firm's variable costs, such as the costs of input or energy used in the production process, divided by the quantity of output produced. Average fixed costs are calculated as the fixed costs of production, such as property taxes and rents, divided by the quantity of output produced.
43 In the Guidance, fn 18, the Commission defines LRAIC as 'the average of all the (variable and fixed) costs that a company incurs to produce a particular product'.
44 The Guidance, [26].

'sacrifice'), and obtain a long-term profit, by raising and maintaining anti-competitive prices, thereby causing consumer harm.

The Guidance provides that the Commission will take the AAC[45] as a starting point in the assessment of whether the dominant undertaking incurred or is incurring losses. Charging prices below the AAC will be indicative of sacrifice and therefore such prices will be predatory. If prices are above the AAC, but below the LRAIC, the Commission will assess, on a case-by-case basis, whether there is evidence of a predatory strategy on the part of the undertaking concerned. Prices above the LRAIC will normally not amount to predatory prices capable of foreclosing competition.

The contentious matter relating to predation relates to recoupment – that is, the ability of a dominant undertaking to obtain additional profits that more than offset sacrifices stemming from predatory pricing. It is accepted by economists that predation makes sense only if the alleged predator expects to recoup short-term losses that it has incurred in the form of the long-term profits to be earned once its rivals are destroyed.[46] Despite the views of economists, under Article 102 TFEU, recoupment is not required for establishing predatory conduct.[47] This differs from the position of US anti-trust law, which requires recoupment for a finding of predatory pricing.[48]

7.4.1.2 Loyalty discounts or concessions

Loyalty discounts and concessions are prohibited under Article 177(2)(i) RTC. However, rebates that do not induce loyalty are not in themselves in breach of CSME competition law. They constitute a form of price competition and encourage a customer to do business with a supplier on a long-term basis. However, discounts or concessions that seek to tie dealers to an enterprise in a dominant position by granting advantages that are not based on a countervailing economic advantage, and act to prevent those dealers from obtaining their supplies from the enterprise's competitors, will infringe Article 177(2)(i) RTC. Such rebates are loyalty-inducing rebates and have exclusionary effect.

45 AAC is normally identical to AVC, but in some situations AAC will capture costs that are fixed. The following example illustrates this point. If a firm decides to expand its production and purchases a licence to use a particular patent, this will not be part of AVC because the cost of purchase does not vary with output. Accordingly, the increase in fixed costs attributable to acquisition of the licence is avoidable and thus will be part of AAC.

46 See S. Bishop and M. Walker, *The Economics of EC Competition Law: Concepts, Application and Measurement*, 3rd edn, 2010, London: Sweet and Maxwell, pp 308–310.

47 See Case C-202/07 *France Telecom SA v Commission* [2009] ECR I-2369, [113]; Commission Decision COMP/38.233 *Wanadoo Interactive* [2005] 5 CMLR 120, [335].

48 *Pacific Bell Telephone v. LinkLine Communications Inc.*, 555 US 438 (2009).

The European Commission's Guidance makes clear that it will intervene if rebates are likely to lead to anti-competitive foreclosure of actual or potential competitors 'as efficient' as a dominant undertaking.[49] It also lists factors that it will take into account when analysing potential anti-competitive foreclosure.[50] The Guidance makes a distinction between single-product rebates and multi-product, or 'bundle', rebates. Bundle rebates are discussed in the Guidance in respect of tying, but it seems appropriate to examine them in this section.

With regard to single-product rebates, the Commission will use the 'effective price' test (a variant of the AEC test) to determine what effective price a competitor would have to offer in order to compensate a customer for the loss of rebates if the customer were to switch part of its demand (referred in the Guidance as the 'relevant range') within the relevant time period to a competitor of the dominant undertaking. The Guidance states that:

> "The effective price that the competitor will have to match is not the average price of the dominant undertaking, but the normal (list) price less the rebate the customer loses by switching, calculated over the relevant range of sales and in the relevant period of time."[51]

The Guidance makes a distinction between a 'non-contestable portion' and a 'contestable portion' of the demand of each customer. The 'non-contestable portion' of the demand refers to the amount that a customer would, in any event, purchase from the dominant undertaking because there is no proper substitute, whilst a 'contestable portion' refers to the portion of the customer's demand for which substitutes are available elsewhere.

The determination of the relevant range depends on the facts of each case and whether a conditional rebate is incremental (given on purchases made in excess of those required to achieve the threshold) or retroactive (given retrospectively on all purchases made in the reference period after the threshold is reached). For incremental rebates, the relevant range is normally the incremental purchases that the customer is considering making from an undertaking that competes with the dominant undertaking. For retroactive rebates, it will generally be relevant to assess, in the specific market context, how much of a customer's purchase requirements can realistically be switched to a competitor (that is, the 'contestable portion').

49 The Guidance attempts to respond to the criticism of the ECJ's approach to rebates and discounts, which treats them as abuses *per se* on the ground that they have exclusionary capabilities, instead of examining their effect on the relevant market. On this topic, see H. Zenger, 'Loyalty Rebates and the Competitive Process' (2012) 8 J Comp L & Econ 717; J. Temple Lang, 'How Can the Problem of Exclusionary Abuses under Article 102 TFEU be Resolved?' (2012) 37 EL Rev 136.

50 The Guidance, [38]*ff.*

51 Ibid., [41].

The European Commission will not intervene if the effective price – that is, the price charged by a competitor for the relevant range – is higher than or equal to the dominant undertaking's LRAIC for the relevant range. If the effective price is below the LRAIC of the dominant undertaking, the rebate scheme is likely to foreclose an equally efficient competitor. If the effective price is between the AAC and the LRAIC, the European Commission will examine additional factors to establish whether the rebate scheme will affect entry and expansion of an as efficient competitor. In this respect, the Guidance states:

> [T]he Commission will investigate whether and to what extent competitors have realistic and effective counterstrategies at their disposal, for instance their capacity to also use a 'non contestable' portion of their buyers' demand as leverage to decrease the price for the relevant range. Where competitors do not have such counterstrategies at their disposal, the Commission will consider that the rebate scheme is capable of foreclosing equally efficient competitors.[52]

With regard to bundle rebates, the Guidance states that the Commission will not intervene if the incremental price that customers pay for each of the dominant undertaking's products in the bundle, including the bundled product, remains above the LRAIC of the dominant undertaking.[53]

7.4.1.3 Margin, or price, squeeze

The RTC does not mention the so-called 'margin squeeze', also known as a 'price squeeze'. However, Article 179(d) RTC, as well as Article 179(1)(g) RTC, cover this kind of abuse.

A margin squeeze leads to anti-competitive foreclosure when a dominant enterprise in an upstream market that supplies goods or services to its rivals, who use them to compete with that dominant enterprise in one or more downstream markets, squeezes its downstream rivals by charging prices that do not allow rivals as efficient as the dominant enterprise to make a living profit. As a result of the upstream price (which is set by the dominant enterprise), the prevailing price in the downstream market is such that a rival or potential rival is forced out of the downstream market.

The Guidance treats margin squeezes and refusals to supply as one and the same thing. However, the ECJ, in *Deutsche Telecom*[54] and *TeliaSonera*,[55] confirmed that a margin squeeze is an entirely separate abuse – that is, that it is independent

52 Ibid., [44].
53 Ibid., [60].
54 Case C-280/08P *Deutsche Telekom AG v Commission* [2010] ECR I-9555.
55 Case C-52/09 *Konkurrensverket v TeliaSonera Sverige AB* [2011] ECR I-527.

from refusal to supply. In *TeliaSonera*, the ECJ provided a test for determining the circumstances in which a margin squeeze will constitute an abuse. The ECJ used the AEC test to determine the level of margin squeeze of competitors. It accepted the proposition that unlawful margin squeeze takes place in a situation in which competitors would need to offer goods or services either at a loss or 'at artificially reduced levels of profitability'. The Court also established that it is necessary to demonstrate the anti-competitive effect, at least the potential anti-competitive effect, of the practice on the relevant market. The Court found that, when establishing whether a margin squeeze infringes Article 102 TFEU:

- it is irrelevant whether the dominant undertaking is dominant in the downstream market;
- it is irrelevant whether the dominant undertaking has a legal obligation to supply its downstream competitors;
- it is irrelevant whether customers to whom the margin squeeze is applied are new or existing customers of the dominant undertaking;
- the degree of dominance is irrelevant;
- the inability by a dominant undertaking to recoup losses is irrelevant; and
- the fact that the relevant market concerns new technology, as opposed to established technology, is irrelevant.

7.4.2 Non-price-based exclusionary conduct

Examples of non-price-based exclusionary conduct include tying and bundling, exclusive dealing, and refusal to deal, or to continue to deal, with existing and potential customers. Each of these is considered in turn below.

7.4.2.1 Tying and bundling

Tying and bundling, both of which lead to anti-competitive foreclosure, are examples of exclusionary vertical restraints prohibited by Article 177(2)(j) RTC.

In tying arrangements, an enterprise obliges customers to purchase not only the one product or service that they want to purchase, but also an additional item, or items, or service, whether they want to do so or not. Thus the purchase of the main product or service (the 'tying product') is conditional upon the purchase of another product or service (the 'tied product'). In bundling, the additional product is already incorporated into the main product. In both tying and bundling, the customer has no choice other than to buy both products or services, or not to buy at all.

The Guidance restates the case law of the ECJ on tying and bundling. Tying, in the context of Article 102 TFEU, was examined in depth in *Tetra Pak II*.[56] In

56 Case C-333/94P *Tetra Pak International SA v Commission* [1996] ECR I-5951.

this case, the ECJ held that, when an undertaking in a dominant position makes the purchase of one product (the tying product) conditional on the purchase of a second product (the tied product), this may amount to an abuse of a dominant position, even though such sales are in conformity with commercial usages and even though the two products are closely associated, unless the 'natural link' between them can be objectively justified. Tetra Pak argued that both products (that is, the carton-filling machinery and the requisite cartons for milk products) constituted an 'integrated service'. The ECJ rejected this argument. It held that it would be justified to consider the manufacturing equipment and the cartons as forming a natural link, and thus being treated as an integrated service, only if there were no other independent manufacturer specialising in the production of non-aseptic cartons, or if it were impossible for other manufacturers to start producing non-aseptic cartons for reasons relating to intellectual property rights.

In the *Microsoft* decision,[57] the European Commission clarified its approach to the matter of tying. The Commission found that Microsoft, by tying Windows Media Player (WMP) to its desktop operating system (OS), was in breach of Article 102(d) TFEU. This was an example of technical tying, which occurs where the tied product is physically integrated into the tying product so that it is impossible to buy one product without the other. In *Microsoft*, the Commission set out the criteria (which apply to both tying and bundling) that have to be satisfied for an abuse under Article 102(d) TFEU to be established. These criteria are as follows.

1. The tying and tied goods must not be within the same product market. In *Microsoft*, the Commission found that there were two separate product markets: one for the OS and one for WMP.
2. The undertaking concerned must be in a dominant position in the tying product market. In this respect, Microsoft was in a position of 'super-dominance' in the OS market.
3. The undertaking concerned does not give customers a choice to obtain the tying product without the tied product. WMP was sold as a package with the OS. Users could not get the OS without WMP. Therefore, as the Commission stated, the issue was not whether users were forced to use WMP, but whether they had the choice to get the OS without WMP. Because WMP was a built-in feature of the OS, consumers obviously had no choice. The argument of Microsoft that the customers were not required to pay separately for WMP was rejected.
4. The tying must foreclose competition. The Commission stated that:

> "[T]ying WMP with the dominant Windows makes WMP the platform of choice for complementary content and applications which in turn risks foreclosing competition in the market for media players.

57 COMP/C3/37.792 *Microsoft* [2005] 4 CMLR 965.

> This has spillover effects on competition in related products such as media encoding and management software (often server-side), but also in client PC operating systems for which media players compatible with quality content are an important application. Microsoft's tying practice creates a serious risk of foreclosing competition and stifling innovation."[58]

The Commission established that the above criteria were met in *Microsoft*. It was left to Microsoft to attempt to show that the efficiencies of tying prevailed over the harm to competition. The argument of Microsoft was that the pro-competitive effects of tying – that is, distribution efficiency, platform efficiency, the desirability of one unique media player worldwide, and so on – outweighed the harm to competition. The Commission stated that these argued benefits of tying could be achieved in the absence of Microsoft tying WMP with its OS. The major benefit, according to the Commission was 'Microsoft's own profitability', which, being disproportionate to the anti-competitive effect of tying, could not be accepted as an objective justification. It is to be remembered that the burden of proof to establish an objective, proportional justification is on the undertaking concerned.

Finally, the European Commission assessed the potential effect of tying in light of the probability, and the possible magnitude, of harm to competition. It established that there was a reasonable likelihood that tying WMP with the OS would lead to a lessening of competition, so that if the tying were to continue, the maintenance of an effective competition structure in the relevant product market would not be ensured in the foreseeable future.

With regard to tying, Microsoft was ordered by the European Commission to prepare and market a version of its OS without WMP, although it was allowed to continue selling its OS tied with WMP.[59]

The Commission's Guidance confirms the criteria used in *Microsoft* as decisive in the determination of anti-competitive foreclosure. The Guidance sets out the distinct products test as follows:

> "Two products are distinct if, in the absence of tying or bundling, a substantial number of customers would purchase or would have purchased the tying product without also buying the tied product from the same supplier, thereby allowing stand-alone production for both the tying and the tied product."[60]

In order to show that products are distinct, the Commission will use direct evidence (such as evidence based on whether, when they have a choice to

58 Ibid., [842].
59 The European Commission decision was upheld by the General Court: see Case T-201/04 *Microsoft Corp. v Commission* [2007] ECR II-3601.
60 The Guidance, [51].

purchase the tying and the tied product from different sources of supply, customers will choose to do so) and indirect evidence (such as the presence on the market of undertakings that manufacture and sell the tied product without the tying product, or the fact that undertakings with little market power, particularly in a competitive market, tend not to tie or to bundle such products).

7.4.2.2 Exclusive dealing

Exclusive sales, or exclusive purchasing, agreements aim at creating an obligation or an incentive, as a result of which the buyer makes all of its purchases on the relevant market from one dealer alone.

Exclusive purchasing or dealing agreements may lead to the foreclosure of a market if purchasers are tied to an enterprise enjoying a dominant position. In such circumstances, the ability of new competitors to enter the market is restricted, as well as the ability of the existing competitors to expand their market share.[61]

The Guidance states that the European Commission will concentrate on cases in which consumers, as a whole, do not benefit as a result of an exclusive purchasing obligation. This will occur, in particular, where there are many customers and where the exclusive purchasing obligations imposed by a dominant undertaking, taken together, will have the effect of preventing the entry or expansion of competitors. Other factors will also be taken into account.[62] In general, the likelihood of anti-competitive foreclosure will increase the longer the duration of the exclusive purchasing agreement. However, in a situation in which the dominant undertaking is an unavoidable trading partner for all or most customers, even an exclusive purchasing obligation of short duration can lead to anti-competitive foreclosure.

7.4.2.3 Refusal to deal, or to continue to deal, with existing and potential customers, and the doctrine of 'essential facility'

It is important to make a distinction between the situation in which a dominant enterprise refuses to deal with existing customers and that in which such an undertaking decides to deny access to an essential facility – that is, when a dominant enterprise is in possession of a scarce resource or facility that cannot be duplicated, such as access to a port, or a railway station, or other facility protected by intellectual property rights.

61 See D. Ridyard, 'Exclusive Contracts and Article 82 Enforcement: An Effects-Based Perspective' (2008) 4 EuroCJ 579.

62 The Guidance, [20].

A Refusal to deal, or to continue to deal, on a non-discriminatory basis with existing or potential customers

The principle of the freedom of contract entails that an enterprise, whether dominant or not, should be free to decide with whom it wants to do business. The importance of preserving the freedom of contract is recognised by the Guidance, which emphasises that to force a dominant undertaking to supply, even for a fair remuneration, may undermine that undertaking's incentive to invest and innovate, and thus harm consumers.[63]

The Guidance recognises that, in some circumstances, refusal to supply will have anti-competitive effects – namely, where the dominant undertaking is vertically integrated (that is, where it is active on both the upstream and downstream markets) and refuses to supply a buyer on the downstream market with which it competes on that market, or refuses to supply a buyer in order to punish that buyer for dealing with competitors or for its refusal to accept a tying agreement. The last of these is an example of horizontal foreclosure, and may also involve situations in which refusal to supply will prevent parallel imports and exports, and may thus be harmful to the internal market.

The Guidance deals directly with only two situations:

- a refusal of a dominant undertaking to supply a buyer on the downstream market on which it competes with that buyer; and
- a situation in which a dominant undertaking charges a buyer in a downstream market, in which it competes with that buyer, a price for its upstream products that does not allow even an equally efficient competitor to trade profitably in the downstream market on a lasting basis – a situation known as 'margin squeeze' (see section 7.4.1.3).

With regard to refusal to supply, the European Commission considers that it is not necessary for the refused product to have been already traded. Accordingly, it is sufficient that there is demand from potential buyers and that a potential market for the product in question can be identified. Further, not only actual refusal to supply, but also 'constructive refusal', such as undue delay in supplying the product or the supplying of a lower quality product, may constitute an abuse.

The Guidance identifies three conditions that must be satisfied in order for a refusal to supply to constitute an abuse:

- the refusal relates to a product or service that is objectively necessary to be able to compete effectively on a downstream market;
- the refusal is likely to lead to the elimination of effective competition on the downstream market; and
- the refusal is likely to lead to consumer harm.[64]

63 Ibid., [75].
64 Ibid., [81].

These three conditions are also applicable in the context of the doctrine of 'essential facility'.

B The doctrine of 'essential facility'

Article 177(2)(f) RTC states that unauthorised denial of access to network or essential infrastructure constitutes an abuse. This provision embraces the doctrine of 'essential facility'.

To understand the doctrine of essential facility, it is necessary to determine what facilities should be considered to be essential. This is done on a case-by-case basis. Advocate General Jacobs, in his Opinion in *Oscar Bronner*,[65] stated that a facility is considered to be essential if access to it is indispensable in order to compete in a related market and duplication of that facility is impossible, or extremely difficult, owing to physical, geographic or legal constraints, or is highly undesirable for reasons of public policy.

Examples of essential facilities are ports, airports, bus stations, gas pipelines, telecommunication networks and intellectual property rights.

As explained above, only in exceptional cases – that is, those in which the three conditions set out in paragraph 81 of the Guidance are satisfied – will refusal of access to an essential facility constitute an abuse. The burden of proof lies with the alleged victim.

7.5 Exploitative abuses

Article 179(1)(d) RTC prohibits the imposition of unfair purchase or selling prices, or other restrictive practices, by a dominant enterprise, whilst Article 179(1)(g) RTC prohibits a dominant enterprise from engaging in any business conduct that results in the exploitation of its customers or suppliers. Exploitative abuses may take many forms, including the charging of excessively high or low prices, and the imposition of unfair contractual terms and conditions.

An abuse consisting of the charging by a dominant enterprise of excessively high prices seems to be the most controversial. This is because, in some circumstances, prices may, at first glance, seem excessive, but in fact may be justified by objective considerations.[66] Such objective considerations include a temporary increase of demand, greater efficiency of an enterprise than that of its competitors in the relevant market and the introduction of an innovation, on which the profits earned are necessary to provide a fair return on the cost of the development and a fair reward for the risks taken by an enterprise in developing and introducing the innovation to the market. For these reasons, normally, it is very difficult to assess

65 Case C-7/97 *Oscar Bronner GmbH & Co. KG v Mediaprint Zeitungs- und Zeitschriftenverlag GmbH & Co. KG* [1998] ECR I-7791.

66 On this topic, see L. Hou, 'Excessive Prices within EU Competition Law' (2011) 7 EuroCJ 47.

whether high prices are excessive and thus amount to an abuse. For example, in 1999, the European Commission started an inquiry into excessive 'roaming' charges imposed by mobile phone operators in the European Union.[67] The inquiry was dropped in 2007 without any mobile operator being found guilty of charging excessive prices. Although the Commission established that, on average, roaming charges were four times higher than national mobile calls and that this difference could not be explained by the cost incurred by the network operator, it was unable to show analytically the existence of an abuse. As a result, the Commission decided to regulate roaming charges *via* secondary legislation.[68]

In the European Union, case law on excessive pricing is scarce. This paucity can be explained by three factors, as follows.

1. It is assumed that competitive forces within the relevant market can readjust excessive pricing. In particular, in the absence of entry and expansion barriers, new entrants will be attracted to enter the relevant market and to compete with a dominant undertaking.
2. Standards for assessment of the exploitative nature of high-prices are notoriously difficult to find and to apply.[69]
3. If prices are found to be excessive, it is difficult to establish what would be the right price. In this respect, it must be remembered that competition authorities should not act as price regulators; this task should be left to specialised authorities.

Charging excessive prices will constitute an exclusionary abuse when a dominant enterprise charges excessive prices for access to an essential facility (see section 7.4.2.3B) and, when, in the context of aftermarkets, it levies excessive prices for spare parts or complementary products.[70]

7.6 Price discrimination

Article 177(2)(h) RTC prohibits price discrimination. The interpretation of this provision raises a number of difficulties. First, the concept of price discrimination

67 Roaming relates to the use of a mobile phone when abroad. Because a home network operator cannot provide a service in another country, when a person travels to another country, and in that country receives or makes calls, the person is using the network of an operator in that country, i.e. 'roaming' on a foreign network. For this, the foreign network operator charges the home network operator a wholesale rate. The home operator then charges its customer a retail price for using a mobile phone abroad.

68 Regulation 717/2007 on Roaming in Public Mobile Communications Networks within the Community [2004] OJ L 171/32.

69 See D. Evans and J. Padilla, 'Excessive Prices: Using Economics to Define Administrable Legal Rules' (2005) 1 J Comp L & Econ 97.

70 Case 238/87 *AB Volvo v Eric Veng* [1988] ECR 6211.

applies to many practices. Examples include rebates, tying, selective price-cutting, the imposition of discriminatory prices by a vertically integrated enterprise on its downstream competitors and geographic discrimination. Each practice has a different objective, and thus it is impossible to establish a single analytical framework capable of dealing with all of them appropriately.

Second, according to economists, price discrimination can have beneficial effects on consumer welfare in some circumstances. To condemn all of them would be counter-productive.[71]

Third, economists divide discriminatory practices into three categories, depending on whether they create primary line injury (which injures rivals of a dominant enterprise), secondary line injury (which harms consumers) or geographic discrimination (which consists of applying differing prices depending on the geographical location of the customer, without any objective justification, with the consequence that the Community market is divided along national lines).

- With regard to primary line price discrimination, Article 177(i) and (j) RTC will be used to condemn loyalty discounts or concessions or some exclusionary vertical restrictions.
- With regard to secondary line price discrimination, Article 179(1)(d) and (g) will be relevant.
- With regard to geographic price discrimination, the matter of whether such discrimination will constitute an abuse will depend on the objectives of CSME competition law.

In the context of EU law, *United Brands*,[72] although decided a long time ago, is still one of the leading cases on Article 102 TFEU and one that exemplifies many aspects of the Article. In this case, the matter of geographic price discrimination was also at issue.

Case 27/76 *United Brands Company and United Brands Continentaal BV v Commission* [1978] ECR 207

Facts

United Brands (UB), a multinational US corporation, shipped bananas from its own plantations in South America to Rotterdam and Bremerhaven using its own ships. In both ports, unloading costs were almost identical. The bananas

71 S. Bishop and M. Walker, *The Economics of EC Competition Law: Concepts, Application and Measurement*, 3rd edn, 2010, London: Sweet and Maxwell, pp 252–256.

72 Case 27/76 *United Brands Company and United Brands Continentaal BV v Commission* [1978] ECR 207.

were sold at those ports, at prices that differed substantially, to customers (distributors or ripeners) from different Member States. The customers then transported the bananas at their own cost to ripening rooms in their Member States. UB explained that it fixed the prices taking into account what the market in a particular Member State would bear. Further, under contractual arrangements between UB and its distributors, the latter were prevented from exporting green, unripened bananas. As a result, any parallel import from one Member State to another was prevented by practical considerations relating to ripeness.

Held

First, the ECJ held that UB's prices were discriminatory because bananas unloaded in two EU ports on practically identical terms as regards costs, quality and quantity were sold to the customers at prices which differed considerably – by between 30 and 50 per cent – from one Member State to another, although the services offered were identical in each case. The ECJ stated that:

> These discriminatory prices, which varied according to the circumstances of the Member States, were just so many obstacles to the free movement of goods and their effect was intensified by the clause forbidding the resale of bananas while still green and by reducing the deliveries of the quantities ordered.
>
> A rigid partitioning of national markets was thus created at price levels, which were artificially different, placing certain distributors/ripeners at a competitive disadvantage, since compared with what it should have been competition had thereby been distorted.
>
> Consequently, the policy of differing prices enabling [UB] to apply dissimilar conditions to equivalent transactions with other trading parties, thereby placing them at a competitive disadvantage, was an abuse of a dominant position.[73]

The ECJ rejected the explanation submitted by UB and stated that differences in prices can be justified only on the basis of objective criteria, such as differences in transport costs, taxation, customs duties, labour wages, and so on.

73 Ibid., [232]–[234].

Second, the ECJ held that the clause seeking to prevent parallel imports constituted an abuse, since it limited markets to the prejudice of consumers and affected trade between Member States, in particular by partitioning the internal market along national borders.

Comment

This judgment has been criticised for the following reasons.[74]

1. Only the clause prohibiting parallel import should have been condemned, bearing in mind that its consequence was that the internal market was partitioned and that UB could charge discriminatory prices.
2. Distributors were not placed at a comparative disadvantage, bearing in mind that, when the market for the resale of bananas was partitioned, they were not in competition with each other.
3. It suggests that a dominant undertaking should charge uniform prices throughout the European Union. In this respect, economists submit that 'price discrimination unambiguously reduces welfare only when it does not raise total output, whereas the sign of welfare change is ambiguous in all other cases'.[75] Accordingly, discrimination should not be condemned merely because some consumers are deemed to be 'exploited' by having to pay higher prices than other consumers, because this may have negative effects on consumer welfare. For example, if price discrimination increases the number of sales to customers who would have been left out of the market if uniform prices had been charged, and there is no decrease or likely decrease in consumer welfare, there should be no abuse under Article 102 TFEU.

Notwithstanding the above criticism, geographic price discrimination constitutes an abuse under EU law, as was confirmed in *Tetra Pak II*.[76]

74 W. Bishop, 'Price Discrimination under Article 86: Political Economy in the European Court' (1981) 44 MLR 282; L. Zanon, 'Price Discrimination under Article 86 of the EEC Treaty: The *United Brands* Case' (1982) 31 ICLQ 36.

75 M. Motta, *Competition Policy: Theory and Practice*, 2004, Cambridge: CUP, p 496.

76 Commission Decision 92/163/EEC *Tetra Pak II* [1992] OJ L 72/1, [154], [155] and [160], upheld by the General Court in Case T-83/91 *Tetra Pak International SA v Commission* [1994] ECR II-755 and on appeal to the ECJ in Case C-333/94P *Tetra Pak International SA v Commission* [1996] ECR I-5951.

7.7 Justifications available to dominant enterprises

Articles 177(4) and 179(3) RTC provide justifications that may be relied upon by a dominant undertaking to avoid being found to have abused a dominant position. Both Articles are, however, unclear.

7.7.1 The exemption set out in Article 177(4) RTC

The defence based on Article 177(4) RTC raises many issues, most prominent among which is whether all four of the criteria for exemption set out in Article 177(4) RTC apply cumulatively, or whether a business practice will merit exemption when the two positive criteria and either of the negative criteria are met (see Chapter 6, section 6.6).

The second issue is that the four criteria set out in Article 177(4) RTC are perhaps not appropriate to deal with unilateral conduct of a dominant enterprise. In this respect, each criterion set out in Article 177(4) RTC is now examined separately.

7.7.1.1 Article 177(4)(a) RTC: Positive criteria 1 and 2 – efficiency gains and consumer benefit

In order to satisfy the two positive criteria, a dominant enterprise must show that its behaviour has achieved an economic or non-economic improvement, or both, in production, distribution, etc. (see Chapter 6, section 6.6.1) that outweighs the negative effects that it may have on consumers. The greater the restriction that its behaviour imposes on competition, the greater must be the efficiency gain and the benefit for consumers. It is submitted that the positive criteria raise the following issues.

1. It will be very difficult for a dominant enterprise to assess the restriction on competition that its conduct imposes without detailed information relating to the relevant market. In light of Article 177(1)(a) RTC, which prohibits any anti-competitive exchange of information, the issue of how a dominant enterprises is to obtain relevant information is critical.
2. If CSME competition law is about protecting consumers from abuses by dominant enterprises, it is the task of the CCC to establish whether a particular practice impacts adversely on consumer welfare. If it does so, a balancing of improvements against benefits to consumers is not necessary. Such conduct is anti-competitive and constitutes an abuse.
3. By its very nature, a dominant enterprise acts independently of its competitors, its customers and its consumers. It generates benefits that are passed on to its shareholders, not to customers or consumers. However, if efficiencies are enjoyed by shareholders only, a dominant enterprise will fail to satisfy the criterion requiring that consumers must receive a fair share of

the benefits. It seems that if a dominant enterprise is required to pass on cost savings derived from efficiency gains to its final or intermediate consumers, it will be required to act contrary to the interest of its shareholders, or it will no longer be in a dominant position, because its behaviour will be dependent on consumers.

7.7.1.2 Article 177(4)(b) RTC: First negative criterion – indispensable restrictions

With regard to the first negative criterion under Article 177(4) RTC – that is, the indispensability – it is suitable in the context of exemption relating to prohibited agreements, decisions and concerted practices, but not with regard to abusive behaviour of dominant enterprises. This is for the following reasons.

1. The application of this criterion will require a dominant enterprise to do no more than is indispensible to maintain its position on the relevant market. This is contrary to the objectives of competition law, which encourage enterprises, irrespective of their position on the market, to compete fiercely on the relevant market.
2. A dominant enterprise acts on its own when granting discounts, setting its pricing policy and indeed when taking any decision relating to its conduct on the relevant market. Whilst, in the context of agreements, decisions and concerted practices, enterprises act jointly and can easily assess the impact of their conduct on the relevant market, and thus assess whether a restriction on competition is indispensible for the achievement of the objective sought, a dominant enterprise acts unilaterally, without any information from competitors (otherwise it will be in breach of Article 177(1)(a) RTC). Therefore it will be very difficult, if not impossible, for such an enterprise to assess the indispensability of its conduct – that is, to decide whether there are no other economically practicable or less restrictive means of achieving its objectives.
3. It raises the question of what standard of conduct on the market should apply to a dominant enterprise. Only when such a standard is established will it be possible to decide whether a particular practice is indispensable.

7.7.1.3 Article 177(4)(c) RTC: Second negative criterion – no possibility of eliminating competition

Under Article 177(4)(c) RTC, conduct of a dominant enterprise must not eliminate competition in respect of a substantial part of the market in goods and services concerned. Whilst this criterion is appropriate to deal with prohibited agreements, decisions and concerted practices, it is less suitable for application to the conduct of dominant enterprises. This is for the following reasons.

1. This criterion seems to impose on a dominant enterprise an obligation to ensure that its conduct does not eliminate competitors. Therefore if, by reason of innovation, a dominant enterprise charges lower prices and thus eliminates inefficient competitors, it will have to justify conduct that is pro-competitive and beneficial to consumers.
2. Dominant enterprises may fear being investigated and punished if their competitors leave the market. As a result, they may forgo initiation of legitimate competitive action that would benefit consumers.

It is submitted that Article 179(c) RTC creates a presumption of culpability with regard to dominant enterprises. Unlike enterprises operating in a competitive market, dominant enterprises compete in a market in which effective competition is already restricted. This entails, first, that the criterion embodied in Article 177(4)(c) can be applied only if and when the competition authorities clearly establish what kind of behaviour is regarded as 'normal' in such a market; second, exclusionary abuses, by their very nature, eliminate competition and thus the exemption set out in Article 177(4) RTC will not be available to justify such abuses; third, this criterion may have chilling effects on competition in that a dominant enterprise may be deterred from taking competitive initiatives because of fear of punishment.

It is to be noted, however, that the literal interpretation of Article 174(4) RTC means that the criterion set out in Article 177(4)(c) RTC may not be applicable to dominant enterprises (see Chapter 6, section 6.6).

7.7.1.4 Conclusion

It is submitted that the criteria set out in Article 177(4) RTC are not the most appropriate for the purposes of assessing whether a practice of a dominant enterprise merits exemption under Article 177(4) RTC. These criteria need clarification from the CCC, in particular in terms of what should be considered to be 'normal' behaviour in a market in which the very presence of a dominant enterprise has already significantly restricted competition. Only by reference to the appropriate standard of conduct expected from a dominant enterprise is it possible to decide how to apply the criteria set out in Article 177(4)(b) and (c) RTC. Further, Article 177(4)(c) RTC seems to remove the presumption that any type of abusive conduct, whatever it is, may merit exemption. It suggests that exclusionary abuses will never qualify for exemption.

It may well be thought that Article 177(4) RTC imposes an unreasonable burden of proof on a dominant enterprise. Whilst it is relatively easy to establish whether an agreement, decision or concerted practice has as its object or effect the elimination of competition, the same cannot be said in respect of dominant enterprises: first, they do not have access to information allowing them to assess the impact of their practice on the relevant market; and second, because they do not operate in a competitive market, almost any new strategy or practice may result in the elimination of competitors.

7.7.2 Justifications set out in Article 179(3) RTC

Article 179(3) RTC states that:

> "An enterprise shall not be treated as abusing its dominant position if it establishes that:
>
> (a) its behaviour was directed exclusively to increasing efficiency in the production, provision or distribution of goods or services or to promoting technical or economic progress and that consumers were allowed a fair share of the resulting benefit;
> (b) it reasonably enforces or seeks to enforce a right under or existing by virtue of a copyright, patent, registered trade mark or design; or
> (c) the effect or likely effect of its behaviour on the market is the result of superior competitive performance of the enterprise concerned."

The literal interpretation of Article 179(3) RTC means that a dominant enterprise will have to satisfy, in addition to the condition set out in Article 179(3)(a) RTC, either condition (b) or (c). This interpretation does not seem to be appropriate. For example, if the behaviour of a dominant enterprise is the result of its superior competitive performance, why should it prove the existence of efficiencies? If its behaviour is lawful, it does not have to be justified in any way.

It is submitted that the literal interpretation of Article 179(3) RTC should be rejected and, instead, that Article interpreted teleologically. When interpreted in light of the objectives of the RTC, it is clear that Article 179(3) RTC sets three separate defences on the basis of which behaviour of a dominant enterprise should not be regarded as abusive.

The three defences set out in Article 179(3) are as follows.

7.7.2.1 The efficiency defence

The efficiency defence is examined in Chapter 6, section 6.6.1.

7.7.2.2 Defence based on the reasonable enforcement of intellectual property rights

The holding of intellectual property rights (IPRs) may confer on an enterprise a dominant position in the relevant market or even a *de facto* monopoly. However, CSME competition law does not prohibit the creation or holding of such a dominant position; only its abuse.

Article 179(3)(b) RTC clearly states that a dominant enterprise does not abuse its dominant position when it 'reasonably' enforces or seeks to enforce its IPRs. The interpretation of what is 'reasonable' is therefore essential for determining whether the behaviour of a dominant enterprise may be justified by the acquisition, holding and exploitation of IPRs. In this context, the meaning of the words 'enforces or seeks to enforce' needs to be clarified. It is submitted that these words should be generously interpreted – that is, that a dominant enterprise 'enforces or seeks to enforce its IPRs' not only when it starts legal proceedings against unlawful use by a rival of its IPRs, but also when it exercises them. Such exercise must be in conformity with CSME competition law – that is, it must be reasonable.

The approach of EU competition law to the relationship between the prohibition of abuses of a dominant position and IPRs may be relevant to the determination of the word 'reasonably'. The main concern of EU competition law is the prevention of anti-competitive leveraging of market power from one market into another by means of IPRs. Having said this, the EU case law also shows that, in some circumstances, abusive use of IPRs may occur when a dominant undertaking is active on one market only.

A Leveraging: compulsory licensing

'Leveraging' refers to a practice whereby an enterprise in a dominant position uses its power in one market to gain advantages in a related market. This practice is used mainly by a dominant enterprise in an upstream market to gain advantage in a downstream market, although leveraging may also take place in aftermarket products or services, and in a primary market when a dominant enterprise uses its power in one geographical area of that market to gain advantage in another area. Tying, bundling and the essential facility principles are examples of leverage.

The main issue with regard to the interface between IPRs and the prohibition of abuses of a dominant position concerns the determination of conditions under which a refusal by a dominant enterprise to grant a licence to a third party to exploit its IPRs may amount to an abuse. If such an abuse is established, the enforcement authority, for example the European Commission, usually orders the dominant enterprise to grant a licence. This is known as 'compulsory licensing'.

EU law on this matter can be summarised as follows.

If a dominant undertaking operates on two distinct markets, its refusal to license IPRs will amount to an abuse 'only in exceptional circumstances' – that is, if the following conditions set out by the ECJ in *IMS Health*[77] and refined by the General Court in the *Microsoft* case[78] are met. These conditions are cumulative.

1. The product protected by the IPR must be indispensable for operating in a secondary market. Thus a secondary market must be clearly identified. This

77 Case C-418/01 *IMS Health GmbH & Co. OHG v NDC Health GmbH & Co. KG* [2004] ECR I-5039.

78 Case T-201/04 *Microsoft Corp. v Commission* [2007] ECR II-3601.

is essentially a matter for expert economic evidence. For this condition to be met, there must not only be a secondary market, but also the product must be indispensable to the exercise of a particular activity in a secondary market. The ECJ held that preventing duplication (which really means plagiarism) could not be considered to be an abuse. The Court stated that 'indispensable' means 'indispensable in practical terms' – that is, intended to produce new goods or services not offered by the holder of IPRs. However, in the *Microsoft* case, the General Court held that the emergence of a new product was not the only relevant parameter; it stated that any refusal to license the use of IPRs that has the effect of limiting technical developments to the prejudice of consumers is also within the scope of Article 102(b) TFEU.[79]

2. There must be potential consumer demand on the secondary market for a new product, or service, or technical development.
3. The refusal must not be justified by objective considerations.
4. The refusal must risk excluding competition in a secondary market.

The European Commission and then the General Court applied these conditions in the *Microsoft* case.[80] The European Commission found that Microsoft was abusing its position in two ways, the first of which was by refusing to disclose interoperability information to its rivals in the secondary market, identified by the Commission as being a market for workgroup server operating systems (WGOSs), which information was needed by those rivals to be able to compete effectively against Microsoft's own supply of server operating systems. This was the so-called 'interoperability' abuse.[81] The second abuse consisted of the tying of Windows Media Player (WMP) with its desktop operating system (OS) (see section 7.4.2.1).

With regard to the interoperability abuse, the General Court emphasised that a refusal to license is an abuse 'only in exceptional circumstances'. The European Commission considered that Microsoft, which had a monopoly on the PC OS market (of which Windows controled over 95 per cent), deliberately restricted interoperability between Windows PCs and non-Microsoft workgroup servers. As a result, Microsoft had extended its market power from the PC OS into a neighbouring market – that is, the WGOS. One of the remedies ordered by the European Commission was for Microsoft to disclose complete and accurate

79 Ibid., [646]–[647].

80 COMP/C3/37.792 *Microsoft* [2005] 4 CMLR 965, upheld by the General Court in Case T-201/04 *Microsoft Corp. v Commission* [2007] ECR II-3601.

81 'Interoperability' refers to the need of providers of software to be able to make products that can operate in conjunction with the systems and programmes of other producers. In order to ensure interoperability, providers of software must have access to interface information, i.e. information relating to systems and programmes of other producers, if they are to make their products compatible with and usable alongside the products of other producers.

interface information, which would allow non-Microsoft workgroup servers to achieve full interoperability with Windows PCs and servers. This information was protected by IPRs.

The European Commission found that the disclosure of interoperability information (that is, the information on how Microsoft's server software worked) was indispensable in order to ensure that those of Microsoft's competitors that provided WGOSs could compete viably on the market and that this market remained innovative, so ensuring that consumers' choices were not diminished by locking them into a homogeneous Microsoft solution.[82] Accordingly, the European Commission used a twofold test to assess indispensability, considering first the degree of interoperability necessary for the Windows WGOS to remain viable on the secondary market, and second, whether the disclosure of interface information by Microsoft was indispensible in order to ensure the viability of competitors of Microsoft on the market. The European Commission found that there were no substitutes for disclosure, such as reverse engineering, because this required 'considerable efforts with uncertain chances of success'.[83]

The condition relating to a new product or service was extensively interpreted by the General Court. In this case, there was no new product or service. Despite this, the Court held that this condition applies when the refusal to grant a licence limits 'technical development'. This was the case in *Microsoft*, given that its refusal created 'artificial interoperability advantage', which, in conjunction with its dominant position, discouraged development of competing WGOSs.[84]

With regard to the elimination of competition, the General Court considered that, without the disclosure of interoperability information, there was a considerable risk that competition in the secondary market would be eliminated. The argument submitted by Microsoft was that, for the condition relating to elimination of competition to be met, it was necessary for the European Commission to show that the refusal eliminated all competition on the secondary market, and that the possibility of eliminating competition had to be 'immediate' and 'real'.[85] The Court stated that it is sufficient that the refusal creates a risk of elimination of all effective competition. It also stated that 'a marginal presence in certain niches on the market cannot suffice to substantiate the existence of such competition'.[86] In the case of Microsoft, such a risk existed on the grounds that Microsoft's share in the market for WGOSs was increasing, whilst its competitors' shares were declining, mainly owing to the interoperability problems.

The General Court rejected Microsoft's defences based on freedom of contract and the protection of IPRs. With regard to the latter, Microsoft argued that the disclosure of interoperability information would lessen its incentive to innovate.

82 COMP/C3/37.792 *Microsoft* [2005] 4 CMLR 965, [693]–[708], [782].
83 Ibid., [685].
84 Case T-201/04 *Microsoft Corp. v Commission* [2007] ECR II-3601, [653].
85 Ibid., [439]–[440].
86 Ibid., [563]–[564].

In this respect, the European Commission stated that, 'on balance, the possible negative impact of an order to supply on Microsoft's incentives to innovate is outweighed by its positive impact on the level of innovation of the whole industry (including Microsoft)'.[87] The General Court found that there were three reasons why the disclosure would not have 'significant negative impact' on Microsoft's incentive to innovate:

- the compulsory licences would not allow Microsoft's competitors to clone Microsoft's products;
- the sharing of interoperability information was a standard practice in the software industry; and
- under the terms of settlement of a case against Microsoft in the United States,[88] an obligation imposed on Microsoft to share its interoperability information had not adversely affected Microsoft's incentive to innovate.[89]

B Abuses of intellectual property rights when a dominant undertaking is active on one market only

In some cases, the European Commission, and subsequently the EU courts, has found that a dominant undertaking was abusing its position by reliance on IPRs despite the fact that it was active on one market only. Some of the situations that emerged in the case law are examined below.

1. Where a dominant undertaking acquires IPRs in order to reinforce an existing barrier to entry into the market on which it is already in a dominant position. This situation occurred in *Tetra Pak (No. 1)*.[90] Tetra Pak had approximately 90 per cent of the market in the European Union, and thus enjoyed a dominant position in machinery for manufacturing both brick-shaped cartons and the aseptic cartons in which UHT milk was sold. Consumers preferred 'gable-shaped' cartons, in which only fresh milk could be sold. For that reason, for many years, Liquipak, an American company, was developing a gable-shaped carton for milk and the necessary filling machinery. The only rival of Tetra Pak on the market, Elopak, also began developing gable-shaped cartons. When Elopak was ready to launch its product, Tetra Pak acquired Liquipak, together with the exclusive licence for developing the gable-shaped aseptic milk cartons and necessary filling machinery. Elopak complained to the Commission.

87 COMP/C3/37.792 *Microsoft* [2005] 4 CMLR 965, [783].
88 *US v. Microsoft Corp.*, 231 F.Supp.2d 144 (D.DC 2002). It is to be noted that there were important differences between the case against Microsoft in the United States and that in the European Union. Accordingly, the obligation imposed on Microsoft in the United States was not as expansive as that imposed on it by the General Court.
89 Case T-201/04 *Microsoft Corp. v Commission* [2007] ECR II-3601, [699]–[703].
90 Case T-51/89 *Tetra Pak Rausing SA v Commission* [1990] ECR II-309.

The Commission, and subsequently the General Court, decided that Tetra Pak, by acquiring an undertaking possessing an exclusive licence for rival technology, had abused its dominant position. The Court ruled that the acquisition by an undertaking in a dominant position of an exclusive licence did not, in itself, constitute an abuse – but in the circumstances of this case, in particular taking into account the very high barrier to entry to the relevant product market, the acquisition of the exclusive licence not only strengthened the dominant position of Tetra Pak, but also reinforced the barriers to entry of new competitors into the market.

On appeal, this was confirmed by the ECJ in *Tetra Pak (No. 2)*,[91] in which the Court ruled that Tetra Pak was trying to eliminate its competitors and imposed a fine of €75 million on Tetra Pak.

2. Where a collecting society abuses its dominant position. The main features of collecting societies are described in Chapter 6, section 6.3.3.3. Collecting societies may abuse their dominant position in two ways:

   (a) in respect of their members, by imposing discriminatory terms on nationals of other Member States,[92] or in respect of the unduly broad rights that they require their members to assign to them;[93] and
   (b) in respect of those who seek a licence to exploit rights in a work or works controlled by collecting societies, mainly by imposing unfair and unreasonable terms on users of copyright works.[94]

3. Where a dominant undertaking charges excessive royalties for granting a licence. The European Commission in *Eurofix-Bauco*[95] found that charging excessive royalties was an abuse in a situation in which the sole objective of fixing excessive royalties was 'to block or at the very least unreasonably to delay' that granting of a patent licence, which was available under UK patent law.
4. Where a dominant undertaking misuses the patent system. In *AstraZeneca (AZ)*,[96] the General Court held that AZ, the Anglo-Swedish pharmaceutical group active worldwide in the sector of inventing, developing and marketing innovative pharmaceutical products, was in breach of Article 102 TFEU in relation to the ulcer treatment drug Losec. The General Court confirmed

91 Case C-333/94 P *Tetra Pak International SA v Commission* [1996] ECR I-5951.

92 Commission Decision 71/224/EEC *GEMA* [1971] OJ L 134/15, [1971] CMLR D 35.

93 Case 127/73 *Belgische Radio en Télévisie (BRT) v SV SABAM* [1974] ECR 313. SABAM required the assignment of the author's copyrights for all categories of work and manners of exploitation, and for the whole world. This was considered to be an abuse under Article 102 TFEU.

94 In Commission Decision 71/224/EEC *GEMA* [1971] OJ L 134/15, [1971] CMLR D 35.

95 Commission Decision 88/138/EEC *Eurofix-Bauco v Hilti* [1998] OJ L 65/19, [78].

96 Case T-321/05 *AstraZeneca AB and AstraZeneca plc (AZ) v Commission* [2010] ECR II-2805.

the Commission Decision adopted in 2005[97] that AZ had committed two abuses of a dominant position:

(a) making misleading representations to the patent offices and national courts of several Member States in order to obtain extended patent protection for Losec, which would allow AZ to block, or to delay, its competitors from entering the market for generic versions of Losec; and
(b) the submission of requests for deregistration of the marketing authorisations for Losec capsules in Denmark, Norway and Sweden, combined with the withdrawal from the market of Losec capsules and the launch of Losec multiple unit pellet system ('Losec MUPS') tablets in those three countries, the purpose of deregistration being to delay the marketing of generic versions of Losec by AZ's competitors.

With regard to the first abuse, AZ argued that it had not intentionally provided misleading information to national patent offices and national courts in several Member States in order to obtain supplementary protection certificates (SPCs), which would allow AZ to extend the basic patent protection for Losec beyond the initial protection period.

The General Court found that AZ did, in fact, make misleading representations to obtain SPCs to which it was not entitled. The Court emphasised that the concept of an abuse is an objective concept and therefore the misleading nature of representations made to public authorities must be assessed on the basis of objective factors; thus proof of intent or bad faith on the part of a dominant undertaking is not required for the purposes of identifying an abuse. This means that, first, proof of bad faith or bad intent is not sufficient to establish an abuse, and second, even a genuine error in information provided by a dominant undertaking could amount to an abuse under Article 102 TFEU. If an error occurs in communication with public authorities, the dominant undertaking is required to inform the relevant authorities in order to enable them to rectify the error. If it fails to do so, the fact that it holds the patent or SPC to which it is not entitled can, in itself, be regarded as an abuse, even if the public authorities later revoke those rights, either on their own initiative or following a third-party complaint.

With regard to the second abuse, AZ argued that the introduction of a new Losec formulation and the withdrawal of Losec capsules were part of its legitimate business strategy aimed at protecting AZ's interests from competition from generic producers and parallel importers. The General Court agreed that those activities were not abusive, because they were not capable of blocking competition from generic producers and parallel importers. However, the deregistration of marketing authorisations for Losec capsules had the effect of preventing the use by AZ's competitors of a simplified authorisation procedure, and thus created obstacles to the market

97 Commission Decision 2006/857/EC *AstraZeneca* [2006] OJ L 332/24.

entry of generic products and parallel imports. As a result, the use of deregistration procedures by AZ was outside the scope of competition on the merits and constituted an abuse under Article 102 TFEU.

The *AstraZeneca* judgment clearly shows that the General Court interpreted the concept of an abuse broadly and that the special responsibility imposed on dominant undertakings, irrespective of the industry in which they operate, entails that they should take particular care when implementing their business strategies, so as to ensure that they do not use practices falling outside the scope of competition on the merits.

5. Where a dominant undertaking pursues vexatious litigation involving the protection of IPRs. In Case *ITT Promedia*,[98] the General Court implicitly confirmed that vexatious litigation by a dominant undertaking before a national court may constitute an abuse, but only when two cumulative criteria are met:

   (a) when the relevant national legal proceedings cannot reasonably be considered to be an attempt to assert the rights of the dominant undertaking, and thus serve only to harass the opposing party; and
   (b) when the national legal proceedings have been commence as part of a plan, the goal of which is to eliminate competition

   The Court stated that these criteria must be interpreted narrowly, so as not to undermine the right to access to the courts, which is protected by the European Convention on Human Rights (ECHR) and constitutes a general principle of EU law. However, in this case, the General Court did not find an abuse.

The exercise of IPRs by a dominant enterprise always creates difficulties for competitors. Those difficulties derive from the very nature of IPRs. CSME competition law will not intervene when a dominant enterprise 'reasonably' enforces or seeks to enforce its IPRs. The case law of the ECJ shows that a refusal to license IPRs is never in itself an abuse. However, it becomes so when it causes prejudice to consumers.

7.7.2.3 A defence based on the superior competitive performance of a dominant enterprise

The defence based on superior competitive performance is puzzling, but can perhaps be understood in light of Article 179(1)(a)–(c) RTC, which states that a dominant enterprise abuses its position when its behaviour:

> "(a) restricts the entry of any enterprise into a market;
> (b) prevents or deters any enterprises from engaging in competition in a market;
> (c) eliminates or removes any enterprise from a market . . ."

98 Case T-111/96 *ITT Promedia NV v Commission* [1998] ECR II-2937.

These three so-called 'abuses' are, in fact, possible consequences of conduct of a dominant enterprise, which may be lawful or unlawful, rather than abuses in the strict sense. Article 179(1)(a)–(c) RTC seems to suggest that it will be sufficient for the CCC to establish an abuse entirely based on the fact that competitors of a dominant enterprise have left the market. If this interpretation is correct, it means that Article 179(1)(a)–(c) RTC establishes a presumption that, when any of the three situations set out in that Article occurs, a dominant enterprise will, in order to avoid liability, have to rebut the presumption. Accordingly, it will be for a dominant enterprise to show that whilst its conduct eliminated competitors, it nevertheless resulted only from its superior performance on the relevant market. This reversal of the burden of proof, although advantageous for the CCC, cannot be accepted. This is because such a presumption of 'guilt' is in breach of the principle of the presumption of innocence. An enterprise should be presumed innocent unless and until the contrary is established by the CCC. Further, this interpretation is incompatible with Article 179(2) RTC, which lists the factors to be taken into account when determining whether an enterprise has abused its dominant position.

8

THE OBLIGATIONS OF MEMBER STATES UNDER CSME COMPETITION LAW

Chapter contents

8.1 Introduction

Under the Revised Treaty of Chaguaramas (RTC), Member States have general and specific obligations to ensure the enactment, proper enforcement and efficiency of CSME competition law. In light of those obligations, the treatment of public undertakings and State monopolies merits examination – in particular, the question of whether and to what extent CSME competition law applies to a situation in which a State is engaged in economic activities through enterprises that it controls, or owns, or to which it has granted special rights, by virtue of which those enterprises are put in a privileged position within the relevant market. This chapter does not, however, deal with the topic of State aid, which is outside the scope of this book.

8.2 General and specific obligations imposed on a Member State concerning implementation and enforcement of CSME competition law

The general and specific obligations imposed by the RTC on a Member State relating to CSME competition law are examined below.

8.2.1 Article 9 RTC: 'General Undertaking on Implementation'

Article 9 RTC, entitled 'General Undertaking on Implementation', is central to the achievements of the objectives of the CARICOM Single Market and Economy (CSME) set out in Article 6 RTC. That Article applies to all provisions of the RTC, including those on competition law. It imposes a positive and a negative obligation on a Member State.

The positive obligation requires Member States to facilitate the achievement of the Community's tasks. To this end, they must take all appropriate measures, whether general or particular, to ensure the fulfilment of their obligations under the Treaty, or their obligations resulting from decisions taken by the organs and bodies of the Community. This includes decisions and determinations of the CARICOM Competition Commission (CCC). Article 174(6) RTC states that each Member State shall enact legislation to ensure that determinations of the CCC are enforceable in its jurisdiction. It flows from Article 174 RTC that a Member State is required to ensure that not only determinations of the CCC are enforceable in its territory, but also its decisions adopted during investigations. This is supported by Article 174(2) RTC, under which the CCC may request a Member State to secure the attendance of any person before it to give evidence, may require the discovery or production of any document and may take other action as may be necessary in furtherance of its investigations. Accordingly, a Member State must ensure that decisions of the CCC relating to the conduct of its investigations are enforceable under national law.

The negative obligation requires Member States to abstain from taking any measures that could jeopardise the attainment of the objectives of the RTC. The case law of the European Court of Justice (ECJ) demonstrates that any measure adopted by a Member State that requires, or favours, the adoption of an anti-competitive agreement, decision or concerted practice, or strengthens any such effect, or deprives national legislation of its official character by delegating price-setting powers to private operators, will infringe Article 101 TFEU in conjunction with Article 4(3) TFEU,[1] which latter Article bears close similarity to Article 9 RTC. With regard to abuses of a dominant position, measures adopted by a Member State are assessed in the light of Article 106 TFEU in conjunction with Article 102 TFEU, rather than Article 4(3) TFEU in conjunction with Article 102

1 See Case 267/86 *Pascal Van Eycke v ASPA NV* [1988] ECR 4769, [16].

TFEU (see section 8.3.3.1). It is submitted that, under CSME competition law, reliance on Article 9 RTC may be limited, given that the provisions of Chapter VIII, Part One – in particular Article 170 RTC – impose specific obligations on Member States relating to the implementation of Community competition policy. These obligations are examined below.

8.2.1.1 The assessment of existing national legislation, agreements and administrative practices in light of their compatibility with CSME competition law

Article 170(5) RTC requires that each Member State, within 24 months of the entry into force of the RTC, notifies to the Council for Trade and Economic Development (COTED) all of its existing legislation, agreements and administrative practices that are inconsistent with the provisions of Chapter VIII. Then, within 36 months of entry into force of the RTC, COTED is to establish a programme providing for the repeal of conflicting legislation, and for the termination of agreements and administrative practices inconsistent with Chapter VIII.

It is submitted that Article 170(5) RTC is likely to become a major source of dispute between Member States and the CCC, unless the CCC provides guidance as to how the screening of existing measures in terms of their compatibility with CSME competition law is to be effected. Article 170(5) RTC is very broad: it refers to any measure that renders CSME competition rules ineffective. The identification of national measures, whether legislative, administrative, or a combination of both, which could breach Article 177(1) RTC and thus are subject to Article 170(5) RTC is to be made by each Member State itself. It can be said that most Member States have little, or no, experience in the area of competition law. Therefore, even if they genuinely wish to comply with Article 170(5) RTC, they may find the identification of national measures within the scope of Article 170(5) RTC a daunting and complex task, with the potential result that, when in doubt, national measures will not to be notified to COTED. It is submitted that the CCC should consider ensuring not only that existing State measures restricting competition are properly identified and negated, but also that Member States take a proactive approach to combating any proposed new State restrictions. In this respect, the CCC might well consider it important to provide guidelines to each Member State on how to assess the impact of its legislative proposals and policy on competition in the CSME, with a view to ensuring their compatibility with CSME competition law.[2]

2 In the EU context, see the European Commission, *Better Regulation: A Guide to Competition Screening*, available at http://ec.europa.eu/competition/publications/legis_test.pdf [accessed 13 December 2013].

8.2.1.2 The obligation to enact appropriate national legislation

Under Article 170(1)(b) RTC, Member States are required to take all necessary legislative measures to ensure consistency and compliance with CSME competition law, and also to introduce penalties for anti-competitive business conduct. As at September 2013, only four Member States had enacted national competition legislation: Barbados, Guyana, Jamaica, and Trinidad and Tobago.[3]

8.2.1.3 The obligation to establish and maintain a national competition authority

Under Article 170(2) RTC, a Member State has a duty to establish and maintain a national competition authority (NCA). As at September 2013, only Barbados, Guyana and Jamaica had functioning NCAs.[4]

8.2.1.4 The obligation to ensure that an NCA co-operates with the CCC and other NCAs

Under Article 170(3)(a), every Member State must ensure that its NCA co-operates with the CCC and with other NCAs. As at September 2013, only Barbados and Guyana had incorporated provisions into their national competition legislation to facilitate co-operation between NCAs and with the CCC.[5]

8.2.1.5 Conclusion

As can be seen from the above, the level of implementation of CSME competition law is low. This means that the CCC is prevented from carrying out its task, bearing in mind its reliance on national law and co-operation with the relevant NCAs (see Chapter 9, section 9.7.1.3). However, two particular factors are expected to force Member States to comply with their obligations under Article 9 RTC and the relevant provisions of Chapter VIII, Part One, RTC:, as follows.

1. The CCJ in *Myrie*[6] held that:

   > "The Court is . . . entitled if not required, to adjudicate complaints of alleged breaches of Community law even where Community law is

3 See Latin American Competition Forum, 'Session II: Regional Competition Agreements – Contribution from the CARICOM Competition Commission', 3–4 September 2013, Lima, Peru, 4, available at http://search.oecd.org/officialdocuments/displaydocumentpdf/?cote=DAF/COMP/LACF%282013%2929&docLanguage=En [accessed 1 December 2013].

4 Ibid.

5 Ibid.

6 *Shanique Myrie v Barbados* [2013] CCJ 3 (OJ).

> inconsistent with domestic law. It is the obligation of each State, having consented to the creation of a Community obligation, to ensure that its domestic law, at least in its application, reflects and supports Community law."[7]

This statement means that non-implementation of obligations set out in Article 170 RTC will not prevent enterprises from bringing proceedings before the CCJ. Accordingly, private enforcement of CSME competition law may force reluctant Member States to enact legislation and to adopt appropriate measures to comply with the general obligation set out in Article 9 RTC, in conjunction with the relevant provisions of Chapter VIII.

2. The RTC does not impose any deadline on Member States in terms of implementation of the obligations set out in Article 170 RTC. This is to be contrasted with the Economic Partnership Agreement (EPA), signed between the CARIFORUM States, on the one hand, and the European Union and its Member States, on the other.[8] All CARICOM Member States are signatories of the EPA, which came into effect through provisional application in December 2008. Under Article 127 EPA, the parties to the EPA must ensure that, within five years of its entry into force, they have laws in force addressing the restrictions on competition specified in Article 126 EPA. Further, they must, within that period, establish competition authorities. In the case of the CARICOM States, the authority in question is the CCC. Article 127 EPA imposes an obligation on the CARICOM Member States to enact competition legislation, which must prohibit both:

   (a) agreements and concerted practices between undertakings, which have as their object or effect preventing, or substantially lessening, competition in the territory of the CARIFORUM States or in a substantial part thereof; and
   (b) abuses of a dominant position by one or more undertakings in the territory of the CARIFORUM States or a substantial part thereof.

   The obligations imposed by Article 127 EPA are to be compared with those contained in Article 177 RTC, which requires a Member State to have national legislation prohibiting similar infringements to those specified in Article 126 EPA. It is therefore submitted that if a Member State of CARICOM fails to enact national competition legislation, it will be in breach of both the EPA and the RTC. However, the EPA imposes a strict time frame for enactment of national legislation. This entails that the EPA will force CARICOM Member States to comply with Article 170(1)(b) RTC by enacting legislation that complies with both the EPA and the RTC.

7 Ibid., [53].
8 [2008] OJ L 289/1.

8.2.2 Article 8 RTC: 'Most Favoured Nation (MFN) Treatment'

Article 8 RTC contains the 'most favoured nation (MFN) treatment' clause. It states that:

> "Subject to the provisions of this Treaty, each Member State shall, with respect to any rights covered by this Treaty, accord to another Member State treatment not less favourable than that accorded to
>
> (a) a third Member State; or
> (b) third States."

The CCJ in *Myrie* explained the meaning of the MFN obligation as follows:

> "The right to Most Favoured Nation (MFN) treatment set out in Article 8 RTC applies to all rights conferred by or under the RTC. It is a right that enures to Member States and, so far as applicable, to their nationals. The right to MFN treatment guarantees to Community nationals treatment by the defendant State that is no less favourable than is extended by that State to nationals of other States (whether CARICOM States or otherwise)."[9]

Amongst the multilateral and bilateral agreements entered into by Member States of CARICOM,[10] the most relevant from the perspective of the application of

9 *Shanique Myrie v Barbados* [2013] CCJ 3 (OJ), [92].

10 With regard to the WTO agreements, the divergences between developing and developed countries regarding the content of common multilateral rules on competition under the WTO resulted in the decision of the WTO General Council to suspend the WTO's work in this area and to terminate the mandate of the *ad hoc* WTO Working Group on Trade and Competition Policy, which was created in 1994 to discuss the appropriateness of the establishment of common multilateral rules on competition under the WTO. See WTO General Council, Decision on the Doha Agenda Work Programme (the 'July package') 2 August 2004, WT/L/579, [1(g)]. The existing WTO rules have a very limited impact on competition policy. The most important rules are set out in TRIPS (Article 8(8)), and in the GATT and GATS. Article XVII GATT on 'State Trading Enterprises' provides that such enterprises must operate in a non-discriminatory manner in their sales or purchases of imports and exports. Article VIII GATS on 'Monopolies and Exclusive Service Supplies' provides that each Member State must ensure that any monopoly supplier of a service respects the MFN clause and that each WTO Member State respects its sectoral commitments in services.

It is to be noted that the CARICOM–Canada FTA is in the advanced process of negotiations. The sixth and latest round of negotiations took place in March and April 2014: see Foreign Affairs, Trade and Development Canada, *Canada–Caribbean Community (CARICOM) Trade Agreement Negotiations*, April 2014, available at http://www.international.gc.ca/trade-agreements-accords-commerciaux/agr-acc/caricom/index.aspx?lang=eng [accessed 25 May 2014]. It seems, however, that in terms of the removal of State restrictions on competition it will not go beyond the obligations imposed on CARIFORUM Member States by the EPA: see Foreign Affairs, Trade and

Article 8 RTC is the EPA, because it contains a separate Chapter on competition (Articles 125–130 EPA). In particular, its Article 129 deals with public enterprises and enterprises entrusted with special or exclusive rights, including State monopolies. Article 129 EPA imposes restrictions on such enterprises that go beyond those imposed by the RTC, or indeed the World Trade Organisation (WTO) agreements (see section 8.5).[11]

Article 238(2) EPA states that: 'Any more favourable treatment and advantage that may be granted under this Agreement by any Signatory CARIFORUM state to the EU Party shall also be enjoyed by each Signatory CARIFORM State.' Accordingly, under Article 238(2) EPA, each CARIFORUM State is obliged, with regard to any other CARIFORUM State, to ensure that its own treatment of public enterprises, and enterprises to which it has granted special or exclusive rights, conforms to Article 129 EPA. By virtue of Article 8 RTC, Article 129 EPA will be within the scope of CSME competition law in that a CARICOM Member State and, if appropriate, its nationals may rely on Article 8 RTC to ensure that another CARICOM Member State treats enterprises and nationals of that State in the manner prescribed by Article 129 EPA in a situation in which a national measure or practice has a cross-border effect on competition and trade within the CSME.

It is to be noted that the European Union insisted on the insertion of a Chapter on competition in the EPA and on the use of wordings that show a great similarity to Article 106 TFEU (see section 8.3.3). The matter of inclusion of Article 129 into the EPA was, together with Chapters on other trade-related issues, one of the most sensitive and divisive matters during negotiations between the CARIFORUM States and the European Union. The South Centre notes that the inclusion of Article 129 EPA 'represents major concessions of Caribbean negotiators to the EU. Moreover, there could be conflict between competition provisions and those regarding government procurement and trade in services.'[12]

8.2.3 Article 7 RTC: The principle of non-discrimination

A general principle of non-discrimination based on nationality is embodied in Article 7 RTC. It requires goods, persons, services and capital to enjoy the same treatment in a host Member State as that given by that State to domestic goods,

Development Canada, *Canada–CARICOM Free Trade Negotiations*, July 2008, available at http://www.international.gc.ca/trade-agreements-accords-commerciaux/agr-acc/caricom/caricom-initial-initiale.aspx [accessed 20 December 13].

11 On the status of implementation of the EPA in CARIFORUM States, see C. Lindsay, 'The EU–CARIFORUM EPA: Regulatory and Policy Changes and Lessons for Other ACP Countries' (2013) 1 Caribbean Journal of International Relations & Diplomacy 5.

12 South Centre, *Fact Sheet No. 8: Competition Policy in Economic Partnership Agreements (CARIFORUM Text)*, March 2008, SC/AN/TDP/EPA/15, [48].

services, capital and national workers. The main benefit of 'national treatment' is that it does not interfere with national regulatory autonomy. Consequently, a Member State remains free to regulate the way in which goods are produced, services are provided and workers are treated on its national territory. Any discrimination measure based on nationality can be justified only on grounds provided by the Treaty, and must be necessary and proportionate to the objectives that it seeks to achieve.

The CCJ in *Myrie* described the meaning of the principle of non-discrimination based on nationality as follows:

> "Discrimination in the context of Caribbean Community law occurs where, within the scope of application of the Treaty, the facts of the case disclose treatment that is worse or less favourable than is accorded to a person whose circumstances are similar to those of the complainant except for their and the complainant's nationality, with no objective and reasonable justification for the difference in treatment."[13]

It is submitted that CSME competition law, on the one hand, goes beyond the prohibition of discrimination based on nationality and, on the other, allows such discrimination. It allows discrimination because it recognises State trading through enterprises that have been granted monopolistic rights by a Member State. The existence and operation of such enterprises is, by definition, discriminatory. It goes beyond the prohibition of discrimination based on nationality, because many provisions of CSME competition law prohibit discriminatory practices irrespective of whether they are directed against competitors from other Member States or against national enterprises. For example Article 177(2)(d) prohibits the imposition of discriminatory conditions on equivalent transactions.

The principle of non-discrimination based on nationality will be of great relevance to nationals of the CARICOM States in connection with private enforcement of CSME competition law. Article 170(1)(b)(iv) RTC requires a Member State to take effective measures to ensure access by nationals of other Member States to its own enforcement authorities, including its courts, on an equitable, transparent and non-discriminatory basis.

8.3 Competition law and public undertakings, and undertakings to which special or exclusive rights have been granted by a State, including State monopolies

The treatment of public enterprises under competition law raises many questions. Should competition law endorse the principle of competitive neutrality, which would mean that public and private enterprises should operate upon a level

13 *Shanique Myrie v Barbados* [2013] CCJ 3 (OJ), [84].

playing field when carrying out commercial transactions, and thus that public undertakings should not enjoy any competitive advantage merely by virtue of State ownership or control? Should some exemptions from the application of competition law to such enterprises be allowed? In this respect, Article 129(2) EPA provides that public enterprises, and enterprises to which special or exclusive rights have been granted, are subject to competition rules 'in so far as the application of such rules does not obstruct the performance, in law or in fact, of the particular tasks assigned to them'.

The treatment of public enterprises under competition law is an important matter for the following reasons.

1. Public enterprises and enterprises to which a State has granted special and exclusive rights are often in a dominant position in the relevant national market, and therefore may also be found to be in a dominant position in the relevant Community market (see Chapter 7).
2. Public enterprises that perform State prerogatives are excluded from the scope of competition law. Accordingly, only enterprises within the meaning of CSME competition law are within the scope of competition law (see Chapter 4, section 4.5).
3. Public enterprises and enterprises to which special or exclusive rights have been granted by a State are in a peculiar situation in the relevant market when they provide universal services. Perhaps the best definition of 'universal services' was provided by the European Commission in its White Paper on Services of General Interest.[14] It reads as follows: 'It establishes the right of everyone to access certain services considered as essential and imposes obligations on service providers to offer defined services to specified conditions including complete territorial coverage and at an affordable price.'[15] Examples of universal services include telecommunication, postal and sewage services.

   An enterprise providing commercial services of a universal nature often subsidises non-profitable parts of its operation from profitable parts. Accordingly, to submit such an enterprise to the full application of competition law would result in 'cream-skimming' – that is, a situation in which profitable parts of its operation would attract competitors, whilst non-profitable parts would be carried out by the enterprise providing services of a universal nature. If competitors were allowed to cream-skim, in the long run this would lead to the collapse of the universal service concerned. Accordingly, it is reasonable to suggest that a public undertaking should be shielded from the application of competition law in order to avoid cream-skimming, particularly in light of the fact that the provision of universal

14 European Commission, *White Paper on Services of General Interest*, May 2004, COM(2004)374 final.

15 Ibid., p 8.

services is essential to ensure the social inclusion of and a high quality of life for citizens (see section 8.4.2.1).

4. A State may be tempted to protect 'national champions' from competitive pressures. In developed countries, 'national champions' are large enterprises or industries that are expected to become major international players in the relevant market, and thus governments justify protectionist measures for their champions on the basis of the need to strengthen the competitiveness of the national economy.[16] The European Union considers that competition law should apply to national champions, and condemns attempts by the Member States to create and promote national champions.[17] Small developing countries argue that the protection of national champions in the early stage of a country's industrialisation is necessary to ensure that they will, with time, be able to compete in international markets. However, the Organisation for Economic Co-operation and Development (OECD) Global Forum on Competition found that:

> "The empirical evidence shows that, in a globalised world, emerging firms grow better by first competing at home without State support, and thus prepare themselves better to compete on international markets. Indeed, intense rivalry between firms and the permanent threat to incumbents posed by innovative entrants are a far better engine of growth than industrial policies run by bureaucrats who are not subject to market discipline, but are capable of being captured by vested interests. There is also ample evidence of the failure of many national champions, which can often be ascribed to a lack of accountability, and to economically irrational decisions resulting from politicized governance."[18]

5. State monopolies often produce revenue for a State. For example, profits from gambling may be an important or even an essential source of revenue for a State. Further, a State monopoly on goods such as tobacco and alcohol not only brings revenue for a State, but also may be considered to be a potentially effective instrument for the protection of public health.

16 See J. Galloway, 'The Pursuit of National Champions: The Intersection of Competition and Industrial Policy' (2007) 28 ECLR 172.

17 See European Commission, *Communication on Pro-active Competition Policy for a Competitive Europe*, April 2004, (COM)2004 0293 final, [2.1(5)]: 'The benefits of competition . . . demonstrate the danger in arguments about the creation of "national champions". There is nothing improper in companies growing into a sufficient scale to compete globally. However, this has to come about within a competitive environment and in full compliance with the competition rules. Competition at home enhances a firm's ability to compete abroad.'

18 See OECD, *Policy Roundtables: Competition Policy, Industrial Policy and National Champions*, 2009, available at http://www.oecd.org/daf/competition/44548025.pdf [accessed 13 December 2013], p 16.

6. A State monopoly may be a major source of employment, in particular in a small country. Additionally, employees of a State monopoly may enjoy advantages not necessarily provided by the private sector, such as higher pay, generous health insurance and generous retirement arrangements. Accordingly, any attempt at privatisation of a State monopoly may result in politicians being subjected to strong public pressure. In those circumstances, maintenance of a State monopoly may be necessary to ensure political stability and to achieve social objectives, such as full employment of labour, or both.
7. A State may establish a monopoly in order to ensure that some strategic sectors of economy are controlled by the government, for example a State monopoly on import of gas or oil to ensure security of supplies, or a State monopoly to protect national natural resources in terms of the rate of exploitation.
8. The very existence of national monopolies of a commercial nature, or character, undermines the CSME. It partitions the Community market and prevents operators from other Member States from competing, thereby obstructing the free movement of goods and services. Further, State monopolies are inherently less efficient and responsive to consumers' needs than private enterprises.

In light of these considerations, the extent to which competition law should apply to public enterprises, and enterprises to which special or exclusive rights have been granted, including State monopolies, is very controversial. The next section examines the treatment of such enterprises under the RTC and under Article 129 EPA.

8.3.1 Definition of 'public undertakings'

Article 94(10) RTC states that 'public undertakings' means 'central, regional, or local government authorities, public enterprises and any other organisation by means of which a Member State by law or in practice controls or appreciably influences imports from, or exports to any other part of the Community'. Although this definition of public undertakings is provided in Part Two of the RTC, which concerns 'Trade Liberalisation', it is useful for the purposes of competition law. It emphasises that, in order to decide whether a particular entity is to be regarded as a public undertaking, the degree of State control, rather than the legal form of the entity in question, should be decisive. A State may control an enterprise by virtue either of ownership, or of some structural, contractual or other arrangements.

Unlike the Treaty on the Functioning of the European Union (TFEU),[19] the RTC contains no specific provisions dealing with the application of competition

19 See Article 106 TFEU, discussed at section 8.3.3.1.

law to public undertakings. However, Article 94 RTC provides some general prohibitions, whilst Article 31 RTC deals with the treatment of State monopolies. Furthermore, Article 129 EPA, which deals with public enterprises and enterprises entrusted with special or exclusive rights, including designated monopolies, may, because of the MFN obligation enshrined in Article 8 RTC, be useful in the clarification of the treatment of public undertakings under CSME competition law.

8.3.2 Article 94 RTC

Article 94(1) RTC imposes an obligation on a Member State to ensure that its public undertakings do not take protectionist or discriminatory measures with regards to goods coming from other Member States. Such measures may not only be in breach of the rules on the free movement of goods, but also contrary to Article 177(1)(b) RTC, which prohibits abuses of a dominant position. This is acknowledged in Article 94(3(b) RTC, which states that it applies not only to measures relating to the free movement of goods, but also to any measure or practice introduced by a public undertaking that 'in law or in effect, results in limiting access to any market, distorts competition or fair trade, or otherwise nullifies or impairs benefits expected from the establishment of the CSME'. It is to be noted that Article 94(9) RTC prohibits the introduction of new practices of the kind described in Article 94(3) RTC.

Article 94 RTC sets out the procedure to be adopted in a situation in which a national measure or practice may, *inter alia*, distort competition within the Community. Under Article 94(3) RTC, an aggrieved Member State may request consultation with the offending Member State and is required to notify COTED of its request promptly. If the offending Member State, which, under Article 94(4) RTC, is required to give favourable consideration to such a request, fails to reach a mutually acceptable solution with the aggrieved Member State, within 30 days of the date of request for consultation, COTED becomes involved in the matter if the aggrieved Member State so wishes. Under Article 94(5) RTC, COTED will have 60 days from receipt of notification from the aggrieved Member State of its consultation request in which to investigate the matter, and prepare and submit to the Member States concerned a report, which will serve as the basis for further consultation between them. If no mutually acceptable solution is achieved within 15 days of submission of COTED's report and if COTED is satisfied that the rights of the aggrieved Member State have been infringed, it shall request the offending Member State to withdraw the offending measure or practice. If the offending Member State refuses to comply with that request within 60 days of receipt of that request, COTED may authorise the aggrieved Member State to suspend, in relation to the offending Member State, the application of such provisions of the RTC as COTED may decide.

The procedure set out in Article 94 RTC allows only the aggrieved Member State to act. Accordingly, there is no direct redress available to a private party either under the RTC or under the national law of the offending Member State. Further, no application of CSME competition law is provided to solve a dispute relating to measures or practices that may distort competition. As a result, any solution to a dispute will be based on political, rather than legal, grounds. This entails a lack of transparency and random political settlement of legal problems, which may be of concern to other Member States.

It is submitted that the RTC clearly excludes the application of CSME competition law to public undertakings when they take measures distorting competition in the Community. However, by virtue of Article 8 RTC, any dispute relating to alleged anti-competitive measures or practices of public undertakings may be brought within the scope of the RTC. For that reason, it is important to examine Article 129(2) EPA in light of Article 106 TFEU.

8.3.3 Article 106 TFEU and Article 129(2) EPA

Article 106 TFEU deals with public undertakings and undertakings to which a Member State has granted special rights or exclusive rights. It comprises three parts.

- Article 106(1) TFEU is addressed to Member States. It prohibits them, in relation to public undertakings or undertakings to which a Member State has granted special or exclusive rights, from enacting or maintaining in force any measures contrary to the EU Treaties – in particular, any measures contrary to the principle of non-discrimination and to the EU rules on competition.
- Article 106(2) TFEU is addressed to undertakings that have been entrusted with the operation of services of general economic interest (SGEIs) (see section 8.4.2.1) and State monopolies producing revenue for a Member State. It allows such undertakings to be exempted from the application of EU competition law in so far as this is necessary for carrying out their tasks. The exact words of Article 106(2) are that undertakings are subject to the rules of competition 'in so far as the application of such rules does not obstruct the performance, in law or in fact, of the particular tasks assigned to them'.
- Article 106(3) TFEU gives the European Commission the power, first, to ensure that Member States respect Article 106 TFEU and, second, to legislate to ensure the proper application of Article 106 TFEU.

Article 129(2) EPA contains many elements of Article 106(1) and (2) TFEU. It states that:

> "With regard to public enterprises and enterprises to which special or exclusive rights have been granted, the Parties and the Signatory CARIFORUM States shall ensure that, following the date of entry into

force of this Agreement, there is neither enacted or maintained any measure distorting trade in goods or services between the Parties to an extent contrary to the Parties interest, and that such enterprises shall be subject to the rules of competition in so far as the application of such rules does not obstruct the performance, in law or in fact, of the particular tasks assigned to them."

In light of the similarity between Article 106(1) and (2) TFEU and Article 129 EPA, it seems useful to define the concepts of special and exclusive rights.

- Exclusive rights are monopoly rights granted to enterprises, either public or private.
- Special rights are more difficult to define, but the European Commission has identified them as those that are granted by a State to a limited number of undertakings, through any legislative, regulatory or administrative instrument. Such undertakings are chosen in a subjective and discriminatory manner by a State, and the rights granted to them substantially affect the ability of any other undertaking to provide that same service in the same geographical area and under substantially equivalent conditions.[20]

8.3.3.1 'Measures' that may affect competition

With regard to measures that may affect competition and which are within the scope of Article 106(1) TFEU, the necessity for providing exclusivity or special rights to a public undertaking has been challenged in many cases before the ECJ. However, the case law of the ECJ clearly shows that the granting of exclusive or special rights by itself is not in breach of Article 106(1) TFEU.[21] A Member State will be in breach of Article 106(1) TFEU, in conjunction with Article 102 TFEU, only when an undertaking to which such rights have been granted cannot avoid

20 See Preamble to Directive 94/46 amending Directive 88/301/EEC and Directive 90/388/EEC in particular with regard to satellite communications [1994] OJ L 268/15.

21 However, see Case C–320/91 *Criminal Proceedings against Paul Corbeau* [1993] ECR I-2533, in which the ECJ seems to suggest that the grant of monopoly rights itself may breach Article 106(1) TFEU unless the rights at issue can be justified under Article 106(2) TFEU. In this case, there were none of: an abuse of rights granted to the Belgian Post Office; the extension of the monopoly into a neighbouring market; a conflict of interest; or the bundling of regulatory functions with commercial activities. However, the ECJ subsequently retreated from the position adopted in *Corbeau*: see, e.g., Case C-323/93 *Société Civile Agricole du Centre d'Insémination de la Crespelle v Coopérative d'Elevage et d'Insémination Artificielle du Département de la Mayenne* [1994] ECR I-5077. On this topic, see D. Edward and M. Hoskins, 'Art. 90: Deregulation and EC Law – Reflections Arising from the XVI FIDE Conference' (1996) 32 CML Rev 157.

abusing its dominant position, or when a Member State creates a situation in which an undertaking is led to abuse its dominant position.

It seems appropriate to provide a short examination of the way in which the ECJ approaches the treatment of public undertakings, and undertakings to which a Member State has granted exclusive or special rights. Although any categorisation of measures that will infringe Article 106(1) TFEU is not possible, it is useful to comment on the case law of the ECJ in order to identify measures that are likely to make it unavoidable for an undertaking to which exclusive or special rights have been granted to abuse its dominant position, or likely to create a situation in which it is led into abusing its dominant position. The most likely situations in which a Member State will be liable for breach of Article 106(1) TFEU, in conjunction with Article 102 TFEU, are examined below.

A Where a statutory monopoly is manifestly unable to meet demand because of the manner in which it has been set up

In *Höfner*,[22] the German Federal Office for Employment (GFOE), which was granted exclusive rights of employment procurement, was not able to meet demands for placement of business executives. Under German law, the provision of such services by private companies was prohibited. The ECJ found Germany in breach of Article 106(1) TFEU because it created a situation in which the GFOE could not avoid infringing Article 102(b) TFEU – that is, the GFOE was manifestly incapable of satisfying demand in the market for executive recruitment agency services, but the provision of these services by private recruitment agencies was rendered impossible by the maintenance in force of a statutory provision under which provision of those services was prohibited, and non-compliance with that prohibition rendered the relevant contractual arrangements between private recruitment agencies and their clients void.

In *Merci Convenzionali Porto di Genova*,[23] under Italian law, all dock work was reserved to dock-work undertakings. In the Port of Genoa, all dock work was granted to Merci – a dock-work undertaking, which held the concession to organize dock work in that port, but which was required, under Italian law, to call upon dock-work companies to actually perform the dock work.

Siderurgica made a request to Merci for the unloading in the port of Genoa of a consignment of steel, which had been brought from Germany. Merci then called upon a dock-work company operating in the port of Genoa to actually perform the unloading. Owing to strikes among that dock-work company's workforce, the unloading was substantially delayed, as was the subsequent transportation of the steel to Siderurgica's required destination. Under Italian law, the crew of the ship that had transported steel to Genoa was not allowed to

22 Case C-41/90 *Klaus Höfner and Fritz Elser v Macrotron GmbH* [1991] ECR I-1979.

23 Case C-179/90 *Merci Convenzionali Porto di Genova SpA v Siderurgica Gabrielli SpA* [1991] ECR I-5889.

unload it, although the ship was equipped for that purpose. Further, Siderurgica was prevented from collecting the steel itself in circumstances under which, after the unloading, Merci failed, for a considerable period of time, to deliver it to Siderurgica. Despite all of the delays, Siderurgica was required to pay to Merci the compulsory standard charges for handling its consignment.

Siderurgica brought proceedings against Merci both for damages that it had suffered as a result of the delay in unloading and for reimbursement of sums that it alleged had been wrongfully charged for dock-work services that it had been required under Italian legislation to use, but had never requested and which, in fact, it did not use.

The ECJ held that Italy was, *inter alia*, in breach of Articles 102(b) and 106(1) TFEU on the ground that Merci had been inefficient, had exploited its customers and had refused to modernise.[24] The Italian law created a situation in which Merci was induced to, or led to, abuse its dominant position.

It is to be noted that Articles 177(2)(b) and 179(1)(e) RTC set out a prohibition similar to that set out in Article 102(b) TFEU.

B Where rights conferred on an undertaking holding exclusive or special rights create a conflict of interest

In *ERT*,[25] the ECJ condemned Greek law, which granted to ERT, a Greek radio and television undertaking, a monopoly to broadcast national programmes – that is, its own programmes – as well as to retransmit foreign programmes, including those from other EU Member States. The ECJ held that the double monopoly created by Greek law was liable 'to create a situation in which [ERT] is led to infringe Article [102] by virtue of a discriminatory broadcasting policy which favours its own programmes'.[26]

In *Silvano Raso*,[27] following the judgment of the ECJ in *Merci Convenzionali Porto di Genova*, Italy amended its law granting exclusive rights to organise dock work at Italian ports. Under that law, dock-work companies were granted a monopoly in respect of the supply of temporary labour. Further, they could compete with undertakings that, under Italian law, were authorised to carry out actual dock work in the supply of services to port users. Authorised undertakings were allowed to use their own employees to execute dock work, but when they were unable to meet the demand, they had to have recourse to dock-work companies to provide the necessary labour. As a result, dock-work companies could both compete with undertakings authorised to carry out dock work in the supply of services to port users and, simultaneously, enjoy an exclusive right

24 Ibid., [19].

25 Case C-260/89 *Elliniki Radiophonia Tiléorassi AE (ERT) and Panellinia Omospondia Syllogon Prossopikou v Dimotiki Etairia Pliroforissis and Sotirios Kouvelas and Nicolaos Avdellas and ors* [1991] ECR I-2925.

26 Ibid., [37].

27 Case C-163/96 *Criminal Proceedings against Silvano Raso and ors* [1998] ECR I-533.

regarding the provision of temporary labour to authorised undertakings. This, according to the ECJ, created a 'conflict of interest', because it distorted, in favour of the dock-work companies, the equal conditions of competition between various operators on the market in dock-work services. The conflict of interest led to an abuse by dock-work companies of their dominant position 'by imposing on its competitors in the dock-work market unduly high costs for the supply of labour or by supplying them with labour less suited to the work to be done'.[28] Accordingly, Italy was in breach of Article 90(1) TFEU, in conjunction with Article 102 TFEU.

C Where rights conferred on an undertaking holding exclusive or special rights extend to a neighbouring, but separate, market

In *RTT*,[29] the ECJ dealt solely with a situation in which national law extended exclusive rights of an undertaking to a neighbouring, but separate, market. In this case, under Belgian law, RTT, a company operating the public telephone network in Belgium, was granted a monopoly over the establishment and operation of the Belgian public telephone system. Belgian law also provided that only equipment supplied by RTT or approved by it could be connected to the Belgian public network. GB-INNO sold, in its shops, non-approved telephones for use as second telephones at a price lower than the prices charged by RTT. RTT brought proceedings for an order that GB-INNO cease selling telephones without informing the purchasers that they were not approved by RTT. GB-INNO challenged the Belgian law in the Belgian Commercial Court, which referred to the ECJ, *inter alia*, the question of whether Article 106(1) TFEU, in conjunction with Article 102 TFEU, precluded Belgium from granting to RTT the power to lay down the standards for telephone equipment in Belgium and to check that economic operators met those standards, in a situation in which RTT was competing with those operators on the market for terminals.

The ECJ found RTT in breach of Article 102 TFEU. It held that there is a breach of that Article when an undertaking that holds a monopoly in the market for the establishment, and operation, of a telephone network, without any objective necessity, reserves to itself a neighbouring, but separate, market (that is, the market for importation, marketing, connection, commissioning and maintenance of equipment for connection to its network), thereby eliminating all competition from that market. However, because Article 102 TFEU applies only to undertakings that engage in anti-competitive conduct on their own initiative, not to measures taken by a Member State, the extension of the dominant position of a public undertaking, or undertaking to which a Member State has granted exclusive or special rights, to a neighbouring market is attributable to the

28 Ibid., [30].
29 Case C-18/88 *Régie des Télégraphes et des Téléphones (RTT) v GB-Inno-BM SA* [1991] ECR I-5941.

Member State only when that Article is applied, in conjunction with Article 106(1) TFEU. The ECJ applied those Articles jointly and found that Belgian law had created a situation that led to an abuse of a dominant position by RTT.

In *ERT*,[30] the Greek law had granted ERT exclusive rights not only in respect of broadcasting its own programmes, but also in respect of the retransmission of foreign programmes. This extension of monopoly rights to a neighbouring, but separate, market constituted a breach of Article 106(1) TFEU, in conjunction with Article 102 TFEU.

In its *Slovakian Hybrid Mail* decision,[31] the European Commission found Slovakia in breach of Articles 106(1) and 102 TFEU on the ground that 2008 Slovakian legislation re-monopolised business activities that had been successfully liberalised under the relevant EU directive. In this case, Slovakia enacted legislation under which the delivery of hybrid mail[32] was given back to the Slovenská Pošta, a public undertaking holding a postal monopoly in Slovakia. The delivery of hybrid post was, prior to the enactment of the 2008 legislation, carried out by private undertakings. According to the European Commission, the 2008 Slovakian legislation extended the statutory monopoly of the Slovenská Pošta into the neighbouring market of hybrid mail services without any objective justification, and thus harmed consumers and postal operators that had already entered the hybrid mail market.

D Where a dominant public undertaking refuses to supply its services to other undertakings

This mainly occurs in cases involving 'essential facilities' (see Chapter 7, section 7.4.2.3). For example, in the *Port of Rødby* decision,[33] the European Commission found Denmark in breach of Article 106(1) TFEU, in conjunction with Article 102 TFEU, for refusing to allow 'Euro-Port A/S', a subsidiary of the Swedish group 'Stena Rederi AB' (Stena) to build a new port in the immediate vicinity of the port of Rødby or to operate from the existing port facilities at Rødby. In this case, DSB, a Danish public undertaking, owned and managed the

30 Case C-260/89 *Elliniki Radiophonia Tiléorassi AE (ERT) and Panellinia Omospondia Syllogon Prossopikou v Dimotiki Etairia Pliroforissis and Sotirios Kouvelas and Nicolaos Avdellas and ors* [1991] ECR I-2925.

31 Case COMP/F-1/39.562 *Slovakian Hybrid Mail* [2008] OJ C 322/10, [2009] 4 CMLR 663. It should be noted that Slovakia has brought proceedings for the annulment of the decision in Case T-556/08 *Slovenská Pošta v Commission* (pending) on the ground, *inter alia*, that the European Commission committed manifest errors in assessment and interpretation, in fact and in law, of the lawfulness of the granting of exclusive rights in the postal sector, as a result of which it wrongly applied Articles 106 and 102 TFEU.

32 Hybrid mail is a specific form of postal service whereby printable content is electronically transferred from the sender to the postal service operator, who then prints, envelopes, and delivers the postal items. Hybrid mail is mainly used by companies that send large amounts of mail (e.g. invoices), such as banks and insurance companies.

33 Commission Decision 94/119/EC *Port of Rødby* [1994] OJ L 55/52.

port of Rødby, and provided, together with a German public undertaking named DB, ferry services between the port of Rødby and the port of Puttgarden. The port of Rødby handled more than 70 per cent of the passengers, and approximately 90 per cent of the lorries, crossing between Denmark and Germany. Although DSB did not hold any exclusive rights to ferry services, upon its recommendation, the Danish Transport Ministry had been granting authorisations to potential competitors of DSB to use the port terminal. Denmark's refusal was given to Euro-Port A/S on the grounds that, first, the building of a new terminal was unjustified because Euro-Port A/S had not established that there was an unsatisfied demand for ferry services between the port of Rødby and the port of Puttgarden and, second, if Euro-Port A/S had been given access to the existing terminal, its operation would have the effect of preventing DBS and DB, which were already operating in the port, from expanding their activities. The European Commission established that both grounds were unjustified. It found that both refusals constituted 'measures' within the meaning of Article 106(1) and that they had the effect of eliminating potential competitors on the Rødby–Puttgarden route, and hence of strengthening the joint dominant position of DSB and DB on that route.

E Where a dominant public undertaking applies dissimilar conditions to equivalent transactions with other trading parties, thereby placing them at a competitive disadvantage, irrespective of whether such discrimination is linked to nationality

Discrimination on this basis usually takes the form of price discrimination. For example, in *GT-Link A/S*,[34] the ECJ found that when a public undertaking, which operated services and owned a commercial port (the business of the latter of which constituted a substantial part of the internal market), waived harbour duties on its own ferries and reciprocally on those of some of its commercial partners, while charging the full duties to other commercial partners, there could be a breach of Article 102(2)(c) TFEU.[35] The ECJ left to the referring court the assessment of whether the exemption from payments of harbour duties amounted to the application of dissimilar conditions to equivalent transactions, but indicated that an abuse would have occurred with regard to exemption of the public undertaking's own ferry services:

> . . . if it appeared that in its accounts the public undertaking did not allocate a sum equivalent to the total sum of port duties ordinarily payable to that part of its activity concerned with operating ferry services. In the absence of transparent accounts, the fact that the prices charged for its ferry services

34 Case C-242/95 *GT-Link A/S v De Danske Statsbaner (DSB)* [1997] ECR I-4449.
35 Article 177(2)(d) RTC contains a prohibition similar to that contained in Article 102(2)(c) TFEU.

are unusually low compared with those charged by competitor ferry companies could constitute evidence that there was no such allocation.[36]

In *Portugal v Commission (Landing Fees at Portuguese Airports)*,[37] Portugal set up a scheme for granting discounts on landing fees to airlines depending on the number of planes that they landed. In fact, only two airlines, both Portuguese, qualified for the highest rate discount. The ECJ held that a non-abusive discount system must be non-discriminatory in fact. The Court emphasised that while it was inherent in any quantity discount system that the largest buyers obtained the highest reduction, nevertheless it could be discriminatory if the system were to set out thresholds that only a few very large users could reach and which gave them disproportionate rewards. Further, under the Portuguese scheme, different landing charges were applied for domestic and international flights (in particular for intra-EEA flights). This, the ECJ held, was discriminatory within the meaning of Article 102(c) TFEU, because the landing and take-off services provided by airports are the same irrespective of the destination of flights.

In many cases relating to charges imposed by public undertakings holding a legal monopoly on ownership and operation of services relating to ports and airports, the ECJ and the European Commission have found a breach of Article 102(2)(c) TFEU.[38]

8.4 Exemptions from the application of competition law enjoyed by public undertakings, and by undertakings to which exclusive and special rights have been granted by a State

Article 129(2) EPA and Article 106(2) TFEU set out exemptions from the application of competition law. There are differences between Article 129(2) EPA and Article 106(2) TFEU, which can be explained by the fact that each treaty has a different role to play, and that differing levels of regional integration have been achieved by the EU and the CARIFORUM States. Despite this, for the interpretation of the exemption set out in Article 129(2) EPA, it will be instructive to examine the case law of the ECJ relating to the interpretation of Article 106(2) TFEU. This is because, under both treaties, enterprises may qualify for exemption in circumstances under which the application of competition law would render them incapable of fulfilling their mission. Under Article 106(2) TFEU, the ECJ's assessment of whether the application of competition law obstructs the performance of particular tasks assigned to

36 Case C-242/95 *GT-Link A/S v De Danske Statsbaner (DSB)* [1997] ECR I-4449, [42].

37 Case C-163/99 *Portugal v Commission (Landing Fees at Portuguese Airports)* [2001] ECR I-2613.

38 See, e.g., Commission Decision 1999/199/EC *Portuguese Airports* [1999] OJ L 69/31, [24]–[40]; Commission Decision 2000/521/EC *Spanish Airports* [2000] OJ L 208/36, [45]–[56].

enterprises is made in light of the principle of proportionality. It is submitted that the case law of the ECJ on this point may well be of relevance in the application of the 'obstruct the performance' test set out in Article 129(2) EPA.

8.4.1 Exemption from the application of competition law under Article 129 EPA

With regard to Article 129 EPA, it exempts from the scope of competition law the following.

1. Public enterprises and enterprises to which special or exclusive rights have been granted in the Signatory CARIFORM States, which 'are subject to specific sectoral rules as mandated by their respective regulatory frameworks'.[39] It is to be noted that COTED, under Article 182 RTC, 'shall develop and establish appropriate policies and rules of competition within the Community including rules for particular sectors'. It is therefore submitted that special sectoral rules are likely to be harmonised. In this respect, the CCC has expressed its intention to press COTED for removal of sectoral exemptions in situations in which anti-competitive conduct that could be exempted nationally has cross-border effects on markets in the CSME.[40]

   It is to be noted that Article 129(5) EPA states that the CARIFORUM–EU Trade and Development Committee must be informed about the enactment of sectoral rules provided for in Article 129(3) EPA. This will ensure that the discretion of a Member State to enact new rules will be subject to scrutiny.
2. Public enterprises and enterprises to which special or exclusive rights have been granted, in so far as rules of competition obstruct the performance in law or in fact of the task assigned to them.
3. Measures under Article 129(2) EPA, which are justified 'by the Parties' interest. Under this provision, CARIFORUM States are prohibited from enacting and maintaining any measures distorting trade in goods and services between 'the Parties' that are contrary to 'the Parties' interests'. However, the EPA does not define the concept of 'Parties' interests'. The South Centre notes that:

   > "[N]o indication of what could constitute the Parties' interests under this provision is given. Presumably, the text refers to the overall commercial interests of the parties or the commercial interests of their nationals (e.g. importers or exporters of services and goods), that is a

39 Article 129(3) EPA. Sectoral rules regulate a specific sector of economy, e.g. telecommunication, broadcasting, banking, or supply of electricity or water.

40 See Chapter 9, section 9.5.

> very vague notion, potentially encompassing any government (behind-the-border) measure.'[41]

If the South Centre's interpretation is correct, it entails, first, that a Member State will not be allowed to justify such a measure on the ground of public policy and, second, that measures examined in Chapter 8, section 8.3.3.1, which distort competition, will be within the scope of Article 129(2) EPA, because they cannot be justified by any commercial interest, and undoubtedly distort trade in goods and services between the Signatories of the EPA.

8.4.2 The Article 106(2) TFEU exemption from the application of EU competition law: the 'obstruct the performance' test

Under Article 106(2) TFEU, exemption applies only to undertakings entrusted with the operation of SGEIs and State monopolies producing revenue for a State. In the context of Article 106(2) TFEU, it is necessary to define the concept of SGEIs.

8.4.2.1 The definition of 'service of general economic interest'

The European Commission considers the term 'public service' to be confusing;[42] instead, it uses the terms 'service of general economic interest' (SGEI) and 'service of general interest' (SGI). Neither has been defined by the TFEU or by secondary legislation. However, the European Commission describes SGIs as being 'services that public authorities of the Member States at national, regional or local level classify as being of general interest and, therefore, subject to specific public service obligations (PSO)'.[43]

The term 'SGI' covers both economic activities and non-economic services. Non-economic services are outside the scope of the TFEU, and thus not subject to EU competition law, although they may be subject to other provisions of the EU Treaties, such as those that prohibit discrimination.

SGEIs are defined as:

> ". . . economic activities which deliver outcomes in the overall public good that would not be supplied (or would be supplied under different conditions in terms of objective quality, safety, affordability, equal treatment or

41 South Centre, *Fact Sheet No. 8: Competition Policy in Economic Partnership Agreements (CARIFORUM Text)*, March 2008, SC/AN/TDP/EPA/15, [42].

42 See European Commission, *Green Paper on Services of General Interest*, May 2003, COM(2003) 270 final, [19].

43 See European Commission, *Guide to the Application of the European Union Rules on State Aid, Public Procurement and the Internal Market to Services of General Economic Interest, and in Particular to Social Services of General Interest*, April 2013, SWD(2013) 53 final/2, p 21.

universal access) by the market without public intervention. The PSO is imposed on the provider by way of an entrustment and on the basis of a general interest criterion which ensures that the service is provided under conditions allowing it to fulfil its mission."[44]

Accordingly, under EU law, SGEIs are subject to competition rules and rules of the internal market, because they are of an economic nature.

Under Article 106(2) TFEU, State monopolies that raise revenue for the State and undertakings entrusted with the operation of SGEIs may claim an exemption from competition law. With regard to undertakings entrusted with the operation of SGEIs, for the application of Article 106(2) TFEU, it is immaterial whether an undertaking is public or private; what is important is that it has been entrusted by a Member State with the operation of SGEIs and that the services being provided exhibit special characteristics that qualify them as SGEIs.

Under EU law, it is for the public authorities of a Member State, whether at national, regional or local levels, to decide whether a service at issue is a SGEI.[45] The discretion given to every Member State is explained by the fact that each Member State has its own social, cultural and historical conditions influencing its decision when determining the scope and nature of a SGEI. However, when a Member State makes a manifest error in assessment, the European Union will intervene. For that reason, a Member State, when making a determination, must provide reasons why it considers that a particular service, because of its specific nature, deserves to be classified as a SGEI and thereby be distinguished from other economic activities. This enables the European Commission, and subsequently the European courts, to decide whether there is a manifest error in assessment on the part of a Member State. For example, in *Merci*,[46] Italy claimed that the performance of all dock work was a SGEI. The ECJ disagreed. It held that the operation of a commercial port does not necessarily constitute operation of a SGEI.

In order to qualify as a SGEI, the following criteria must be satisfied.

- The public service duty must be entrusted to the undertaking concerned by the public authorities of the Member State. The case law of the ECJ shows that the act of entrustment has been interpreted broadly, so encompassing regulatory and administrative acts and contracts. Entrustment can also be granted at the request of the service provider.[47] An act of entrustment must

44 European Commission, *Communication on a Quality Framework for Services of General Interest (SGI) in the EU*, December 2011, COM(2011) 900 final, p 3.

45 See T-289/03 *BUPA and ors v Commission* [2008] ECR II-81, [166]–[169].

46 Case C-179/90 *Merci Convenzionali Porto di Genova SpA v Siderurgica Gabrielli SpA* [1991] ECR I-5889/90, [27]; Case C-242/95 *GT-Link A/S v De Danske Statsbaner (DSB)* [1997] ECR I-4449, [53]; Joined Cases C-34/01–C38/01 *Enirisorse SpA v Ministero delle Finanze* [2003] ECR I-14243, [33]–[34].

47 Case T-17/02 *Fred Olsen, SA v Commission* [2005] ECR II-2031, [187]–[190].

be legally binding. For that reason, approval or authorisation by a public authority given to the provider of a service does not constitute an act of entrustment, because such acts do not create an obligation for the operator to provide the service. It is not necessary for an undertaking to be granted special or exclusive rights. A regulatory act may entrust the SGEI mission to all undertakings operating in a particular sector and thus it is not necessary that each undertaking is individually entrusted with the SGEI mission. Although no particular form is prescribed, an act of entrustment must clearly state the nature of the tasks, scope and general operational conditions of the SGEI. This is consistent with the principle of transparency.

- Advocate General Colomer, in his Opinion in *Federutility*,[48] defined the main characteristics of a SGEI as being continuity, universality, equality, transparency and affordability.
    - Continuity means that a SGEI must be provided without interruption.
    - Universality entails that it must be provided to all citizens, for example that a postal service must be supplied throughout the territory of a Member State, although universality is not compromised when a service is supplied by a particular group of persons in a particular part of the Member State. In *BUPA*,[49] the General Court held that:

        > "[T]he fact that the SGEI obligations in question have only limited territorial or material application or that the services concerned are enjoyed by only a relatively limited group of users does not necessarily call in question the universal nature of an SGEI mission within the meaning of [EU] law."[50]

    - Equality requires that the operator must provide a given product or service at the same price to all consumers, regardless of any differences in the cost of supplying different groups. For example, a telecommunications undertaking must ensure access to its network for all wishing to use it, irrespective of the fact that it will normally incur a higher cost for linking to its network an additional residential user located in an isolated rural area than an additional user located in a big city.
    - Affordability entails that an undertaking entrusted with the SGEI mission must provide the product or service at 'an affordable price'. Affordability is the main reason for public intervention, because often,

48 Case C-265/08 *Federutility and ors v Autorità per l'Energia Elettrica e il Gas* [2010] ECR I-3377, [54]–[55].
49 T-289/03 *BUPA and ors v Commission* [2008] ECR II-81.
50 Ibid., [187].

without it, some deserving group of users will be unable to acquire access to the relevant product or service.

The case law of the ECJ shows that, apart from the most obvious SGEIs concerning public utilities, such as the provision of electricity, gas, water, sewage disposal and basic postal services, the Court has recognised as SGEIs, *inter alia*, the administration of major waterways,[51] the operation of non-economically viable air routes,[52] the provision of sectoral supplementary pension funds,[53] the provision of emergency ambulance services,[54] the treatment of waste material[55] and the provision of private medical insurance.[56]

The existence and continuity of SGEIs is of great social and political importance for the Member States of the European Union. The European Commission stated in its 2007 Communication that SGEIs are:

> ". . . essential for the daily life of citizens and enterprises, and reflect Europe's model of society. They play a major role in ensuring social, economic, and territorial cohesion throughout the Union and are vital for the sustainable development of the EU in terms of higher levels of employment, social inclusion, economic growth and environmental quality."[57]

The importance of SGEIs has been recognised in Article 14 TFEU, and in Protocol 26 to the Treaty on European Union (TEU) and TFEU.

It is interesting to note that Article 106(2) TFEU, although numbered differently, appeared in the 1957 Treaty creating the European Economic Community (the Treaty of Rome), but was used once only in some thirty years of its existence.[58] It became relevant to the development of the European Union with the creation of the internal market, initiated by the 1986 Single European Act, and technical developments that eroded the traditional view that the maintenance of public monopolies is the only way of ensuring that public services are delivered. Further, with the development of competition law, it became evident that many State monopolies were economically inefficient and thus

51 Case 10/71 *Ministère Public Luxembourgeois v Madeleine Muller* [1971] ECR 723.

52 Case 66/86 *Ahmed Saeed Flugreisen and Silver Line Reisebüro GmbH v Zentrale zur Bekämpfung unlauteren Wettbewerbs e.V.* [1989] ECR 803.

53 Case C-67/96 *Albany International BV v Stichting Bedrijfspensioenfonds Textielindustrie* [1999] ECR I-5751.

54 Case C-475/99 *Firma Ambulanz Glöckner v Landkreis Südwestpfalz* [2001] ECR I-8089.

55 Case C-203/96 *Chemische Afvalstoffen Dusseldorp BV and ors v Minister van Volkshuisvesting, Ruimtelijke Ordening en Milieubeheer* [1998] ECR I-4075.

56 See T-289/03 *BUPA and ors v Commission* [2008] ECR II-8.

57 European Commission, *Communication on Services of General Interest, Including Social Services of General Interest: A New European Commitment*, November 2007, COM(2007) 725 final, [2].

58 Case 155/73 *Giuseppe Sacchi* [1974] ECR 409.

imposed restrictions on competition. In those circumstances, the European Commission commenced the process of liberalisation in public industries, first in the telecommunication sector, and then in transport, energy, insurance, postal services, etc., in order to open up to competition areas that were 'protected' by monopolies or exclusive or special rights. However, total liberalisation is not desirable, bearing in mind that it leads to social dumping and thus is contrary to the European social model. In those circumstances, a balance had to be struck between the requirements of competition law and those concerning legitimate national interests. The application of Article 106(2) TFEU makes possible the reconciliation of the objective of an open and competitive market with the objective of developing high-quality, accessible and affordable SGEIs.

8.4.2.2 The 'obstruct the performance' test'

The ECJ interpreted the 'obstruct the performance' test set out in Article 106(2) TFEU as being, in effect, the proportionality test. In early cases, the ECJ adopted a very restrictive approach to the application of the principle of proportionality. It held that an exception to the application of competition law was justified only if it was completely impossible for the undertaking concerned to perform the general interest mission. Accordingly, only restrictions that were indispensable were allowed. This approach was understandable in the context of the building up of the EU internal market. It was relaxed in *Corbeau*,[59] in which Corbeau had set up a private postal service in the Liège area in competition with the Belgian Post Office, which had a monopoly on postal services in Belgium. Criminal proceedings were commenced against Corbeau for infringing the postal monopoly. When the case reached the ECJ *via* the preliminary rulings procedure, the Court held that postal services were SGEIs and that the exception in Article 106(2) TFEU applied, because it was necessary for the Belgian Post Office to provide basic postal services at a uniform price throughout Belgium, irrespective of the specific situations or the degree of economic profitability of each individual operation. The ECJ held that the Belgian Post Office must have 'economically acceptable conditions', and must be able to perform its task in 'conditions of economic equilibrium' and thus preserve its cross-subsidy – that is, offset less profitable sectors against the profitable sectors. Accordingly, if competitors were allowed to 'cream-skim' the profitable operations, the Belgian Post Office would not be operating in 'conditions of economic equilibrium'.[60] However, the ECJ also held that if it were possible to dissociate some postal services from the SGEI without compromising the economic viability of the Belgian Post Office, those services would have been outside the scope of Article 106(2) TFEU – that is, they would have been subject to competition rules.

59 Case C-320/91 *Criminal Proceedings against Paul Corbeau* [1993] ECR I-2533.
60 Ibid., [17].

It flows from *Corbeau* that the proportionality test is no longer whether the public service mission would be impossible if competition rules were applied, but whether the application of competition law would undermine the economic equilibrium of the monopolist. In *Commission v Netherlands*,[61] the ECJ reiterated its ruling in *Corbeau* and elucidated the matter of the proof required from a Member State. It held that a Member State is not required to show that there is no other conceivable measure that could enable the undertaking holding a monopoly to fulfil the tasks assigned to it under economically acceptable conditions.

In *Ambulanz Glöckner*,[62] the question was whether the cross-subsidization of emergency ambulance services by non-emergency ambulances was within the scope of the exemption set out in Article 106(2) TFEU. The ECJ held that the provision of emergency ambulance services with universal round-the-clock availability was a SGEI. It also stated that the provision of non-emergency ambulance services was so closely connected to the provision of emergency ambulance services that it fell within the SGEI. This extension of exclusive rights to the non-emergency services was justified, because it enabled the holder of exclusive rights to discharge its SGEI mission in conditions of economic equilibrium. Indeed, had competitors been allowed to enter the market for non-emergency ambulance services, on profitable routes, in densely populated areas, at profitable peak hours, this could have affected the economic viability of the holder of exclusive rights, and consequently jeopardised the quality and reliability of emergency ambulance services. Advocate General Jacobs stated, in his Opinion in this case, that such 'cream-skimming', if allowed, would create a serious risk that 'inevitable losses of the public ambulances service are socialised, whilst its potential profits are privatised'.[63] The Court added that only in a situation in which the holder of exclusive rights entrusted with SGEIs was manifestly unable to satisfy demand for emergency ambulance services and for patient transport at all times could the justification for extending the exclusive rights to non-emergency ambulance services be accepted.

8.4.3 Conclusions

It is submitted that Article 129(2) EPA may have important consequences for the development of CSME competition law. It may be used to require and, at the same time, justify liberalisation of many sectors of the economy of CARIFORUM Member States, whilst ensuring that the objectives of developing high-quality, accessible and affordable public services are achieved. It is important to note that, in CARICOM, State monopolies are common.

61 Case C-157/94 *Commission v Netherlands* [1997] ECR I-5699, [43] and [58].
62 Case C-475/99 *Firma Ambulanz Glöckner v Landkreis Südwestpfalz* [2001] ECR I-8089. For the facts, see Chapter 5, section 5.3.3.
63 Ibid., Opinion of AG Jacobs, [182].

With regard to Article 129(2) EPA, it is submitted that EU law can assist with the definition of a 'measure' or 'practice' contrary to the 'Parties' interests'. The granting of exclusive or special rights by public authorities is, in itself, neither a breach of EU competition law nor of CSME competition law, bearing in mind the wording of Article 31 RTC (see Chapter 4, section 4.5). However, it is clear from the case law of the ECJ that Member States do not have unlimited discretion to create legal monopolies under whatever conditions they consider appropriate. Accordingly, when a public undertaking, merely by exercising the monopoly rights that have been granted to it, cannot avoid abusing its dominant position, or when such monopoly rights are liable to create a situation in which the monopoly is induced to, or led to, commit an abuse, a Member State will be in breach of competition law. Such measures distort trade in goods and services, and are unlikely to be justified by the Party's interest.

EU competition law may be seen as a useful guide in the matter of exemption from the application of competition law to public undertakings. Any exemption should be strictly interpreted. Under EU law, exemption from competition law is allowed in only two situations: first, when an undertaking carries out an SGEI mission; and second, when an undertaking is a State monopoly raising revenue for a Member State. However, in such situations, exemption will be granted if the application of competition law will obstruct, in law or in fact, the performance of the particular tasks assigned to the undertaking concerned, and if exemption does not affect trade to an extent contrary to the interests of the European Union.

Under Article 129(2) EPA, public enterprises and enterprises to which exclusive or special rights have been granted, including State commercial monopolies, are exempted from the application of competition law 'in so far as the application of such rules does not obstruct the performance, in law or in fact, of the particular tasks assigned to them'. The application of the principle of proportionality will determine whether the application of competition rules obstructs the performance of tasks assigned to such enterprises.

8.5 Monopolies of a commercial nature or character under Article 31 RTC and Article 129(4) EPA

This section examines provisions of the RTC and the EPA on monopolies of a commercial nature or character.

8.5.1 Monopolies of a commercial nature under Article 31 RTC

Article 31 RTC states:

> "1. The Member States may determine that the public interest requires the exclusion or restriction of the right of establishment in any industry or in a particular sector of an industry.
> 2. Where such a determination has been made:

(a) if the determination results in the continuation or establishment of a government monopoly, the Member State shall adopt appropriate measures to ensure that the monopoly does not discriminate between nationals of Member States, save as otherwise provided in this Treaty, and is subject to the agreed rules of competition established for Community economic enterprises;
(b) if the determination results in the continuation or establishment of a private sector monopoly, the Member State shall, subject to the provisions of this Treaty, adopt appropriate measures to ensure that national treatment is accorded to nationals of other Member States in terms of participating in its Operations."

Article 31 RTC is addressed to Member States. It confirms that State monopolies are not prohibited under the RTC. It concerns the treatment of monopolies of a commercial character or nature, in that it refers to both 'economic enterprises' and 'private sector monopolies'. Article 31(1) RTC allows a Member State to impose restrictions, or even to exclude the right of establishment, 'in any particular sector of an industry' when the public interest so requires. This has the following implications.

1. Article 31(1) RTC confirms the obvious consequences flowing from the existence of a State monopoly, or a private sector monopoly to which a State has granted exclusive rights, on the right of establishment. Indeed, the very nature of such monopolies is that they are sole providers of particular goods or services in the territory of a Member State. Competitors, whether national or foreign, are prohibited from carrying out activities that are performed by a monopoly. If competitors were allowed to compete in the provision of particular goods or services, the monopoly would disappear.
2. A Member State claiming the benefit of derogation from the freedom of establishment must show that such derogation is justified by the public interest. The question that arises here is whether justification based on the public interest will be assessed by the CCJ in light of the principle of proportionality. If it will, then even if the justification is acceptable, it may nevertheless fail if it is established that the objective sought by the Member State could be achieved by a measure less restrictive of the freedom of establishment.
3. The public interest derogation applies only to the right of establishment. This means that the restrictions on competition law relating to the existence and operation of a State monopoly of a commercial nature will not be examined from the perspective of its compliance with competition law, but only in light of the rules on establishment set out in the RTC.

It is submitted that an assessment of compatibility of a derogation based on the ground of public interest under the provisions of the RTC relating to the right of establishment may lead to a different outcome from one made under CSME competition rules. *Höfner*[64] may serve as an example in this regard.

If a State monopoly has been granted exclusive rights to put prospective employees and employers in contact with each other, and the Member State concerned justifies the existence and operation of that monopoly on the ground of the need to promote employment, the derogation based on the public interest may be acceptable even when, as in the *Höfner* case, the State monopoly is unable to meet the demand for executive recruitment. However, the principle of proportionality may challenge this. If the existence and operation of a State monopoly is assessed in light of the principle of proportionality, it will be clear that, because of the fact that the State monopoly is unable, on its own, to meet the demand for executive recruitment, the Member State may be in breach of Article 31(1) RTC, with the result that it will have to change some of the statutory provisions relating to the operation of the State monopoly, or employ more consultants to deal with executive recruitment. Alternatively, under Article 31(1)(a) RTC, nothing can prevent the Member State from establishing a new monopoly that will offer recruitment services to executives only. Accordingly, a Member State will be able to maintain the existing monopoly, or even to establish a new monopoly, without opening up the relevant market to competition.

If the existence and operation of a State monopoly is assessed under competition law, the outcome may be different from what it would be if it were assessed under the provisions on the freedom of establishment. In circumstances like those of *Höfner*, the State monopoly will be found in breach of Article 31(1)(a) RTC, in conjunction with Article 179(1)(e) RTC, for abusing its dominant position. This is because the State monopoly, by merely exercising monopoly rights granted to it, will not be able to avoid abusing its dominant position, because it will not be able to satisfy the demand for recruitment of executives. The limitation on the service offered to customers – that is, the fact that the (in this case) German agency was not able to satisfy the demand for recruitment of executives – will be in breach of Article 179(1)(e) RTC, which states that an abuse of a dominant position occurs if an enterprise concerned limits the production of goods or services for a market to the prejudice of consumers. Whilst, under Article 31(1)(a) RTC, a Member State may claim the benefit of derogation from provisions of the RTC relating to the freedom of establishment, in particular if the principle of proportionality does not apply, under Article 177(1(e) RTC, in conjunction with Article 31(1)(a) RTC, a Member State will be in breach of CSME competition law, and accordingly will be required to allow private consultancy companies to enter the market for executive recruitment services. This is justified in particular in a situation in which private operators have already exercised their activity in that market.[65]

64 Case C-41/90 *Klaus Höfner and Fritz Elser v Macrotron GmbH* [1991] ECR I-1979.
65 See COMP/F-1/39.562 *Slovakian Hybrid Mail* [2008] OJ C 322/10, [2009] 4 CMLR 663.

It is to be noted that, in *Höfner*, the ECJ rejected the argument that private recruitment companies could rely on the principle of non-discrimination and the provision relating to the free movement of services, because the situation was purely internal – that is, it concerned a dispute between German recruitment consultants and a German State monopoly involved in the recruitment of a German national. It is important to highlight that, in many cases in which the ECJ found abuse of a dominant position by a State monopoly, the matter at issue concerned situations in which national private companies operating in a Member State had challenged national rules relating to the existence and operation of a monopoly established by that Member State. Therefore no provisions of the EU Treaties relating to the right of establishment or the right to provide services were relevant to the dispute. In other words, claimants had a claim only under EU competition law.

Article 31(2) RTC is not easy to interpret. Article 31(2)(a) RTC refers to State monopolies, whilst Article 31(2)(b) refers to a situation in which a Member State has granted exclusive rights to a private enterprise to perform a particular commercial activity.

Under Article 31(2)(a) RTC, a Member State is required to ensure that any State monopoly of a commercial nature does not discriminate between nationals of Member States – that is, nationals of all other Member States must be treated in exactly the same way. This provision does not require a Member State to ensure national treatment to nationals of other Member States.

Article 31(2)(a) RTC states that, unless otherwise provided by the Treaty, State monopolies are subject to 'the agreed rules of competition established for Community economic enterprises'. It is submitted that this reference is to the rules of competition set out in Chapter VIII, Part One, of the RTC. It is further submitted that those rules apply only to anti-competitive business conduct that is outside the monopoly designation – that is, conduct that is not required or covered by statutory rules relating to the existence and operation of a monopoly. Such conduct therefore will be *ultra vires* and is unlikely to occur. As a result, State monopolies of a commercial nature are well shielded from the application of CSME competition law. Additionally, the principle of non-discrimination further restricts the circumstances in which conduct of a State monopoly will be within the scope of CSME competition law. Under Article 31(1)(a) RTC, a State monopoly must not discriminate between nationals of Member States. This means that, for example, a State monopoly must not discriminate between nationals of other Member States in relation to importing and exporting goods and services, but is allowed to discriminate with regard to the domestic sale and purchase of goods and services. It is to be noted that Article 129(4) EPA grants national treatment to EU citizens and, by virtue of Article 238(2) EPA, to citizens from other CARIFORUM countries in domestic markets of a Member State – that is, it prohibits discrimination with regard to domestic sales and purchases of goods and services. Therefore it ensures a much larger market penetration for EU nationals of markets in the CARIFORUM States than does the RTC with regard to CARICOM citizens.

Under Article 31(2)(b) RTC, a Member State may determine that the public interest requires the continuation, or establishment, of a private sector monopoly. In such a case, a Member State, when granting exclusive rights to a private enterprise to pursue commercial activities on the relevant market, is required to adopt appropriate measures to ensure that, unless otherwise provided by the Treaty, national treatment is accorded to nationals of other Member States in terms of their participation in the operation of such a monopoly. With regard to Article 31(2)(b) RTC, it is submitted that:

- a Member State is required to ensure that national treatment is accorded to nationals of other Member States in terms of their participation in the operation of a private monopoly, which requires that a Member State must enact procurement regulations that will ensure that a private sector monopoly gives no preference to national producers or national service suppliers over those from other Member States; and
- CSME competition law fully applies to the business conduct of a private sector monopoly operating on the basis of Article 31(2)(b) RTC.

8.5.2 State monopolies of a commercial nature or character under the EPA

Article 129(4) EPA contains provisions applicable only to State monopolies of a commercial nature. This provision is modelled, to some extent, on Article 37 TFEU. It imposes far-reaching obligations on CARIFORUM States. They must adjust, without prejudice to their obligations under the WTO Agreements, any State monopoly of a commercial nature so as to ensure that, by the end of the fifth year following the entry into force of the EPA, there is no discrimination between goods and services originating in the European Union and those originating in the CARIFORUM States, or between nationals of the EU Member States and those of the CARIFORM States regarding the conditions under which goods and services are brought or sold, unless such discrimination is inherent in the existence of the monopoly in question.

Under Article 129(5) EPA, measures adopted to implement Article 129(4) EPA must be notified to the CARIFORUM–EU Trade Development Committee.

With regard to Article 129(4) EPA, the following should be noted.

1. Whilst the RTC does not require a Member State to adjust its monopolies of a commercial nature or character, the EPA not only requires an adjustment, but also imposes a very strict and short deadline on CARIFORUM States for making it.
2. Article 129(4) EPA refers to trade in goods and to the provision of services. Article 37 TFEU prohibits discrimination based on nationality in respect of the conditions under which goods are procured and manufactured. The ECJ has consistently held that Article 37 TFEU does not apply to provision of

services, although it has recognised that a State monopoly providing services may indirectly influence trade in goods.[66] However, a State monopoly may be in breach of Article 18 TFEU, which contains a general prohibition of discrimination on the ground of nationality, when it provides services and operates in a discriminatory manner contrary to Article 18 TFEU. Further, it is subject to the provisions of the EU Treaties relating to the free movement of services and to EU competition rules, in particular Article 102 TFEU, which prohibits abuses of a dominant position.

3. Article 129(4) refers to 'conditions under which goods and services are sold or purchased'. The term 'conditions' is all-encompassing: it refers not only to any specific discriminatory measure taken by a Member State, but also to any national rule, and any practice of a State monopoly, which discriminates against goods and services originating in another State.[67] It is submitted that the terms of designation of a State monopoly are likely to be within the scope of Article 129(4) EPA in a situation in which a State monopoly, by merely exercising powers granted to it, cannot avoid abusing its dominant position, or where such terms are liable to create a situation in which a State monopoly, in effect, is forced or compelled to infringe competition law, given the impact that such terms of designation may have on the free movement of goods and services. Accordingly, it is submitted that the terms of designation that hinder the free movement of goods and services could be justified only if they pass the 'obstruct the performance' test set out in Article 129(2) EPA.

   This submission can be justified on two grounds: first, a State monopoly is *per se* a public undertaking within the meaning of Article 129(2) EPA; and second this submission is supported by the case law of the ECJ on Article 37 TFEU. With regard to sales monopolies,[68] the ECJ has made a distinction between, on the one hand, the existence and operation of a State monopoly, and, on the other, activities of such a monopoly that are separable from its operations, but have bearing on it. Whilst the existence and the operation of a State monopoly is examined in light of Article 37 TFEU and may be justified under Article 106 (2) TFEU, activities that are separable from the operation of the monopoly, but which have bearing on it, are subject to Article 34 TFEU – that is, subject to the prohibition of quantitative restrictions (QRs) and measures equivalent to quantitative restrictions (MEQRs). Such measures may be justified under Article 36 TFEU, which provides a limited number of derogations based, *inter alia*, on the protection

66 See Case 155/73 *Giuseppe Sacchi* [1974] ECR 409, [10]; Case 271/81 *Société Coopérative d'Amélioration de l'élevage et d'Insémination Artificielle du Béarn v Lucien J.M. Mialocq and ors* [1983] ECR 2057, [8].

67 It is to be noted that, in light of Article 8 RTC, 'another State' means another CARICOM State.

68 There is a distinction between a sales monopoly and a production monopoly: the latter is regulated under Article 106 TFEU.

of public morality, public policy, and the health and life of humans, animals and plants.

This is exemplified in *Franzén*,[69] in which, under Swedish law on alcohol, Systembolaget had a State monopoly over the sale of alcoholic beverages, and also subjected the production and importation of alcoholic beverages to the possession of a production or wholesale licence. Licences were granted, at the discretion of the Swedish Alcohol Inspectorate, upon the making of an application and payment of a high fee, which was not reimbursed if the application was rejected. Additionally, a high annual payment was required of all licence holders. The purpose of this law was to protect human health against harmful effects of alcohol. Mr Franzén was prosecuted for selling, without a licence, wine imported from Denmark or purchased from Systembolaget. He claimed that the Swedish law was in breach of Articles 34 and 37 TFEU.

The ECJ assessed the compatibility of rules relating to the existence and operation of the State monopoly in light of Article 37 TFEU. It then held that the Swedish law relating to the operation of the monopoly did not discriminate against nationals from other Member States – that is, the ECJ found that none of the production selection, the limited number of 'shops' that sold alcoholic beverages in Sweden and the national promotion scheme were discriminatory, and thus contrary to Article 37 TFEU. However, the provision of Swedish law bearing upon the operation of the licensing system, which required a holder of a licence, *inter alia*, to maintain storage capacity in Sweden, to pay a high fee when submitting an application for a licence and to make high annual payments constituted MEQRs and could not be justified under Article 36 TFEU. This judgment shows that, under EU law, it is difficult to draw a line between national provisions that relate to mere existence and operation of a State monopoly of a commercial nature, and those that bear on its operation.

This is further illustrated in *Rosengren*,[70] in which the ECJ found that a national measure that prohibited a private individual from directly importing alcoholic beverages, without personally transporting them, which appeared in a national law that also granted exclusive rights to a State monopoly to retail sales of alcoholic beverages, was neither related to the existence nor the operation of the monopoly. As a result, the measure was assessed in light of Article 34 TFEU. The ECJ recognised that, although a ban on importation of alcoholic beverages had the effect 'of channeling consumers who wish to acquire such beverages towards the monopoly',[71] which seems to be the very purpose of the existence and operation of a State monopoly, the ban

69 Case C-189/95 *Criminal Proceedings against Harry Franzén* [1997] ECR I-5909.
70 Case C-170/04 *Rosengren and ors v Riksåklagaren* [2007] ECR I-4071.
71 Ibid., [23].

nevertheless did not regulate the operation of the monopoly, because 'it is not intended to govern either the system for selection of goods by the monopoly, its sales network, or the organisation of the marketing or advertising of goods distributed by that monopoly'.[72]

It is submitted that the compatibility of the terms of designation of a State monopoly will be assessed in light of Article 129(2) EPA, whilst activities bearing on its operation will be examined in light of the EPA provisions relating to trade in goods and services.

4. With regard to purchase of goods and services by a State monopoly, Article 129(4) EPA is more generous than Article 31(1)(a) RTC. Article 129(4) EPA prohibits a State monopoly from giving preference to national producers or national service providers, whilst, by virtue of Article 8 RTC, a State monopoly will have to apply national treatment to enterprises from other CARICOM Member States.
5. The South Centre notes that the relationship between Article 129(4) EPA and exclusions contained in the EPA 'Service' Chapter is unclear. It notes:

> "For instance, if a country has deliberately excluded a specific services sector from the EPA, say, transports, would it have to still have to ensure the activities of its national rail company treats ACP and EU nationals equally whenever selling or buying goods? It would appear that would be the case. In other words, the state monopoly would be able to continue to operate without accepting foreign competition, but it would have to refrain from supporting local ACP service providers or producers of goods to the detriment of EU nationals."[73]

6. Article 129(4) EPA requires that, at the end of the transitional period, any discrimination based on nationality must cease with regard to the free movement of goods and services between the Parties. Only discrimination inherent in the existence of a state monopoly of a commercial nature is allowed. This is because such discrimination has its source in the very nature of a monopoly, that is the fact that imports and/or exports of goods or the provision of services are effected exclusively by the state, or under its control.

72 Ibid., [24].

73 South Centre, *Fact Sheet No. 8: Competition Policy in Economic Partnership Agreements (CARIFORUM Text)*, March 2008, SC/AN/TDP/EPA/15, [44].

9

THE ENFORCEMENT OF CSME COMPETITION LAW BY THE CARICOM COMPETITION COMMISSION

Chapter contents

9.1 Introduction

The CARICOM Competition Commission (CCC), the main body to enforce CSME competition law, was established on the basis of Article 171 RTC. In accordance with the decision of the Heads of Government made at their 10th Special Session held in Port of Spain in November 2004, the CCC has its headquarters in Paramaribo, Suriname. It came into existence on 18 January 2008.

This chapter examines the main features of the enforcement of CSME competition law by the CCC.

9.2 The composition of the CCC

The CCC consists of seven members,[1] each being appointed for a term of five years[2] by the Regional Judicial and Legal Services Commission (RJLSC). The RJLSC also appoints the chairman from among the Commissioners.

Commissioners must be citizens or nationals of a CARICOM Member State.

Under Article 172(2) RTC, the members of the CCC are required collectively to have 'expertise in commerce, finance, law, competition policy and practice, international trade and such other areas of expertise or experience as may be necessary'.

Under Article 172(6) RTC, a Commissioner may resign at any time by submitting a written communication to this effect addressed to the chairman of the RJLSC. A Commissioner may also be removed from office for incompetence or misbehaviour. Such removal is subject to a vote by no fewer than three-quarters of all members of the RJLSC.

9.3 The conduct of Commissioners

Commissioners are required to take an Oath of Office, the text of which is attached to Annex V to the RTC, incorrectly named as 'Oath of Office of Judges of the Court'. Under the Oath, Commissioners are required to exercise the office of Commissioner 'without fear or favour, affection or ill-will'. This is obviously insufficient to ensure that they are independent and act only in the interests of the Community. Even though Article 172(4) RTC states that the RJLSC may impose disciplinary measures for misbehaviour, the most serious being removal from the CCC,[3] such sanctions do not apply for behaviour of Commissioners after the termination of their membership of the CCC. It is instructive to examine the approach of the European Commission to this matter, particularly following the dismissal of the European Commission presided over by Jacques Santer.

On 16 March 1999, for the first time in the history of the European Union, a President of the Commission, Jacques Santer, together with all Commissioners, was forced to resign. Under the principle of 'collegiate responsibility', the entire European Commission, including its President, was in effect dismissed. Mismanagement, fraud, the awarding of financial contracts and other irregularities committed by some Commissioners were confirmed by the 'Comité de sages' set up jointly by the European Parliament and the European Commission following a Resolution of the Parliament on 14 January 1999 on improving the

1 Article 171(1) RTC.
2 Under Article 172(3) RTC, members of the CCC may be appointed for one further period of no more than five years.
3 Article 172(5) RTC.

financial management of the European Commission.[4] The subsequent European Commission asked the European Court of Justice (ECJ) to declare that conduct of a member of Jacques Santer's Commission, Mrs Cresson, amounted to favouritism, or if not that, then to gross negligence in breach of Article 245 TFEU, which imposes a duty on Commissioners to act independently and in the interests of the European Union, and consequently to order that she be deprived wholly or partly of a pension or other benefits in its stead.[5] The ECJ found that Mrs Cresson was in breach of her duties as a Commissioner, but did not impose any sanctions on her, because it considered that, 'having regard to the circumstances of the case, the finding of breach constitutes, itself, an appropriate penalty'.[6]

Another member of the European Commission presided over by Jacques Santer, Mr Martin Martin Bangemann, was also involved in serious misbehaviour. He was Commissioner for Industry and Telecommunications. Subsequent to the expiry of his term of office, he accepted a post with Telefónica, the Spanish telecom group, which he had previously regulated as a Commissioner. The Council decided to bring proceedings against him before the ECJ,[7] based on Article 245 TFEU – particularly Article 245(3) TFEU, which provides that Commissioners:

> "... shall give a solemn undertaking that, both during and after their term of office, they will respect the obligations therefrom and in particular their duty to behave with integrity and discretion as regards the acceptance, after they have ceased to hold office, of certain appointments or benefits."

Unfortunately, the Council decided to withdraw its decision, subject to conditions including that Mr Bangemann would not accept any position in Telefónica until 1 July 2000 and would not represent any third party, including Telefónica, until 31 December 2001.[8]

Following the resignation of the European Commission presided over by Jacques Santer, the subsequent Commission adopted a very strict Code of Conduct,[9] under which:

4 [1999] OJ C 104/106.
5 Case C-432/04 *Commission v Cresson* [2006] ECR I-6387.
6 Ibid., [150].
7 Council Decision 1999/494/EC, ECSC, Euratom of 9 July 1999 on the referral of the case of Mr Bangemann to the Court of Justice [1999] OJ L 192/1.
8 Council Decision 2000/44/EC, ECSC, Euratom of 17 December 1999 on the settlement of the Bangemann Case [2000] OJ L 16/73.
9 See European Commission, *Code of Conduct for Commissioners*, 2004, SEC(2004) 1487/2.

- a Commissioner is required to act in accordance with the highest standards of public life;
- in order to avoid any conflict of interests, a Commissioner is subject to a one-year 'cooling-off period' after leaving office, during which his or her prospective jobs may be vetoed by a special ethics committee; and
- a Commissioner is required to declare any pecuniary interests and all substantial assets, including those of a spouse or partner. Access to such information is available to the general public.

The CCC Rules of Procedure do not contain any rule relating to ethical issues. It is submitted that the CCC should include such a rule or adopt a Code of Conduct for Commissioners. This can be justified in light of the following.

1. Commissioners are in charge of the enforcement of CSME competition law. Accordingly, they have access to confidential information that could be used to further their own personal interests or to the detriment of enterprises. Neither outside activities nor Commissioners' personal or professional relationships should give any impression of a conflict of interest. or of favouritism, or of an abuse of the privileges and immunities conferred upon them by CARICOM.
2. Commissioners would have a clear understanding of the standard of conduct expected of them. Being holders of very important posts in the region, they may benefit from published guidelines that clearly set out the conduct expected or required when the proper conduct is not necessarily self-evident. In this respect, it is suggested that any guidelines should state that, when a Commissioner is in doubt concerning a matter of conduct, he or she should seek advice from an ad hoc Ethical Advice Committee of available Commissioners established to consider the relevant matter and provide the advice sought. The composition of any such committee should be decided by the CCC.
3. Such a rule would enhance the link between Commissioners and CARICOM, in that it would emphasise that Commissioners have important obligations, including those of a moral nature, with regard to CARICOM. Accordingly, when they make public statements expressing their personal views and convictions, for example, or accept gifts or honorary titles, Commissioners should ensure that their conduct does not compromise, or appear to compromise, the interests or the reputation of the CCC or CARICOM.
4. The need to avoid any debacle such as that suffered by the European Commission under Jacques Santer.

It is also submitted that a rule on ethical issues should impose on every Commissioner a duty to give notice to the CCC of any intention to engage in any occupation immediately following cessation of his or her office. Upon receipt of any such notice, the CCC should consider the intended occupation and, if in doubt as to it its propriety, seek the advice of an ad hoc Ethical Advice Committee. However, no duty to give notice to the CCC should exist if the planned occupation concerns employment in the public sector or as an international civil servant. Furthermore, a rule on ethical issues should also impose a duty on a Commissioner to disclose all of his or her pecuniary and non-pecuniary interests and assets, as well as those of his or her spouse or partner and dependent children, which might create a conflict of interests in the performance of his or her duties. This would be in accordance with the principles of transparency, accountability and openness, and would enhance public confidence in the integrity of the Commissioners.

The importance of dealing with ethical issues is emphasised by the fact that the CCC is financed mainly by subventions from Member States, some of which may try to exercise pressure on some Commissioners when important personal or national interests are at issue.

9.4 The juridical personality of the CCC

The CCC was granted 'full juridical personality', first under Article II of the Agreement between the Republic of Suriname and the Caribbean Community Establishing the Seat and the Office of the Competition Commission,[10] and then under Article II(1) of the Protocol on the Privileges and Immunities of the Competition Commission.[11]

In *Trinidad Cement Ltd v CCC*,[12] the Caribbean Court of Justice (CCJ) confirmed that the CCC can sue and be sued in the Court in respect of all practices and procedures, at any stage of proceedings carried out by the CCC.

9.5 The functions of the CCC

The CCC has two main functions: one relating to the development, promotion, protection and enforcement of CSME competition law; and the other relating to the promotion and protection of consumer interests in the Community.[13]

Under Article 173(2) RTC, the CCC, when discharging the above functions shall:

10 Available at http://www.caricom.org/jsp/secretariat/legal_instruments/competition_commission_seat.pdf [accessed 10 November 2013].

11 Available at http://www.caricomcompetitioncommission.com/images/registry/protocol-on-the-privileges-immunities-of-the-ccc.pdf [accessed 10 November 2013].

12 [2012] CCJ 4 (OJ).

13 See Article 173(1) RTC, which states: 'The Commission shall: (a) apply the rules of competition in respect of anti-competitive cross-border business conduct; (b) promote and protect competition in the Community and co-ordinate the implementation of the Community Competition Policy; and (c) perform any other function conferred on it by any competent body of the Community.'

"(a) monitor anti-competitive practices of enterprises operating in the CSME, and investigate and arbitrate cross-border disputes;
(b) keep the Community Competition Policy under review and advise and make recommendations to COTED to enhance its effectiveness;
(c) promote the establishment of institutions and the development and implementation of harmonised competition laws and practices by the Member States to achieve uniformity in the administration of applicable rules;
(d) review the progress made by the Member States in the implementation of the legal and institutional framework for enforcement;
(e) co-operate with competent authorities in the Member States;
(f) provide support to the Member States in promoting and protecting consumer welfare;
(g) facilitate the exchange of relevant information and expertise; and
(h) develop and disseminate information about competition policy, and consumer protection policy."

Under Article 173(2) RTC, the CCC is required to carry out an impressive number of tasks. Although the CCC is a young competition agency, it has already made important contributions to the development of a competition culture in CARICOM by:

- Encouraging Member States to enact necessary legislation and to establish national competition authorities (NCAs), in particular providing technical support to Suriname and Belize. With regard to Belize, the CCC assisted that country in drafting legislation on competition law. In respect of Suriname, the CCC provided technical assistance in finalising documents necessary to access funding under the 10th European Development Funds, which will allow Suriname to finance the establishment of its NCA. Additionally, the CCC provided technical assistance and knowledge-sharing to the Organisation of Eastern Caribbean States (OECS) in the area of competition law.[14]
- Increasing the awareness of the general public, the judiciary, consumers, businesses and governmental agencies of the advantages of competition law. In this respect, the CCC established its own website, published booklets on competition law and organised educational activities, such as workshops and conferences.

14 See K. Haraksingh, 'SURINAME: CARICOM Competition Commission', in Global Competition Review, *The Antitrust Review of the Americas 2014*, available at http://globalcompetitionreview.com/reviews/54/sections/191/chapters/2162/suriname-caricom-competition-commission [accessed 20 January 2014]. See also CCC, 'Implementation and Enforcement of Community Competition Policy: The Next 5 Years' (2014) 18 Competition Matters 26.

The CCC has also completed its first investigation, this being into business practices of the Trinidad Cement Limited (TCL) group of companies, and has successfully defended the first case brought against it before the CCJ.[15] It has also taken part in regional and international conferences, and events.[16] Further, on the basis of Article 174(7) RTC, the CCC has established its Rules of Procedure.[17] It is to be noted that Article 173(2)(a) RTC states that the CCC will arbitrate in cross-border disputes. The word 'arbitrate' should be understood in terms of its common usage – that is, attempting to settling arguments between two parties after hearing their arguments – rather than as referring to arbitration in terms of the method of dispute settlement set out in Chapter IX RTC.

Article 173(2)(b) RTC imposes on the CCC a duty to review CARICOM competition policy and to make recommendations to the Council for Trade and Economic Development (COTED) with a view to enhancing the effectiveness of CSME competition law. In this regard, the CCC is well aware that the absence from the Revised Treaty of Chaguaramas (RTC) of any provisions on merger control constitutes a serious *lacuna* that weakens the effectiveness of CSME competition law. This *lacuna* is expected to be filled. In 2011, COTED agreed to incorporate merger provisions into Chapter VIII. However, there is no consensus among the Member States 'with regard to the methodology for assessing regional mergers'.[18] Accordingly, it will be the task of the CCC to persist in its recommendations to COTED to ensure that merger provisions are incorporated into CSME competition law.

Another matter that needs to be addressed by the CCC, and which is on its agenda, is the impact of national sectorial exemptions from competition law on the functioning of the CARICOM Single Market and Economy (CSME). The CCC intends to press for the removal of exemptions in a situation in which anti-competitive conduct that could be exempted nationally has cross-border effect on markets in the CSME.[19]

15 *Trinidad Cement Limited v CCC* [2012] CCJ 4 (OJ).

16 See CCC, 'Celebrating 5 Years of Service', available at http://www.caricomcompetitioncommission.com/en/publications/newspaper-articles [accessed 20 January 2014].

17 See CCC, *CCC Rules of Procedure 2011*, available at http://www.caricomcompetitioncommission.com/images/registry/CCC-Rules-of-Procedure-2011.pdf [accessed 15 March 2014].

18 See K. Haraksingh, 'SURINAME: CARICOM Competition Commission', in Global Competition Review, *The Antitrust Review of the Americas 2014*, available at http://globalcompetitionreview.com/reviews/54/sections/191/chapters/2162/suriname-caricom-competition-commission [accessed 20 January 2014].

19 Ibid.

The CCC has undertaken a review of Chapter VIII, with a view to making recommendations to COTED for necessary amendments reflecting the experience of the CCC, developments in CSME completion policy and law, and international best practice. Any recommendation, once approved by COTED, will be incorporated into Chapter VIII.

Article 173(2) RTC lists tasks that the CCC is required to carry out in order to discharge its function of promoting and protecting CSME competition law, and co-ordinating its implementation. They consist, *inter alia*, of:

- promoting and supporting the establishment of NCAs;
- developing and implementing harmonised competition laws and practices among the Member States, with a view to achieving uniformity in the administration of CSME competition rules;
- facilitating the exchange of relevant information and expertise;
- developing and disseminating information about CSME competition law;
- examining progress made by the Member States in the implementation of legal and institutional framework for enforcement of CSME competition law;
- reporting to COTED on the achievements relating to the performance of tasks assigned to it under Chapter VIII RTC; and
- co-operating with NCAs.

In order to fulfil the functions set out in Article 173(1) RTC, the CCC is assisted by a Secretariat, which is headed by an Executive Director and comprises professional staff, with expertise in law, economics, and administration. The Secretariat, under the direction of the Commissioners:

- receives complaints, and requests for investigations
- opens and maintains case files
- organises and conducts investigations
- prepares investigation reports
- represents the Commission in the CCJ
- follows up cases, and
- maintains records.[20]

9.6 Enforcement of CSME competition law by the CCC and the protection of fundamental rights of enterprises

Recital 8 of the Preamble to the CCC Rules of Procedure states that the Rules:

20 CCC, *Building Competitive Markets*, 2008, available at http://www.caricomcompetitioncommission.com/en/publications/booklets [accessed 15 January 2014], p 4.

> ". . . should address the principles (i) that the person carrying out investigations should not be the same as those adjudicating on the case, and vice versa, (ii) that the rights of the defence should be respected and notably the right to know the case against one and the right to a hearing, and (iii) that confidential and propriety information should be protected but that abridged versions of such information should, to the extent reasonably practicable, be made available to the parties concerned . . . ."

Recital 8 acknowledges the importance of ensuring that the CCC's enforcement proceedings respect the fundamental rights of enterprises. This section focuses on the principle of separation of investigating powers from adjudicating powers of the CCC, whilst the principles relating to the rights of the defence and the right to confidentiality are dealt with in context throughout this chapter.

In order to ensure the impartiality of the CCC's proceedings, Commissioners divide themselves into two groups: one group of Commissioners – that is, the Investigating Panel – is responsible for investigating alleged anti-competitive conduct; the other – that is, the Adjudicating Panel – is responsible for adjudicating the matter after hearing both parties to the proceedings. This division, which may seem artificial, is better understood in light of the judgment of the Jamaican Court of Appeal in *The Jamaica Stock Exchange v The Fair Trading Commission*,[21] in which the Court held that the merger of the investigative and adjudicating functions of the Jamaican Fair Trading Commission, which had been based on sections 5 and 7 of the Jamaican Fair Competition Act of 1993, was in breach of section 20(3) of the Jamaican Constitution with regard to the guarantee of the right to natural justice. In other words, the Jamaican Court of Appeal held that one and the same body cannot be prosecutor, judge and jury.[22]

It is submitted that the EU experience is instructive in the examination of whether the internal division of tasks between CCC Commissioners will be sufficient to ensure the proper protection of the right to natural justice. The European Court of Human Rights (ECtHR)[23] has dealt with the issues, first, of whether sanctions for infringements of competition law should be considered to be criminal sanctions, and second, whether there is a breach of Article 6(1) of the

21 Jamaican Supreme Court Civil Appeal No. 92/97.

22 On the possible implications of the judgment for the Jamaican Fair Trading Commission, see D. V. McKoy, 'The Courts as the Preferred Means of Competition Law Enforcement' (2010) 35(1) WILJ 249; P.-J. Gordon, 'The Case for Maintaining a Single Competition Agency for Investigation and Adjudication of all Competition Matters' (2010) 35(1) WILJ 256; and B. St M. Hylton, 'An Independent Tribunal as an Alternative Avenue for Adjudication' (2010)35(1) WILJ 241.

23 It is to be noted that, in the European Union, the system of enforcement of competition law must comply with the EU Charter of Fundamental Rights of the European Union, and that the European Union is in the process of acceding to the ECHR.

European Convention on Human Rights (ECHR)[24] when an NCA exercises both investigating and adjudicating powers without any internal division of those tasks, as does the European Commission. In this context, it can be said that the CCC is one body, whatever its internal divisions, and therefore if the merger of investigative and adjudicative powers in one body is in breach of the right to a fair trial, such division will not be sufficient to ensure compliance with the international and constitutional requirements of the right to a fair trial.

9.6.1 Whether an infringement of competition law constitutes a criminal offence?

Determination of whether an infringement of EU competition law constitutes a criminal offence is vital. This is because, under Article 6(2) and (3) ECHR, defendants in criminal proceedings enjoy rights additional to those specified in Article 6(1) ECHR, which sets out the general requirements for a 'fair trial' in criminal and civil proceedings. Among rights relating to criminal trials only, Article 6(2) ECHR guarantees the right to be presumed innocent until proven guilty, the right to remain silent and the right not to incriminate oneself.

The only EU legislation that expressly determines the nature of competition law infringements is Article 23(5) of Regulation 1/2003,[25] which states that decisions imposing fines 'shall not be of a criminal law nature'. However, in *Engel*,[26] the ECtHR held that, for the purpose of applying Article 6 ECHR:

> "If the Contracting States were able at their discretion to classify an offence as disciplinary instead of criminal, or to prosecute the author of a 'mixed' offence on the disciplinary rather than on the criminal plane, the operation of the fundamental clauses of Articles 6 and 7 would be subordinated to their sovereign will. A latitude extending this far might lead to results incompatible with the purpose and object of the Convention."[27]

In *Menarini*,[28] the ECtHR stated that three criteria, which are not cumulative, are to be applied to decide whether a procedure is of a criminal nature within the meaning of Article 6 ECHR. The criteria are:

24 Article 6(1) ECHR states: 'In the determination of his civil rights and obligations or of any criminal charge against him, everyone is entitled to a fair and public hearing within a reasonable time by an independent and impartial tribunal established by law'.

25 Regulation 1/2003 on the Implementation of the Rules on Competition Laid down in Articles [101 and 102 TFEU] [2003] OJ L 1/1.

26 App. nos 5100/71, 5101/71, 5102/71, 5354/72, and 5370/72 *Engel and ors v The Netherlands* (1979–80) 1 EHRR 647.

27 Ibid., [81].

28 App. no. 43509/08 *A. Menarini Diagnostics SRL v Italy* (ECtHR, 27 September 2011).

- the classification of the offence by national legislation;
- the nature of the offence; and
- the nature and severity of the applied penalty.

In *Menarini*, an Italian pharmaceutical company was found by the Italian competition authority to be in breach of national competition law by price-fixing and market-sharing in the national diabetes test market. A fine of €6 million was imposed on Menarini. The ECtHR applied the above criteria. It held that the fact that, under Italian law, the offence was classified as being of an administrative nature was not determinative. With regard to the nature of the offence, the ECtHR confirmed its previous judgment in *Stenuit*,[29] in which it had held that the application of competition law by a competition authority affecting general interests of society was of a criminal nature within the meaning of Article 6 ECHR. As to the nature and severity of the fine, its amount and deterrent effect led the ECtHR to conclude that the fine was a criminal sanction.

In *Jussila*,[30] the ECtHR made a distinction between the 'hard core of criminal law' and 'cases not strictly belonging to the traditional categories of criminal law, for example . . . competition law', to which 'the criminal head guarantees will not necessarily apply with their full stringency'. What are the implications of this distinction? In this respect, the ECtHR in *Menarini* was not entirely clear. However, the European Free Trade Association (EFTA) Court,[31] in *PostenNorge*,[32] held that the guarantees provided by the criminal head of Article 6 ECHR apply in a differentiated manner depending upon the nature of the case and 'the degree of stigma carried by certain criminal cases'.[33] In this case, the EFTA Surveillance Authority (ESA) found Norway Post, a Norwegian postal service owned by the

29 App. no. 11598/85 *Société Stenuit v France* [1992] ECHR 34.

30 App. no. 73053/01 *Jussila v Finland* (ECtHR, 23 November 2006), [43].

31 EFTA is an international free-trade organisation created in 1960 by the United Kingdom to counterbalance the creation in 1957 of the European Economic Community (EEC). Members of EFTA cannot concurrently be Member States of the European Union. As a result, currently, EFTA has only four Member States: Iceland; Lichtenstein; Norway; and Switzerland. In 1992, the European Union entered into an agreement with EFTA countries, creating the European Economic Area (EEA). Switzerland, as a result of a negative referendum, entered into separate agreements with the European Union. In the EEA, EU rules on free movement of persons, goods, capital, competition law and non-discrimination on the ground of nationality apply. In order to ensure the uniform application of EEA rules in EFTA countries, two institutions were created, the ESA, which has powers corresponding to those of the European Commission, and the EFTA Court, which has jurisdiction corresponding to that of the ECJ. The EFTA Court exercises its jurisdiction over the three EFTA countries that are party to the EEA.

32 Case E-15/10 *PostenNorge AS v EFTA Surveillance Authority* (ECTA Ct, 18 April 2012), available at http://www.eftacourt.int/uploads/tx_nvcases/15_10_Judgment_EN.pdf [accessed 27 April 2013].

33 Ibid., [89].

Norwegian State, to be in breach of Article 54 of the EEA Agreement (which is identical to Article 102 TFEU) by abusing its dominant position in the business-to-consumer parcel market in Norway between 2000 and 2006. A fine of €12.89 million was imposed on Norway Post. On appeal, the EFTA Court held that, bearing in mind the gravity and severity of the offence, and the considerable stigma attached to the finding that Norway Post had abused its dominant position, the guarantees provided by the criminal head of Article 6 ECHR applied with their full stringency. Although judgments of the EFTA Court are not binding on EU courts, the facts that EEA competition law mirrors EU competition law and that, often, EU Advocates General refer to the case law of the EFTA Court,[34] may not be completely ignored by the ECJ.

9.6.2 Whether a merger of investigative and adjudicative powers is in breach of Article 6(1) ECHR?

Article 6(1) ECHR requires that a court, tribunal, etc. determining civil rights and obligations or a criminal charge must be, and must appear to be, 'independent and impartial'. In *Menarini*,[35] the ECtHR held that an administrative authority can lawfully impose a criminal sanction within the meaning of Article 6(1) ECHR as long as the decision imposing that criminal sanction is subject to review by a court having 'full jurisdiction' – that is, as long as the court reviews all of the aspects of a case, factual and legal, including complex economic assessments. It is important to bear in mind that the enforcement of Italian competition law is modelled on EU competition law, in that the Italian competition authority has similar powers to those of the European Commission. Accordingly, the fact that the European Commission acts as prosecutor, jury and judge in competition matters raises no issues under the ECHR, provided that the EU courts effectively exercise 'full jurisdiction'. In the European Union, the ECJ and the General Court have been criticised for failure to ensure effective judicial review of the Commission's decisions in competition matters, because they defer, to an excessive and unreasonable extent, to the Commission's discretion regarding assessment of complex economic and technical matters. As a result, it is alleged that the EU courts perform only limited reviews of these matters – that is, that the EU courts' review is limited to procedural rules, factual errors, errors of law and manifest errors of appraisal, which, if the allegation is correct, is incompatible with the right to a fair trial as guaranteed under Article 6 ECHR.[36] The position

34 See, e.g., Case C-49/11 *Content Services Ltd v Bundesarbeitskammer* (ECJ, 5 July 2012), Opinion of AG Mengozzi, [39].

35 App. no. 43509/08 *A. Menarini Diagnostics SRL v Italy* (ECtHR, 27 September 2011). See section 9.6.1 above.

36 On this topic, see R. Nazzini, 'Administrative Enforcement, Judicial Review and Fundamental Rights in EU Competition Law: A Comparative Contextual-Functionalist Perspective' (2012) 49 CML Rev 971.

of the ECJ was stated in the *Plain Copper Plumbing Tubes Cartel* cases,[37] in which it found that the rules of judicial review in the European Union are in conformity with the principle of effective judicial protection enshrined in Article 47 of the EU Charter of Fundamental Rights.

It is submitted that merger of investigating and adjudicating powers exercised by a body entrusted with enforcement of competition law, even when such a body imposes criminal sanctions, has not been found to be in breach of the right to a fair trial by the ECtHR, provided that decisions of such a body are subject to 'full jurisdiction' of a court. Accordingly, it is submitted that the exercise by the CCC of both investigative and adjudicating powers, irrespective of the internal division of its task, is in conformity with the requirements of natural justice. It is also submitted that the internal division of tasks within the CCC is to be approved. Indeed, a body with important coercive powers must do its best to ensure compliance with requirements of fundamental rights. In this respect, it is important to note that, in the European Union, the office of 'Hearing Officer' was created in 1982 to respond to criticism that the Commission acts as prosecutor, jury and judge, and uses biased evidence against the defendant.[38] The Hearing Officer, an independent person (although appointed by the Commission and attached to the Commissioner in charge of competition) experienced in competition matters and of high moral standing, is familiar with the file, and ensures that the hearing is properly conducted and that the requirements of due process are respected.[39] The Hearing Officer may intervene in the investigation stage (that is, not only at the stage of a formal hearing conducted after a 'statement of objections' has been forwarded by the Commission to the defendant), when a dispute arises between the Commission and the undertaking concerned, with regard to, *inter alia*:

- claims of legal professional privilege (LLP) over documents required by the Commission in the context of requests for information, investigations or investigatory measures;[40]

37 Case C-272/09 P *KME Germany AG, KME France SAS, KME Italy SpA, v Commission* [2011] I-12789; Case C-386/10P *Chalkor v Commission* [2011] I-13085; Case C-389/10P *KME Germany and ors v Commission* [2011] I-13125.

38 European Commission, *Notice on Procedures for Applying Competition Rules of the EEC and ECSC Treaties* [1982] OJ C 251/2; Commission Decision 94/810/ECSC on the Terms of Reference of Hearing Officers in Competition Procedures before the Commission [1994] OJ L 330/67.

39 The powers of the Hearing Officer are listed in Commission Decision 2001/462/EC on the Terms of Reference of Hearing Officers in Certain Competition Proceedings [2001] OJ L 162/21 and Commission Decision 2011/695/EU on the Function and Terms of Reference of the Hearing Officer in Certain Competition Proceedings [2011] OJ L 275/29. On the role of the Hearing Officer, see S. Durante and K. Williams, 'The Practical Impact of the Exercise of the Right to be Heard: A Special Focus on the Effect of Oral Hearings and the Role of the Hearing Officer' (2005) 2 Competition Policy Newsletter 22.

40 Commission Decision 2011/695/EU, op. cit. Article 4(2)(a).

- claims that replying to a question in a request for information would breach the privilege against self-incrimination;[41]
- claims that time limits imposed by a Commission decision for replying to a request for information are too short;[42] and
- claims that an undertaking or association of undertakings has not been informed of its procedural status.[43]

Additionally, in the European Union, between the investigation stage and the imposition of any sanctions, there are both an oral hearing and subsequent consultations between the European Commission and the Advisory Committee on Restrictive Practices and Dominant Positions.[44]

9.7 The powers of the CCC

Article 174 RTC, entitled 'Powers of the Commission', lists the powers granted to the CCC relating to investigations and punishment of anti-competitive conduct of enterprises. However, the powers of the CCC are not limited to those enumerated in Article 174 RTC; additionally, the CCC is empowered, either expressly or by implication, to take measures ensuring the proper application and enforcement of CSME competition law. This section deals with the exercise by the CCC of, first, the powers enumerated in Article 174 RTC, and second, those deriving from other provisions of Chapter VIII, Part One, of the RTC.

9.7.1 The powers of the CCC under Article 174 RTC

The powers of the CCC that can be exercised on the basis of Article 174 RTC are here examined in light of consecutive stages of enquiry proceedings. The CCC Rules of Procedure are of assistance in this examination.

9.7.1.1 The initiation of proceedings by the CCC

There are three ways in which the CCC may commence an investigation into an alleged infringement of CSME competition law.

1. Under Article 175(1) RTC, a Member State may request the CCC to commence an investigation into the business conduct of an enterprise located in another Member State when such conduct prejudices trade, or restricts or distorts competition in the territory of that State.

41 Ibid., Article 4(2)(b).
42 Ibid., Article 4(2)(c).
43 Ibid., Article 4(2)(d).
44 This Committee is made up of representatives of NCAs from each EU Member State. The Committee comments on draft decisions of the European Commission, and considers draft legislation and the development of competition policy generally.

2. Under Article 175(2) RTC, COTED may request the CCC to commence an investigation when it believes that allegedly anti-competitive conduct of an enterprise prejudices trade and restricts competition within the CSME, and has, or is likely to have, cross-border effects.
3. Under Article 176 RTC, the CCC may commence investigation *proprio motu* (that is, of its own motion).

Because Article 175 RTC deals with the first two ways of commencing investigation together and the third way separately, this section follows the same course.

A Initiation of investigation at the initiative of a Member State or COTED

The CCC has prepared 'Information on Preparing a Complaint'[45] under Article 175(1) and (2) RTC. Such a complaint must be made in writing and be substantiated, so as to allow the CCC to make a preliminary assessment of whether it should proceed with the investigation.

In *Trinidad Cement Ltd v CCC*,[46] one of the complaints submitted to the CCJ by the claimant (TCL, a company established in Trinidad and Tobago, engaged in the production and marketing of cement and ready-mix products, which has subsidiaries in many CARICOM States) was that the CCC was not properly seized with the complaint from COTED. It appears from the facts that COTED, at its 26th Meeting in November 2008, on the basis of repeated complaints of Member States concerning the alleged anti-competitive conduct of TCL, recorded in minutes of the meeting a resolution that the CCC be requested to 'advise whether there was evidence sufficient to enable a preliminary assessment of whether there was anti-competitive conduct by the TCL Group'.[47] Accordingly, the wording of the resolution was inconsistent with Article 175(2) RTC, which refers to a request for an investigation, not advice. Subsequently, the Secretary-General of CARICOM, who attended the 26 November meeting in his capacity as Assistant Secretary-General for Trade and Economic Integration, wrote a letter to the CCC giving effect to his understanding of COTED's intention. Because this letter was not received by the CCC, the Secretary-General wrote a second letter, entitled 'Request for the CARICOM Competition Commission to Investigate the Operation of the Market for the Production and Sale of Cement in CARICOM', in which he quoted the resolution and attached a copy of a document called 'Audit', which indicated details of TCL's operations in the CARICOM. The letter also stated that the Secretary-General, on behalf of

45 See the official website of the CCC, available at http://www.caricomcompetitioncommission.com/ [accessed 10 January 2014].
46 [2012] CCJ 4 (OJ).
47 Ibid., [31].

COTED, requested the CCC to initiate an investigation into the operation of the TCL Group in order to make a determination as to whether TCL's conduct prejudiced trade and/or prevented, restricted or distorted competition within the CSME. The letter also invited the CCC to 'take any other action the Commission deems necessary'.

The CCJ noted that it was at least arguable whether the Secretary-General had competence to make such a request in light of the wording of the resolution, because his letter stated that COTED had reason to believe that TCL was engaged in anti-competitive conduct, which was the condition for making the request under Article 175(2) RTC. In response, the CCC asked the Secretary-General to clarify what was being requested from the CCC – that is, a request for advice, or a request for an investigation. In those circumstances, the Secretary-General dispatched a communication referred to as 'Savigram' to COTED's Ministers, proposing that COTED might wish expressly to request the CCC to initiate an investigation. However, before COTED responded, the CCC wrote to the Secretary-General stating that it had decided to commence an investigation on the basis of: (i) the clear request for investigation provided for in the letter of the Secretary-General; (ii) indications by the CCJ in *Trinidad Cement Ltd and TCL Guyana Inc. v The Co-operative Republic of Guyana*[48] that issues raised in that case concerning claims of abuse of dominance by TCL fell within the jurisdiction of the CCC; and (iii) the CCC's authority to initiate an investigation where it has reason to believe that competition is being distorted within the Community.

The CCJ noted that only the first reason was consistent with the RTC, although even that reason was not entirely satisfactory in that it reflected a reversal of the CCC's original position that the original request made by the Secretary-General on behalf of COTED was ambiguous. With regard to the second reason, the CCJ said that the observations made by the Court could not serve as a basis for initiating an investigation, bearing in mind that the RTC is itself very specific as to the procedure relating to the initiation of an investigation. The third reason was inconsistent with the RTC in that, although under Article 176 RTC the CCC may initiate proceedings on its own motion, this can occur only following a CCC request submitted to the relevant NCA to undertake a preliminary examination. It was clear from evidence submitted to the CCJ that this had not occurred.

After the CCC initiated the investigation, COTED, at its 13 Meeting held in June 2010, confirmed the request made by the Secretary-General.

The CCJ held that, despite the irregularity relating to the request for an investigation, COTED had made a proper request under Article 175(2) RTC, by validating *post factum* the request made by the Secretary-General. The CCJ stated that TCL should have addressed its concerns relating to the request to an Enquiry Panel of the CCC. It stated that it was also clear from the facts that no harm had

48 [2009] CCJ 5 (OJ).

been suffered by TCL as a result of irregularities relating to the initiation of the investigation. Nevertheless, it is worrying that the CCC, in its first case under the RTC, made blatant mistakes as to the application of Articles 175(2) and 176 RTC, and made contradictory statements relating to its understanding of the letter from the Secretary-General.

Under Article 175(4) RTC, the CCC, upon receipt of a request either from a Member State or from COTED:

> ". . . shall consult the interested parties and shall determine:
>
> (a) whether investigation is within the jurisdiction of the Commission; and
>
> (b) whether the investigation is justified in all circumstances of the case."

Such a consultation must be concluded within 30 days of the date of receipt of the request for investigation. However, this time limit may be extended upon the agreement of the parties.

Under Article 175(6) RTC, when the CCC decides to conduct investigation, it is required to notify the interested parties and COTED, and to complete the investigation within 120 days from the date of receipt of the request for investigation. This period may be extended if necessary, but all interested parties must be notified of any such extension.

The term 'all interested parties' used in Article 175 RTC was interpreted by the CCJ in *Trinidad Cement Ltd v CCC*,[49] in which the claimant argued that it was such an 'interested party'. The CCJ duly examined the arguments submitted by the claimant. It justified its conclusion that the claimant was not 'an interested party' within the meaning of Article 175(4) RTC on the following grounds.

1. At the stage of proceedings at which the CCC deals with truly preliminary discussions relating to whether the potential investigation is within its jurisdiction and whether it is justified in any event, it is for the CCC itself to decide such matters and, if appropriate, to consult the Member State concerned, and possibly NCAs. Neither of Articles 175 or 176 RTC provides for any role of a targeted enterprise to play in consultations as to jurisdiction to initiate an investigation and its appropriateness. The CCJ noted that although it could be argued that a targeted enterprise has an interest in being able to persuade the CCC that the proposed investigation is not justified, such an interest is outweighed by other considerations – mainly, the effectiveness of the investigation.[50]

49 [2012] CCJ 4 (OJ).
50 Ibid., [25].

2. The exclusion of a targeted enterprise from the scope of 'interested parties' has no prejudicial effects on the legitimate interests of a claimant, bearing in mind that, at this stage of the proceedings, matters of jurisdiction and appropriateness of a possible investigation are discussed. Further, as the CCJ stated, 'there is no legitimate interest which would require a targeted enterprise to be notified of the commencement of the investigation'.[51]
3. Article 175(8) RTC, which states that, '[a]t the conclusion of an enquiry, the Commission shall notify the interested parties of its determination', indicates that 'interested parties' are those who are not involved in the enquiry. Indeed, when the CCC makes a negative determination – that is, when it decides not to initiate an investigation – why should it inform a targeted enterprise?
4. The CCJ noted that, despite differences between EU and CSME competition law, in both regimes:

> "[I]t is not until the inter parties stage of the proceedings that an enterprise is able to rely on rights akin to those of a defendant and that at the investigation stage the Commission must see to it and the Court would always ensure that nothing is done that would irremediably impair those rights."[52]

Under Article 175(12) RTC, any party that is aggrieved by a determination of the CCC made under Article 175(4) RTC may apply to the CCJ for a review of that determination.

Under Article 175(7) RTC, when, following an investigation, the CCC decides to conduct an enquiry, it 'shall afford any party complained of the opportunity to defend its interest'. Accordingly, it is during the enquiry stage that a targeted enterprise's rights of defence must be fully respected.

B Initiation of an investigation at the initiative of the CCC

Under Article 176 RTC, the CCC is empowered to initiate an investigation if it has reason to believe that anti-competitive conduct by an enterprise prejudices trade and restricts competition within the CSME. The CCC may become aware of something that may be an infringement of CSME competition law through any source, for example the press, the television, complaints from competitors and complaints from the general public. However, neither the RTC nor the CCC Rules of Procedure impose on the CCC an obligation to pursue complaints

51 Ibid., [26].
52 Ibid., [27]. See also, *CCC Rules of Procedure 2011*, available at http://www.caricom competitioncommission.com/images/registry/CCC-Rules-of-Procedure-2011.pdf [accessed 15 March 2014], r 3(1).

from natural or legal persons. Unlike the European Commission, the CCC is not required, within a reasonable time, to state its definite position as to whether it intends to proceed with a complaint.[53] If the European Commission adopts a final decision on rejection or acceptance of a complaint from a natural or legal person, the complainant has *locus standi* to seek judicial review of that decision under Article 263 TFEU.[54] This is not the case under the RTC. However, it is submitted that, under the RTC, it may be possible for an aggrieved party to bring proceedings against the CCC if action or inaction on the part of the CCC has caused damage to the applicant, although this may not be easy for the applicant to establish.[55]

Article 176 RTC imposes restrictions on the CCC's power to initiate an investigation *propru motu* in that Article 176(1) RTC requires that the CCC first requests the relevant NCA to undertake a preliminary examination of the alleged anti-competitive conduct of an enterprise. Under Article 176(2) RTC, the relevant NCA is required to examine the matter and report to the CCC within a time frame specified by the CCC. It is only when the CCC is not satisfied with the outcome of its request that it may initiate its own preliminary examination of the matter.

The requirement that the CCC must request the relevant NCA to conduct a preliminary examination of alleged anti-competitive conduct may seriously obstruct the work of the CCC. First, the criterion of the cross-border effect of anti-competitive conduct entails that, in almost every case of interest to the CCC, at least two NCAs will be involved. Accordingly, it seems impracticable to require the CCC to ask, say, eight NCAs to undertake a preliminary examination.

Second, this requirement could compromise the investigation in that there may be complications with ensuring confidentially of an investigation involving many NCAs.

Third, the main reason for establishing the CCC is to ensure the prompt and efficient enforcement of CSME competition law. In this respect, it can be said that unless clear principles are established regarding co-operation between the CCC and NCAs, the system established under Article 176 RTC is unlikely to contribute to efficient and prompt enforcement of CSME competition law. Additionally, Article 176(4) RTC emphasises the detrimental consequences of the requirements set out in Article 176(1) RTC relating to the initiation of an investigation. It provides that, in a situation in which a preliminary examination indicates that there is a need for investigation, the CCC and the Member State concerned 'shall hold consultation to determine and agree on who should have

53 Case T-127/98 *UPS Europe SA v Commission* [1999] ECR II-2633.

54 Case 26/76 *Metro v Commission* [1977] ECR 1875.

55 See *Doreen Johnson v Caribbean Centre for Development Administration* [2009] CCJ 3 (OJ).

jurisdiction to investigate'. In the context of, say, eight Member States concerned, agreement may take time to materialise, or if there is a disagreement, then, under Article 176(5) RTC, the CCC shall cease any further examination and refer the matter to COTED for its decision. Obviously, while COTED deliberates, irreparable harm may be inflicted on competition within the CSME. Further, it is unlikely that a Member State that has refused to agree to the CCC's jurisdiction will change its position when the matter reaches COTED. Accordingly, in cases of a disagreement between a Member State and the CCC, the matter will be likely to end up before the CCJ.[56] This will mean yet further delays.

It is submitted that the CCC, being an independent Community body, should be entitled to initiate an investigation on its own motion without any preliminary conditions imposed upon it regarding the involvement of NCAs. If it needs assistance from the relevant NCA, it may rely on Article 170(3)(a) RTC, which requires that every Member State must ensure that its NCA co-operates with the CCC.

Under Article 176(6) RTC, when the CCC has jurisdiction to investigate an alleged infringement, it must, *inter alia*, notify the interested parties and COTED, and complete the investigation within 120 days, unless an extension is necessary, in which case the CCC is obliged to notify the interested parties. Under Article 176(7) RTC, the CCC, at the conclusion of an enquiry, must notify the interested parties of its determination.

C Uncertainty relating to the determination of whether the CCC has jurisdiction to proceed to an investigation

Article 175(5) RTC states that, unless otherwise agreed with all interested parties, the CCC has 30 days within which to conclude its consultation relating to jurisdictional matters. Rule 8 of the CCC Rules of Procedure states that, once the CCC's Investigation Panel has completed its investigation, it should draw up a report of its findings, stating with reasons whether an infringement has been committed, the nature of the offence and whether the CCC has jurisdiction to pursue the matter. This report is confidential.

In *Trinidad Cement Ltd v CCC*,[57] the CCJ found Rule 8 to be inconsistent with Article 175(4) RTC. Indeed, at the consultation stage, it is not the task of the CCC to carry out a full investigation. As the CCJ noted, at this stage, 'a *prima facie* case that an offence has been committed' is sufficient to justify the CCC jurisdiction,[58] and therefore there is no need for the CCC to establish the existence and nature of the infringement.

56 See Article 176(6) RTC, which states: 'Nothing in this Article shall prejudice the right of the Member State to initiate proceedings before the Court at any time.'

57 [2012] CCJ 4 (OJ).

58 Ibid., [47].

It is submitted that, at the consultation stage, when the jurisdiction of the CCC to deal with an allegation of an infringement is being examined, the establishment of a *prima facie* case should not be required. The CCC should be required to establish only that alleged anti-competitive conduct has cross-border effects on trade and competition within the Community – that is, the conduct is within the jurisdiction of the CCC. In any event, as the CCJ noted, the Investigating Panel's report did not comply with Rule 8 in that it did not state with reason 'whether an offence has been committed' and the 'nature of that offence'; instead, the report stated only that the Panel found 'evidence that the TCL Group has engaged in price discrimination' and that the 'formal enquiry should look into the concerns that the TCL Group may be engaged in price discrimination in terms of Article 179(1)(g) of the Revised Treaty of Chaguaramas'.[59]

9.7.1.2 Investigation procedure: obtaining information

Article 174(2)(b) RTC states that the CCC may, in the conduct of its investigation and in accordance with applicable national law, '[r]equire the discovery or production of any document or part thereof'.

Rule 5 of the CCC Rules of Procedure specifies the power of the Investigating Panel to request documents or information that the Panel considers relevant to any aspect of the investigation.

Under Rule 5(2), the Investigation Panel may make a request (referred to in the Rule as a 'notice') to any person for the production of a specific document or specific information, or both. Such request must state the subject matter of the request, the reason for the request and the purpose of investigation, make reference to the relevant provisions of the RTC or the relevant provision of the national law of the State in which the investigation is taking place, and specify any penalty applicable under the relevant national law for failure to comply with the request. Rule 5(2) provides important clarifications as to the content of the notice: such notice must not be a 'fishing expedition' by the CCC, bearing in mind that the CCC must specify in the notice the nature of the alleged infringement, the purpose of investigation and the legal basis of the investigation.

It is to be noted that Rule 5(2) requires that the notice should include 'a reference to . . . the relevant national provisions under which the investigation takes place', whilst Rule 4(1) states that the Commission may conduct an investigation if it has reason to believe 'that there has been an infringement of national provisions implementing Articles 177(1)(a), (b) or (c) of the Treaty'. The reference to national law is odd, in that the CCC has no competence to deal with national competition law. In *Trinidad Cement Ltd v CCC*,[60] the CCJ expressed its concerns about the content of some CCC Rules of Procedure, including, *inter alia*, Rule 4(1), which

59 Ibid.
60 Ibid.

in the Court's view seemed not to be required by the RTC and in respect of which the Court stated 'it is difficult to see how an investigation of the regional Competition Commission could deal with cross-border anti-competitive business conduct by focusing on the infringement of national provisions'.[61]

The notice must also specify the time, place and manner in which the requested documents or information must be provided. Under Rule 5(4), the Investigating Panel may, when a document is produced, take copies of the whole or part of it and may require the person producing the document, or any person who is a current or past employee of the investigated enterprise, to provide explanation of the document. If the document is not produced, the Investigating Panel may require the person concerned to assist the Panel in locating it.

Rule 5(6) is rather mysterious, because it states that all information obtained pursuant to Rule 5 shall be treated as confidential and not disclosed in public hearings before an Adjudicating Panel unless the provider of it agrees otherwise. This Rule needs to be amended to take account of the fact that only some documents or information justify confidentiality.

The words in Rule 5(1) stating that the Investigating Panel may require any person to produce for the Investigating Panel 'a specified document, or any specific information, which the Panel considers relevant to any aspect of the investigation', need clarification. On the one hand, it is understandable that it is not possible to specify in advance what kind of documents or information will be relevant to the investigation. On the other, in light of Rule 5(c), under which penalties available under the relevant national law may be imposed on the addressee of the notice for failure to comply, it is appropriate to:

- specify what documents or information may be considered as 'relevant to any aspect of the investigation';
- examine whether the word 'any person', includes governments of Member States;
- address the issue of self-incriminating documents or information; and,
- comment on communications covered by legal profession privilege (LPP).

A The meaning of 'a specified document, or any specific information . . . relevant to any aspect of the investigation' in Rule 5(1) of the CCC Rules of Procedure

In order to elucidate the meaning of 'a specified document, or any specific information . . . relevant to any aspect of the investigation', it is useful to examine the case law of the ECJ on the meaning of 'necessary information', which is used in Article 18 of Regulation 1/2003 under which the European Commission has

61 Ibid., [48].

power to compel undertakings to provide 'all necessary information'. In *Orkem*,[62] the ECJ held that it is up to the European Commission to decide what information is 'necessary', and that 'necessary information' relates to anything that is connected to, or has some relationship with, the information requested and the infringement under investigation. Further, in *SEP*,[63] the ECJ held that information should be regarded as necessary if it has some connection with the alleged infringement, if it assists detection of, or confirmation of, the alleged infringement or if it confirms evidence already gathered by the Commission. It is submitted that a meaning similar to that which was given by the ECJ to the words 'necessary information' should be attributed to the words 'specified document, or any specific information . . . relevant to any aspect of the investigation which are contained in Rule 5(1) of the CCC Rules of Procedure.

It is to be noted that Rule 5 of the CCC Rules of Procedure does not specify what occurs if there is a disagreement between the addressee of the notice and the Investigating Panel as to whether particular information or a particular document is relevant to any aspect of the investigation. This is a gap that should be filled by the CCC. In any event, the fact that a notice must contain the information specified in Rule 5(2) will allow the CCJ to review notices in order to decide whether a requested document or information is of relevance to the investigation.

It is also interesting to note that Rule 5 refers only to 'failure' to provide documents or information, and does not include any reference to a situation in which an addressee of a notice provides incorrect, incomplete or misleading information. Will national penalties apply to the provider of such information?

B The meaning of 'any person' in Rule 5(1) of the CCC Rules of Procedure

Reference to 'any person' does not seem to include requests for information from governments. However, under Article 9 RTC, a government will be required to comply with a notice of the CCC, because it must take all necessary measures to ensure 'the carrying out of obligations arising out of this Treaty or resulting from decisions taken by the Organs and Bodies of the Community'. It is submitted that a notice for supply of documents or information from a government should be considered to be a decision of the CCC and thus to fall within the scope of Article 9 RTC. The inclusion of governments as potential addressees of a notice is implicit in Article 170(4) RTC, which states that a Member State has no duty to disclose confidential information:

62 Case 374/87 *Orkem SA v Commission* [1989] ECR 3283.

63 Case C-36/92P *Samenwerkende Elektriciteits Produktiebedrijven (SEP) NV v Commission* [1994] ECR I-1911.

> "... the disclosure of which would be prejudicial to the public interest or to the legitimate interests of enterprises, public and private. Confidential information or proprietary information disclosed in the course of investigation shall be treated on the same basis as that on which it was provided."

Accordingly, under Article 9 RTC, a Member State will have a duty to disclose information not covered by Article 170(4) RTC.

C Self-incriminatory documents and information

The CCC Rules of Procedure are silent on the very important issue of self-incriminating documents and information. If infringements of CSME competition law are criminal offences, then an addressee's right not to incriminate himself or herself should be respected. The matter will certainly be decided by the CCJ in due course.

The difficulty of dealing with self-incriminating documents and information is emphasised by the approach of the ECJ to that matter. In *Solvay*[64] and in *Orkem*,[65] the issue was whether an undertaking under investigation could refuse to supply requested information by relying on the right not to incriminate oneself. The ECJ held that it is the task of the European Commission to evidence the infringement of EU competition law and that an undertaking cannot be compelled to admit an infringement, because this would undermine its rights to defence, but added that an undertaking is obliged to co-operate with the European Commission, and thus to supply documents requested by it, even though these might serve to establish that undertaking's infringement.[66]

In *PVC Cartel I*,[67] the ECJ stated that the right of undertakings not to be compelled by the European Commission to admit an infringement of EU competition law is to be understood as meaning that:

> "[I]n the event of a dispute as to the scope of a question, it must be determined whether an answer from the undertaking to which the question is addressed is in fact equivalent to the admission of an infringement, such as to undermine the rights of the defence."[68]

64 Case 27/88 *Solvay & Cie v Commission* [1989] ECR 3355.

65 Case 374/87 *Orkem SA v Commission* [1989] ECR 3283.

66 This was confirmed in Case C-301/04P *Commission v SGL Carbon* [2006] ECR I-5915.

67 Joined Cases C-238/99 P, C-244/99 P, C-245/99 P, C-247/99 P, C-250/99 P–C-252/99 P and C-254/99 P *Limburgse Vinyl Maatschappij NV (LVM) (C-238/99 P), DSM NV and DSM Kunststoffen BV (C-244/99 P), Montedison SpA (C-245/99 P), Elf Atochem SA (C-247/99 P), Degussa AG (C-250/99 P), Enichem SpA (C-251/99 P), Wacker-Chemie GmbH and Hoechst AG (C-252/99 P) and Imperial Chemical Industries plc (ICI) (C-254/99 P) v Commission (PVC Cartel I)* [2002] ECR I-8375. See also Case C-301/04P *Commission v SGL Carbon* [2006] ECR I-5915, [44].

68 *PVC Cartel I*, op. cit., [273].

The case law of the ECJ shows that the privilege against self-incrimination:

- applies when a request for information makes provision of information compulsory (under Article 18(3) of Regulation 1/2003), as opposed to not compulsory (under Article 18(2) of Regulation 1/2003);
- applies when a request for information is addressed to an undertaking that is under investigation; and
- covers only the questions addressed by the European Commission to the undertaking under investigation, and does not apply to documents in possession of that undertaking, which, if requested, must be forwarded to the European Commission.

The Notice on Best Practices in the Conduct of Proceedings Concerning Articles 101 and 102 TFEU[69] specifies that, when there is disagreement between an undertaking and the European Commission as to whether the answer to questions asked by the European Commission is covered by the privilege against self-incrimination, the undertaking concerned may, after raising this matter with the European Commission's Directorate-General for Competition, refer it to the Hearing Officer, who will make a reasoned recommendation as to whether or not the privilege applies. The recommendation will be taken into account when the European Commission adopts any decision under Article 18(3) of Regulation 1/2003.

It follows from the above that the ECJ, on the one hand, recognises the right not to self-incriminate in that it does not compel an undertaking to admit an alleged infringement by forcing it to answer questions that might lead to such admission – but, on the other, refuses the right not to provide documents that are incriminating. This position is to be contrasted with that of the EFTA Court in *PostenNorge*.[70]

D Legal professional privilege (LPP)

Rule 7 of the CCC Rules of Procedure provides that LPP applies to communications, documents or other material in possession of a professional legal adviser or his or her client. A definition of 'professional legal adviser' is provided in Rule 2, which states that it includes 'an attorney-at-law, or a legal practitioner, or an advocate or jurist'. It is submitted that the definition is far too extensive. A professor of law would be a jurist within the meaning of the

69 European Commission, *Notice on Best Practices in the Conduct of Proceedings Concerning Articles 101 and 102 TFEU* [2011] OJ C3 08/6.

70 Case E-15/10 *PostenNorge AS v EFTA Surveillance Authority* (EFTA Ct, 18 April 2012), available at http://www.eftacourt.int/uploads/tx_nvcases/15_10_Judgment_EN.pdf [accessed 27 April 2013]. See section 9.6.1.

definition, as would be a former judge and a person who has been awarded an LLB. Such persons are not subject to any professional rules concerning ethical obligations, but under Rule 7 could withhold documents and information from the CCC claiming that they are covered by LPP. Further, Rule 7 does not provide how it is to be determined whether a particular document or information is covered by LPP. In this context, it is unacceptable that a decision of whether the specific document or information is covered by LPP be taken by the CCC.

It is submitted that Rule 7 should be amended. In this respect, the approach adopted by the ECJ may be helpful. EU competition law recognises the principle of lawyer–client confidentiality, but limits its application to communications between a client and his or her independent lawyer[71] – that is, a lawyer who is entitled to practise in one of the Member States. This means that communications between a client and in-house lawyers are excluded from LPP.[72] The reason for exclusion is that in-house lawyers are bound to their clients by an employment relationship and that, in some Member States, there are differing rules of ethics for independent lawyers and in-house lawyers.

A further important point is that only communications between a client and his or her independent lawyer that are made for the specific purpose of, and in the interests of, the client's rights of defence are privileged.

It was expected that the position of the ECJ on LPP may change as a result of the order made by the President of the General Court in *Akzo*.[73] The President of the General Court stated that the arguments presented by Akzo regarding the extension of professional privilege to cover communications with in-house lawyers were not unfounded, in particular (as was the situation in this case) when an in-house-lawyer is subject to professional rules equivalent to those imposed on an independent lawyer. However, on 17 September 2007, the General Court rendered a judgment maintaining the pre-existing position.[74] The Court held that there was no valid reason to reconsider that position, given that comparative examination of national laws of the Member States shows that a large number of them exclude in-house lawyers from the benefit of LPP and that the principle of equal treatment, in the context of the right of establishment and the right to provide services, had not been infringed, given that the situation of an independent lawyer and an in-house lawyer differ as a result of the functional, structural and hierarchical integration of in-house lawyers within the undertakings that employ them.

In the above case, the General Court made the following important findings regarding privileged documents.

71 Case 155/79 *AM and S Ltd v Commission* [1982] ECR 1575.

72 Ibid.

73 Joined Cases T-125/03 and T-253/03 *Akzo Nobel Chemicals Ltd and Akcros Chemicals Ltd v Commission* [2003] ECR II-4771.

74 Joined Cases T-125/03 and T-253/03 *Akzo Nobel Chemicals and Akcros Chemicals v Commission* [2007] ECR II-3523.

- It held that, during investigations, the European Commission is not allowed to take even a cursory look at documents that are claimed by the undertaking concerned as being privileged if that undertaking considers such a cursory look will reveal their content.
- The European Commission is not entitled to read such documents before it adopts a decision refusing to classify them as privileged and before a challenge, if any, to a decision by the undertaking concerned has been rejected by the General Court.
- Documents drafted exclusively for the purpose of seeking legal advice from an independent lawyer in the exercise of the right of defence, even if they have not been communicated with a lawyer, may be classified as privileged.
- Documents that have been discussed between a client and an independent lawyer are not necessarily covered by LPP. This depends on whether they were prepared for the purpose of seeking legal advice.

The ECJ upheld the judgment of the General Court.[75] The ECJ held that communications of lawyers are covered by LPP if two conditions are satisfied: first, the communication must be connected to the client's rights of defence; and second, it must be from an independent lawyer – that is, a lawyer who is not in a relationship of employment with his or her client. The Court specified that the second condition is not satisfied so far as exchanges of communications within a company or group of companies with their in-house lawyers are concerned, because the requirement of independence is absent even when an in-house lawyer is a member of a bar or the Law Society, and thus bound to follow rules of professional ethical obligations. In this respect, the ECJ emphasised that the ability of in-house lawyers to exercise professional independence is affected by the facts that they, being employees, cannot ignore the commercial strategies pursued by their employers and that, depending upon the terms of their employment, they may be required to perform tasks that are not confined to providing legal advice. Accordingly, the ECJ held that in-house lawyers do not enjoy a level of professional independence comparable to that of external lawyers because of their economic dependence on, and close ties with, their employers.[76]

This case confirmed that, where there is a disagreement between an undertaking and the European Commission as to whether documents are covered by LLP, it is the task of the General Court to decide the matter. Accordingly, officials of the European Commission have no right to see those documents, or even to take a cursory look at them, until the disagreement has been resolved,

75 Case C-550/07 P *Akzo Nobel Chemicals Ltd, and Akcros Chemicals Ltd v Commission* [2010] ECR I-8311.

76 The exclusion of in-house lawyers from LPP is a very controversial issue given its practical implications. On this topic, see M. Frese, 'The Development of General Principles for EU Competition Law Enforcement: The Protection of Legal Professional Privilege' (2011) 32 ECLR 196.

because depending upon what they have seen – and what they should not have seen – their final decision may be influenced. The proper procedure for the European Commission is to adopt a decision requiring the documents to be forwarded to it, which decision can then be appealed by the undertaking concerned to the General Court, which will make a final decision on whether the documents are covered by LPP.

It is submitted that Rule 7 of the CCC Rules of Procedure should be amended so that it restricts the scope of LPP as follows.

- With regard to *personal scope*, LPP should apply only to communications between independent lawyers and their clients. Independent lawyers should be defined as those who are members of local bar associations (or similar), and thus subject to rules of professional conduct and discipline, and entitled to practise in one of the Member States of CARICOM. LPP should not apply to communications of in-house lawyers.
- With regard to *communications*, LPP should apply to communications made for the purpose, and in the interest, of the protection of rights to defence of clients of independent lawyers.

In the case of disagreement between the CCC and the person concerned as to whether the relevant communication is covered by LPP, it should ultimately be for the CCJ to decide whether the relevant communication is within the scope of LPP. When officers of the CCC inspect premises of an enterprise, they should not be allowed to take even a cursory look at documents that the enterprise claims to be covered by LPP if such a cursory look may, according to the enterprise, reveal their content. In such a situation, an officer should put the relevant documents into an envelope, seal it and take it with him or her to the headquarters of the CCC, where the envelope should be kept sealed until the disagreement is resolved. This procedure should both avoid the risk of a breach of LPP and ensure that the document(s) will not disappear or be tampered with.

9.7.1.3 The inspection stage

Article 174(2)(c) RTC provides that the CCC may take necessary action in furtherance of the investigation. This, *inter alia*, entails that the CCC may carry out inspections of targeted enterprises' premises. This right to enter premises of a targeted enterprise permits the CCC to obtain evidence of an alleged infringement of CSME competition law in exactly the place where such evidence can often be found – that is, the premises of a targeted enterprise. The right of the CCC to carry out inspections is the best way of discovering information and documents that are not already known, or fully identified, and thus cannot be obtained by requests for information and documents expressly provided for in Article 174(2)(b) RTC. However, the powers granted to the CCC under

Article 174(2) RTC must be exercised in accordance with national law. This means that the CCC will need a warrant in order to enter, search and, if necessary, seal the premises of a targeted enterprise.

Reliance on national law has the following implications.

1. It ensures that targeted enterprises will have to submit to unannounced inspections.
2. It ensures that the nature and degree of protection afforded to premises against inspections by the CCC will be determined in accordance with national laws. In this context, it can be said that although all Member States recognise that any intervention by public authorities must be neither arbitrary, nor disproportionate, the form and the extent to which enterprises are protected under national law may differ from Member State to Member State. In this respect, it is submitted that the CCJ should, in due course, recognise that the protection of fundamental human rights constitutes a general principle of CSME law. This will then ensure that the CCJ has power to determine whether, in any particular case, an inspection ordered by the CCC, despite being in accordance with the relevant national law, conforms with the requirements of fundamental human rights. It is also submitted that when a warrant to enter and search the targeted enterprise's premises is sought, the relevant authority, normally a court, should neither be entitled to call into question the need for the inspection (taking into account the facts that only the CCJ can review the acts of the CCC and that, under Article III(1) of the Protocol on the Privileges and Immunities of the CCC,[77] the CCC enjoys immunity from all legal process), nor demand to be supplied with all of the information in the CCC's possession. A national court should be empowered only to verify whether the coercive measures sought are arbitrary or excessive. If in doubt, a national court may ask the CCC to provide further information.[78]
3. It requires that Member States must ensure that the CCC's action is effective – that is, that mechanisms are put in place that will enable the CCC to obtain the necessary co-operation from national authorities and their NCAs.

Rule 6 of the CCC Rules of Procedure deals with inspections. It provides that the CCC is empowered to:

77 Available at http://www.caricomcompetitioncommission.com/images/registry/protocol-on-the-privileges-immunities-of-the-ccc.pdf [accessed 15 January 2014].

78 See Case C-94/00 *Roquette Frères SA v Commission* [2002] ECR I-9011, in which the ECJ established a similar principle under EU law in a situation in which a targeted undertaking refused to submit to inspection ordered by the European Commission.

- enter and search premises specified in a warrant, search any person on those premises if there are reasonable grounds for believing that such a person has in his or her possession any document, equipment or article relevant to the investigation, and obtain access to and search any computer system or other electronic device on the premises;
- examine any document and other business records;
- take possession of any document or copies of or extracts of it, including copies of any such held in any computer system on the premises;
- ask for immediate oral explanations; and
- seal any business premises and any article or thing found on the premises in accordance with any warrant obtained under national law to this effect.

Rule 6(2) states that if the CCC removes anything from the searched premises, it must provide the owner, or person in control of the premises with a receipt for the item(s) removed.

Rule 6(4) provides that all information obtained pursuant to this Rule must be treated as confidential and not disclosed in any public hearing before an Adjudicating Panel unless otherwise agreed by the person concerned, or unless the information is disclosed in a non-confidential summary form agreed by such a person.

Rule 6 does not address the matter of co-operation between a suspected enterprise and the CCC during an inspection. It is submitted that Rule 6 should be amended to reflect that a refusal to co-operate will be considered by the CCC to be an aggravating factor to be taken into account when, if relevant, it determines the amount of fine for a substantive infringement.[79]

The CCC Rules of Procedure do not specify whether the CCC will be allowed to carry out inspections in premises other than those of an enterprise under investigation. However, the fact that the CCC will need a warrant to enter any premises implies that the CCC will also have power, subject to a warrant being obtained beforehand, to search private homes if relevant documents are likely to be kept there. This is justified in light of Article 174(2)(c) RTC, which permits the CCC to 'take such other action as may be necessary in furtherance of the investigation'.

A The power to take statements

Article 174(2)(b) RTC gives the CCC power to 'secure the attendance of any person before it to give evidence'. This power is to be exercised in accordance with the national law of the person concerned, and thus sanctions for refusal, or

79 For example, in one case, the European Commission had increased the fine imposed on Sony by 30 per cent when an employee refused to answer questions and another shredded documents during the inspection: see European Commission, 'Antitrust: Commission Fines Professional Videotape Producers over €74 Million for Price Fixing Cartel', 20 November 2007, Commission Press Release IP/07/1725.

for the provision of incorrect or misleading information, are also to be in accord with the relevant national law. It is interesting to note that there is no CCC Rule of Procedure relating to this matter.

B The end of the investigation stage

Rule 8 of the CCC Rules of Procedure states that, once the Investigating Panel completes its investigation, it should draw up a report of its findings, stating with reasons whether an infringement has been committed, if appropriate, the nature of the offence and whether the CCC has jurisdiction to pursue the matter. It is submitted that jurisdictional issues should be dealt with before the formal investigation takes place (see section 9.7.1.1). Accordingly, Rule 8 should be amended.

At the end of the investigation stage, the Investigating Panel must decide whether, in its view, an infringement has been committed. If so, the matter proceeds to the next stage – that is, the adjudication stage.

9.7.1.4 The adjudication stage

Rule 10 of the CCC Rules of Procedure provides that if the Investigating Panel recommends an enquiry, it should file a notice, together with a 'statement of issues and material facts', with the Adjudicating Panel. The proceedings before the Adjudicating Panel are aimed at ensuring that the enterprise concerned has an opportunity to be heard before the CCC makes any determination under Article 174(3) RTC. The main purpose for the existence of an Adjudicating Panel is to ensure disinterested objectivity in making a determination pursuant to Article 174(3) RTC.

The procedure before the Adjudicating Panel is divided into pre-hearing procedures, including conferences, and hearings, which may be conducted by means of either a written or an oral procedure.

Rule 11 specifies the content of a notice sent to a respondent found in breach of CSME competition law by the Investigating Panel. The notice must contain:

> "(a) the legal provision under which the notice is issued;
> (b) the nature of the determination that may be made by the Commission including penalties or consequences that may be imposed;
> (c) the name and address of the respondent;
> (d) the disclosure of the failure of the respondent to respond to the notice may result in the Commission taking such steps that are just and reasonable; and
> (e) a clear and concise statement of issues and material facts attached, which shall be divided into consecutively numbered paragraphs."

In addition, every notice must provide any information that may be useful in explaining the content of that notice and must be signed by the Executive Director of the CCC. Upon a notice being filed, the Registrar of the CCC shall serve a copy of it and its annexes on the respondent, who then has 60 business days within which to respond in writing in accord with the requirements of Rule 13.

It is submitted that, although this is not expressly stated in the CCC Rules of Procedure, the service of the notice is the first step in the contentious procedure between an enterprise and the CCC. Accordingly, the final determination of the CCC, if the CCC maintains its allegations, should only repeat the determination made in the notice – that is, the CCC should not be allowed to add any new allegations. This will protect the enterprise's right to a fair trial. However, findings of facts set out in the notice should not be considered to be final, bearing in mind that the final statement of facts will be established during the adjudicating stage.

An enterprise is not obliged to respond to a notice and thus may face consequences specified in Rule 11(d).

While it is not the intention of this book to examine all of the CCC Rules of Procedure relating to the adjudicating stage, a short summary of those procedural steps is set out below.

A Pre-hearing procedures

In the pre-hearing stage, the parties to the proceedings, with leave of the Adjudicating Panel, and the Adjudicating Panel may ask for interrogatories. In the case of the Adjudicating Panel, it may use interrogatories in the hope of clarifying evidence filed by the parties, simplifying issues related to the matter before the Panel, or helping the Panel to gain a full and satisfactory understanding of the matters to be considered.[80] One party to the proceedings may file interrogatories directed to the other, requesting clarification of that other party's evidence, or documents, or both, or requesting other information in that other party's possession relevant to the enquiry.[81] The party to which interrogatories are directed is required to provide a full and adequate response to each interrogatory in the manner specified by Rule 18(1). If no full and adequate response is provided, or if the relevant party is unable or unwilling to provide such a response, it must explain its reasons for failure so to do. If the requesting party is not satisfied with the response, it may bring a motion requesting the matter to be settled by an order, or decision, of the Adjudicating Panel.[82]

80 *CCC Rules of Procedure 2011*, available at http://www.caricomcompetitioncommission.com/images/registry/CCC-Rules-of-Procedure-2011.pdf [accessed 15 March 2014], r 17(1).

81 Ibid., r 17(2).

82 Ibid., r 18(3).

The Adjudicating Panel may direct the parties to participate in the following types of conference:

- *technical conferences*, the purpose of which is to review and clarify 'a notice, and the statement of issues and material facts, a response, the evidence of a party, or matters connected with the interrogatories';[83]
- *issues conferences*, the purpose of which is to identify and clarify 'all the issues raised by the parties and which of those issues are contested, and which are agreed by the parties';[84] and
- *procedural conferences*, the purposes of which are specified in Rule 21(1)(a)–(e).[85]

These conferences, unless otherwise directed by the Adjudicating Panel, are held by way of public oral hearing. As an alternative to requesting participation in a conference, the Adjudicating Panel may direct the parties to provide written submissions.

B Hearings

Hearings may be conducted by means of a written or oral procedure. They may be public or *in camera*. Rule 36 of the CCC Rules of Procedure provides that all hearings, whether of a notice pursuant to Rule 10 or of an interlocutory application by notice of motion, are subject to Part VI of the Rules, entitled 'Hearings'. Rule 37 sets out procedures at the written hearing, whilst Rule 38 and subsequent Rules deal with oral hearings.

Hearings take place *in camera* when the Adjudicating Panel considers that, during a hearing, some confidential information may be disclosed that 'would be prejudicial to the public interest or to the legitimate commercial interest of a party or of a person who provided such party with the information'.[86] When a hearing takes place *in camera*, it may be attended only by the persons testifying before the Adjudicating Panel (the period of whose attendance is limited to that required for their active personal participation), counsel for any of the parties, authorised employees of the CCC and such other persons as the Adjudicating

83 Ibid., r 19.

84 Ibid., r 20.

85 Rule 21(1)(a)–(e) states: 'In addition to technical conferences and issues conferences, the Adjudicating Panel may direct the parties to make submissions in writing or to participate in procedural conferences for the purposes of: admitting certain facts or proof of them by affidavit; permitting the use of documents by any party; recommending the procedures to be adopted before the Adjudicating Panel; setting the date and place for the commencement of the hearing; or deciding any other matter that may aid in the disposing of the enquiry in a just or expeditious manner.'

86 Ibid., r 47(1).

Panel considers should be present. Such attendance will be on conditions specified by the Adjudicating Panel. Any person attending a hearing held *in camera* and who is not bound by an obligation of professional secrecy is required to file a secrecy undertaking, breach of which will be sanctioned in accordance with the law of the place of the hearing.

C Evidence

The rules on evidence set out in Part V of the CCC Rules of Procedure will, doubtless, be tested by the CCJ in the future. Nevertheless, it should be noted that hearsay is acceptable, although the Adjudicating Panel, when considering it, must take into account the doubtful nature of hearsay.

D Determinations

The procedure before the Adjudicating Panel terminates when the Panel makes its determination. A determination must be in writing, signed by all Panel members, stating all issues and material facts, and giving reasons for the determination.

In accordance with Article 174(4) RTC, the Adjudicating Panel may:

> "(b) order the termination or nullification as the case may require, of agreements, conduct, activities or decisions prohibited by Article 170;[87]
> (c) direct the enterprise to cease and desist from anti-competitive business conduct and to take such steps as are necessary to overcome the effects of abuse of its dominant position in the market, or any other business conduct inconsistent with the principles of fair competition set out in this Chapter;
> (i) order payment of compensation to persons affected; and
> (j) impose fines for breaches of the rules of competition."

Additionally, under Rule 52 of the CCC Rules of Procedure, the Adjudicating Panel may make an order requiring a party to compensate another party for the costs incurred by that other party in participating in the enquiry, but only to the extent permitted by the law of any relevant Member State. This is an unclear and unrealistic provision in that, when a targeted enterprise is found by the Adjudicating Panel to be in breach of CSME competition law, it should be fined appropriately and thus the CCC should have no further financial claims on that enterprise. When the Adjudicating Panel decides that there has been no breach of CSME competition law, there is no reason for the CCC to claim any

87 The reference should be to Article 177(1) RTC, not to Article 170 RTC.

compensation. Different when the targeted enterprise is exonerated from all charges, it would be incongruous for it to claim any compensation in a situation in which the CCC has carried out an investigation in a proper manner. However, gross negligence on the part of the CCC in conducting an investigation, or inexcusable errors committed by it, or a manifest and grave lack of diligence on its part when dealing with a particular investigation, should always be compensated in accordance with Community rules on non-contractual liability rather than on the basis of national law, which may differ from Member State to Member State. However, in light of Rule 53(3), which states that '[n]othing in these Rules shall affect the possibility for a party to apply to the Court in relation to any act of the Commission', it can be said that all matters of compensation will, if not otherwise resolved, be decided by the CCJ.

With regard to Article 174(4)(b) RTC, the following is submitted.

1. There are numbering/lettering errors in Article 174(4) RTC. Its paragraphs commence with letter (b), instead of letter (a). Accordingly, Article 174(4)(b) RTC should be identified as Article 174(4)(a) RTC. Additionally, reference contained in Article 174(4)(b) to Article 170 RTC should be to Article 177(1)(a)–(c) RTC.
2. The Article currently identified as Article 174(4)(b) RTC provides that the CCC 'shall order', if it so decides, *inter alia*, the 'nullification' of agreements, conduct, activities or decisions prohibited by Article 177(1)(a)–(c) RTC. Article 174(4)(b) RTC should be read in light of Article 177(3) RTC, which states that, '[s]ubject to Article 168, a Member State shall ensure that all agreements and decisions within the meaning of paragraph 1 of this Article shall be null and void within its jurisdiction'. On the one hand, it can be argued that Article 177(3) RTC implies that no order of the CCC is required to nullify prohibited agreements and decisions of associations of enterprises, because they are null and void in all Member States. On the other, it can be argued that an order from the CCC is necessary to clarify which prohibited agreements or decisions should be rendered void under national law. The latter interpretation is preferable. It is also in line with the approach of the ECJ, in that a very similar provision contained in Article 101(2) TFEU, which provides that agreements and decisions prohibited by Article 101(1) TFEU 'shall be automatically void', was interpreted by the ECJ as meaning that an agreement as a whole is void only if offending clauses cannot be severed from that agreement.[88] Accordingly, it is not necessary for the entire agreement or decision to be declared null and void if it is possible to sever offending clauses without destroying the substance of the agreement or decision. Whether or not it is possible to so do is a matter for national courts

88 Case 56/65 *Société Technique Minière (S.T.M.) v Maschinenbau Ulm GmbH (M.B.U.)* [1966] ECR 235

to decide.[89] Sometimes, EU institutions assist national courts. For example, in *Consten and Grundig*,[90] the ECJ severed the offending clauses of the agreement, being those giving absolute territorial protection. In the context of CSME competition law, it will be for the CCC to specify in its determination whether, and to what extent, the severability rule applies.

It is uncertain whether the nullity referred to in Article 177(3) RTC is absolute – that is, whether it applies *erga omnes* and *ex tunc*. Under EU law, the ECJ held that the nullity referred to in Article 101(2) TFEU is absolute: a prohibited agreement has no effect as between its parties and cannot be set up against a third party.[91] Further, in *Courage*,[92] the ECJ held that the absolute nature of nullity entails that a prohibited agreement has no past or future effects and that even a party to a prohibited agreement may rely upon its nullity to seek compensation from the other party for loss caused by such an agreement. Accordingly, the fact that, under national law, the seeking of compensation was barred was irrelevant; only the fact that the aggrieved party bears significant responsibility for the distortion of competition may deprive it of the right to obtain damages.

The reference in Article 174(4)(b) RTC to 'nullification' of 'conduct, activities' seems odd. How can conduct or an activity be nullified? Only formal arrangements between enterprises or decisions of associations of enterprises can be rendered null.

3. The CCC Rules of Procedure do not deal with the matter of how the CCC will exercise its power to order payment of compensation by an offending enterprise to persons affected by the infringement of CSME competition law. In this context, the issue arises as to how the CCC intends to exercise that power. Will it establish some common rules on this matter? Should the CCC refer to the national law of the victim or that of the offender?

   It is submitted that the possibility for an alleged victim to be awarded damages by the CCC constitutes an important incentive for such a person to participate in proceedings before the CCC. This possibility makes enforcement of CSME competition law relevant to citizens of Member States. It is submitted that the CCC should establish common rules relating to the matter of compensation, because reliance on national laws will undermine uniformity in the application of CSME competition law and may be prejudicial to victims. Substantive conditions relating to awards of compensation, as well as procedural matters, should be the same throughout

89 Case 319/82 *Société de Vente de Ciments et Béton de L'Est v Kerpen and Kerpen GmbH and Co. KG* [1983] ECR 4173.

90 Joined Cases 56 and 58/64 *Établissements Consten SaRL and Grundig-Verkaufs-GmbH v Commission* [1966] ECR 299.

91 Case 22/71 *Béguelin Import Co. v S.A.G.L. Import Export* [1971] ECR 949, [29].

92 Case C-453/99 *Courage Ltd v Bernard Crehan and Bernard Crehan v Courage Ltd and ors* [2001] ECR I-6297.

the Community. It is important to emphasise that to leave to national procedural laws the determination of such important matters as, for example, matters relating to *locus standi*, methods of proof of damage, types of damage for which compensation is recoverable and the principles of damage calculation, many of which differ among Member States, in particular between common law States and civil law States, may result in different outcomes for similar cases under differing national laws.

It is to be noted that, under the national laws of each Member State, victims of anti-competitive conduct of enterprises may initiate proceedings claiming damages from parties to an infringement of CSME competition law. Such proceedings will be facilitated if a determination of the CCC has established the existence of an infringement. Further, if Member States harmonise the rules governing actions for damages – that is, align them with those to be developed by the CCC – such harmonisation will increase legal certainty and facilitate the private enforcement of CSME competition law.

4. Under Article 174(4)(j) RTC (which should rightly be referred to as Article 174(4)(d) RTC – see point 1 above), the CCC is empowered to impose pecuniary sanctions on enterprises that infringe CSME competition law. The CCC has drafted a proposal relating to its fining policy, which is currently being reviewed, and thus is unavailable to the public and cannot be commented upon.[93]

E The right of access to documents in possession of the CCC

In *Trinidad Cement Ltd v CCC*,[94] TCL alleged that the CCC was guilty of bad faith in that it had failed to disclose information relevant to the case. The CCJ did not directly deal with this allegation. The CCJ emphasised that the CCC had supplied all necessary documents to the CCJ and that CARICOM had provided some additional documents that had not been requested by the Court, but which were of relevance to the case. The CCJ was pleased with the attitude adopted by the CCC and CARICOM. With regard to TCL, the CCJ stated that:

> "[T]he information was available to the Claimant in time for use in trial. This removed any complaint about unfairness from non-disclosure. It also prevents possible delays or additional costs that may have become necessary if the information was only revealed during the testimony phase of the proceedings."[95]

93 See CCC, 'Fining Regime', available at http://www.caricomcompetition-commission.com/en/competition/fining-regime [accessed 12 January 2014].

94 [2012] CCJ 4 (OJ).

95 Ibid., [43].

The CCJ also noted that additional documents provided by CARICOM were of such a nature that, normally, the claimant would have no access to them even though they were relevant to the case. The CCJ concluded that, 'despite sympathetic notation of TCL's submission, the Court considers that no further orders are required'.[96] This conclusion indicates that when a claimant has access to documents for the first time during proceedings before the CCJ, but prior to the CCC's making a determination under Article 174(4) RTC, there is no breach of its right of defence.

It is submitted that, in the preliminary stage of proceedings, when the CCC is determining whether it has jurisdiction to act, a claimant should not be entitled to consult documents in the possession of the CCC. However, the situation differs once the CCC has made a determination finding a claimant in breach of CSME competition law. In such a situation, the matter arises whether there is a sufficient ground to annul the CCC's determination when access to documents is given to the claimant, for the first time, at so late a point as during proceedings before the CCJ. In other words, the matter is whether procedural flaws on the part of the CCC should result in annulment of the CCC's determination. In this respect, the case law of the ECJ may be of some interest. In the *Solvay* cases,[97] the ECJ held that, when access to documents is granted for the first time during proceedings before the General Court, the party alleging breach of its rights of defence has to show 'not that if it had had access to the non-disclosed documents, the Commission decision would have been different in content, but only that those documents could have been useful for its defence'.[98] Accordingly, if a claimant's ability to defend itself were prejudiced, the EU courts would annul the decision of the European Commission on the ground of infringement of the claimant's right of the defence.

It is submitted that the right to defence should be one of the fundamental principles of CARICOM law, the observance of which should be ensured by the CCJ. It should not be sufficient to give access to documents prejudicial to the defence at the stage of judicial proceedings before the CCJ. This is because, first, the role of the CCJ is not to replace the full examination of the case carried out by the CCC, and second, as the ECJ held in *Aalborg Portland and ors*:[99]

> "[B]elated disclosure of documents in the file does not return the undertaking which has brought the action against the Commission decision to the situation in which it would have been if it had been able to rely on those documents in presenting its written and oral observations to the Commission."[100]

96 Ibid., [44].

97 Case C-109/10P *Solvay SA v Commission* [2011] ECR I-10329; Case C-110/10P *Solvay SA v Commission* [2011] ECR I-10429.

98 Case C-109/10P *Solvay SA v Commission* [2011] ECR I-I0329, [57].

99 Joined Cases C-204/00 P, C-205/00 P, C-211/00 P, C-213/00 P, C-217/00 P and C-219/00 P *Aalborg Portland and ors v Commission* [2004] ECR I-123.

100 Ibid., [103].

Accordingly, the CCJ might well take the view that, in such a situation, the CCC's determination should be annulled on the ground of a procedural defect, with the result that the CCC will be required to adopt a new determination and conduct a new hearing of the enterprises concerned before the Adjudicating Panel. In other words, the CCC should not be allowed to make a new determination, with substantially the same content and based on the same grounds, without giving the enterprise concerned an opportunity to be heard by the Adjudicating Panel.

It is submitted that, under the CCC Rules of Procedure, a refusal of access to documents held by the CCC will be of relevance only when a document or information is considered by the Adjudicating Panel as confidential (see below). Unlike the European Commission, which makes its final decision as to whether an infringement of EU competition law has occurred on the basis of its entire file,[101] under CSME competition law, the determination is made by the Adjudicating Panel on the basis of documents and information filed by the parties. Accordingly, if access to a document or information is refused, but the CCJ later finds that the Adjudicating Panel made an error by classifying the relevant document as confidential and that non-disclosure of its content to the suspected enterprise has prejudiced its rights to defence, annulment of the CCC's determination will be justified.

In the context of access to documents, a distinction must be made between those that are accessible to the public and those that are not. This is particularly so in light of Rule 67 of the CCC Rules of Procedure, which states that, subject to the rule of confidentiality contained in Rule 68, 'documents filed in respect of an enquiry shall be placed on the public record'.

Rule 68, regarding the treatment of confidential documents, is of vital importance for both the CCC and the targeted enterprise. With regard to the CCC, it will refuse access to documents if:

- they were supplied subject to a condition of non-disclosure;
- disclosure of them would be prejudicial to the public interest; and
- this is necessary to protect the identity of an informer.

With regard to the targeted enterprise, it needs to be assured that documents relating to its business secrets remain confidential. In the European Union, in *Akzo*,[102] the ECJ emphasised that undertakings have a legitimate interest in

101 European Commission, *Notice on the Rules for Access to the Commission's File in Cases Pursuant to Articles [101 and 102 TFEU], Articles 53, 54 and 57 of the EEA Agreement and Council Regulation (EC) No 139/2004* [2005] OJ C 325/7, [8], states: 'The Commission's file in a competition investigation . . . consists of all documents . . ., which have been obtained, produced, and/or assembled by the Commission Directorate General for Competition, during the investigation.'

102 Case 53/85 *AKZO Chemie BV and AKZO Chemie UK Ltd v Commission* [1986] ECR 1965.

protecting their business secrets, taking into account the extremely serious damage that could result from improper communication of documents to a competitor. It then held that it is for the European Commission to judge whether or not a particular document contains business secrets.

Under Rule 68(1) of the CCC Rules of Procedure, a party, upon filing a document with the CCC, may make a request to the Adjudicating Panel for confidentiality in respect of all or part of that document. The request must summarise the nature of the document, explain why the request is made, state any objections to the placing of an abridged version of the document on the public record and the reasons for any such objections, and file the request with the CCC; the Registrar must then serve it on the parties. Under Rule 68(3), a confidentiality request is placed on the public record.

Rule 68(5) states that 'a person may object to a request for confidentiality by filing an objection and the objection shall be served by the Registrar on the parties at least two business days prior to the hearing'. This Rule implies that an objection may be made not only by the parties to the proceedings before the Adjudicating Panel, but also by 'a person'. Accordingly, it appears this should be understood as meaning that a third party may object to a request for confidentiality. If this interpretation is correct, it seems that the power given to the Adjudicating Panel to determine, alone, whether the relevant document or information is to be classified as confidential is excessive. It is submitted that, when there is a disagreement between the Adjudicating Panel and the party to the proceedings as to whether the relevant document or information is of a confidential nature, the final arbitrator should be the CCJ rather than the Adjudicating Panel. In this respect, the EU example may be seen as instructive. First, the right to access the European Commission's file is limited to the targeted enterprise; third parties have no such right. Second, if there is a request from a third party to consult a particular document, the European Commission must inform the undertaking from which this document was taken. If the undertaking concerned identifies that this document is of a confidential nature, the European Commission has two options: it may agree with the undertaking concerned, whereupon this document will not be communicated to a third party; or it may disagree, in which case it must give the undertaking an opportunity to state its views. If the European Commission still disagrees, it must adopt a decision in that regard, which contains an adequate statement of the reasons on which it is based and which must be notified to the undertaking concerned. The European Commission must, before implementing its decision, give the undertaking an opportunity to bring an action before the General Court seeking to have the decision reviewed by it. Accordingly, the undertaking has a route for attempting to stop implemention of the Commission's decisions.

It is to be noted that, under Article 170(4) RTC, a Member State is not required to disclose information that it regards as confidential if to do so 'would be prejudicial to the public interest, or the legitimate interests of enterprises, public or private'. The CCC Rules of Procedure do not address this matter. However, it is submitted that if there is a disagreement between a Member State and the CCC as to whether confidential information required by the CCC is within the scope of Article 170(4) RTC, the matter should be conclusively determined by the CCJ in exercise of its supervisory power over the CCC.

9.7.2 The explicit or implied powers of the CCC deriving from Chapter VIII, Part One, RTC, which are not listed in Article 174 RTC

This section examines the explicit or implied powers of the CCC flowing from Chapter VIII, Part One, RTC, but not listed in Article 174 RTC.

9.7.2.1 The express powers of the CCC additional to those stated in Article 174 RTC

The following express powers, additional to those stated in Article 174 RTC, have been granted to the CCC.

1. Under Article 168(e) RTC, the CCC is empowered to review the conformity with CSME competition law of rules relating to professional standards developed or enforced by professional associations (see Chapter 4, section 4.4.2.3).
2. Under Article 180 RTC, the CCC may issue a 'negative clearance' ruling. This occurs in a situation in which a Member State has doubts as to whether particular business conduct is prohibited by Article 177(1) RTC and makes a request to the CCC to determine whether a breach of CSME competition law has occurred. If the CCC determines that such conduct is not prohibited, it issues a negative clearance ruling. This ruling is conclusive in any judicial proceedings in the Community except when the CCC makes an application to the CCJ to review its own ruling on the ground that it was induced by deceit or improper means.

   It is interesting to note that a Member State that has requested a negative clearance ruling has no *locus standi* to challenge the CCC's negative clearance ruling before the CCJ. This seems very restrictive and suggests that, when a Member State is uncertain whether particular business conduct is prohibited by Article 177(1) RTC, it should request the CCC to investigate that conduct under Article 175(1) RTC rather than apply for a negative clearance ruling under Article 180(1) RTC. This is because any determination pursuant to Article 175(1) is subject to review by the CCJ if a requesting Member State so wishes.
3. Under Article 181 RTC, the CCC may apply the *de minimis* rule (see Chapter 5, section 5.3.2) and so exempt business conduct that, although in breach of CSME competition law, has minimal impact on competition and trade in the CSME.

9.7.2.2 *The implied powers of the CCC*

There is no provision in the RTC that allows the CCC to take interim measures in relation to possible infringements of Article 177(1)(a)–(c) RTC. However, teleological interpretation of the RTC entails that the CCC needs to have such power in order to ensure the effective exercise of its functions.

The CCC has granted to itself the power to take interim measures. Under Rule 55 of the CCC Rules of Procedure, the Executive Director of the CCC may apply to the Adjudicating Panel, once a notice pursuant to Rule 10 has been issued finding an infringement of CSME competition law, to order interim measures to prevent serious and irreparable damage to a particular person, or category of persons, or to protect the public interest. The Adjudicating Panel, before making such an order, is required to follow the procedure set out in Rule 55(2) – that is, it must give a written reasoned notice to the person against whom it proposes to make an order and give that person an opportunity to be heard. The Adjudicating Panel, when considering whether to order interim measures, must balance all of the interests concerned. An order of the Adjudicating Panel must set out the reasons why it has been made. This is an important requirement in that it enables the CCJ to verify whether the order was necessary. Rule 55 ensures that legitimate rights of the person against whom an order is sought are maintained, in particular the right to be heard.

It is submitted that Rule 55 should be amended in that it may become obvious during the investigation stage that the CCC must take interim measures in relation to possible infringements of CSME competition law. Under Rule 55, interim measures can be taken only after an investigation has been completed – that is, after a notice pursuant to Rule 10 has been issued. It is submitted that decisions ordering interim measures should be available to the CCC at any stage of the proceedings if the situation is urgent – that is, if, without an order, serious and irreparable damage is likely to occur. It is further submitted that if there is a need to make an interim measures order before the completion of an investigation by the Investigating Panel, the Executive Director of the CCC should be empowered to make such an order subject to guarantees set out in Rule 55.

INDEX

www.ingramcontent.com/pod-product-compliance
Ingram Content Group UK Ltd.
Pitfield, Milton Keynes, MK11 3LW, UK
UKHW022011180926
475701UK00003B/305
* 9 7 8 1 1 3 8 7 8 7 3 1 5 *